A Line of Blood and Dirt

Creating the Canada–United States Border across Indigenous Lands

BENJAMIN HOY

OXFORD
UNIVERSITY PRESS

OXFORD
UNIVERSITY PRESS

Oxford University Press is a department of the University of Oxford. It furthers the University's objective of excellence in research, scholarship, and education by publishing worldwide. Oxford is a registered trade mark of Oxford University Press in the UK and certain other countries.

Published in the United States of America by Oxford University Press
198 Madison Avenue, New York, NY 10016, United States of America.

Library of Congress Cataloging-in-Publication Data
Names: Hoy, Benjamin, author.
Title: A Line of Blood and Dirt : Creating the Canada–United States
border across indigenous lands / Benjamin Hoy.
Other titles: Creating the Canada–United States border across indigenous lands
Description: New York, NY : Oxford University Press, [2021] |
Includes bibliographical references and index.
Identifiers: LCCN 2020034962 (print) | LCCN 2020034963 (ebook) |
ISBN 9780197528693 (hardback) | ISBN 9780197528716 (epub) | ISBN 9780197528723
Subjects: LCSH: United States—Boundaries—Canada. | Canada—Boundaries—United States. |
Indians of North America—Canadian–American Border Region—Government relations. |
Indians of North America—Canadian–American Border Region—History. |
Indians, Treatment of—United States—History. | Indians, Treatment of—Canada—History. |
Boundaries—Social aspects—United States. | Boundaries—Social aspects—Canada.
Classification: LCC E179.5 .H73 2021 (print) | LCC E179.5 (ebook) |
DDC 320.1/2—dc23
LC record available at https://lccn.loc.gov/2020034962
LC ebook record available at https://lccn.loc.gov/2020034963

DOI: 10.1093/oso/9780197528693.001.0001

To my parents, to whom I owe everything.

CONTENTS

ACKNOWLEDGMENTS

This book, like my childhood, was created in motion. In both instances, the Canada–US border was never far from view. I was born to a Canadian mother and an American father. By the time I was ten years old my family had relocated for my parents' work five times. Most of those transitions crossed the international border. The genesis of this book was no different. I completed parts of it in Ontario, California, and Saskatchewan—Anishinaabe, Muwekma Ohlone, and Treaty 6 territories, respectively. Throughout the process the border divided where I lived, who funded my research, and where I was in relation to my loved ones.

Like the experiences of the people who appear in these pages, my own sense of belonging is complicated. My sister is Cree, my father is Cherokee-Greek, and my mother is Irish. I am a dual citizen with mixed heritage and white skin. I grew up with Métis, Salish, Haudenosaunee, Cherokee, and Anishinaabe men from across the country who got together once a week to sing. None of our identities matched the boxes that administrators liked to create.

This book project might seem like a natural fit for me, a chance to understand the lives of people who crossed borders and categories as my life has. In practice, this work has felt anything but preordained. My initial interest in the topic remained low. When I was young, I was not sure what I wanted to do beyond a desire to avoid the footsteps of my parent who taught English, Indigenous literature and history, and women's studies. I failed. I am indebted to Michelle Hamilton and Kris Inwood for showing me how rich the study of Indigenous history, borders, and quantitative data could be and for fostering my early development as a scholar.

I soon learned that history is a humbling endeavor. While historians often pretend that the practice of history is a solitary activity filled with lonely reflection, little could be further from the truth. Creating a history book requires an endless amount of assistance. The final product is better described as a collection of debts than an individual effort. This book, like so many others, would not have been possible without the support of dozens of funding agencies, universities, students, archives, and colleagues.

The University of Saskatchewan, Stanford University, and the Social Science and Humanities Research Council (SSHRC) ensured I had the resources necessary to sustain a project of this magnitude. Technical and logistical support came from many directions. Stanford's Spatial History Lab and the University of Saskatchewan's historical Geographic Information Systems (HGIS) lab provided my work with a home for many years. Jane Westhouse, Rilla Friesen, Jim Clifford, Jim Handy, Lesley Biggs, Erika Dyck, Keith Carlson, and Geoff Cunfer removed barriers and ensured that I was never far from supporting hands. The Summer University Research Initiative (SURI) exchange program between the University of Saskatchewan and the Indian Institute of Technology Gandhinagar exposed me to new ideas and insightful scholars. The Social Science and Humanities Research Council provided funding at multiple stages of my career and made the scale of this research possible.

Dozens of organizations and people have lent their support in other ways. Rilla Friesen created the index for this book and Anne Sanow did the copyediting. Jeremy Toynbee, at Newgen, oversaw the book's production. The Stó:lō Nation provided me with access to their collections, for which I remain deeply grateful. Archivists from more than thirty institutions helped me navigate a bureaucratic labyrinth. A heartfelt thanks is owed to each of these organizations, people, and institutions.

Friends and colleagues also added their expertise to this project. Just listing the scholars who read sections of the book no longer fits into a comfortable sentence. Keith Carlson, Cameron Blevins, Ashleigh Androsoff, Maurice Labelle, Matthew Neufeld, Valerie Korinek, Erika Dyck, Robert Englebert, Kathryn Labelle, Helen Hoy, Thomas King, Andrew Graybill, and Stephen Aron all read segments. Brian Delay, Geraldo Cadava, Michel Hogue, C. Matthew Snipp, Albert Camarillo, and anonymous reviewers read entire drafts. Each scholar caught mistakes and improved the research and writing in innumerable ways. Any lingering shortcomings or errors, of course, remain my own.

The Building Borders team helped to create many of the visuals that appear in this book. Tyla Betke, Meagan Breault, Katherine McPhee, Erin Isaac, Kevin Winterhalt, Steven Langlois, Olya Sotskaya, Tenille Holm, Himanshu Chauhan, and Kristen Forest helped me digitize, track, and map the thousands of individuals and policies that made the border a reality. So too did graduate students including Tarisa Little, Arya Adityan, Chris Marsh, and Punya Suri. Your collective ability to solve problems and rebuild histories continues to astound me.

I would like to extend a special thanks to both Richard White and Susan Ferber. Richard read more drafts of this work than anyone, no matter their crime, deserved to. I am not sure I will ever be able to repay your generosity. Susan provided expert editorial guidance and endless patience as this book took a long and winding road toward competition.

To my parents, for whom this work is dedicated, thank you for all your support. My successes would not have been possible without your sacrifices. My final debt is to my partner Nadine Zabder. Your love and support are visible through every page of this book. I cannot thank you enough.

A NOTE ON TERMINOLOGY

The terminology used to describe Indigenous communities in this book is complex, in part because a dozen different names may apply to a single group. Historic documents, contemporary sources, and ethnographic/anthropological studies may refer to a group by their autonym (the name it calls itself) or by one of the many exonyms that Europeans or other Indigenous groups created to reference that community. Not all the terms used describe the same thing. Some documents cluster people by the language they spoke, while others use community organization at a variety of scales. Differences in spelling and translation add further complexity.

Throughout this book, I have used the terms each community currently uses to describe itself to outsiders, often derived from each community's website. This creates some inconsistencies in the type of terminology used (some groups prefer autonyms, others prefer tribal categories, and still others use exonyms), but honors the ways each community wishes to present itself to the surrounding world. I have included alternative terms in brackets for some communities to help avoid confusion. The appendix provides a detailed description of many of these names, where they originated, and what alternatives exist. Where I was not able to reconstruct the connection between a historic term and a contemporary community, I have left the terms as they appeared in the original historical documents.

When referring to the first residents of North America in aggregate, I have used the term "Indigenous." This was a complicated decision. Over the past two hundred years, scholars have used a wide array of terms to describe Indigenous people. Some of terms (Indian and Aboriginal) carry specific legal meanings as well as a parallel, but often fuzzier, set of social usage. Other terms carry an implicit sense of geography. The term "First Nations," for example, is only used in Canada, while the terms "Native American" and "American Indian" appear only in the United States. My earlier attempts to apply these geographically constrained terms to communities that crossed the border met with failure. It confused scholars of each respective country more often than it demonstrated to them how inadequate these terms were for describing communities that lived beyond the realms created by nation-states. As a result of this failure, I have prioritized the term "Indigenous" in this book, which the Assembly of First Nations recognizes as its "preferred and accepted" term and which is widely used by both the United Nations and the Canadian government.[1]

Organizing the termoninology used in this book into a cohesive guide, which appears in the appendix, created an array of unexpected challenges. Separating each group by name and including separate entries for each makes it easier to reference a given community. That approach, however, hides the commonality that many of these groups shared. It also makes it difficult to see how overarching cultural/linguistic terms reference multiple communities at once or how geographic concepts like "Northern Indians" shaped settler conceptions of the world around them. The appendix therefore contains a split approach. The first section describes the nine most prominent linguistic and cultural groups that appear in this book as well as their subdivisions. The second section provides shorter descriptions of all of the other Indigenous communities.

The terminology guide in the appendix is not comprehensive. It mentions only the nations that appear in the book and does not include all of the subdivisions that exist for each linguistic or cultural group.

ABBREVIATIONS

AM	Archive Manitoba
AO	Archive of Ontario
BCA	British Columbia Archive
BIA	Bureau of Indian Affairs
CAHAN	Chronicling America Historical American Newspapers
COS Archives	City of Saskatoon Archives
DIA ARO	Department of Indian Affairs Annual Reports Online
DW OHP	U.S.–Dakota War of 1862 Oral History Project
HMSO	Her Majesty's Stationery Office
INS	Immigration and Naturalization Service
LAC	Library and Archives Canada
LOC	Library of Congress
MBHP	Minnesota Black History Project
MHS	Minnesota Historical Society
NARA	National Archives and Records Administration
O CPRC	oURspace Canadian Plains Research Centre
PAS	Provincial Archives of Saskatchewan
RCMP	Royal Canadian Mounted Police
TUS	Traditional Use Study
UDC WDW	U.S. District Courts Western District Washington
UM Mansfield	University of Montana Mansfield
UWDC	University of Wisconsin Digital Collections
OIA ARO	Office of Indian Affairs Annual Reports Online

A Line of Blood and Dirt

Introduction

In 1938, Andrue Berding, an Associated Press staff writer, returned to the United States after almost twelve years abroad in Europe. Born in Ohio, Berding studied at Oxford before becoming the bureau chief for the Associated Press in Rome.[1] After his return, he found himself traveling hundreds of miles along the US border with Canada. The travel, part of his research into the proposed St. Lawrence Seaway, provided Berding with an opportunity to reflect on the differences between North American and European border crossings. In Europe he had come up against endless formalities related to customs, passports, and currency every time he crossed between nations. He became accustomed to spending "the usual half-hour wait beneath the prying eyes and fingers of guards and officials."[2]

In North America, Berding encountered a different kind of border. At 5,525 miles in length, the Canada–US border ran roughly the same distance as between Paris (France) and Nagpur (India) if travelled by land. If such a journey was made by car today, one would pass through Pakistan, Afghanistan, Uzbekistan, Kazakhstan, Georgia, Russia, Ukraine, Poland, the Czech Republic, and Germany in addition to France and India. In North America, travelers could move such vast distances while remaining at the intersection of two nations.

By Berding's time, the Canada–US border had a tangible presence. Both countries had deforested an area twenty feet wide along their border's path across the continent. They placed over 8,000 boundary markers to indicate its location. For all the resources invested in such an undertaking, the impacts of the border on everyday life seemed minimal. In Berding's estimation, the border divided people who seemed essentially the same. They spoke the same language, drove the same cars, and accepted one another's currency without hesitation. Boundary markers, which seemed more ornamental than real, and the occasional French sign seemed all that separated the two nations. When Berding crossed the international boundary along the Great Lakes and St. Lawrence River, border guards let him pass after he declared his American birth. The

A Line of Blood and Dirt. Benjamin Hoy, Oxford University Press (2021). © Oxford University Press.
DOI: 10.1093/oso/9780197528693.003.0001

agents did not even bother to ask him his name. In Berding's words, "the border seemed more symbolic than real."[3]

Berding's statement conveyed the reality of the division in 1930s, but it disguised deeper truths about the border. Compared to Europe's borders on the eve of World War II, the border separating Canada from the United States must have indeed seemed unusual and paltry. The idea that the border was somehow less real, however, missed the significant ways it had shaped life and governance for over a hundred years.

Since the eighteenth century, the Canada–US border had created havens from criminal prosecution that militants, political agitators, and criminals had taken advantage of. It structured the experiences of Chinese migrants who faced exclusion, eastern and southern Europeans who encountered new immigration laws, businesses that built branch plants, and merchants who sent their goods along more expensive routes to avoid customs duties and tariffs. What Berding noticed then was not the border's symbolic or illusory quality, but rather its unevenness.

Four years before Berding declared the border a mere symbol, Walking Earth and Red Dog described their own relationships to borders and territory. The two men, part of the Star Blanket Reserve in Southern Saskatchewan, described the Calling River Cree's (Katepwu-cipi-wiyiniwuk) territory and its relationship to the Canada–US border. The Cree (Nêhiyawak) had long maintained a territorial base in the Qu'Appelle Valley. Their historic hunting grounds spread across the majority of present-day southern Saskatchewan, from the File Hills to Maple Creek and Wood Mountain. As Red Dog recalled, this expansive land base brought the Cree into conflict with the Siksika (Blackfeet), Kainah (Blood), Piikani (Piegan), Tsuut'ina (Sarcee), Salish (Flathead), Crow (Apsáalooke), and A'aninin (Gros Ventre), as well as Canadian and American settlers.[4] The boundaries that Red Dog and Walking Earth described did not remain static. In the mid-nineteenth century, during Walking Earth's great grandfather's time, the community hunted in the United States. By Walking Earth's generation, the practice had all but disappeared. The bison's demise provided a partial explanation. The growth of both the international line and reserve boundaries explained much of the rest.[5]

For Walking Earth, Red Dog, and others like them, the border did not exist as an abstract line. It operated instead as a challenge to the land uses of the Cree, Dakota, Lakota, Nimiipuu (Nez Perce), Métis, Haudenosaunee (Iroquois), Anishinaabe, and Coast Salish.[6] The conflicting claims emphasized a basic truth about territory. Borders, whether national or otherwise, are not created in isolation. They are drawn on top of a territorial tapestry already established, the new form never vivid enough to block out what came before.[7]

Created over more than a century, the Canada–US border did not emerge from a single conflict, act of legislation, or administrative flourish. Boundary negotiations and surveys proliferated on the Atlantic Coast and in the Great Lakes during the eighteenth and early nineteenth centuries. Surveys of the Pacific Coast (1857–1868), Prairies (1872–1874), and Arctic (1904–1918) stretched out across another century. The process jumped around. Surveyors moved from the East Coast to the West Coast before filling in the Prairies. Neither country seemed in a rush. Decades passed between the treaties that defined the border, the surveys that marked it on the land, and placement of the administrators who made it matter. Perceived cost drove much of that delay. Treaties were cheap, sometimes little more than ink and paper. Real power, on the other hand, required real investments.

In practice, border control required a catalyst to offset the expense of the operation. The breadth of the territory claimed by Canada and the United States and the timing of their colonization efforts ensured that no single moment could justify the entire enterprise. Concerns varied by region, but each played a role in shaping where the border ran and how each government policed it. In the Prairies, fears of Indigenous power dominated. On the Pacific Coast, legislators emphasized the threat of a Chinese menace. Desires for gold in the Arctic eventually mixed with older concerns about immorality, immigration, and citizenship that had first arisen across the Great Lakes.

Each set of regional concerns pushed border control in a different direction and left a unique mark on how the border would operate at a continental scale. In that sense, the border had a reactionary quality to it. It served as a tool, however imperfect, for solving regional problems of governance. Once in place, however, the border created problems of its own that soon justified both its own expense and its continued importance.[8]

For all the walls built, treaties signed, and personnel deployed, nation-states have never succeeded in making borders their exclusive domain. States create legal boundaries and recognize legitimacy. They develop complex ways of thinking about territory and aim to stamp those ideas onto the landscape itself. But borders are more than just federal musings. They are, as historian Karl Hele observes, "lived experiences."[9] The Canada–US border grew because of federal investments, but like most borders, it also expanded because it found ways to incorporate ambiguity.

John George Brown (Kootenai Brown) was born in Ireland in 1839. As a young man he worked for the British army in India before coming to British

Columbia in 1862 to prospect for gold. By the end of his life he had worked for the American Army, the Canadian North-West Mounted Police, and the Métis community to which his wife, Olive Lyonnais, belonged. Opportunity, not national boundaries, dictated Brown's movements.[10]

Building a border required assigning men like Brown a singular identity, however, imprecise such a label might be. It required that thousands of people across cultures, locations, classes, and races saw value in the border's existence even though they did not agree on its precise meaning or purpose. That uncertainty produced difficulties for the administrators tasked with enforcing the international divide. It has created similar dilemmas for historians and scholars interested in how borders create a sense of psychological separation between peoples who have much in common.

By the time of Berding's death in 1989, scholars had decades of experience writing about the edges of nations. Early researchers realized that borders, for all their importance, blurred identities better than they divided them.[11] Regional and tribal histories flourished. Increasingly scholars wrote about the border itself, not as a foregone conclusion but as an institution that required explanation. Studies about the US border with Mexico grew numerous, a reflection of an increasingly diverse professoriate and contemporary concerns about Mexican immigration.[12] For all that changed, violence and exclusion remained central to the ways scholars understood America's southern border.[13]

Canada's border with the United States, which Berding dismissed as illusory, has always seemed a little different. Compared to the conflicts associated with the US–Mexico border, Canadians and Americans, past and present alike, have viewed their shared border in a more positive light.[14] They described it as a border between friends, a place of mingling, and an unguarded or friendly frontier.[15] The international line connected "children of a common mother" or, at worst, "ambivalent allies."[16]

The borders that the United States shared with Mexico and Canada contained real differences, but more commonality than such depictions suggested. Racial fears and violence served as a catalyst for the professionalization of border security in the north much as they had in the south.[17] Building borders, regardless of location, displaced Indigenous communities. Deprivation, starvation, status, dispossession, and employment served as the tools of choice.[18] By leaving the Canada–US border out of the equation, scholars of the US–Mexico border have often underplayed the commonalities of violence that spanned the continent. If each border looked quite different by the Great Depression, that divergence was not a forgone conclusion.

For all the outpouring of research, the perennial questions that men like Berding posed in the 1930s still remain. What do borders look like, and how do they close? In Canada and the United States, the parallel sets of literature created by historians of Indigenous people,[19] gender,[20] Chinese Exclusion,[21] immigration,[22] and federal agencies[23] have created vibrant discussions around these issues. Very few of these studies, however, have attempted to understand the border closure experience across multiple races, administrative groups, Indigenous communities, and regions. This has had the unfortunate consequence of obscuring the interactions and connections that made the border feel like a cohesive entity. It is significant because the border never treated people as equals—a feature that makes extrapolating from the history of a single group or agency an uncertain proposition.

This book follows the growth of the Canada–US border through three stages of development: its childhood, adolescence, and early adulthood. From 1775 until 1865, the border found its early life (chapters 1 and 2). Bookended by American Independence and the American Civil War/Canadian Confederation, the border's childhood saw the emergence of new nations and the entrenchment of their power. As the power shifted across the continent, Indigenous people found themselves subjected, in ways they could not have imagined, to a border they had helped create.

From the 1865 until the 1914, the border experienced a short but rapid growth spurt (chapters 3–8). Federal power expanded across the continent, adding new resources and opportunities for border control. Like human adolescents, the border's development during this period was filled with awkwardness, unevenness, and doubt. Regional problems in the Great Lakes, Prairies, and Pacific Coast pulled border policies in different directions. The persistent autonomy of local administrators created wide gaps between federal desires and practical policy. Each challenge left a mark on the border's scope and execution that would remain with it through its later development.

By the early twentieth century, the border had reached its early adulthood (chapters 9 and 10). It had become a stable, well-funded, and centralized process. Permanent organizations managed its operation, and civilian administrators had replaced military ones. Adulthood, however, did not make the border a final product or an all-powerful institution. The speed of change slowed, but administrators continued to redefine the border's goals and operations. It remained permeable and limited. Canada and the United States had failed to build a border that matched their ambitions. By the early twentieth century, however, they had succeeded in creating a fixture of the landscape that often appeared natural and which had the capacity to shape movement across thousands of miles of territory.

For the communities who interacted with the border on a regular basis, the growth of federal power never felt simple or linear. The border began to close for the Oceti Sakowin (Sioux), Nimiipuu, and Métis starting in the 1870s and 1880s. It closed for the Chinese and Coast Salish in the 1880s and 1890s and for

African Americans and Europeans at the turn of the century. It tightened for the Haudenosaunee at the turn of the century only to reopen, as it would for many other Indigenous communities, beginning in the 1920s and 1930s.

These closures and openings did not happen in isolation from one another. Attempts to control Indigenous mobility through status helped develop approaches that officials later used to control the mobility of white women. Support for open or closed borders was never clear-cut. Indigenous people fought for their own rights to cross borders while joining the vigilante mobs that tried to expel Chinese immigrants from the continent. Unevenness and variation served as hallmarks of the border at all stages of its operation.

A Line of Blood and Dirt attempts to combine all of these paths together linking the border closure experiences of Anishinaabe, Haudenosaunee, Métis, Dakota, Lakota, Cree, and Coast Salish communities with the experiences of Chinese, African American, and European immigrants. To do so, it draws from family records, newspapers, diaries, and close to a thousand oral histories from across the continent. Court cases, federal reports, and correspondence helped to rebuild the practical approaches that federal administrators relied upon.

For all its breadth, this book remains limited. The Great Lakes, Prairies, and West Coast loom large in this account. This focus allows for both a comparative and comprehensive overview of a vast contiguous region filled with diverse peoples, patterns of settlement, geographies, and climates. At the same time, the western focus underplays the unique processes that occurred in the Arctic, St. Lawrence, and Atlantic regions. In those areas, linguistic differences, the timing of expansion, and a host of other factors created a different kind of border closure process. The underlying source base also contains limitations. Consulting oral accounts, even hundreds of them, is not a substitute for a community-engaged history, which this work is not. This book will hopefully help provide a larger framework for understanding the hundreds of local, regional, and tribal histories that have flourished in the border's shadow.

Drawing from this evidence and confined by these limitations, *A Line of Blood and Dirt* makes three major arguments. First, the Canada–US border developed differently from the US–Mexico border because of American perceptions of cultural similarity and military prowess. The United States offered a generous hand to Britain, whose military power it respected, and a less forgiving one to Spain and Mexico, whose power it did not.[24] Despite more than enough reason for bad blood, Americans promoted a kind of transnational brotherhood with Canada not as apparent in the south. This perceived brotherhood helps explain why today British Columbia is Canada's gateway to the Pacific rather than America's bridge between Alaska and Washington. Its absence explains, at least in part, why California, New Mexico, and Arizona are part of the American southwest rather than the Mexican north. Geopolitics across an entire continent depended on perceptions of strength and belonging.

These perceptions shaped how the border grew, but have also impacted how each country thinks about its borders today. Canadians and Americans continue to view their border as a site of friendly relations, loose restrictions, and comical rather than ghastly occurrences. Cheese smuggling seems quintessentially Canadian. The traffic of people out of the aptly named Smugglers Inn, a bed and breakfast in Blaine, Washington, seems too brazen, too honest, to be real.[25] Stories of refugees and suffering along the northern border receive only passing coverage. Compared with the accounts along the US–Mexico border of migrants dying in the desert, children held in detention centers, and the construction of a multibillion-dollar wall, the Canada–US border appears well managed and less consequential. This book helps explain that division and the hidden history of a border built in conflict that learned to hide its past.[26]

Second, this book argues that the history of the Canada–US border, and each nation more broadly, are inseparable from histories of colonialism, hunger, dispossession, and Indigenous politics. From the very outset, Canada and the United States believed that building a national border on Indigenous lands required erasing pre-existing territorial boundaries. They saw erasure as a component of creation. This approach, however, remained hard to execute in practice. Government personnel thought of territory as a zero-sum game in which they were the principal actors. The practical realities of power suggested something else entirely. Local communities and Indigenous people held substantial sway.

Indigenous labor and support underwrote the border at all stages of its creation. Indigenous people impacted how Canada and the United States conceptualized their border, demarcated it, and attempted to enforce it. Although Britain, Canada, and the United States excluded Indigenous people from the treaty negotiations that determined the path the border took, the actions of Indigenous people on the battlefield shaped the terms European diplomats pushed for. Indigenous communities provided scouts, translators, guides, haulers, packers, canoe men, and provisioners to the boundary survey projects.[27] Haudenosaunee and Métis communities supported British officials in putting down Canadian rebellions and Irish independence movements.[28] Cheyenne (Tsistsistas), Crow, and Bannock (Nimi) scouts assisted the American army in preventing the Nimiipuu from successfully fleeing across the border into Canada. Indigenous scouts captured army deserters who attempted to cross the border and provisioned the federal outposts from which border patrols operated.[29]

In short, Canada and the United States did not simply force the border upon Indigenous communities. Instead, groups like the Coast Salish, Cree, and Oneida offered selective support when it suited their own purposes. Recognizing their contribution neither diminishes the ways Indigenous people resisted the imposition of national spaces nor the ways Canada and the United States later used the border against them. Rather it suggests the very personal ways that individuals, both native and non-native alike, interacted to create the very edges of each nation.[30]

Finally, this book argues that Canada and the United States designed their border to operate as a prism of control that drew from two distinct forms of power. In the natural world, prisms split white light into rainbows by slowing each band of light to a different degree. The stratification occurs across the entire prism, not at a single discrete point. The border applied a similar set of principles to people, animals, ideas, and goods. It bent and stratified movement across the entire nation, creating thousands of different outcomes.

These kinds of divergences help explain why the Canada–US border, which seemed so trivial to some, was so devastating for others. Regional differences discouraged one-size-fits-all border policies. The location of the crossing mattered, as did the racial, economic, gendered, religious, and cultural background of the migrant. Neither government desired a border that treated people, or movements, equally. Settlers of wealth and education, like Berding, experienced few barriers to their movement. Men like Walking Earth and Red Dog faced far more. Variability was not the unwanted side effect of the border's implementation; it was the whole point.

By the twentieth century, Canada and the United States had succeeded in creating a border quite different from the division that appeared on colonial maps. Most maps depicted it as a clear and narrow line. As both countries invested money, personnel, and attention into their border, however, they prioritized a strategy that pushed the border's presence deeper into the interiors of each country. In doing so, they aimed to force violators to avoid federal demands on a daily basis. They attempted to ensure that citizens of each country felt the border's presence more than a hundred kilometers from the international boundary itself. In a practical sense, the border became wider and more diffuse as it became more powerful. It started to shape movements at the point of departure, not merely at the moment of crossing.

The process of widening the border and intensifying its effects relied on two interwoven forms of power: direct and indirect control. Direct control focused on debarment. It aimed to influence the exact moment an individual attempted to cross the international line. Immigration and customs agents, provincial police forces, and naval units all contributed to this type of policing. As migrants appeared at customs posts and in port cities, federal personnel made decisions about admissibility. They let people pass, held them for questioning, and barred their entry. In practice, neither country possessed enough administrators or troops to guard more than a fraction of the border in this way at any given time.

The inadequacies of direct control encouraged both countries to create barriers in the mind, rather than simply physical borders.[31]

Indirect control worked by shaping motivations rather than by enforcing check points. By the nineteenth century, Canada and the United States had created a suite of policies designed to strip undesired migrants of their rights, wealth, and peace of mind. Canadian Indian agents deprived Indigenous men and women of their status and annuities when they left the country for extended periods. They made life difficult for those they believed did not belong. Throughout Emihana's early life, her family crossed back and forth across the line. Her family enrolled as members of Turtle Mountain Band of Chippewa in North Dakota in 1892. Not long after, they relocated to Canada. Emihana attended the Industrial School in Lebret, Saskatchewan, just as her father became a fugitive from justice and fled back to the United States at the turn of the century. When Emihana attempted to collect annuities north of the line, her family's historic mobility served as a sticking point for Indian agents. It created an opportunity for denial. Requests for recognition and aid gave each federal government a tangible way to punish earlier movements and to discourage future crossings. Stress, uncertainty, and scrutiny served as powerful tools of discouragement.[32]

In adopting this approach, both governments gained the ability to apply their punishments years after the initial crossing in places far removed from the international line. Both countries' reliance on indirect control helps to explain how the border shaped movement and identity without relying on the kinds of invasive searches that Andrue Berding had come to expect from his travels in Europe. Together, direct and indirect control allowed Canada and the United States to extend their reach over the minds and bodies of potential travelers.[33]

If Berding ever recognized that Canada and the United States had built their border through Indigenous territory and at times with Indigenous hands, he did not let on. By the 1930s, the border seemed natural and forgettable. As this book suggests, that outcome required more than just treaties, boundary markers, and guards. It required that both countries learned to hide more than a hundred years of violence, anxiety, and dispute in order to create what seemed at first glance to be the "world's longest undefended border."[34]

1

Building Borders

When a party of Dakota boys travelled north from their encampment, they came across a sight unlike anything they had ever seen. Piles of stones, painted red, stacked five or six feet tall, dotted the landscape east to west with no apparent end in sight. The boys, concerned that they had accidently entered enemy territory, reported back to their elders. The Dakota visited a town near the border and inquired with a man they had worked with during the War of 1812. The man told them that the line of red rocks represented a division. To the south are "people of their own, they have nothing to do with the people on the north side of this here landmark, these red stones." For Robert Goodvoice (Wahpeton Dakota), based on histories passed on to him by Henry Two Bear, "that is the landmark which is known as the boundary between the States and Canada today. That is the way it was first started."[1]

During the eighteenth and early nineteenth centuries, the boundaries that mattered in North America shifted as epidemics, horses, immigration, and violence remade the entire continent.[2] Amidst great change, quill pens and distant promises did a subtle kind of work. Created across sixty years, the Treaty of Paris (1783), Treaty of 1818, Anglo-Russian Treaty (1825), and the Oregon Treaty (1846) established British, American, and Russian territorial claims on paper.[3] While further treaties clarified the exact path each boundary would take in practice, by the 1840s diplomats had roughed out the border that present day Canadians and Americans would inherit.

The border agreements that European politicians constructed created only ripples at first compared with the monumental waves of change sweeping across North America. Early treaties anticipated a desired future more so than the present. They applied across a geography none of the signatories understood and where Indigenous people, not colonial settlers, held power. Without sufficient knowledge of the local topography to draw these borders on maps, each government had succeeded in creating only borders of ink and paper. Meaningful borders, which required both knowledge and power, came years later. Even so,

A Line of Blood and Dirt. Benjamin Hoy, Oxford University Press (2021). © Oxford University Press.
DOI: 10.1093/oso/9780197528693.003.0002

as these ripples created by diplomatic agreements mixed with the waves of immigration, disease, and upheaval, they took on increasingly greater significance. Eventually, they helped to structure the very distribution of power itself.

The transition from diplomatic agreements to boundary surveys to practical control was not a natural progression or part of an unbroken push west. Instead, a rolling set of crises structured the process. Surveyors jumped from the Atlantic Coast to the Pacific Coast before filling in the intervening areas. Local uncertainty and outbreaks of violence dictated the timing and geography of these early national projects. In the east, the War of 1812, the Aroostook War, Indian removal, and the Rebellions of 1837 and 1838 provided the impetus for surveys, territorial clarifications, and a broader reexamination of federal policy. Along the Pacific Coast, the rapid immigration of American settlers encouraged a similar commitment west of the Rocky Mountains by 1857. Neither country spent much effort surveying their border across the Plains until the 1870s or across the Artic until the turn of the century. Children were born, grew old, and died in the gaps between federal pronouncements and the moment either country learned of the basic features of the land they had claimed.

So why did Britain and the United States bother to sign such wide-reaching treaties before gaining the practical knowledge necessary to enact them? Was it just colonial posturing or perhaps a desire for legal clarity in distant lands? Both provide only partial explanations. For Britain and the United States, these early territorial agreements held particular importance because both countries saw border creation as a process of erasure, not simply construction. Early treaties mattered because they unlocked each government to engage in a parallel treaty process. In their eyes, it allowed them to extinguish Indigenous title and to build their nations across Indigenous lands.

Unsurprisingly, the process of building borders on Indigenous territory remained fraught long after each government recognized one another's dominion. As both Britain and the United States attempted to mark their border on the land itself, their ability to overlook Indigenous boundaries and territories diminished. They had set out to draw a series of borders that all but ignored Indigenous people and in the process soon discovered their own reliance on the native inhabitants. On a logistical level, the boundary survey process forced British and American surveyors to travel into Indigenous lands, exposing them to the potential risks such movements created. Moreover, while the surveyors possessed valuable astronomical equipment, they required Indigenous knowledge and labor to make efficient headway. Surveying equipment told surveyors where they were in relation to lines of latitude, but the equipment remained quiet when asked to indicate the location of the closest source of drinkable water.

To offset these challenges, the boundary survey teams hired hundreds of Indigenous guides, laborers, packers, and provisioners. They drew on these men's knowledge and used the partnerships the boundary teams forged with them to enable surveyors to work across Indigenous lands without incident. If Indigenous people participated in these boundary surveys for their own reasons, many did not anticipate the lasting changes this border would bring to their communities. The power to affect lives at a local level came later, long after the Canada–US border had taken its first shape.

American Revolution

Between the 1754 and 1812, the boundaries Europeans drew across North America shifted frequently in response to war. The French Indian War (part of the broader Seven Years War) divided France's territorial claims in North America between the Spanish and British empires. The American Revolution a decade later separated the United States from Britain.[4] In the aftermath of the Revolution, the Treaty of Paris (1783) established a preliminary border between the United States and Britain. The dividing line ran from the Atlantic Ocean up the St. Croix River and through the highlands dividing the St. Lawrence and Atlantic watersheds. From there the border went down to the 45th parallel, through the middle of the Great Lakes, stopping its westward trajectory at the northwestern point of the Lake of the Woods. After that it dropped down the Mississippi River and then back east until it hit the Atlantic Ocean. The resulting border bounded the United States by Spanishcontrolled Florida in the south, the Mississippi in the west, British North America in the north, and the Atlantic Ocean in the east.[5]

While the Treaty of Paris established a preliminary border between the two countries, it failed to disentangle each country's interests or its people. The treaty required the United States to recognize the rights of British creditors and to "earnestly recommend" that each state return the confiscated goods of British subjects. In exchange, Britain provided the United States with fishing rights off the Grand Banks of Newfoundland and Gulf of the Saint Lawrence. It also agreed "with all convenient speed" to withdraw its armies from the territory it recognized as belonging to the United States.[6] Peace remained a messy affair. American ships continued to fish in British waters, British creditors still collected American debts, and British property remained intertwined in the United States. The vague wording of the Treaty of Paris created frustration as both countries honored the words, but not the spirit of the agreement.[7]

As Britain and the United States drew new borders, they created a disconnect between loyalty and patterns of residence. In the aftermath of violence, thousands of loyalists relocated from the United States to Britain's remaining possessions.[8] Problems, however, remained. Following the American Revolution, two thousand Haudenosaunee (Iroquois) loyalists, following Joseph Brant, left New York. They relocated to Garden River in Ontario, where they received six miles of territory on both sides of the river as compensation, however inadequate, for the millions of acres of land they lost in the United States.[9]

For the Mohawk (Kanyen'kehaka), the relocation soon came to symbolize Britain's betrayal. Over time, British settlers reduced the land base granted to Haudenosaunee loyalists, removing much of the compensation Britain had initially offered. The Ojibwe fared far worse. Oral accounts by James Mason, a chief of the Saugeen band, has emphasized that Britain paid for Mohawk loyalty with Ojibwe land. From both Haudenosaunee and Ojibwe perspectives, Britain balanced its debts with land it did not own and with promises it did not keep.[10]

Geographic uncertainty compounded the social and economic difficulties that plagued Britain and the United States. During the initial boundary negotiations the two nations had relied on the Mitchel map, which they soon realized contained significant errors. By the 1790s, both governments expressed concerns that the Lake of the Woods might not intersect with the Mississippi river. If it did not, they would need to renegotiate that portion of the boundary line. In the east, the treaty's reference to the St. Croix River created a similar set of problems. Missionaries had named many rivers the "St. Croix River," making it difficult to determine which river the treaty-makers had intended to reference. Peacemaking would prove just as complicated as war.[11]

Both countries pinned their hopes on the Jay Treaty. Signed in 1794, the treaty created a timetable for Britain's military withdrawal and stipulated that the United States would cover the losses suffered during the war by British merchants. In addition, it provided that citizens of Britain, the United States, and "Indians dwelling on either side of the said boundary Line" shall be free to navigate "all the lakes, rivers and waters thereof, and freely to carry on trade and commerce with each other."[12] In doing so, it emphasized the free movement of goods across national lines and recognized the rights of Indigenous people to move between colonial spaces.

Control over the border, however, remained minimal. The United States opened customs posts near the border beginning in 1799 to collect duties on Canadian goods.[13] The Alien Act of 1798 allowed the United States to apprehend and remove "all natives, citizens, denizens, or subjects of the hostile nation or government, being males of the age of fourteen years and upwards, who shall be within the United States."[14] In practice, however, the act had a limited impact on border crossings. Monitoring the movement of people was expensive and, unlike tracking commercial goods, offered little direct return on investment.[15]

Loyalty and claims of sovereignty mixed in uncomfortable ways. Following the American Revolution, Britain and the United States held conflicting conceptions of belonging. Britain maintained an expansive view, which saw allegiance as a matter of nativity rather than choice. The United States, by contrast, argued that allegiance was an unstable quality that changed in accordance with an individual's convictions.[16] Between 1803 and 1811, Britain impressed an estimated ten thousand American citizens into its navy to help fight a war with France. In doing so, it transformed the doctrinal difference into a diplomatic impasse.[17]

War of 1812

The United States viewed British impressment as flagrant violation of American sovereignty and an attempt to make residual subjects out of American citizens in spite of the War of Independence. The impressment of American sailors served as a diplomatic pressure point. Many more soon appeared. On the continent, American fears of Tecumseh's intertribal alliance and a broader belief that British North America could not resist annexation created a volatile mixture.[18]

On June 18, 1812, the United States declared war on Britain. The war pitted two asymmetrical forces against one another. The United States had a population of 7.7 million compared to only 300,000 in British North America, making an overland war a promising venture for the United States. The army the United States could muster, however, was inexperienced. Lawyers and merchants led fresh soldiers who often broke under stiff resistance. Britain worried about the loyalty of its limited population on the continent. Still, it had a vast empire to draw from, the strongest navy in the world, and an army of battle-hardened soldiers.[19]

Disorganization, decentralization, political infighting, and unfounded optimism sapped the American war effort, turning the liberation of Canada that Thomas Jefferson had announced would "be a mere matter of marching" into an ugly drawn out stalemate.[20] The United States failed to conquer Canada despite several campaigns, and Britain's interest in redeploying its troops for a conflict in Europe resulted in favorable terms for the United States.[21]

The War of 1812 clarified the location of the border and shifted power away from Indigenous communities. Just as importantly, it demonstrated the uneasy associations individuals had toward national governments. The British Governor General reported that two-thirds of the military forces in Canada relied on American beef contractors for their provisions. Merchants in Vermont provided the British army with a wide array of foods despite the Enemy Trade

Acts of 1812 and 1815. They risked imprisonment and fines of up to a thousand dollars to do so.[22]

Lower Canadian merchants sent flour, meat, and grain across the border in the opposite direction. Proximity and market prices dictated many of these economic and social relationships. Faced with marauding soldiers who destroyed the property of friend and foe alike, borderland communities tried to keep military men at arm's length. They created local agreements with one another to minimize the chance of conflict.[23]

If Britain and the United States failed to instill a pervasive sense of national allegiance or duty within their civilian populations, they fared little better with their armed forces. Army officials charged with policing smuggling indulged in the practice themselves, making it difficult to control a line already in flux.[24] Poor conditions, fear, unrest, and offers of better pay resulted in rampant desertion.[25] In the American army, thirteen percent of the recruits deserted, making desertion a far more devastating ailment to the army's ranks than either combat (three percent loss) or disease (eight percent loss). Along the border, merely keeping armies intact was a monumental undertaking. Stopping smuggling, which had support from civilians on both sides of the line, exceeded the capacity of both states.[26]

All told, the War of 1812 demonstrated the tremendous capacity for violence that the United States and Britain could bring to bear. It also outlined the profound limitations of each state. Neither country's military succeeded in capturing much territory and what little was gained came at a heavy cost. If the war had no clear winner, it certainly had losers. Indigenous people, who had been crucial to Britain's war effort, found themselves abandoned during the peace.[27] Tecumseh's death in 1813 eliminated the driving force behind pan-Indigenous resistance. Andrew Jackson's success against the Muscogee (Creek) in 1814 led to millions of acres of land cessions.[28]

Although the Treaty of Ghent specified that the United States would restore "all the possessions, rights and privileges which [Indigenous people] may have enjoyed, or been entitled to in 1811," it did little to protect them in practice.[29] The Ojibwe who had allied with Britain faced the same dilemma the Haudenosaunee had thirty years earlier. They could abandon their homelands in the United States or put themselves at the mercy of their recent enemy whom they believed would treat them "worse than dogs."[30] Movement across the border, even by Indigenous people loyal to the British crown, had lasting implications. Canadian newspapers continued to refer to the Ojibwe who relocated to Manitoulin Island (Lake Huron) after war as foreigners, despite their long-standing connections across the Great Lakes.[31]

For Britain and the United States, the war had demonstrated the uncertainty of day-to-day allegiances, but offered no clear path forward. American born-citizens living in Upper Canada had not risen up during the War of 1812 as American officials had expected. Still, the fears of American annexation was never far from mind. In the aftermath of the war, British Tories demanded American immigrants take oaths of loyalty, while Reformers argued that mandating such action created dissatisfaction even among the loyal. In either case, oaths provided little assurance for the colony's prosperity or protection.[32]

In the immediate aftermath of the War of 1812, both countries experimented with policies designed to help match boundaries of loyalty with the borders of nationality. The American Foreign Enlistment Act of 1818 provided one approach. It prohibited the recruitment of American citizens to fight in foreign wars.[33] The Naturalization Act of 1828 provided another. Under the Naturalization Act, Britain granted American-born residents in Upper Canada who had immigrated to the colony before 1820 the same rights as British born subjects.[34]

The Naturalization Act, however, left open the future of immigration and, with it, a lot of difficult questions. On the one hand, the continued growth of an American population in Britain's remaining territory created the possible groundwork for a future annexation. On the other hand, preventing immigration from the United States deprived the British colonies of an important source of settlers and threatened their economic growth. It also ignored the fact that thousands of Americans already lived peacefully north of the line.[35] Creating a border required more than treaties and map-making. It required changing the beliefs and behaviors of settlers and Indigenous people alike on a grand scale. In practice, that process happened in fits and starts.[36]

Surveying in the East

If restructuring the hearts and minds of a continent remained a long-term goal, Britain and the United States had more than enough short-term problems to keep their administrators occupied. As the guns fell silent, Britain and the United States created a commission to investigate disputes in the Passamaquoddy Bay (Maine-New Brunswick) and along the Northwest Angle (Northern Minnesota). They negotiated the path their border would take across the Plains.[37] Oddities and irregularities, however, remained. Oregon Country, which extended from Spanish territorial claims in the south (42° N) to Russia's claims in the north (54° 40'N), remained under joint ownership. In the absence of a national system of law or governance, fur traders and Hudson's Bay Company employees operated in Oregon Territory with little oversight. They built forts, established trading relationships, and developed social and sexual partnerships with the Indigenous people they encountered. Where possible, the Hudson's Bay Company implemented its own brand of justice that relied on harsh punishments to keep employees in check and to influence and intimidate the Indigenous people with whom they traded.[38]

As Britain and the United States investigated border disputes and surveyed new areas, they drew upon the expertise and assistance of Indigenous guides, pilots, transporters, provisioners, labor recruiters, messengers, and informants.[39] J. L. Tiarks, a British astronomer who worked as part of a joint survey team, utilized "a small plan traced by an Indian" to navigate the river system near Squattuck Lake.[40] Indigenous informants provided Thomas Carlile with the path of the Chaudière, Black, and Ouelle Rivers, which he had little time to explore himself. Indigenous guides took John Johnson, a US surveyor, down the St. Francis River. They also provided transportation to J. M. Partridge, an assistant surveyor on the American boundary team, near Lake Megantic.[41]

British and American surveyors also consulted the historical memory of Indigenous communities in an attempt to fix earlier mistakes. The Treaty of Paris, for example, referenced the St. Croix River. Although both countries had used that river's name in their treaty language, neither had any idea where it ran. They turned to Indigenous people for support. Francis Joseph, a member of the Passamaquoddy tribe, recounted under oath his people's historic interactions with European powers. Joseph noted that his Grandfather Bungawarawit referred to the river then known as Magaguadavic as the St. Croix River and that the French had done so as well. He argued that his community had never referred to the Scoodiac River, another river under consideration, as the St. Croix. Indigenous testimony, like that provided by Joseph, helped clarify the boundaries European powers had created in haste.[42]

Soldiers and surveyors planted oak posts to indicate the border's location. They read proclamations and they fired salutes. For all the exhilaration these kinds of theatrics could create, all the surveyors and soldiers left behind were posts, maps, and a belief that their work would matter more in the future.[43] If they left little tangible presence on the ground, the opposite was true on paper. By 1827, the reports and documents surrounding the boundary line had become "so voluminous and complicated" that both countries worried that would be "improbable that any Sovereign or State should be willing or able" to serve on the arbitration committees.[44]

Indigenous Boundary-Making

The border that British and American officials stamped onto the landscape itself offered only one possible way to organize territory. European borders mattered, but throughout most of the continent, they played second fiddle to the territorial arrangements made by thousands of Indigenous communities that constrained the movements of settlers and Indigenous people alike. These boundaries did not exist in a timeless or unchanging past. Like the borders created by Britain and the United States, the boundaries that Indigenous people developed shifted over time. Warfare, geopolitics, disease, technological advancements, natural disasters, and the reintroduction of horses all shaped territorial control.[45]

On the Prairies, Tom Mutceheu (te-tapaxtoweu "Falling Noise") noted that the South Saskatchewan River served as a boundary between the Siksika (Kaskitiwayasituk) and the Cree (Nêhiyawak). The Tsuut'ina (Sarcee) lived near the Elbow River near the Rocky Mountains but remained scarce because of Cree attacks.[46] In 1934 Sam Belanger, then in his sixties, recounted the territorial boundaries that existed in the early nineteenth century during his grandfather's time. He noted that the Cree group he belonged to once had a territorial base that extended across Saskatchewan and Manitoba, bounded roughly by modern-day Regina, Moose Mountain, the Qu'Appelle River, and Winnipeg.[47]

Feather (Migwan, tipisko tigisikgo-awasis, Child of the Sky Right Above), an Assiniboine-Saulteaux man of the Little Hawk Band (Peepeekisis), provided a similar depiction of Indigenous boundaries. Recorded in the 1930s at the age of eighty-five, Feather noted that in his grandfather's time—roughly 1800—the band defeated the Siksikaitsiitapi (Blackfoot) in order to gain access to buffalo. They maintained a hunting territory that extended from Poplar Creek to Wood Mountain and occasionally engaged in hunts around the Touchwood and Cypress Hills.[48] Although the Siksikaitsiitapi and other Plains groups did not consider land as property in the same way that Europeans did, trespass on another group's territory risked death.[49]

Plains communities found creative ways to mark their territory on the land itself. In the early nineteenth century, the Cree and Siksikaitsiitapi appear to have used fire to establish buffer zones between one another. As Ted Binnema has noted, large-scale fires tended to follow military disputes. If indeed fire was used in this way, it would have been a potent tool of territorial organization. The absence of grass for more than a week's ride created an inhospitable environment for even the most determined riders. Compared with the pillars and wooden posts that colonial regimes relied upon, scorched landscapes provided a real barrier to movement.[50]

Indigenous communities on the Pacific Coast, like those on the Plains, developed effective land-use policies long before the arrival of Europeans. The Nooksack at Matsqui, Kilgard, and Cultus Lake shared much in common. They intermarried with one another, drew their leadership from the same group of people, and recognized one another as neighbors.[51] Despite these connections, oral accounts by Joe Louie emphasized the presence of "boundaries to hunt, to trap, to gather fish, gather roots, [and] gather berries."[52] Communities could gain short-term permissions to use resources in another group's territory, but failure to honor the limitations that a group placed on these visits could lead to dire consequences.

Hereditary ownership, reciprocal exchanges, and long-term stewardship flourished among the Coast Salish. They emphasized nonexclusive control over resources. This maximized the variety of resources each community could draw upon while still allowing for clear ownership and responsibility. Compared to the ways that Canada, the United States, Britain, and many European powers staked claims of sovereignty over land they had no understanding of, much less control over, the Coast Salish's system of territorial control seemed eminently practical.[53]

If Indigenous people found themselves occasionally stumbling across boundaries they did not fully comprehend, the experience was mutual. A Milwaukee deliveryman found himself caught in the middle of a battle between the Oceti Sakowin (Sioux) and Ojibwe (Chippewa) while carrying mail between Hudson and St. Paul. Unbeknownst to him he had entered a buffer zone located between the St. Croix and Mississippi rivers in which both groups hunted but neither lived. Luckily, his captors treated him as an innocent bystander and forgave his trespass. They fed him and treated him respectfully, concerned only that he did not give their position away to their enemy.[54] As the deliveryman no doubt came to realize, attempts to build a singular border across Indigenous lands had not dulled the importance of the pre-existing lines.

Aroostook War and 1837–38 Rebellions

Into the 1830s, the Canada–US border still represented only one border among many and remained a confusing one at that. Treaty negotiations had failed to resolve claims of ownership or reduce disputes.[55] The Treaty of Paris, for example, stipulated that the border would follow the "highlands which divide those Rivers that empty themselves into the River St. Lawrence from those which fall into the Atlantic Ocean."[56] Neither government, however, understood either watershed. Arbitration in 1831 ruled in favor of the United States, but did not grant it the entirety of the territory. Maine refused to recognize the decision and arrested New Brunswick lumbermen who continued operate throughout the region.[57]

Partially drawn borders created more problems than they resolved. Amidst uncertainty, both countries gathered soldiers to defend their claims. While the conflict, known today as the Aroostook War, flared during 1838 and 1839, Britain and the United States avoided outright violence. Both countries agreed to mediation, but the conflict and its resolution left lasting concerns. For the United States, a second mediation in 1842 granted it less than the original 1831 ruling, creating bitterness.[58] For Britain, which fared well in the second agreement, the nature of the conflict was still a sobering reminder of the limits of its control. During the conflict, the United States had built a blockhouse in the disputed lands and sustained it "by supplies ordered and delivered from Quebec over the Temiscouata route patrolled by British troops."[59]

Between 1843 and 1845, the two countries, unsettled from the events along the Maine–New Brunswick border, began to survey and mark the boundary in the eastern portions of each country. This was exhausting work. Marking the line required survey teams to clear-cut a thirty-foot-wide space through the forests they encountered. At times, this cutting slowed the boundary commission's work to a standstill.[60] It took ten men to "cut a quarter of a mile of Boundary in a day; but one-third of their number would be occupied in bringing in supplies for the rest."[61] To help overcome this complication, the British Boundary Commission employed as many as five hundred laborers during parts of the survey.[62] Hiring additional men, however, increased the logistical constraints the team found themselves facing, since each laborer needed food, supplies, transportation, and lodgings.

Canoes operated by Indigenous men as well as flat-bottomed boats operated by settlers conveyed surveyors and laborers to their destinations and provisioned them with supplies. In areas not accessible by rivers, teams of laborers carried provisions on their backs, sometimes as far as forty miles into the interior, to members of the team. Carrying supplies in such a fashion demanded "a constant supply of fresh men . . . for it always happened that many of the men who had made one trip into the woods with a load on their backs, refused, upon their return, to undertake another."[63]

Surveying the border and clarifying territorial claims dealt with only some of the challenges facing Britain and the United States. Without a matching capacity to control movement, clear borders did little to prevent regional disputes from becoming international incidents. The border divided legal policy much better than it did social, economic, or cultural links. If the legal division helped make the border palpable, it also hamstrung British and American officials.

In 1837 and 1838 political unrest in Upper and Lower Canada intensified into open rebellions that revealed the difficulties of maintaining colonial order while border control remained anemic. Tensions between English and French Canadians, patronage appointments, economic friction, and desires for a more democratic system of government fueled discontent against British rule.[64] After the initial fighting for both the Rebels (Upper Canada) and *Patriotes* (Lower Canada) went poorly, supporters of both causes fled across the border into Vermont, New York, Ohio, and Michigan.[65]

To the rebels' delight, the inhabitants of northern border states saw them as proto-American revolutionaries. The perceived brotherhood created a hotbed of support. As many as 200,000 Americans joined Hunter and Patriot Lodges along the frontier. These secret societies aimed to liberate Canada from Britain allowing rebel leaders to find a ready supplies of munitions and recruits. With this support, Rebel and *Patriote* leaders planned additional attacks from the safety of the United States.[66]

In February of 1838, Robert Nelson, a leading *Patriote*, invaded Lower Canada from Vermont, carrying with him an indictment of British crimes and a declaration of Lower Canada's independence. The declaration included provisions for the creation of a republican government with no allegiance to Britain. It granted Indigenous people the same civil rights as other citizens, expanded religious freedoms, abolished seigniorial landholdings, and reduced the punishments for debt. Delegates elected by every male twenty-one years or older would create the new government, using confiscated Crown lands and clergy reserves to fund the new state.[67]

Nelson's attack failed almost immediately. His forces made little headway against stiff resistance, and Nelson was captured and charged with violating American neutrality. Freed by a sympathetic jury, he redoubled his efforts. He reformed the movement's organization, acquired new recruits and supplies, and planned another invasion.[68]

Throughout the conflict, Britain worked in conjunction with the United States to control the border. British and American naval units created joint agreements to search islands throughout the Great Lakes "without regard to the territorial boundary line, in order that the culprits might have less chance of escaping."[69] Authorities transferred prisoners caught in such a manner to the correct jurisdiction, providing military forces with flexibility while keeping legal jurisdictions roughly intact. The process, as with many like it, remained imperfect. American authorities released prisoners captured by Britain without calling upon the testimonies of the British forces that had conducted the initial arrests. For all the practical troubles related to the policy's implementation, the cooperative approach to border control demonstrated the depth of goodwill that existed between the two countries.[70]

Britain also responded to the rebellions with internal measures. It suspended habeas corpus, imposed martial law, made blanket arrests, seized boats, and created legal protections for loyalists who went beyond the scope of the law to apprehend rebels.[71] By 1838, Britain had five thousand troops stationed in Lower Canada to help put down unrest and used militia units to monitor and control suspicious movements across the border.[72]

British forces also recruited Haudenosaunee from Grand River and Kahnawake to assist in policing militants. In 1838, for example, Allan N. MacNab recruited three hundred Haudenosaunee to scout the "the swamps and Morasses between Brantford and Chippawa [*sic*] extending on either side of the Grand River."[73] They were charged with searching for rebels and hidden caches of arms. Haudenosaunee from Grand River protected the Niagara frontier in 1837 during the Navy Island crisis, while the Kahnawake community mobilized to defend Lachine.[74] Men from Kahnawake also captured seventy-five *Patriotes* who attempted to enlist the Kahnawake's aid in the rebellion and volunteered to fight a suspected Patriot army near the Châteauguay River.[75]

British commanders justified their use of Indigenous soldiers to police the boundary through a combination of necessity, racial stereotypes, and genuine admiration of their skill. The British government worried the Haudenosaunee would be unable to remain neutral in the conflict so they offered the Haudenosaunee presents. Enlisting the help of these warriors not only benefited the Crown's military capabilities but also deprived the *Patriotes* and Rebels of a potential source of information, support, and supplies.[76] British commanders also believed Haudenosaunee possessed unique attributes. Allan N. MacNab noted that Indigenous people were better suited for scouting in difficult terrain because their "habits and knowledge of the country [are] much better adapted than the Militia."[77]

Enlisting Haudenosaunee, however, created concerns about the use of "savages" to put down recalcitrant white settlers. Lieutenant Governor George Arthur attempted to allay such fears by noting that the Indigenous soldiers he used were "very different in habits and circumstance from the savages called into the service during the wars of the last century." They followed orders, cultivated land, expressed loyalty, and obeyed the "merciful rules of civilized warfare."[78] Indians still inspired fear in the hearts of their enemies, but to Arthur posed no threat to British sensibilities when commanded by adept British commanders.[79]

The Haudenosaunees' decision to support the British during the 1837–38 Rebellion was not a given. The Haudenosaunee at Kahnawke viewed the *Patriotes* as a threat to their community and feared that they would trespass upon their lands. The *Patriotes'* failed attempt to confiscate the arms of the Kahnawake in 1838 only fueled the Haudenosaunees' distrust further, while British offers of guns, ammunition, and provisions offered an appealing alternative. Warfare also gave Kahnawake soldiers opportunities to pillage and plunder, reaffirm historical alliances and treaties with the British government, acquire additional presents from the Crown, and achieve prestige within their own communities.[80]

By the end of 1838, the momentum of each rebellion had almost completely dissipated. Opportunistic raids, including the destruction of the *Sir Robert Peel* and attacks on the Haudenosaunee village at Kahnawake, damaged property and spread terror. Significant military victories, however, remained far from the rebels' grasp.[81] Britain's victory over the *Patriotes* at the Battle of Windmill in November all but ended the *Patriotes'* campaign. Britain executed nine prisoners of the 140 it captured in the battle, in an attempt to send a clear message to those who still harbored desires for rebellion. The United States, in turn, convicted

William Lyon Mackenzie for violating American neutrality laws in 1839, sentencing him to eighteen months in jail and a meager fine.[82]

The rebellion failed to destroy Britain's control on the continent, but it succeeded in forcing Britain to adjust its colonial policy. Lord Durham's report on the violence in 1839 convinced the British government that the colonies required a new system of management if it wished to maintain its foothold on the continent. In 1841, Britain combined Upper and Lower Canada into the Province of Canada (comprised of Canada East and Canada West) and in 1848 instituted responsible government based on Durham's suggestions.[83] The new distribution of power did not adhere with the visions imagined by the reformers who fought in 1837–38, or with the republican visions created by their American supporters. Britain reduced the power of its appointed governors and expanded self-governance. It did so, however, by increasing the authority of the executive council and local bodies of governance rather than the democratically elected Legislative Assembly.[84]

Not everyone remained to see how these new reforms would unfold. Rebels, sympathizers, and even property owners concerned about the uncertainty created by the rebellion relocated from Upper and Lower Canada into the United States during the rebellions. Some of them returned with the cessation of violence, while many of the most radical supporters chose to remake their lives south of the border. Not all French Canadians had chosen to engage in active rebellion, but all who remained north of the line soon felt the reprisals that followed. For French Canadians, the forced merger between Upper and Lower Canada served as a visible reminder of Britain's continued attempts to stamp out their autonomy.[85]

Indian Removal

While the Rebellions of 1837 and 1838 provided an intense, yet short-lived challenge to British authority along the boundary line, British and American approaches to Indian policy emphasized the longer-term problems both countries faced. Until the 1840s, British officials provided gifts to the Anishinaabe who traveled from the United States to places like Manitoulin Island for annual ceremonies where they could renew their alliances with the British crown.[86] Lewis Cass, the governor of Michigan Territory, warned against the problems such policies created. He believed it was incompatible that "a foreign power should thus subsidize a body of people living within our jurisdiction" and felt the matter warranted the attention of the War Department.[87] Henry Schoolcraft, the acting Indian Superintendent of Michigan, came to similar conclusions. Schoolcraft warned that "the British Government held out inducements" in this fashion "more from the hope of securing the service of the Indians in any future difficulties with the United States, than from any other cause."[88]

The fears Cass and Schoolcraft expressed became all the more significant as the United States adopted Indian removal as a national policy. Beginning in the early nineteenth century and intensifying in the 1830s, Indian removal aimed to relocate Indigenous people living in the eastern United States to lands west of the Mississippi River. Proponents of Indian removal argued that their policies opened up land for settlement and gave Indigenous people more time to assimilate. In the Great Lakes, however, British offers of alliance and permanent relocation put a damper on American attempts to force relocation beyond the Mississippi.[89]

In the fall of 1839, Schoolcraft's frustrations boiled over. He complained that unless the United States abandoned its removal efforts, the Odawa living in the Lower Peninsula of Michigan would move into British territory, where they maintained familial and social connections.[90] Differences in colonial policies created opportunities for resistance and strategic weaknesses at the edges of the nation. Schoolcraft beseeched Major General Winfield Scott to strengthen the defenses along the border. At the same time, he informed the Odawa that those who relocated across the line would forfeit the annuities and treaty goods provided to them in the Treaties of 1836 and 1837.[91] He hoped indirect forms of control would shore up the direct kinds of power he lacked.

Similar measures followed for other groups, creating widespread ambiguity. The Potawatomi's decision to resist removal in the United States by fleeing to British North America emphasized the power the border could have in regional disputes, but also the ways it could leave groups in limbo. In a similar set of migrations regarding the Oneida, the United States had ruled that Indigenous migrants remained "wards of the United States . . . [who had] no right of expatriation."[92] In the case of the Oneida, that ruling secured their rights to a share of the treaty fund. When applied more broadly to groups like the Odawa and Potawatomi, it emphasized the ways the United States could claim power over people even when they attempted to live beyond its explicit jurisdiction. Indirect power had a significant reach.

Britain, for its part, continued to treat the Indigenous migrants from the United States as American Indians regardless of their desire to relocate permanently to British territory. The Potawatomi who moved north did not receive a reserve in British North America and had no access to a trust fund. Many eventually incorporated themselves into Indigenous communities at Sarnia, Cape Croker, Thessalon, Spanish River, Christian Island, and elsewhere. British ambivalence and pre-existing social connections with communities north of the border made the movement possible. British ambivalence also ensured such movements came at a significant cost.[93]

For Americans, Britain's approach to Indigenous mobility represented a violation of American jurisdiction. Britain's lack of support for permanent migrations mattered little. Americans viewed Britain's actions as an attack on the civilizing efforts of the United States and a strategic threat along Michigan's northern frontier. Gift-giving provided a visible reminder of warfare and alliances, a reminder that violence underlay the basic geography of power in the Great Lakes.[94]

Although Britain undermined American removal efforts, it relied on the same kinds of indirect control to shape the transnational mobility of Indigenous people. In 1843 George Ironside, a superintendent of Indian Affairs, learned of a group of Wendat who left British territory to take up lands along the Mississippi River. Ironside requested the support of the Wendat chiefs who remained in British territory. Together they prevented the migrants from leasing out the farms they left behind. The approach deprived the migrants of important financial resources and created internal divisions within the community.[95]

Indirect forms of control, enacted by men like Schoolcraft and Ironside, did not prevent the Ojibwe, Odawa, Wendat, and Potawatomi from crossing the border, nor did they prevent them from returning home in the years that followed. Fears that the Anishinabek collected treaty benefits on both sides of the line continued into the twentieth century.[96] Still, the array of threats that Schoolcraft and Ironside helped to develop had wide reaching implications. They formed the early underpinnings of indirect border control strategies that Britain and the United States would rely on to police movement across the Great Lakes, Prairies and Pacific Coast.[97] They managed to create a border that mattered. It remained, however, only one border among many.

At the same moment that the Rebellion of 1837–38 and Indian removal challenged British and American authority along the boundary line, Indigenous people rethought their own boundaries and challenged European ones. After years of fighting, the Cheyenne (Tsistsistas), Arapahos (Hinono'ei), Lakota, Comanche (Nimini), and Kiowas came to a peace agreement in 1840. The agreement extended from British North America into Mexico and from the Rocky Mountains to the eastern edge of the Great Plains.[98]

Oregon Boundary Dispute

By 1842, Britain and the United States had cleared up most of their remaining questions about their border's path from the Atlantic Ocean to the Lake of the Woods. Across the rest of the continent, however, the situation remained less certain. No boundary markers indicated the border's path west of the Lake of the Woods, and the arrival of thousands of American settlers in the 1840s to the jointly managed Oregon Territory put pressure on the existing relationship.[99]

American expansionists rallied behind the slogan "Fifty-Four Forty or Fight!" but neither country relished the thought of war.[100]

The Treaty of Oregon, signed in 1846, attempted to fix the impasse and settle disputes between the Hudson's Bay Company and American expansionists.[101] It established the 49th parallel of latitude as the boundary between the two countries west of the Rocky Mountains. In choosing that location, the two countries committed to following abstract parallels rather than a natural feature like the Columbia River.[102]

Like the boundary agreements the two countries had signed in the past, the Treaty of Oregon ignored existing Indigenous boundaries and created an agreement on paper rather than in practice. Vague language and limited geographical knowledge compounded matters. As part of the treaty, both countries agreed that their maritime border would stretch from Vancouver Island through the middle of the Strait of Juan de Fuca. Neither country, however, could agree on which of the three possible channels constituted the "middle."[103] It took until 1872 for an international arbitrator to rule in favor of the United States' claim to the San Juan Islands. In the meantime, the United States and Britain sent warships and soldiers to the islands.[104]

The process of claiming territory, surveying it, and settling land caused friction and violence, particularly south of the 49th parallel. The Cayuse War (1847–1855), Puget Sound War (1855–56), Yakama War (1855–1858), and persistent coastal raiding escalated regional violence into matters of international concern. In 1855 tensions boiled over when the Yakama killed A. J. Bolen, a sub-Indian agent, leading to the short-term mobilization of the militia and rumors of a pan-Indigenous alliance that persisted years after the conflict.[105]

In reality, the possibility of a pan-Indigenous alliance existed more as a specter than a reality. While the Nisqually decided to fight, others such as the Snoqualmie led by chief Patkanim provided troops to the United States to help put down resistance. In Puget Sound, Leschi (Nisqually), his brother Quiemuth, and a few hundred of their followers fought for close to a year against regular troops, militia units, and Indigenous auxiliaries. The combat was sporadic and most battles produced few casualties.[106] By April 1856, the war had all but ended. The United States branded Leschi a domestic traitor and executed him for murder, a crime inapplicable among wartime combatants.[107]

Britain and the United States demonstrated that they could field impressive militaries to fight wars in the 1850s, but they struggled to police their border on a day-to-day basis. During the 1850s, both countries worried that successful Indigenous opposition on one side of the border could increase boldness and resistance on the other. Mutual fear created opportunities for cooperation.[108] On November 1, 1855, James Tilton, adjutant-general of Washington Territory, requested that Britain send a ship to assist the American government in Puget Sound against Indigenous resistance. James Douglas, the governor of the colony of Vancouver Island, agreed to help. He sent rifles, ammunition, a company steamer, and money out of his personal supply to assist the Americans. The British ship would not engage directly in military conflicts, but acted in a supporting role. By the time hostilities in Puget Sound abated in 1856, Douglas estimated that the United States owed at least $40,000 to Britain for the use of British ships and for supplies. The United States took until 1859 to repay these debts, disipating some of the goodwill that existed between officers in the two countries.[109]

Despite this setback, the two countries sent ships and information to assist one another into the 1880s to ensure that a pan-Indigenous alliance never materialized. They justified this cooperation along practical lines.[110] British and American military victories "had a very quieting effect on both sides of the line."[111] In this context, subduing Indigenous people, no matter where they were located, benefited colonial policy on both sides of the border.

While violence against settlers motivated British and American action, Tsimshian (ćmsyan), Tlingit, and Haida raids against Coast Salish communities also drew concern. The Pacific Coast had witnessed raiding long before the arrival of Europeans, and the practice continued well after their arrival. Both countries worried, however, that raiding encouraged reciprocal violence and blurred the lines of nationality.[112] Patterns of settlement and the newly formed border made the problem difficult to ignore. The creation of Fort Victoria in 1843, for example, provided incentives for the Tsimshian, Tlingit, and Haida to make the arduous trek all the way down the Pacific Coast from as far north as what would become Alaska to the northern edge of Washington. The journey gave these groups access to the preferential goods and wage labor markets of Puget Sound. It also provided northern groups with access to a variety of coastal communities, which they could raid for slaves and other spoils.[113]

In the 1850s, the growth of settler populations led officials on both sides of the border to engage more directly with raiding parties. Britain sent a gunboat to the Haida Gwaii in 1851 and to New Caledonia in 1858. Gunboats provided moments of intense authority, but did not establish the consistent kind of power necessary to creating a long-term border policy.[114] During the 1850s and 1860s, thousands of Haida, Tsimshian, Tlingit, and other "northern Indians" still traveled hundreds of miles south to trade and work. If soldiers attempted to engage raiding parties, they crossed the boundary line to evade pursuit. The Sqilxw (Okanogan) might not recognize the validity of European territorial boundaries, but they understood the restrictions these borders created. When threatened, they exploited the limitations that national borders put on colonial soldiers.[115]

Pacific Coast Boundary Survey

For all the ways the international line west of the Rocky Mountains impeded the efforts of federal administrators, it remained a border without much form. From 1857 until 1868, the Northwest Boundary team aimed to change that. It surveyed eight hundred miles of border and gathered information on over thirty thousand square miles of territory. Manual laborers cut through dense forests and hauled supplies.[116] Skilled laborers and technical experts built bridges, set up astronomical stations, drew maps, and traversed land "almost unknown" to both governments.[117] Finding the border, marking it on the land, and making the surveys legible to distant administrators required time and money. The American team alone required $400,000 in wages to offset the 120,000 days' worth of labor required by the process.[118]

Supplies, provisions, transportation, and accommodations added at least another $200,000 in costs.[119] Unsurprisingly, the scale of the operation created significant logistical challenges. Utilitarian supplies—including 966 pounds of hard bread and 645 pounds of soap—mixed with chronometers, telescopes, and other technical equipment in their cargo manifests. If the surveyors refrained from bringing fully completed buildings with them, it was a matter of logistics rather than desire. In the fall of 1857 they purchased 35 windows, 54,000 shingles, and over 40,000 feet of lumber, batten, and scantling from J. P. Keller in a single purchase. The surveyors came to stay.[120]

The surveyors brought china plates, cups, and saucers as well as chocolate, assorted jellies, English mustard, and curry powder. Luxury items provided the officers, at least, with a reprieve from the drudgeries of their work. While many of these comforts weighed little, the 1,420 pounds of Sandwich Island sugar, 710 pounds of crushed sugar, and 46.5 gallons of Sandwich Island syrup purchased from W. S. Ladd in the fall of 1857 did not. The survey team packed for utility and pleasure, but undesired contingencies did not stray far from their minds. In their medical kits, they included bullet forceps and an array of "penis syringes" used in the treatment of syphilis. Unsure if they would be fighting or fornicating, the surveyors erred on the side of caution and prepared for both.[121]

Both countries imagined the border as a clear line without ambiguity. For the laborers who tried to make that vision a reality, border-making was often miserable work. Complications, discomforts, and setbacks mired the process. Steep mountains and dense forests mixed with persistent rain, tedious marches, and unexpected dangers.[122] Swarms of mosquitoes, known by surveyors as "our tormentors," took advantage of the men's helplessness as they crossed difficult terrain.[123] Tired from long treks and limited diets, laborers looked for simple pleasures. They delayed marches, for example, at every opportunity to gorge themselves on delicious Hookle berries.[124]

In 1858, shortly after the survey began, news of a gold discovery on the Fraser River reached California, altering the logistics of the entire survey.[125] In four months, thirty thousand settlers flooded onto the Fraser River. The news crippled regional military and commercial ventures as wageworkers and soldiers alike deserted their posts. Worse still, the influx of American settlers threatened to destabilize the region and undermine Britain's territorial claim. Britain established the Colony of British Columbia in 1858, expanded its administration, and sent gunboats and troops to help enforce order in its new colony. The creation of the colony helped reinforce Britain's territorial claims on the West Coast, but did not end the friction between Britain and the United States.[126]

For the Stó:lō, whose territory the miners entered, the challenges brought by a sudden demographic upheaval were even harder to ignore. The Xwelítem ("the starving ones," as the Stó:lō knew them) brought disease. They also destroyed longhouses and excavated the river fronts where the Stó:lō made their summer residences.[127] The Stó:lō had participated in the gold trade in the past and took advantage of the economic opportunities the gold rush created. They offered their services as guides, provisioners, packers, and freighters and conducted their own mining operations. While the gold rush provided the Stó:lō and Nlaka-pamux with opportunities, they could not ignore the miner's disrespect of their territory or the overlaps between productive mining claims and their salmon fishing and processing sites. The miners' militancy, which peaked with destruction of five Indigenous settlements near Spuzzum, required immediate action.[128]

For Britain and the United States, the miner's attacks and the Stó:lō's response provided a unsettling reminder of how little control they maintained on the coast as they prepared to define their shared border. Neither country could control the movements of miners or the attacks they launched. Nor could they control the peace that followed.[129] According to oral accounts by Elder Patrick Charlie, the Stó:lō chief Liquitem and Major Snyder (a leading miner) established a peace agreement long before Britain's Colonial Office could respond to the violence.[130] The lag time between local problems and colonial responses created an environment where regional solutions could flourish. For the survey teams themselves, the Gold Rush drove up the price of labor and supplies, causing "considerable embarrassment, delay, and additional expense in the field operations."[131] The eruption of the American Civil War a few years later diverted resources from the survey, causing it to drag on until 1868.[132]

Building borders in regions in which neither country had much control or knowledge required a mixture of unbridled optimism and legions of workers. When mixed correctly, the result was potent. Unskilled laborers and

Table 1.1 **Distribution by Occupation in the Northwest Boundary Survey Paylists and Special Paylists, 1857–1868**

Occupation Type	*Days Worked*	*%*	*Pay Received*	*%*
Administration	16,720.0	13.5	$84,610.66	21.0
Misc	11,186.5	9.0	$75,499.55	18.8
Skilled Labor	8,676.0	7.0	$37,998.22	9.4
Technical Experts	17,443.0	14.1	$87,464.91	21.7
Transportation	27,941.0	22.5	$52,298.58	13.0
Unskilled Labor	42,116.5	33.9	$64,428.82	16.0
Total	124,083.0	100.0	$402,300.74	100.0

Source: Andrew Johnson, "Message from the President of the United States Concerning the Northwest Boundary Commission, February 13, 1869" (hereafter "Northwest Boundary Survey Disbursements"), 1869. 40th Congress, 3d Session, Ex. Doc. No. 86, 2-92. In the original records, 200 days of labor are not associated with any occupation and therefore are not included in this chart. The boundary commission records note 124,283 worth of labor in total. For a detailed description of occupational classifications see the User Guide at www.buildingborders.com.

transporters—measured in either days worked or people employed—did the bulk of the work. Axemen on the American team, for example, spent 8,754 days cutting down trees on either side of the boundary line so that travelers could see the border as it passed through the forests. Technical experts and administrators, while a much smaller contingent in the parties, worked full time for most of the survey and drew disproportionate salaries.

If the survey teams represented the vanguard of federal power on the Pacific Coast, it was a power contingent on local cooperation. American surveyors had drawn on Indigenous guides and provisioners in the Great Lakes during the early nineteenth century and similarly relied on them as they surveyed their border with Mexico.[133] They approached the Pacific border in much the same way.

The Stó:lō, Semiahmoo, Lummi, Nooksack, Colville, and Uhiloweyuks provided the survey team with saddles, canoes, sleighs, planks of wood, and a wide array of food. They piloted steamers, ferried parties across the Chilliwack River, cared for animals, rented out their cabins, and served as guides. Most of all, they provided crucial information and allowed British and American surveyors to pass through their territory unmolested. The United States boundary team likely employed between 200 and 300 Indigenous laborers, although inconsistencies in record keeping has meant that as few as 150 and as many as 600 may have participated.[134]

Table 1.2 **Indigenous Laborers in the United States Northwest Boundary Survey**

	Indigenous	*Likely Indigenous*	*Total*
Entries of Work*	538	209	747
Days Worked (paylists)	1,811	723.5	2,534.5
Days Worked (total)**	–	–	7,873
Pay Received	$4,922.92	$2,865.25	$7,788.17

Source: Northwest Boundary Survey Disbursements, 2-92.

*Entries of work include each reference to a laborer even if they appear multiple times in the paylists.

** Days worked (total) refers to the number of days the Boundary Commission claims to have hired Indigenous workers. It recorded only about a third of these (days worked—paylists) with any detail.

Ská ákle, for example, worked for the boundary survey team as an expressman, packer, laborer, and transporter on at least fifteen separate occasions between 1857 and 1859. Ská ákle served as the representative for groups of laborers ranging from six to 39 people.[135] The individuals Ská ákle recruited on each team likely overlapped, but the boundary commission's records make discerning these patterns impossible. In many instances, the boundary commission recorded Coast Salish and other Indigenous participants as "Indians," leaving out their names, genders, tribal affiliations, days worked, rates of pay, and even the exact number of people employed. What they did note, however, suggests that Indigenous laborers worked primarily in transportation related industries. Many received one dollar a day for their labor plus fifty cents a day per canoe—a rate on par with what many non-Indigenous manual laborers received.[136]

While the survey team hired at least two Indigenous women, the unnamed wives of La Hache and La-Hark, as transporters, they avoided the practice where possible.[137] When Tuk-Tuk refused to join a survey party unless a female companion accompanied him, Henry Custer, one of the team's topographers, replaced him with a more "reflective" Indian. Custer feared that "the disturbance which these Indian damsels produce in a party by their willfulness and extent of influence over their stronger companions" would be a significant impediment to his party's progress.[138]

Considered together, Indigenous people provided roughly 6.3 percent of the days of labor noted by the Northwest Boundary Survey's records. Their labor, however, mattered far more than their numbers suggested. In 1859, as the joint boundary commission surveyed the Northern Cascade Mountains in present-day Washington State, they drew on detailed maps created by Thiusoloc and his father.

Table 1.3 **Occupations of Indigenous Workers on the Northwest Boundary Survey**

Occupation	**Entries of work***		**Days Worked****		**Pay**	
	No.	%	**No.**	%	**$**	%
Canoeman	316	42.3%	582	23.0%	$2,326.35	29.9%
Packer	176	23.6%	450	17.8%	$2,699.50	34.7%
Transporter	70	9.4%	31	1.2%	$498.72	6.4%
Expressman	50	6.7%	443	17.5%	$710.60	9.1%
Laborer	40	5.4%	225	8.9%	$262.00	3.4%
Misc	31	4.1%	107	4.2%	$176.00	2.3%
Guide	26	3.5%	371.5	14.7%	$745.00	9.6%
Supplier	16	2.1%	10	0.4%	$10.00	0.1%
Provisioner	13	1.7%	20	0.8%	$20.00	0.3%
Herder	9	1.2%	295	11.6%	$340.00	4.4%
Grand Total	747	100.0%	2,534.5	100.0%	$7,788.17	100.0%

Source: Northwest Boundary Survey Disbursements.

Note: *Entries of work include each reference to a laborer even if they appear multiple times in the paylists. ** Days worked (total) refers to the number of days the Boundary Commission claims to have hired Indigenous workers. It recorded only about a third of these with any detail.

Both men provided information on the pertinent river systems the surveyors would encounter and the Halq'eméylem place names that surrounded them.[139] Indigenous guides carried messages between astronomical stations serving as a backbone of communication.[140] They portaged heavy canoes over obstructed terrain and hunted, fished, and gathered food necessary for the survey's success.[141] Nooksack men constructed river canoes in the field, allowing surveyors to explore long distances without having to portage canoes across the entire distance.[142]

In a number of regions, such as along the interior portions of the Cascade Mountains, the reconnaissance team required Indigenous guides and carriers.[143] Henry Custer believed that the Indigenous people he worked with possessed differing ranges of geographical expertise, but all possessed "the most minute topographical knowledge, of a certain portion of the country."[144] As the guides moved beyond their own territorial boundaries, however, he noted that "the country is perfect terra incognita to them, which they neither need or care or have the curiosity to explore."[145] Custer's statement acknowledged the ways Indigenous territories and boundaries shaped the world he encountered, even as he worked to create colonial borders on top of them.

If Custer hesitated to hire Indigenous women, he displayed no such reluctance with Indigenous men. On July 14, he gathered a party "consisting of 11 Indians, 2 white men . . . every one of the Indians loaded with a Pak [*sic*] of about 50–60 lb."[146] The ratio of Indigenous workers to white surveyors (11 to 3) and the ability of Indigenous workers to carry heavy packs over difficult terrain emphasized their importance. Without Indigenous participants, the party of 14, which was supported by more than 600 pounds of goods, became a party of three hungry and undersupplied surveyors.

If Britain and the United States desired to use the boundary survey to project federal power onto local communities, the men who worked on it learned a conflicting lesson through experience. Local knowledge made national borders feasible. Surveying equipment had powerful applications, but could not select optimal routes or approaches. For that, Custer relied heavily on his Stó:lō guide, who could follow "faint traces [of Indian trails] with remarkable expertness."[147] Without skilled Coast Salish guides, Custer worried he would have to turn to white settlers who "unused to travel in these woods . . . [are] sure, to select always the most awkward place of the route."[148]

By the time Custer planned his trip along the Whatcomb trail, he had employed Indigenous guides and laborers for several months. He expressed his gratitude for their efforts, emphasizing the "almost incredible amount of labor [that] may be gotten out of them" when treated with respect.[149] If boundary surveyors did not bother to consistently record the name or the tribe of the Indigenous laborers, guides, packers, and navigators they relied upon, they did not hesitate to recognize their value to the project's success.

The Coast Salish offered laborers to the boundary team on good faith. Colonial officials rarely lived up to the expectations the Coast Salish placed on them in return. Neither Britain nor the United States consulted the Coast Salish when designing the border and showed little interest in consulting them about it after the survey. Local knowledge might have underwritten the success of the boundary survey, but Britain and the United States soon forgot about it. They dreamed of federal governments who monopolized what borders meant and how they affected the Indigenous systems of territory and governance.

***

By the time the Northwest Boundary team had finished their work in 1868, Britain and the United States had succeeded in establishing lasting territorial agreements with one another. They had demarcated their border in the Atlantic, Pacific, and Great Lakes regions, giving substance to the division they had once imagined. The border they created, however, did not exist in isolation. It served as only one way to organize territory and coexisted with hundreds of Indigenous borders on the continent. The process had not been easy. From 1775 until 1861, the border provided as much grief as it did clarity.

The Rebellions of Upper and Lower Canada (1837), the bloodless Aroostook War between New Brunswick and Maine in 1839, the Oregon boundary dispute of 1846, and the San Juan affair of 1859 on the Pacific Coast ensured that war and territory remained on the minds of federal officials in both countries.[150] Britain and the United States stationed troops near the border as markers of national power and as practical contingencies against the possibility of war. Once stationed in the borderland, these soldiers acted as a rudimentary border control force.

In practice, however, soldiers attacked fortified locations and held strategic points better than they provided any kind of comprehensive control. Soldiers enforced order with a kind of brutality and immediacy unmatched by any of the other agencies that would eventually help to enforce the border. Faced with an expansive, amorphous, and dangerous borderland, most units confined their attention to the immediate vicinity of their posts and ignored much of the day-to-day traffic that crossed the border.[151] Part of the problem they faced was inherent in the border itself.

Creating colonial borders without knowledge of where they actually ran resulted in decades of problems and disputes. Boundary surveys clarified the border's location, but created problems of their own. As the Rebellions of 1837–38 and the Odawa's resistance to Indian Removal had demonstrated, the border outlined the limits of federal power better than it constrained the social and economic connections that crossed it. Exerting consistent control across that line took decades to establish. Before the United States and Britain could achieve that kind of power, a Civil War and a political reorganization called both countries' futures into question.

2

The Civil and Dakota Wars

In the 1860s, the American Civil War and the Dakota War provided sobering reminders of the ineffectiveness of federal border controls. The border succeeded in creating havens that defectors, draft dodgers, smugglers, refugees, soldiers, and Confederate raiders all exploited. It contributed little to the ways Britain maintained its neutrality and actively reduced the ways the United States could exercise power. Even federal employees ignored the border when possible. In such an environment, the border provided neither government with the ability to shape violence or handle the resulting fallout.

Just as troubling, the wars underscored just how much Indigenous territorial boundaries still mattered. After the Dakotas' defeat in 1862, many relocated north. Crossing the international line offered a viable means of avoiding violence with American settlers and soldiers, but it required entering territory claimed by the Métis, Oceti Sakowin (Sioux), Cree, Ojibwe, and British. That the Dakota needed to construct multiple diplomatic agreements in order to remain north of the line provided a reminder to the ways the Canada–US border still operated as partial fiction. The Civil War provided no more reassurance. Soldiers who fled onto Indigenous lands disappeared, and communities located near Indigenous nations attempted to skirt their recruitment quotas on the grounds that they might need to fight frontier wars at any moment. For all the thousands of soldiers both countries invested into policing the edges of their territories, the continent's geopolitical environment continued to bear little resemblance to the clean lines federal diplomats had set out to create.

Despite frequent setbacks in direct approaches to policing, both governments found success exerting power in indirect ways. American soldiers, for example, funded kidnappers to enter British territory, showcasing both the visceral and psychological ways that it could extend power across national lines. For the Dakota, even those living two hundred kilometers into the interior of British North America, the specter of American power loomed large years after the conflict. Indigenous communities continued to skip over and ignore boundary

A Line of Blood and Dirt. Benjamin Hoy, Oxford University Press (2021). © Oxford University Press.
DOI: 10.1093/oso/9780197528693.003.0003

stones. Fear, however, lingered and shaped behavior decades later in ways border guards never could.

The Civil War

In April 1861 Confederate forces fired on Fort Sumter, beginning a Civil War that would consume the United States for the next four years. From the outset, the war put Britain in an uncomfortable position. On an ideological level, British North Americans hoped that the Civil War, while unfortunate, would end slavery. At the same time, a southern victory, although ideologically abhorrent, held practical value for Britain. If the South remained independent, British North America might hold the balance of power on the continent.[1]

By the end of 1861, British hopes had faded. The North showed little interest in abolishing slavery, and British military experts worried that if the war ended quickly, Union soldiers might turn north and march into Canada. With only a 4,300 regular troops, 10,000 inconsistently trained volunteers, and a deficit of naval vessels on the Great Lakes caused by the United States' violation of the Rush-Bagot agreement, Britain stood little chance on land. If war broke out, British forces in the interior could only hope to stall against a Union army that had swelled to 700,000 men and hope that the British navy could force a peace.[2]

In response to the dilemma created by the Civil War, Queen Victoria declared Britain's neutrality in May of 1861. The declaration, combined with colonial laws passed subsequently, banned the enlistment of British subjects in the foreign war and prohibited British merchants from contributing weapons, ammunition, and coal to the belligerents. These laws, however, left open other avenues for profit. British subjects remained free to sell food and medicine to both sides. Britain's desire for profit prevented its full divestment from American commerce.[3] Even if it had not, British neutrality depended on its ability to control economic and military movements across its borders. It had failed in that respect in 1812 and again in 1837. By the 1860s, it had years of experience putting out diplomatic fires, but had shown little capacity for rooting out the underlying problems.

To the surprise of few, Britain's attempted neutrality quickly ran into problems. In November of 1861, Captain Charles Wilkes of the Union's *San Jacinto* stopped the British ship *Trent* on its way from Havana to England and arrested Confederate envoys John Slidell and James Mason. The capture violated British sovereignty and put Britain in an awkward diplomatic position. It had no interest in fighting the United States, but neither would it let the United States board its ships. Britain sent 14,436 soldiers with artillery support and military supplies to North America. Canada called up its militia. The increase in forces provided Britain with a stronger foothold on the continent, but fell well short of the 150,000 soldiers that British military experts estimated would be needed to defend its North American territory. The Union, in no condition to begin an unnecessary war with Britain, backed down and turned over the two prisoners.[4]

In the aftermath of the *Trent* affair, Britain and the United States enacted policies designed to discourage Confederate soldiers from using British North America as a staging ground and British citizens from seeking enlistment south of the line. The plan relied on large numbers of soldiers. Britain built and repaired forts along the border and hoped that direct approaches to control would suffice. In practice, policing the border required fewer men than active warfare, but continued to exceed the capacity of the British and American personnel.[5]

The Union's attempt to control the transit of goods fared no better. The South lacked the manufacturing industry necessary to produce enough arms, rails, cloth, pig iron, and shoes necessary for supply its war effort. Facing shortages, it turned to smugglers to make up the difference. For all the strategic importance that rested on controlling maritime trade, Union blockade attempts sputtered. Goods from Britain, Canada, Mexico, Bermuda, Nassau, and even from the North entered the South.[6] Historian Stephen R. Wise estimates that blockade-runners supplied the Confederacy with 60 percent of its weapons and three-fourths of its gunpowder.[7] Female smugglers and foreigners, in particular, found success. Union soldiers showed reluctance to search women and often refused to prosecute British smugglers out of fear of diplomatic reprisals. The Confederacy's lifeline remained open. Both Britain and the United States had failed to curb smuggling during times of peace and found it an even more daunting task in times of war.[8]

The problem stemmed from the approach, not simply the execution. In 1864 N. Sargent, the American commissioner of customs, toured the customshouses located along the eastern portion of Canada–US border and along the Atlantic seaboard. Despite the heavy concentration of customs posts in the area he toured, Sargent expressed dismay at what he saw. The thousands of bays, rivers, inlets, and islands on the coast of Maine created ample opportunity for smugglers from New Brunswick and Nova Scotia to bring cargo uncontested into the United States. In Maine, the border was an "imaginary one, running through a wild country, sparsely settled in some places, and with no inhabitants in others, for hundreds of miles."[9]

Sargent commended the customs officers in Maine for their tenacity and skill. Unless they received more people and faster boats, however, he believed smuggling would remain easy and profitable. Both the presence and absence of people created difficulties for border enforcement. Along the Quebec-Vermont border, Sargent noted that thick forests inhibited the movement of customs officers, while dense settlement on adjoining parts of the border made it difficult for federal personnel to separate local from international traffic. Smugglers exploited the noticeable gaps in enforcement. In a wartime environment, failing to prevent smuggling was more than a missed opportunity to secure revenue. It often put guns and bullets in the hands of enemies.[10]

Breaking the social bonds that connected communities provided an alternative way to control movement. So long as borderland communities prioritized their own economic success and their social connections with their neighbors, neutrality would remain difficult to police. To address these challenges, the US State Department created a passport system in 1861 designed to create economic and social distance by adding annoyance and delay to transnational travel. Confusion marred the plan from its outset. Although Congress had claimed the exclusive right to issue passports since 1856, mayors of Canadian towns issued their own certifications of nationality as substitutes for passports, hoping to provide a less intrusive means of identification. This alternate system made Canadian bureaucrats wealthy, while creating a creating a market for counterfeit papers.[11]

In the end, the passport system ignited public resentment better than it contained Confederate operatives. Canadian newspapers panned the idea of a national passport system as both impractical and disastrous. Toronto's *Globe and Mail* argued that "on so extensive a frontier as that between the United States and Canada, thirty thousand men would be needed to carry out a passport system with efficiency."[12] The paper stated that even in Europe, which had relatively short borders, many countries had already abandoned passports as "utterly inoperative to prevent the transit of political conspirators."[13] It further complained that the passport system added two and a half dollars to travel costs between the two countries and created long delays at major railway hubs. Pressed by the logistics of policing such an extensive border and by the tepid Canadian response, the United States rescinded its passport order on March 8, 1865.[14]

The failure of military patrols, blockades, and passports created a disheartening environment. The countries' inability to control even their own soldiers and agents only made matters worse. By 1865 approximately 508,000 men deserted the Union army, out of an estimated two million enlisted men.[15] In New York, deserters simply walked across the border to escape service. By 1865, an estimated fifteen thousand soldiers had made the united Canadas their temporary home.[16]

British soldiers deserted their posts in the opposite direction to enlist with the Union or Confederate armies, which paid higher wages and bounties for enlistment.[17] Federal bounties of $100 to $300 and local bounties of as much as $1,000 offered soldiers the equivalent of several years of pay as a laborer.[18] Prospective soldiers could cross the border to collect bounties and then flee back to Canada to avoid military service, a process that could be repeated multiple times. Police Sergeant George Blanke summarized the problem in the spring of 1863. Blanke lamented that a large number of deserters had arrived in Victoria from Puget Sound, "most of them are deserters from the American Army . . . some of them were originally deserters from the English Service."[19] Desertion of any kind risked incarceration and possible execution. Deserting from both the British and American armed forces added an additional layer of risk that only the most reckless took. Still, these kinds of decisions made quick money for those who successfully navigated national jurisdictions.[20]

For Indigenous soldiers who chose to desert, nearby reservations and Indigenous communities created additional places to seek asylum. While this kind of movement did not put these deserters outside of the territory claimed by the American government, it often put them outside its practical reach. Colonial maps recorded borders agreed upon by European diplomats, but these served as only a portion of the many borders that mattered to everyday life. Despite having an employee follow a "half breed" deserter for more than one hundred and fifty miles along the Snake River, the Provost Marshal General's Bureau in Minnesota failed to capture him after he took "up his quarters among the Indians."[21] The Bureau came up short again in their attempt to find John Ayers, a deserter who they believed had fled to an Ojibwe (Chippewa) community near Sunrise, Minnesota.[22]

Recruitment efforts faced the same bevy of challenges that retention did, creating a dual drain on the Union's war effort. In an effort to hit recruitment targets, the Union turned to crimpers (recruitment agents) to try to expand their potential pool of applicants. The system encouraged all kinds of graft. Crimpers enlisted men they knew carried diseases, gathered recruits from British territory in violation of its neutrality, and kidnapped both British and Indigenous men to force them into service. Crimpers in Minnesota rounded up wagonloads of Ojibwe, intoxicated them, and attempted to sell them as substitutes until the Provost Marshal General's office intervened.[23] For all the problems, the possibility of recruiting willing soldiers from British soil offered a welcome relief to the northern enlistment system. The system only succeeded in getting 3 percent of those it drafted to serve, the remainder either deserting, paying commutations, or gaining suspicious exemptions.[24]

Far reaching recruitment efforts restructured life outside of the United States. Two-thirds of the young men from the Elgin Settlement, Canada West, left their homes after the Union opened military service to African American men. By the war's end 2,500 African American volunteers from British North America crossed the line to serve, believing they had a personal stake in the conflict being fought south of the border.[25] The breadth of transnational life remained hard to ignore. A reward pamphlet for deserters in the second Congressional district of Minnesota noted that from June to August 1864 more than 259 men failed to report to headquarters after being drafted; 28 of these men had a Canadian birthplace. This indicated the ways that nationality spilled across borders and the opportunities the border offered for escape.[26]

The proximity of Indigenous nations put pressure on nearby settler communities, amplifying the impact of the Canada–US border. The Beaver Bay community in northern Minnesota, for example, complained that the draft being held in Lake County would ruin their community. Many of the men who the Deputy Marshall had included in the draft pool had already left for Canada creating an unfair burden on those who remained. With the majority of able-body men drafted or absent, members of the community feared that the women of their community "could not protect herself and home against the Indians."[27]

The petitions by the Beaver Bay community for draft relief highlighted two important boundaries that shaped their experiences: the Canada–US border and American-Ojibwe boundary. The former border provided an asylum from the draft that drained the labor force of Beaver Bay as eligible men crossed the line. While colonial maps did not reflect Ojibwe power, the fear expressed by the Beaver Bay community reflected the presence of alternative territorial systems and boundaries. Residents of Beaver Bay lived not only within the Canada–US borderlands but, as their high emotions suggested, within Ojibwe borderlands as well.[28]

Like the deserters who crossed national lines and the crimpers who looked beyond them for recruits, the men tasked with policing the border paid little respect for the boundaries. In 1863, Union soldiers crossed the border in pursuit of Ebenezer Tyler, a deserter from the Union army who had fled Wolfe Island in Canada West. The soldiers succeeded in capturing Tyler and dragging him back into the United States, although pressure from the British government forced Tyler's release. More often the United States and Britain reprimanded their soldiers for abducting deserters, but they rarely repatriated the accused. Illegal abductions resulted in apologies but few changes in policy.[29]

The Civil War exposed the limitations of border control, but also emphasized what was at stake. The *Trent* affair, transnational crimping, and illegal operations of law enforcement personnel exacerbated an already tense diplomatic situation. Local violations across the border threatened to spark national outrage and push the two countries closer to a conflict neither had any interest in. This possibility became more disturbing by the middle of the war when the Confederacy began a more open policy of violating British neutrality in the hopes of fostering a conflict between Britain and the northern states.[30] Confederate sympathizers, for example, built ammunition, grenades, and a cannon at a foundry in Guelph, Canada West. They hoped to smuggle the canon in a crate marked "potatoes" onto Lake Michigan, where they intended to use it to free Confederate prisoners on Johnson's Island. The plan failed, but it demonstrated the creativity smugglers and militants used to exploit the boundary line.[31]

Although the Confederates and their sympathizers engaged in a variety of operations, including inciting Indigenous resistance to disrupt union communication and supply lines, the most spectacular event occurred at St. Albans, Vermont.[32] On October 19, 1864, twenty Confederates supporters led by Bennett Young seized the town of St. Albans, robbed three banks, killed one person, set a number of buildings on fire, and fled with $200,000 back across the line. An American posse pursued and overtook the robbers on British soil. The local militia intervened, took the prisoners and some of the money into custody, and reprimanded the American posse for operating across the international boundary.[33]

What would become of these men remained up for debate. The American government pressed for the raider's extradition, without luck. Bennett and his men justified their actions as wartime activities outside of the extradition system and found sympathy with Charles-Joseph Coursol, the presiding magistrate. Coursol claimed that the warrants for the men's arrest had not been properly issued and set them free with $84,000 of their spoils. The prisoners escaped to Montreal, and Coursol was suspended amidst accusations that he had accepted stolen money from the prisoners in exchange for their freedom.[34]

In response to Coursol's bungling of the situation, John Dix, a Union general, ordered his troops to capture the St. Albans raiders wherever they disappeared to. If that meant crossing the border and ignoring British neutrality, so be it. The approach had precedence in the way both countries had responded to the *Caroline* affair in 1837–1840 and in international law. Border crossings could occur if in hot pursuit of the enemy, but precedence did not ensure peaceful relations. Dix's policy threatened to exacerbate an already incendiary issue and forced Lincoln to intervene on December 17, 1864. Lincoln demanded that American troops crossing the border receive authorization from Washington before proceeding. A war with Britain would open new fronts and could breathe life back into the South's military efforts. Lincoln's policy kept the border crossing options open, but aimed to place the decision in the hands of the president alone rather than leaving it to an errant general.[35]

At the same moment, Britain worked to relieve tensions along the border. It recaptured the St. Albans raiders and, when it failed to secure convictions, the Canadian government paid over $30,000 in bank notes and $39,000 in gold to compensate the American banks for losses due to improper handling. Britain also passed a new neutrality act to help ease tensions over the debacle and established a Western Frontier Constabulary force to coordinate border patrols. Under the new act, Britain could fine and expel foreign nationals it suspected of using the united Canadas as a base to launch hostile actions against friendly nations. The United States used Britain's failure during the St. Albans raid as a precursor to abrogate their reciprocity agreement, but the two countries never came as close to warfare as they had been during the *Trent* affair. War weariness and an acceptance of the practical limitations of border control overcame the possibility of conflict between the two nations.[36]

By the Civil War's end, the Union and Confederacy had suffered approximately 750,000 casualties, with thousands more permanently injured.[37] Indigenous and African American communities suffered alongside American settlers as the war took its deadly toll. The Wisconsin Oneida, for example, enlisted over one hundred volunteers in the 14th Wisconsin Volunteer Regiment from a reservation of 1,100 residents. Well over a third of those soldiers never returned home. African American communities suffered likewise. Two-thirds of the young men at Buxton, Canada West, left to enlist in the Union army between 1863 and 1865, undercutting the basis of the community for the duration of the war. The border helped shape which communities took part in the violence and to what extent that violence later made its way back home. Death and suffering, however, did not confine themselves within national borders.[38]

The Dakota War

As civil war focused the Union's attention on the South, it exacerbated longstanding problems with Indigenous nations. Although the Dakota had ceded parts of Minnesota, Iowa, and the Dakotas to the United States throughout the early nineteenth century, they found themselves in an untenable situation by the 1860s. The US government refused to pay the Dakota the annuities it had promised and located the promised mills, physicians, and schools close to a hundred miles from the Sisseton. Traders soon stopped supplying goods on credit, exacerbating an already dire situation.[39] Andrew J. Myrick, a Minnesotan trader who refused to extend credit, noted: "If they are hungry, let them eat grass."[40] Starvation resulted. Settlers, lumbermen, and traders violated treaty agreements, fueling the animosity. The Dakota believed that the American government, which could not even honor its most basic treaty provisions, was falling apart.[41]

Amidst tension and suffering, individual skirmishes risked widespread violence. Robert Goodvoice (Wahpeton Dakota) has noted that the violence in Minnesota began when four young Dakota men cut through a farmer's field on their way back from hunting deer. The men got into a skirmish with the farmer, who struck one of them with his broom. The man, humiliated and goaded on by his friends, shot the farmer and killed his family. The men's actions divided the Dakota. One side called for war. The other, led by Tarasota, argued that the Dakota should avoid fighting a foolish war with the Wasitiu (white men). If warfare happened, Dakota children and elderly would suffer and American soldiers would cut the Dakota off from necessary supplies. Tarasota's pleas failed.[42]

In the middle of August 1862, Dakota launched a series of attacks throughout southwestern Minnesota. From August 18 to 23, the Dakota, led by Little Crow, killed hundreds of settlers in Minnesota, including Andrew J. Myrick.[43] Before they left, Pazeda-yapa and Inkpaduta stuffed Myrick's mouth with grass.[44] Interwoven identities made violence a messy affair. The Dakota had comingled, established friendships, intermarried, and traded with settlers.[45] According Walter LaBatte, his great-grandfather Francois, a mixed Dakota/Frenchman, stood outside his store when the violence began saying " 'Makte sni, makte sni, damakota do, damakota do' . . . 'Don't kill me, don't kill me I'm Dakota, I'm a Dakota.' They shot him, killed him."[46]

Many others caught in the middle had more success. Half a dozen Canadians, who had intermarried and lived with the Dakota for two or three decades, remained in an uncomfortable limbo. They retained access to their property and limited amounts of personal freedom, but remained under careful watch until the Dakota could ascertain their loyalties.[47] Even settlers who spoke poorly of Indigenous people maintained significant personal connections. George Spencer Jr., for example, believed that Indians possessed only a clouded intellect, loved to wash their hands in the blood of others, were incapable of diplomacy, and served as the connecting link between man and beasts.[48] Despite Spencer's perceptions, which were low even by the standards of his time, he still maintained a decade-long friendship with His Thunder (Wa-kin-yan-or-in). When violence broke out, His Thunder protected Spencer at great personal risk and later helped him escape.[49]

Early victories bolstered the Dakota's cause. The Civil War consumed the resources and attention the United States might have otherwise expended to resolve the violence. Minnesota's military forces remained underfunded and in disarray, and the Dakota pressed their advantage. Spencer estimated that Dakota wagons filled with plunder from their attacks stretched for five miles. These wagon trains flew American flags the Dakota had captured during their attacks as well as Hudson's Bay Company flags, which the Dakota had acquired years earlier from British diplomats and traders. The flags served as an eerie reminder of the transnational identities of groups like the Dakota and the limits of federal control.[50]

Success, however, remained fleeting. The Dakota sent messengers to the "Sissetons, Yanctons, Yanktonnais and the Governor of Selkirk Settlement," hoping to enlist broader support for their attacks but without much luck.[51] By late September the American military rebounded, forcing the Dakota into retreat. Goodvoice's grandparents and Tarasota fled the battle zone with many of the noncombatants.[52]

Both sides paid heavily for the war. By the end of the violence, the state of Minnesota claimed it had incurred more than $320,000 in expenses.[53] The human cost far outweighed the financial. By legal historian Carol Chomsky's estimate, between August 18 and September 26 "77 American soldiers, 29 citizen-soldiers, approximately 358 settlers, and an estimated 29 Dakota soldiers" died as open warfare consumed the region.[54] In the aftermath of the war, the US government arrested and tried close to four hundred Dakota for their involvement in the violence. The American military commission convicted 303 Dakota to death in cases that sometimes lasted less than five minutes. In the face of uncertainty, President Abraham Lincoln commuted most of the death sentences to prison terms. Even so, he upheld the military commission's decision to execute 38 Dakota, leading to what became the largest single execution in American history.[55]

If executions had a finality, the long-term outcome of the violence remained far less certain. Dakota who had escaped the American military fled in all directions. Parents lost contact with their children. Fearing retaliation, many Dakota moved toward the Canada–US border, often travelling by night to avoid detection. This was not the Dakota's first experience in this area.[56] Oral accounts by Melvin Littlecrow note, for example, that "we were always in this country [Canada]. . . . At one time back in those days there was no border. We hunted all over the place, north of the present day border."[57]

Even so, the journey north required substantial perseverance. LaVonne Swenson noted that her relative's grandmother took seven years to travel on foot from the Lower Sioux (Minnesota) to Sioux Valley (Manitoba), surviving off berries and dried food. During the day they would "dig down into the ground and lay that buffalo robe over the top . . . So when the troops were coming looking for them, they'd look and see nobody and keep going."[58] The lack of border guards meant that for some, it was not until "they met some wagons coming and they had a Canadian flag" that the Dakota knew they no longer needed to hide.[59] For those travelling at night, the flags of merchants, rather than boundary stones or soldiers, served as the only visible marker that they had crossed national boundaries.

The Canada–US border was not the only border that the Dakota had to contend with after being forced into retreat. According to Robert Goodvoice, Tachamishota found out about the war while returning from a hunt. He fled with his young sister Goweegaway and his wife, who informed him that the American military "is just killing everything that is in their path."[60] The party followed tracks to the west hoping to reunite with the Tachamishota's family. The path they followed took them into Teton territory. While there they stumbled onto a large camp and quickly found themselves surrounded by groups of riders the camp sent to capture them. Tachamishota stood under a white cloth and a peace pipe and yelled, "I am a Dakota. I am not an enemy, I am a Dakota, the same as you people."[61]

Tachamishota learned that the Teton had followed the Dakota's war with the United States with great interest. The Teton told Tachamishota that they had "men watching this part. We don't allow nobody to come here. Even the American soldiers, if they come here, we are going to see if we can stop them and if they don't listen to us, well we will make them listen."[62] As Tachamishota soon learned, regional violence had convinced the Teton to police their own territorial boundaries with more fervor. That put Tachamishota in a dangerous position.

After a tense first encounter, the Teton provided Tachamishiota, Goweegaway, and his wife with a tent, food, and supplies.[63] Despite this assistance, the Dakota travelers remained in a precarious position. The Teton party insisted that Goweegaway marry one of their men and Tachamishota feared that "if we don't do as they say, they might kill us and they will still take you."[64] Goweegaway married the man, but later escaped and rejoined her brother. After almost three months of searching, they found some of their people. Tachamishota would never see his parents or many of his other family members again.[65] He relocated to Prince Albert, Saskatchewan in 1876, where he remained until his death.[66]

Throughout the immediate aftermath of violence, the American army hampered the Dakota's relocation efforts. Cavalry led by Generals Alfred Sully and Henry Sibley pursued, ambushed, and slaughtered those who remained below the line. Battles at Big Mound, Dead Buffalo Lake, Stony Lake, and Whitestone Hill left 350 Dakota dead and destroyed many of their remaining supplies. Those who remained in Minnesota continued to suffer. Little Crow, a leader in the conflict, went north for a time but returned to Minnesota in June of 1863.[67] Little Crow's move proved ill fated. On July 3, a settler discovered him while he was picking fruit and shot him. The death occurred just in time for the town of Hutchinson to incorporate the desecration of Little Crow's body into their Fourth of July celebrations.[68]

The Dakota who relocated to British territory fared better but encountered a different set of challenges and hardships.[69] By the winter of 1862, hundreds of Dakota who had escaped capture had relocated to the Red River Settlement in British Territory. The Dakota found themselves short on supplies. They immediately set about strengthening their ties with the British and securing a separate peace with the Red River Métis.[70]

The Dakota recognized at least two important sets of borders they had crossed, one Indigenous, the other European.[71] To secure British support the Dakota relied on the presence of a historical alliance. The Oceti Sakowin (Sioux) had assisted the English during the War of 1812. In return they had received a promise from the British that should they need assistance the British would provide it, and now called upon them to make good on their words. The approach produced only minimal success.[72]

By 1863 Medicine Bottle, Little Six, and close to six hundred Dakota had arrived at the Red River Settlement. Those fleeing violence continued to come. The sudden influx of people stretched the limits of the Métis and put the British government in a tricky position. The presence of the Dakota increased tensions with the United States, and the Red River Settlement lacked a proper police force should any conflict break out.[73] Alexander Dallas, the British governor appointed by the Hudson's Bay Company, considered drastic measures. Governor Dallas feared that he could not provision the Dakota and that they would attack settlers in order to secure enough food for their survival. Lacking a military force, and unable to get either Britain or the Hudson's Bay Company to supply the necessary funds for troops, he began to consider the possibility of using the American army to remove the Dakota from British territory.[74]

Previously, Major Edwin A. C. Hatch had offered to let the British command his troops should he be allowed to operate on British soil. The offer created concerns in the middle of the Civil War. Britain already worried about its inability to appear neutral as soldiers from both countries violated each other's sovereignty while searching for deserters. By March 1864, Dallas relented. He requested that Hatch help expel the Dakota from British lands. By that time, however, Hatch had abandoned the plan for an American intervention. The cold winter and lack of shelter had killed most of Hatch's horses and rendered many of his troops unfit for duty.[75]

The Aftermath of the Dakota War

Although the Dakota had successfully evaded the American army by relocating north into British territory, their place in the new region remained precarious. In May, Plains Ojibwe killed approximately twenty Dakota in a single raid. The Dakotas' prolonged stay also put pressure on their relationship with the Cree. Faced with continued conflicts and limited food, the Dakota turned west in search of hunting grounds.[76]

In the end, fear shaped movement just as clearly as guns and cannons. Around 1875–76, a settler named McKay sought help for his ill wife from the Dakota Medicine Man Hoopayakta. McKay, grateful for the care, relayed information to the Dakota that he had heard in a nearby village. McKay told Hoopayakta that the American government would promise to feed and house the Dakota, but their real goal was to gather all the Dakota in one spot.[77] American soldiers would then capture and torture them: "They are going to hang you, they are going to kill most of you, maybe all of you."[78] According to Robert Goodvoice, McKay advised the Dakota to flee north where "you will be safe" in lands where there were lots of lakes, natural resources, and fur bearing animals.[79] Dozens of families heeded McKay's advice. They moved north to present-day Portage la Prairie (120km north of the border) where they wintered, drawing on social connections set up by McKay.

Once spring arrived, the group traveled north to Prince Albert in present-day central Saskatchewan. They did so on foot, a journey of roughly 700 kilometers, with children as young as four in their party. McKay later introduced the Dakota to his relatives in Prince Albert, ensuring that they had initial support while rebuilding their lives.[80] Economic factors, fear of continued violence with the United States, and networks of personal relationships motivated both the timing and path of their relocation. By the end of the journey from Minnesota to Prince Albert, the Dakota had travelled close to 1,500 km—equivalent to crossing through France, Germany, Austria, and Hungary in a transit between Paris and Budapest. Many of the Dakota who relocated to Prince Albert would not make a return trip home.[81]

Despite traveling so deep into British territory, the Dakota never shook their fears of American retribution. They worried that the American army would cross into Canada and "carry them all to the States there to punish their former misdeeds."[82] Dakota oral histories noted at least four occasions when Wasitu men and women operating on behalf of the American government tried to kill the Dakota. The attempts came by poisoning bread or by tampering with goods like underwear that the Wasitu passed off as charity. Those who fell prey to the trap suffered from a wide variety of ailments including itching, hemorrhagic fevers, foaming at the mouth, and other signs of poisoning.[83] Dakota preacher Masawakeean, who lived in the United States, supported these assertions, declaring that the American government had paid men and women to "kill off all the Dakotas around Prince Albert. They would get so many thousands of dollars for doing that. That is why these people came over here and poisoned them."[84] Cree and Blood communities echoed similar concerns about poisoned food.[85]

The Dakota complained to the police about their fears of American intervention, but the people who had supplied them with the dangerous goods left behind few traces. Whether the suffering experienced by the Dakota was the direct result of American machinations or simply a correlation between outbreaks of disease and genuine acts of charity is hard to determine. Regardless, these worries shaped the lives of the Dakota living north of the line in tangible ways. Many refused to accept goods from white settlers and the Dakota remained in fear of American military forays, poisonings, interference, and transnational kidnappings for decades.[86]

Fears of American interference also manifested in subtler ways. According to David Pasche, his great grandfather Pazeda-yapa had helped stuff Andrew Myrick's mouth with grass. Although Pazeda-yapa evaded American attempts to drag him back to the United States throughout his life, he failed in his death.[87]

Pasche, drawing on stories from his aunties and grandmother, noted that "when he [Pazeda-yapa] died the U.S. government came during the night and paid one of our family members here to show them where his grave was . . . and they dug his grave out in the middle of the night" and took his body to New York to display in a museum.[88] As late as 2012 Pasche was still attempting to locate Pazeda-yapa's remains for repartition, hoping this would help his present-day community "come back together some day" and live harmoniously.[89] For Pasche, historic conflicts did not exist in a distant past. They served as continuous impediments to the present-day well-being of his community.

American military sources confirm some, but not all, of the ways the American army influenced Dakota lives from afar. Following the violence, Major Hatch attempted to get the rations supplied by Britain to the Dakotas limited or annulled. He also hired auxiliaries to kidnap Little Six and Medicine Bottle. The move risked an international conflict, but not as seriously as the movements of the army would have. The US government declared its innocence in the matter, stating it had not authorized Major Hatch's action. The United States had no qualms, however, benefiting from the kidnapping. It convicted the two chiefs for murder and sentenced them to death in November 1865.[90]

Dakota histories of the events confirm many of the basic details found in settler accounts, while providing a far greater context for the event's long-term impact.[91] Robert Goodvoice noted that after the battles of 1862 a Wasitiu (white man) came to the Dakota camp in Manitoba looking for Eeotokta. Eeotokta, though suspicious of the man's motives, agreed to go on the journey with his brother-in law Tatayjusnomonee. The white man provided Eeotokta and Tatayjusnomonee with food and whisky, and they quickly fell asleep. While unconscious, white men bundled the Dakota in blankets, loaded them onto a toboggan, and "shipped them to New York under the influence of liquor and chloroform" in exchange for a $500 reward for each of them.[92]

These captures and deaths were not forgotten. Goodvoice recalled that Tataytunkowee, Tatayjusnomonee's wife, frequently spoke of her husband's kidnapping until her death in 1922.[93] Dakota who believed they had a bounty on their head stayed protected and out of sight. Red Top, for example, ensured that while he "was asleep there [was] somebody sitting beside him awake. And they had two vicious dogs. They watch him day and night."[94] Fear of foreign interference did not end with death. When Red Top died of natural causes near Macdowell, Saskatchewan, his family buried him and leveled the grave site so that his body could not be dug up.

As accounts by Goodvoice and others suggested, the United States continued to influence Dakota lives decades after they had left the territorial boundaries of the country. The United States sent Dakota speakers to Canada to offer the communities north of the border land, houses, teachers, and an absence of retribution should they return.[95] According to Goodvoice's grandfather, only Wasoosomacanow took up the American offer after he had been whipped by members of his community for violating hunting norms.[96]

Despite the depth of prevailing fears, many Dakota also stayed behind. Even the Dakota who remained in Minnesota, however, generally chose to remain within the border's shadow. They posted regular sentries at night and stayed within a few miles of the border so that they could cross at a moment's notice. Living south of the border, however, had long-term consequences. The Dakota who remained in the United States feared engaging in wage labor opportunities or seeking medical attention in Wasitu communities along the border because they could find themselves working for a white man who "will report them or he might give them away."[97] Settler families searched for Dakota to get revenge, reinforcing Dakota concerns about their safety.[98]

In at least a handful of cases, families who had crossed into Canada later reconstructed lives south of the line. Ta Sina Suspe Becawin's family learned of the violence while gathering pipestone. Seeing plumes of smoke and gathering news of the Dakota's defeat from those fleeing the violence, her family headed for Canada. They took Ta Sina Suspe Becawin, no older than twelve, with them. In the 1890s, as a middle-aged woman, Ta Sina Suspe Becawin returned to Minnesota where she married Joseph Amos (Hototona). The coupled lived at Sisseton, South Dakota, until Hotonona's illness prompted him to go back to Minnesota.[99] Ta Sina Suspe Becawin was not alone. While Inyangmani Hoksida (Running Walker Boy, John Roberts) and Tiwacktag-win Provincial lost relatives during the violence and fled across the line, both chose to return to the United States. After the war, Provincial relocated near Turtle Mountain, in Dakota Territory where she was married around 1877. Like many others, she was careful to stay near the international line.[100]

For those who made their way to Canada, the border continued to hang over their heads. In the early 1870s the Dominion Government offered hundreds of Dakota a permanent reserve. Relocating the Dakota to a reserve appealed to the Canadian government because it increased Canadian control, ended the uncertainty over the Dakota's future, allowed for assimilation, and relieved tensions.[101] The Canadian offer came with two sets of stipulations. First, William Sprague, Indian commissioner in the North-West Territories, emphasized that Canada offered to set aside the land as a sign of good faith rather than as an obligation on the government's part. Sprague viewed the Dakota as pseudo-immigrants. Second, the Canadian offer would not apply to Sioux currently living in the United States who wished to join those who had already made the trek north. He believed that if white immigrants could apply for land, it seemed disingenuous to bar Indigenous ones. Still, the Canadian government did not consider the Dakota to be treaty Indians and gave them no annuities.[102]

White Cap and Standing Buffalo's son argued on behalf of the Dakota that they were in fact British Indians. To both men, being British meant two things: a connection to the territory claimed by the Canadian government, and a reference to the historical alliance that the Dakota had with the British.[103] In the eyes of Canadian agents, however, the Dakota remained ambiguously American Indians for decades to come. The annual reports of the Department of Indian Affairs in Canada emphasized the Dakota's historical ties to the United States and their uncertain place in Canada. Reference to the Dakota's American origin appeared in the annual reports decades after they had received a Canadian reserve. The annual report in 1911, for example, included a note that the Dakota "came to the Dominion of Canada after the Minnesota massacre, and who refused to return to the United States."[104] By this point the children of the original Dakota migrants, many of whom had been born in Canada, had reached adulthood.

The ongoing references to the Dakota's American origin served two purposes. It allowed Canadian agents to compare their country favorably with the United States, as a refuge from American aggression. It also showed Canada's reluctance to allow wards of the United States to be integrated into Canada. Canada gave them land to defuse a tense situation, but it did not see the Dakota as immigrants who could change their national allegiances through relocation or naturalization. Instead, the Dakota remained American Indians living permanently abroad. The Dakota carried the stigma of their American origin and their unusual legal status—as nontreaty Indians in possession of reserve—into the twentieth century.[105]

***

Violence throughout the 1860s shaped British and American conceptions of their shared border and the practical policies they attempted to implement. Blockade runners demonstrated the inability of both countries to control transnational commerce, while draft dodgers emphasized the fluidity with which people moved. In both cases, violations of the border had immediate consequences within a wartime environment. British enlisters and smugglers undermined Britain's claims to neutrality, while blockade runners and draft dodgers impeded the Union's ability to fight the Confederacy. Crimpers and overzealous soldiers created diplomatic incidents of their own as their pursued their duties on both sides of the line.

While unsanctioned and illicit mobility provided uncomfortable reminders of the limits of federal power, this mobility also indicated the growing significance of international borders in North America by the 1860s. Illicit movements across a border only made sense if the border divided policies, peoples, and markets. The unevenness of this process rewarded movement. As Ebenezer

Tyler's case suggests, the border never operated as a complete barrier. Instead it increased the difficulty, effort, and risk associated with certain kinds of movements, but left other types relatively untouched. Law enforcement officers and military personnel failed to control how this process played out in practice, often finding the border inhibited their own movements more than those of the people they chased.

At the same moment that the Civil War made the dilemmas of international borders inescapable, the Dakota War of 1862 demonstrated the dangers of taking a narrow viewpoint on territorial divisions. In the 1860s, the United States shared borders with Britain and Mexico, but it also maintained borders with hundreds of Indigenous communities. Although it often conceptualized its boundaries with Indigenous nations as internal or domestic, treaty agreements governed these divisions and set clear expectations for both parties. Failing to abide by the terms of these agreements risked war for the same reasons that a failure to honor treaty agreements with European powers did. Overlapping territorial claims created a difficult, complex, and variable environment. In this context officers of the state attempted to achieve what they saw as justice, even if it meant violating their own borders to do so.

3

New Countries, Old Problems

In the span of less than a decade, violence and a shifting political landscape created the continent of North America anew. The Civil War tore the United States apart, spawning questions about what kind of country would rise from the ashes. The Union's victory allowed for the accession of a free labor ideology and a broad reconceptualization of citizenship. Victory also provided the North with an opportunity to remake the South and the West in its image.[1] While Confederate attempts to split from the United States failed, Canadian attempts at independence succeeded. In 1867 Ontario, Quebec, New Brunswick, and Nova Scotia began a slow separation from Britain. While the Dominion of Canada would handle its own day-to-day affairs, foreign policy remained in British hands and Canada retained Britain's monarch. Even so, change progressed at a rapid pace.[2]

In less than five years, British North America transitioned from a colony of Britain to a largely independent nation with colonial aspirations of its own. In 1869 the Dominion purchased three million square miles of territory, known as Rupert's Land, from the Hudson's Bay Company.[3] The purchase occurred primarily on paper. First Nations and Métis controlled most of the land in question but were neither consulted nor compensated by Britain, the Hudson's Bay Company, or the Dominion of Canada. Instead, Canada began a concerted push to reinforce its territorial claims over both its new lands and its old ones. High tariffs, a transcontinental railway, and rapid settlement of the Canadian West were its methods of choice.[4]

The American Civil War and Canadian Confederation had failed to provide either country with the necessary power to enforce their borders, but both events served as important catalysts for change. In their aftermath, the three countries began to build a border across North America designed to amplify and control difference. In a world that appeared uncertain, the border increasingly seemed like a practical tool for social control. By creating a border that embraced unevenness at its very core, each country could prioritize its resources

A Line of Blood and Dirt. Benjamin Hoy, Oxford University Press (2021). © Oxford University Press.
DOI: 10.1093/oso/9780197528693.003.0004

in strategic ways. They policed undesired people fiercely, often long after their initial crossings, and left most other kinds of movements and activities unguarded.

For all that changed in the 1860s, 1870s, and 1880s, old problems continued to vex each nation. The regional variation of the challenges, however, had an important legacy. As both governments created national solutions to solve regional concerns, they entrenched the basic components of how the border would operate into the fabric of each nation. In the Great Lakes region, where the density of settlers was high, federal concerns around the border prioritized resolving questions around emancipation, transnational crime, economic mobility, and the home. Fears of degeneracy ushered in new immigration laws and extradition provisions as officials and the broader public reimagined how African Americans, Indigenous people, immigrants, and settlers fit into each country. Those concerns shifted the border's vision in particular ways, ensuring it never treated all movements or people quite the same way.

Citizenship and the Home

In the 1860s, violence and political reorganization created an opportunity for two of the largest powers in North America to reimagine who belonged within their expanding territorial control. For Americans, the home served as the basic building block of society. Belonging require civilization, and civilization, in turn, required the home. Presidents, suffragettes, entertainers, and vigilantes all found the idea appealing. Defense of the home helped to push forward social reform and justified violence. The Morrill Act (1862) and Edmunds Act (1882) attacked Mormon polygamy.[5] The Dawes Allotment Act (1887) targeted Indigenous communalism. The Page Law (1875), Chinese Restriction Act (1882), and Chinese Exclusion Act (1888) curtailed Chinese immigration and impeded the creation of Chinese families on the continent. All became realities because they appeared to defend the home and America alongside it.[6]

Like most powerful concepts, the home did not have a stable or natural definition. Context forever shaped its form. For the unnamed writer of Tinsley's magazine, the home consisted of men who gave their lives for their country and bore the hardships of life. The home also consisted of women whose beauty, smiles, and kindnesses softened life's trials and provided a necessary complement. In this imagination, the home had little need for masculine women or feckless men.[7] For others, the homes created through marriage served as the legitimation of a natural balance. Wives served as the "balancewheel, the regulator, the guardian angel of a husbands' trust, confidence, and prosperity."[8] Without creating a home, men left no legacies and deserved no respect. Despite the variability in definition, monogamous marriages and divided gender roles often provided a basic outline of what Americans believed a proper home looked like. Economic independence (competence), private property, and control over one's own labor (contract freedom) provided important considerations as well.[9]

To the horrors of many Americans, the basic features of the home seemed at odds with one another after the Civil War. As historian Richard White suggests, Americans "gauged the success of an economy, and a life, more by its ability to produce homes than its ability to produce wealth."[10] Industrialization attacked the basic competence of working-class Americans. Men struggled to provide for their families, forcing their wives to work. Fears of alienated affections and disappearing manhood proliferated. Young women relocated to the cities where new opportunities existed for an independent living outside of patriarchal relationships.[11] Suffrage added new wrinkles to an already fraught set of questions. If African American men could vote and become citizens, what about white women? All social relationships suddenly seemed up for renegotiation. In that context, who people married, who could vote, and how individuals defined their allegiance appeared more and more important.[12]

In the eighteenth century, European powers had accepted "permeable borders, relational rather than territorial allegiance, and overlapping, royal, noble and ecclesiastical jurisdictions."[13] The modern nation-states that came of age during the nineteenth century believed in clearly demarcated borders and exclusive sovereignty. This idealized vision of territory operated as a zero-sum game. Every person had one and only one place they belonged.[14] Prior to the Civil War, the United States left individual states to define the rights, qualifications, and privileges they associated with citizenship. The mismatched mosaic that emerged did not separate citizens from inhabitants, nor did it specify a citizen's rights, except in a handful of cases.[15] For Indigenous people, citizenship remained murky. Supreme Court decisions in the 1830s characterized Indigenous communities as "domestic, dependent, nations," a classification that created more confusion than it resolved.[16]

The Civil War increased the power of the federal government and created an opportunity for the country to rethink who "the people" were on a national scale. After the war, the federal government superseded individual states as the adjudicator of citizenship. In doing so, it centralized who defined belonging. The Thirteenth Amendment emancipated slaves. The Fourteenth and Fifteenth Amendments provided them equal protection under the law, granted them the ability to vote, and declared that naturalized citizens would enjoy the same rights as American-born ones. Radical republicans pushed for land redistribution, fearing that without property freedmen could not create proper homes or become proper citizens.[17]

Figure 3.1 A political cartoon attacking George C. Gorham's support African American suffrage. Gorham stands at the bottom with a black man, an Indigenous man, and a Chinese man on his shoulders. Beside Gorham, a man with a monkey remarks "Say, Gorham! put this Brother up." Another blocks the ballot box remarking "Young Man! Read the history of your Country, and learn that this ballot box was dedicated to the white race alone. The load you are carrying will sink you in perdition, where you belong . . ." *The Reconstruction Policy of Congress, as illustrated in Canada,* 1867. Library of Congress Prints and Photographs Division, LC-DIG-ds-14037.

The reimagining of citizenship south of the border had important implications for Britain and Canada. In 1868, Congress declared that choice and not birth would determine allegiance. Building the right to expatriate into the United States' definitions of belonging risked aggravating old conflicts with Britain. To the United States' relief, Britain simplified the matter two years later when it signed a mutual naturalization treaty. Under the treaty Britain abandoned its commitment to the doctrine of perpetual allegiance, which had brought the two countries to war in 1812.[18] Together, Britain and the United States increasingly viewed citizenship as a voluntary association with the federal government that defined both a national belonging and a series of protections. The similarities in policy in both countries made immigration and expatriation less complicated and simplified border control.[19]

Everyday movements across the border, however, created unanticipated challenges to the ways both countries conceptualized identity. In 1886, J. J. Elder left Ireland. He travelled to Canada, settling in Woodstock, New Brunswick, for a few years before relocating in the United States. By 1900, Elder understood borders better than he understood tact. He sent an inquiry to the Under-Secretary of State asking about the long-term implications that he would create for himself if he renounced forever his allegiance to the British crown as part of the American naturalization process. With a bluntness that few mustered, Elder stated that he wished to naturalize in the United States but noted that "it is quite possible that I may return to Canada (where I have two brothers) and may wish to resume my allegiance to the British Crown (having a government appointment or something of that kind in view!)."[20] Forever seemed far too long a commitment for a man who had dreams on both sides of the line.

Elder's case landed on the desk of Joseph Pope, the Undersecretary of State. Pope responded to Elder's inquiry with the kind of official advice that was hardly worth the postage. If Elder wished to resume his allegiance, Pope recommended he employ a lawyer. Pope, however, could not pass up the opportunity to include his own private opinions on the matter. He believed that making an oath Elder later intended to break was a "matter of conscience rather than law."[21] Familial and economic connections drew people like Elder back and forth across the border. If Britain and the United States conceptualized citizenship as matter of choice rather than a condition of birth, they had to contend with the possibility that men like Elder would change their allegiance not simply once, but multiple times, over the course of their lives.

While constitutional reforms clarified the legal status of African Americans and started a long road toward clarifying the rights of expatriation, the status of Indigenous people remained in flux. The nationwide enfranchisement of Indigenous people did not occur until 1924 in the United States and until 1960 in Canada.[22] In the interim, both countries developed a complicated series of half-measures. By 1922, at least nine unique pathways including marriage, special acts of congress, military service, assimilation, allotment, and treaty provisions could grant citizenship to Indigenous people. Even the apathetic and inattentive found themselves reeling in the eddies produced by such a wide-reaching set of measures.[23]

On a local level, questions about suffrage and citizenship had important implications on governance. In 1870 Thomas B. White, a Wendat from southern Ontario, defeated Dallas Norvell for the office of Reeve (the head of a town council) in the Township of Anderdon. Norvell possessed more grit than grace. Not one to approach a loss with dignity, Norvell attempted to have White disqualified on the basis of his race. White owned enough land to meet the provincial property requirements, but received annuities as part of the Wendat and had never enfranchised.[24] During the ensuing court case Judge Dalton ruled in favor of White. In presenting his ruling, Dalton took the opportunity to point out that there was a "marked difference" between Ontario and the United States; "there, the Indian is an alien, not a citizen."[25] Dalton's statements touched on actual differences but valorized Canada better than they reflected the realities of life.

The benefits of citizenship and the liabilities of its absence had rested on uncertain ground for some time. In 1835, Michigan Territory had granted the right to vote to white male citizens at least twenty one years old who met a residency requirement.[26] Michigan's 1850 Constitution expanded the definition, granting suffrage to "every civilized male inhabitant of Indian descent, a native of the United States and not a member of any tribe."[27] The definition separated men from women, Americans from Canadians, and the civilized and nontribal from their counterparts.

If the three provisions served as a lock, it was a fixture that many keys could soon pick. A treaty signed with the Odawa and Ojibwe in 1855 dissolved tribal organizations "except so far as may be necessary to carry out the purposes of the treaty."[28] Michigan had created tribal categories to assist in land cessions and then dissolved them when it no longer needed them. On a practical level, the change made only a few differences. The organization and identity of Anishinaabe communities focused on the band, rather than the tribe, and continued to function. The legal sleight of hand, however, gave the Anishinaabe of Michigan the right to vote.

Politicians like Perley Bills worried about the logical implications this kind of policy created. During Michigan's failed attempt to reform its constitution in 1867, Bills argued that the United States should not consider Indigenous people as citizens. He believed they maintained independent tribal identities and "acknowledge no allegiance to our Government."[29] Loyalty could not be split. Either Indigenous people remained Indians or they became fully white. From Bills's perspective there existed no opportunity for hybridity. Legal theorists supported similar assertions. Alexander Porter Morris, writing just over a decade later, argued that the United States could not afford to accept "abnormal and monstrous" categories like dual citizenship or a lack of nationality.[30] The situation only rectified itself, in Morris's eyes, when Indians renounced their tribal identity and became fully American.[31]

For Omar Conger and other proponents of Indigenous suffrage, the fact that Indigenous people made homes in accordance with "the rules of civilized life" justified their inclusion.[32] Even without that capacity, Conger argued, the United States had a moral obligation to grant them the vote as one "last lingering boon that civilization can extend" before they disappeared like "the failing leaves of the forest." [33] He believed that fear motivated their exclusion more than practice. With only one exception in 1861, when forty-one Indigenous men swayed an election at Arenac Michigan, the constitutional commission could find no instance where the Indigenous voters held the balance of power. Opponents of suffrage, however, continued to flaunt the possibility that unscrupulous men would recruit to Indigenous men from Canada in order to disrupt local elections in Michigan.[34]

Debates across the Canadian Senate and other branches of government in 1885 reflected the same kinds of concerns, which emerged south of the line.[35] For John A. Macdonald, Canada's first prime minister, the matter seemed clear. Indigenous people purchased taxed clothes and drank taxed tea. If they had sufficient property, he believed they had a right to vote.[36] Senator Alex Campbell made a similar argument, noting that the Mohawk of Tyendinaga owned property and had achieved high levels of literacy. More to the point, "they were the owners of the country before we were, have always been loyal to the Crown, and they are educated."[37] Campbell's and Macdonald's opponents disagreed but, like Campbell, played a familiar tune. They worried that Indian agents would exploit naïve communities and organize them into powerful voting blocs.[38]

Charges against Indian Agent John Crowe of Chippewa Hill, Ontario seemed to confirm fears of foul play. In 1896, at least six members of the Saugeen Agency accused John Crowe of offering timber privileges and small cash payments to those who voted on behalf of the local conservative candidate. A lack of corroboration and the presence of competing statements created muddy water.[39] Chief Thomas Solomon defended Crowe, arguing that he had told the Ojibwe of the Saugeen "to pick their candidates as they chose."[40] After a lengthy investigation, the Canadian government dismissed Crow for his improper handling of timber. The investigators declined to address the impact, if any, he had on the election.[41]

Other politicians, like Thomas Elliott, a member of the Liberal Conservative Association of South Brant, saw tremendous potential in Indigenous voters. A margin of only 176 votes had separated victory and defeat in the last election. In that context, Elliot saw the potential of 400 Tuscarora (Skaru:reh) and 350 Onondaga voters as potentially game-changing.[42] He petitioned John A. Macdonald for the appointment of a new forest warden on the nearby reserve. He hoped that placing key conservative supporters on the reservation would help secure the votes of the nearby residents.[43]

If politicians such as Campbell and judges like Dalton took pride in the inclusivity of Canada, the expected beneficiaries of suffrage showed less enthusiasm. Given the option, only 250 Indigenous people opted to officially enfranchise in Canada between 1876 and 1920. Indigenous resistance to suffrage baffled federal administrators, especially in the United States. African Americans fought and died for equality, hedging their bets on citizenship and suffrage rights. Indigenous people had different inclinations. They could push for their economic and social rights through the adoption of suffrage, but more often emphasized their rights as independent nations.[44]

Undeterred, social reformers in both countries pressed onward. Contract freedoms, monogamous marriage, and private property would serve as the gateways to civilization and incorporation. American politicians and courts ruled that Indians existed as wards—tribes as semisovereign nations.[45] If Indigenous people wished to vote, they had to naturalize and assimilate. What that exactly that entailed, however, remained unclear. The Fourteenth Amendment would not apply. In the absence of clear direction, politicians and Indian agents developed their own, often personalized, criteria for assessment. Whether a family slept on beds, ate at a table, or used cutlery became focal points for assessing a suitability for suffrage and citizenship.[46]

The transformative power of land also took center stage. By 1887, the Dawes Allotment Act established a clear process and pathway for incorporating Indigenous tribes into American society. Under the Act, Indigenous communities surrendered their rights to their land either by force or by choice. In return, the federal government granted private land held in trust for twenty-five years to the head of the household.[47] Land under the policy served dual purposes. Private property would help Indigenous people establish nuclear families and encourage them to adopt American ways of life. Excess land would make American expansion possible. It would also provide a venue for the transformation of immigrants into American citizens.[48]

Heralded by its proponents as something of a Magna Carta, the Dawes Allotment Act was a disaster even by the low standards set by Indian policies. In 1881, Indigenous communities controlled approximately 242,000 square miles of land (155 million acres), which would be equivalent of the third largest state in the United States today, a fraction smaller than Texas and quite a bit larger than California. Twenty year later, Indigenous people had lost half their lands. Nevada could fit into the gap left by Dawes, with room for Connecticut, Delaware, and Rhode Island left over. Suffering proliferated on a sickening scale.[49]

If reformers had approached the transformative power of land with a reckless enthusiasm, they approached the power of marriage with far more trepidation. In 1855, Congress ruled that a woman's citizenship followed her husband, so long as she might be "lawfully naturalized."[50] The ruling entrenched marriage as a crucial mechanism through which citizenship travelled, while leaving open the possibility for federal intervention in the case of excluded or undesired populations.[51]

Congress later passed the Intermarriage Act of 1888, which was designed to discourage miscegenation. Citizenship became a cudgel rather than a gift. Under the act, if an Indigenous woman married an American she gained the citizenship of her husband. Her husband did not gain access to his wife's property, and her gain in citizenship came at the cost of her tribal status. Any children from such a union were "not entitled to share in the property of the tribe except such as they might take by representation of their mother."[52] Congress relied on the undesirability of both provisions to discourage unwanted unions.[53]

Canada used marriage—and the homes it created—as a similar underpinning for belonging. According to the Canadian Indian Act of 1876, settler women who married Indigenous men became Indian by law. Indigenous women became white in the opposite direction. The shifting racial categories caused by marriage had unexpected implications.[54] In 1876, J. R. Innus sentenced Charles Mahoy to three years' hard labor for supplying malt liquor to Sarah Meadsul, a conviction that rested on Meadsulf's legal status as an Indian. Upper Canada had prohibited the sale of liquor to Indians in 1835, and the Indian Act of 1876 had created broad restrictions across the country. To Innus's dismay, he soon found out that Meadsulf had married a white man. Although Indigenous by most other metrics, she was no longer an Indian by law. Innus consented to have his conviction overturned.[55]

The border created a similar kind of instability in identity and belonging. Three years earlier, the Superintendent of Indian Affairs in Washington Territory complained that his attempts to prevent Indians from buying liquor had failed because the legislation in the United States only applied to American Indians. This oversight meant that British Indians had the same rights as British citizens when travelling south of the line.[56] Indigenous men and women at St. Regis (Quebec), Sarnia (Ontario), Lake of the Woods (Keewatin), and Emerson (Manitoba) took advantage of similar opportunities to buy alcohol.[57] In British Columbia, this loophole allowed Coast Salish from Canada to provide liquor to their American brethren with whom they were "more or less intermarried."[58] At the edges of each nation, federal and state policies surrounding citizenship, family, and assimilation collided with one another. The resulting fault lines underscored the unstable ground on which borderland residents worked and lived.

Migration, Travel, and Identity

Politicians, judges, social reformers, and administrators wielded power, but as their battles over suffrage and alcohol suggested, they did not possess a monopoly over either movement or belonging. Throughout the nineteenth century, individuals and communities voted with their feet more often than with ballots. Americans provided technical expertise on Canadian industrial projects. American business integrated Canadian resources and farmlands into the American hinterlands.[59] Canadian wageworkers crossed into New England, New York, and Michigan in pursuit of better wages. Between 1840 and 1940 as many as three million Canadians settled in the United States, many of them in the Great Lakes region.[60] Despite the scale of the exodus the *Butte Weekly Miner* accused Canadian newspapers of preserving an "unbroken silence on the subject."[61] Pretending transnational mobility did not exist resolved few problems.

Migration worked in both directions, creating questions about how to define citizenship, belonging, and loyalty amidst shifting patterns of residency. The life of James Ryerson emphasized the impossibility of the task. James Ryerson's mother was a native of New York. His grandfather had served in the US Army during the War of 1812 and his father was American, at least later in life. Born in Canada in 1846, Ryerson's father relocated to New York where he naturalized. Canadian by birth, he became American by choice.

Ryerson's life took him back and forth across the line. Born in Canada, he attended at Allegheny College in Meadville, Pennsylvania, after an early education in Canada. At the age of seventeen, he joined Company E of the Thirteenth Ohio Calvary and worked as a teamster during the American Civil War. The position that cost him dearly. At the battle of Crater, an explosion ripped apart his left leg and damaged his right foot. Ryerson convalesced in Ohio, his left leg amputated just below the knee. The physical damage required healing, but witnessing a battle where his unit lost 181 of its 350 men undoubtedly took a mental toll as well. Ryerson returned to Canada in 1871 and continued to draw a pension from the United States.[62]

At the age of fifty-two, Ryerson lived in Hamilton, Ontario. He expressed enthusiasm for naturalization as an American citizen, but had never done so. Interested in supplementing his Civil War pension, he applied for the vacant American consul position at Galt, Ontario. In his application, he emphasized both his own loyalty to the United States and that of his family. Although he had spent much of his life in Canada, he argued that his actions, rather than his residency or legal status, defined his belonging. Ryerson's ability to position himself as American despite his mixed identity secured him the appointment, which he held from 1899 until 1925.[63]

Throughout the late nineteenth century, Indigenous workers, much like their European counterparts, ignored the implications of the Canada–US border as much as possible. Men from the Grand Portage Band in Wisconsin chopped wood and mined precious metals in Canada. Ojibwe from Garden River, Ontario made a considerable portion of their income selling berries in the

United States.[64] The Haudenosaunee of St. Regis, Caughnawaga, and Lake of Two Mountains crossed the border to sell patent medicine, baskets, beadwork, and snowshoes as well as to work as laborers, shantymen, steamship operators, and bridge-builders.[65] The Abenakis spent the spring and summer selling their wares across the border and guiding sportsmen, while the Red Rock Band of Ojibwe supplied American tourists with canoemen. Personal and economic circumstances mattered more to an individual's mobility than did international policy.[66]

Migration undermined national boundaries and drew communities across the Great Lakes together. In 1860 Canadians represented 14.5 percent of Detroit's foreign-born population and by 1880 they represented 23.6 percent. Intermarriages between Canadians and Americans further blurred lines between nationalities, making accurate counts difficult to establish.[67] When oil was discovered in 1864 on Manitoulin Island, prospectors came from both Canada and the United States to try to make their fortunes. W. L. Baby of Windsor and J. R. Berthelott of Milwaukee worked together in the pursuit of oil reserves on the island. The border provided little barrier to their partnership.[68]

On a larger scale, persistent migrations for personal and economic reasons made separating who was Canadian from who was American a daunting task. By 1870, 14 percent of Canada's population lived in the United States. Border inspections could not keep up. Michigan, for example, possessed no formal commission to supervise alien immigration until 1881. Out migrations created difficult bureaucratic questions. For a young nation it produced soul-searching as well.[69]

Slavery and Sanctuary

The absence of a comprehensive borderland bureaucracy limited the ways the state could respond to crisis and shifting social environments. War created change, which federal administrators soon discovered, came like a landslide. The American Civil War clogged old streams of movement and dredged new ones. The flows of people across national borders persisted, but the direction they moved, the barriers they faced, and their motivations changed in response to violence and upheaval.

Since the late eighteen century, fugitive slaves exploited the border between United States and Canada to secure their freedom. Slaves swam across the Detroit River in the summer and walked across it in the winter. By the 1830s, African Americans had settled in urban areas like Toronto, London, St. Catharines, and Windsor. They settled in rural locations as well as predominately black communities such as Dawn, Wilberforce, and Buxton. They enlisted in the militia by the hundreds, and they made British North America their home.[70]

Britain's prohibition of slavery across its empire in 1834 and shifts within the United States itself made the asymmetry created by the border more pronounced. American slave laws grew harsher, and northern states became less welcoming. In 1829, Cincinnati officials began to require that black residents provide certificates of freedom and $500 bonds or leave the state of Ohio within 30 days. The law did not have to come into effect to shape movement. Expanding violence and legal threats across the northern United States encouraged thousands to leave voluntarily, convinced that mobs would drive them out if they did not.[71]

The Fugitive Slave Act of 1850 eliminated the legal protections freedmen and freedwomen could expect to find in the northern states and deepened the risks they took while they remained there. In the first three months of the act's operation, three thousand African Americans made their way to British North America. In the decade that followed thousands more crossed the border, bringing the number of African Americans in Canada to twenty thousand. The secretive nature of their journeys, the continued mobility of migrants after they arrived, and the limitations of nineteenth-century censuses make exact numbers difficult to pin down.[72]

If freedmen and freedwomen dreamed of finding the Promised Land or a haven from racial abuse, they found neither in British North America. British subjects denied former slaves admittance to schools and limited their access to financial opportunities and accommodations. Southern slave owners staged kidnappings and sent a bevy of extradition requests to regain control over those who made their way north. British North America provided an unwelcoming and at times uncertain refuge. Still, it granted African American men the right to serve on juries, participate in political processes, control their own land, and fight on behalf of the country. Britain's general refusal to extradite provided a heft to the border that the line between slave and free states no longer carried.[73]

The Union's victory during the Civil War changed the nature of transnational mobility but did not eliminate it. Between 1861 and 1871, between 20 and 30 percent of the African American population living in Canada returned to the United States.[74] Many returned to the communities they grew up in or set out to find family members they had been separated from during slavery. The exodus changed the communities that remained north of the line. Buxton ceased to be an exclusively black settlement in 1860, and by 1873 the Elgin Association, which had managed the community, had dissolved.[75]

Those who returned to the southern United States faced concerted opposition. Southern states introduced black codes and attempted to recreate slavery in all but name. The federal government had its own conceptions of what peace would look like, but struggled under the magnitude of reform. During Reconstruction, American troops occupied 750,000 square miles of land and attempted to hold nine million people under their control. By January 1866, only 90,000 Union soldiers remained in the south to complete that task.[76] Militant organizations such as the Ku Klux Klan (KKK) assassinated black leaders, intimidated white abolitionists, and disrupted Reconstruction policies. The Ku Klux Klan Act, signed into law in 1871, empowered President Ulysses S. Grant to suspend the writ of habeus corpus and use troops to put down internal disorder. Grant authorized mass arrests to stamp out what he saw as a continued rebellion. Prominent Klansmen fled.[77]

Canada, which had been a refuge for fugitive slaves before the war, became a sanctuary for their oppressors after it. White supremacists, like earlier fugitive slaves, needed to move beyond the borders of the United States to escape its criminal jurisdiction. Many southerners drew on friends, family, and business associates north of the line.[78] As the case of Major James W. Avery and Dr. Rufus Bratton suggested, relocation to Canada never provided a complete sanctuary from American interference, but it offered far more security than hiding out in the nearby mountains or crossing state lines. The cases also served as a reminder of how deep into each country transnational connections and problems ran.[79]

In 1871, residents of Yorkville, South Carolina accused James W. Avery of murder—no less than eleven counts of it, if the US Secretary of State had his numbers correct. Avery had served as a surgeon for the Confederacy, and witnesses believed that after the war he had led the local chapter of the Ku Klux Klan. Accused of a bevy of serious crimes and fearful of the judicial and political ramifications of Reconstruction, Avery took no chances in the courtroom. He fled to Canada, a gamble that paid off. Canada treated him as a political refugee and refused the extradition request.[80] Despite his legal victory, Avery remained in a precarious situation. An enormous bounty on his head soon drew the attention of Joseph G. Hester, an American detective, and Isaac Bell Cornwall, a British deputy to a Crown Attorney. Kidnapping was not easy, but for Hester and Cornwall, it seemed worth the risk. One way or another Avery was coming home.[81]

Cornwall and Hester located the man they believed to be Avery in London, Ontario. Their target, a tall gaunt man in his mid-forties, bore the appearance of "a respectable well-to-do farmer" who operated under the alias James Simpson.[82] Undeterred by the light cast by the afternoon sun, Cornwall and Hester made their move. At knifepoint, and with the aid of chloroform, they handcuffed Avery, shoved him into a horse-drawn cab, and took him to a nearby train station. By the time they had gotten Avery to Detroit, they realized their mistake. Avery remained at large. Instead they had captured Dr. Rufus Bratton, one of Avery's compatriots and a wanted man in his own right.[83] While Cornwall and Hester might have salvaged the botched arrest, and may have even plotted to use Avery's warrant as a pretense to capture Bratton, they could do little to subdue the international attention that their bold scheme had drawn. Newspapers demanded Bratton's repatriation and swift punishments for those who sullied the British flag.[84]

The Governor General's Office, Canadian Prime Minister, the US Attorney General, and the Secretary of State for the Colonies all took interest. Cornwall received three years in a Dominion penitentiary, a decision that provided little respite for Bratton, who faced a trial of his own in South Carolina.[85] Allowed out of jail on a $12,000-dollar bond, Bratton fled back to Canada. The border had failed to protect him once, but he kept his faith in its efficacy. His faith proved well-placed. While Avery and Bratton viewed exile as preferable to incarceration, neither man made Canada their home. After a general amnesty to Klansmen in 1876, both men rebuilt their lives south of the border.[86]

Fears that the border could serve as a shield for criminals continued to create widespread unease, even when the facts of the cases failed to live up to the public's initial expectations. On January 4, 1883, Kitty Marsh, a thirteen-year-old girl from Rochester, Vermont, disappeared. The blond-haired, blue-eyed Marsh was tall, slim, and graceful. The day she disappeared, only a thin shawl and her school dress braced her against the winter's cold.[87] Marsh's schoolmates reported they had last seen her at noon entering a sleigh driven by John Edwards, a thirty-year-old man of mixed African and European descent. Edwards lived in a house owned by Marsh's father and had known the girl for some time. That same day Edwards, a team of horses, and a sleigh owned by Edward's employer vanished as well. Communities along Lake Champlain searched in vain, but could not locate the missing girl.[88]

When evidence began to suggest that Edwards and Marsh had headed north, newspapers around the country expressed concern that they were witnessing a transnational kidnapping case in progress. The respective races of the victim and perpetrator added to the concern. The *National Republican* of Washington, DC mourned the possibility that "the pair will reach Canada before they can be overtaken."[89] Within a week and a half, a pursuit party discovered Marsh and Edwards residing in Willsboro, New York, less than a hundred miles from their homes in Vermont. Fears of elopement replaced those of kidnapping.

Marsh professed her desire marry Edwards and noted they had been in a relationship for a year before absconding. She showed little interest in returning to her parents, who she claimed had treated her poorly. Only concerted pressure convinced Marsh and Edwards to return to Vermont, where Edwards was arrested, likely for the theft of the horses. While much of the coverage of the case provided no indication that the couple intended to make their way to Canada, the specter of the border shaped early interpretations of their movement. Border anxiety applied to communities adjacent to it. As Marsh's case attested, it also extended to communities, like Rochester, located 150km from the border as well.[90]

While Bratton's abduction and Marsh's flight played to common border anxieties, the fears of the 1870s differed from those of the 1880s. In 1873 Reconstruction faltered, and by 1877 it began to fall apart. As federal troops withdrew, the incentives for movement changed. Incidents of lynching skyrocketed across the South. Redeemers used poll taxes, registration laws, literacy tests, and residency requirements to disenfranchise black citizens, and to a lesser extent working-class white citizens as well. In short order, the United States became a less democratic nation.[91]

In Canada, the thought of renewed immigration by African Americans from the United States, and later the West Indies, created long-lasting concerns. While the fears eventually culminated into a short-lived ban of "any immigrants belonging to the Negro race" in 1911, Canadians by that point had years of experience making border crossings less appealing for African American migrants.[92] Canadian newspapers and politicians depicted Black men and women as racially unsuited for Canada's cold climate. Immigration officials limited access to information, found reasons to debar when possible, and pressured railway companies to charge additional money to black passengers heading to Canada.[93]

If the "cold climate" argument provided a color-blind way of justifying exclusion, it had wider reaching implications. Commentators used the distinction to separate blacks from whites, but also applied it to Americans and Canadians of any race. For the *Maysville Evening Bulletin* of Kentucky, the practice of pulling down winter caps over the skull made ears stick out and "grow in an unnatural way."[94] Although members of either nation suffered under such conditions, "it is only American ears which get frostbitten in Canada. The ears of the natives are inured to excessive cold."[95] The statements, which betrayed both an ignorance of ears and functional winter hats, pointed to the novel ways people conceptualized national identity. If frostbite had indeed separated Canadians from Americans, immigration agents would have faced a much simpler task ahead of them. Ears, however, offered no more accurate a reading of identity than skin color.

Waves of transnational laborers, fugitive slaves, KKK members, and returning freedmen betrayed easy identification. As they moved across national borders they underscored both the limitations and potentials of federal power. Direct power—the ability to prevent border crossings themselves—remained a distant dream. The ability to influence the motivations for crossings, however, provided a potent, if indirect, alternative. Changes in federal policies drew African Americans across the border and pushed them back in the other direction. A legal refuge for slaves soon became a haven for white supremacists. Control over perceived risks and rewards remade the border in ways that a thousand soldiers could not. Canada and the United States used indirect approaches to border control on African Americans adeptly, but it was a tool they first developed and later perfected on Indigenous communities.

Leech Lake and White Earth

Around 1880, Nay Nah Arrug Abe, then in his late fifties, left the Leech Lake area in Minnesota for Rainy Lake in Ontario. During his three-year absence, Indian agents at Leech Lake developed a band enrollment list that excluded many of the American Ojibwe living in Canada. Nay Nah Arrug Abe's residency abroad and his later request for inclusion in the Leech Lake Band put power in the hands of C. P. Luse. Luse, the Farmer in Charge at the White Earth Agency, supported Nay Nah Arrug Abe's enrollment.[96] Abe's failure to participate in annuity payments north of the line helped to justify his access to resources south of it. Simplified ideas of belonging had a seductive appeal.

Mobility, however, remained an ever-present part of life at Leech Lake and Rainy River. Marriages, divorces, adoptions, and death all encouraged mobility. The death of Way Me Sho Me As Nind's and Now E Sis Wann Abe's mother prompted their decision to relocate. At the same moment, Ne Ghe Kay Woub E Quay and her son Quay Quay Cub crossed in the opposite direction to join her husband's community at Rainy Lake. Agents like Luse recognized the need to allow for some level of mobility. Belonging could shift, but Luse believed that no person could claim belonging in two countries at once.[97]

The Anishinaabeg understood the power Americans attached to simple identities and national belonging. In the same year that C. P. Luse defended the inclusion of Nay Nah Arrug Abe, he fielded complaints by settlers of Kanabec County, Minnesota. If the settler's statements could be trusted, the Snake River Band of Mississippi Chippewa (Ojibwe) acted as drunken nuisances.[98] The Anishinaabeg disparaged their accusers in return. Ju Yahn, a chief of the Snake River Band, noted that many of the settlers who signed the petition were "Norwegian or foreigners," and that "they make it a point to show us their hatred."[99]

Ju Yahn's approach marshaled American fears of immigration to defend Ojibwe property and territorial boundaries. Glossing over the troubled history between the Americans and the Ojibwe, he emphasized the peaceful relations that had long existed between the two groups. The approach provided Yahn with an opportunity to compliment the people he requested aid from, while attacking those he believed did not belong. Yahn demanded that the United States honor the promises it had made to Indigenous people and called upon the American government to help enforce their rights against a Norwegian menace. Penned in 1885, Yahn's petition came out amidst intensifying concerns across the country over Chinese immigration. The petition played to the same concerns that nativists used to justify Chinese exclusion: foreigners failed to integrate and deprived native-born residents of their opportunities.[100]

Yahn's strategy, for all its inventiveness, played poorly with Luse. Luse could conceptualize transnational mobility in nuanced ways, but he had a very simplistic idea of belonging. Luse ignored the personal claims to land made by Yahn, May Yaw Ub, and others. He asked two simple questions: "Do you not know that you have no rights as a tribe to inhabit the country where you now make it your homes in the snake river [*sic*] Country (Kemabec)?" and "Why do you not remain at Mille Lac where you properly belong and evade all the controversies with the settlers?"[101] For Luse, the Snake River Ojibwe's only home remained Mille Lac. Luse's decision, which he forwarded to the Commissioner of Indian Affairs, removed the Ojibwe's hope that they could draw on the federal government to protect their land from outsiders.

Staying put on Mille Lac, as Luse suggested, did little to reduce tensions. In 1887, Ojibwe men from Mille Lac discharged their weapons into some houses that settlers had abandoned as a way to pass time and relieve stress. For the settlers who had reoccupied the dwellings since the last time the Mille Lac had checked their occupancy, terror better described the experience.[102] T. J. Sheehan, the Indian agent at White Earth, blamed the poor judgment surrounding the discharge of weapons on whiskey, but the Ojibwe's frustrations ran much deeper. Over the previous five years settlers had tried to swindle the Ojibwe out of money, Indian agents had refused to honor Ojibwe property and territory, and a growing reliance on federal annuities had made it harder for the Ojibwe to cross borders without repercussions. On an even more basic level, the Ojibwe were angry because the United States failed to offer them even the most basic levels of protection from nearby settlers.[103]

Sheehan noted that he could not, in good conscience, report on his basic duties without mentioning the horrific ways white settlers treated their Anishinaabe neighbors. Ojibwe women between Little Falls and White Oak Point begged him "to get their young daughters back from white men who had taken them from home and kept them in the woods; sometimes leaving a few dollars or a sack of flour" behind. The unwanted gifts did little to pacify "the minds of the mothers of those poor girls who are the victims of those inhumane brutes."[104]

The conditions the Ojibwe lived under created little more to be proud of. Mille Lac consisted of 1,500 people, but lacked a school, passable dwelling houses, basic tools, or enough food to stave off starvation. In that context, Ojibwe men firing into buildings they believed settlers had abandoned or leaving the area to join their relatives in Canada displayed a patience well beyond what the United States deserved. If Luse earnestly thought that the Ojibwe belonged at Mille Lac, the Ojibwe could certainly be excused for believing that there were better places to live.[105]

Still, Luse acted as a gatekeeper for each individual's annuities, adding stress and uncertainty to those who relocated north of the line. The denial of recognition or services only worked well for communities that depended on the federal government in some way. In other cases, Britain and the United States used formalized processes like their extradition system to limit the ways that individuals could use the border to dampen federal authority.

Extradition

Prior to the Civil War, Britain approached extradition with some trepidation. While the United States had signed fourteen extradition agreements by 1870, Britain had only signed extradition agreements with the United States, France, and Denmark.[106] An initial agreement between Britain and the United States allowed for the extradition of individuals for violent crimes (murder) and property crimes (robbery, arson, forgery).[107] For judges along the border, the approach had significant merit. If extradition had a problem, Judge John Hawkins Hagarty of Upper Canada noted, it was that the provisions only applied to only the most serious of offenses and left the vast majority of felonies untouched.[108]

The system, although popular with men like Hagarty, limped along for three decades. With the Civil War, extradition held a new promise. The war ended Britain's concerns about extraditing slaves back into captivity or Confederate soldiers back to unfair trials. The emergence of new kinds of crimes also added incentives to find creative solutions. Embezzlers fled with thousands of dollars in loot, choosing to live within sight of the country that wished to extradite them.[109]

While the Union's victory solved some problems, persistent disputes remained. Political prisoners and speciality—the practice of requiring the extraditing country to charge only wanted men with the crimes listed on the extradition request—grew increasingly difficult to ignore. Disagreements between American courts and the Foreign Office in Britain came to a head in 1876 when United States refused to abide by the protections for criminals that Britain demanded. In response, Britain released Ezra Dyer Winslow, instead of extraditing him. In outrage, the United States suspended its adherence to the Webster Ashburton Treaty. From June until December 1876, Britain, the United States, and Canada possessed no extradition agreement.[110]

Doctrinal differences became local nightmares for communities along the border. Police officers and judges attempted to create a stopgap measure for transnational crime, but doing so required exceeding their legal mandates.

Canadian officers held Maraine Smith, believed to have committed homicide in Detroit, for over a month, despite no clear precedent for such a detention. Criminals flaunted the gaps in the system. According to the *Winnipeg Free Press*, E. G. Mellor removed $100,000 worth of merchandise from his Montreal jewelry store before setting it aflame. He then claimed the losses against his insurance company. When his claims were found to be fraudulent, Mellor fled to the United States.[111]

Mellor's brilliance came when he crossed the border. Rather than trying to hide his luggage, he paid all the necessary duties on his stolen goods and even left "bullion and jewelry in the Custom House at Plattsburg for safe keeping."[112] What he could not carry, he left for his family to bring across the line. As his sisters crossed the border at Malones, New York, they replaced Mellor's brazenness with a common kind of subterfuge.[113] Customs agents discovered $15,000 worth of jewelry secreted "in flower pots, cocoanut [*sic*] shells, children's toys and bars of soap."[114]

Newspapers joked about the discovery of jewelry in household items, but the challenges facing customs agents had real ramifications.[115] Smugglers caught in the act faced punishments. Those who declared their cargos and paid duties on

Figure 3.2 The Interior of E. G. Mellor's Jewellery Store in Montreal five years before the fire. *Canadian Illustrated News*, December 1871, Vol. IV, No. 25, Page 389. Reproduced from Library and Archives Canada's website: *Canadian Illustrated News*, 1869–1883.

stolen goods had no easy answers. The absence of extradition provisions created a sobering reminder to how much both countries relied on cooperation to capture criminals who crossed borders.[116] Britain backed down over the question of political prisoners and the doctrine of specialty in December of 1876. The reinstatement of the extradition agreement closed the gaps in policy that men like Mellor exploited. Britain's concession provided only a temporary fix. A more comprehensive set of revisions was clearly needed.[117]

The amendments to extradition that occurred over the subsequent decades emphasized the value Britain and the United States placed on eliminating legal refuges. New extradition provisions pertaining to embezzlement, counterfeiting, voluntary manslaughter, and burglary reinforced both countries' commitment to policing financial and violent crimes. They also added new laws designed to protect the family and sexual morality.[118] By 1901, rape, abortions, and child stealing became part of the agreements. Over the next three decades Britain and the United States added statutory rape, bigamy, transporting women for immoral purposes, and indecent assault to the list of crimes worthy of an international agreement.[119] Immigration restrictions against moral turpitude—an amorphous category that could include adultery, bigamy, sodomy, and polygamy—reinforced the options both countries had for policing sexuality across borders.[120]

The United States' commitment to extradition with Britain, even when it waned, deviated from its approach to international justice with other countries. The US–Mexico Treaty of 1861 provided the opportunity to extradite but no gave compulsion to do so. While the United States respected the military capacity of Britain, it gave little credit to the capabilities of Mexico. That distinction provided the United States with greater flexibility along its southern border and served as a reminder of the subtle ways that perceptions of cultural similarity or military prowess structured transnational policy.[121]

On June 1, 1877, the Ord Order authorized General E. O. C. order to enter Mexico in pursuit of Indigenous and Mexican raiders. Extradition offered a diplomatic means to get wanted men back across the line, but for the commander of the Army Department of Texas, it offered only one option. Ord wished to minimize the offense caused by sending American troops into a foreign country, but he maintained the right to do so if Mexico failed to stop raiders. President Hayes soon rescinded the pronouncement, but the attempt reflected a visible distinction between policies along the northern and the southern borders.[122]

In other instances, the United States extorted Mexico for transnational crimes. In 1888 a group of Mexican soldiers crossed into the United States with the simple goal of capturing a deserter hiding out at Eagle Pass and bringing him home for justice. After an American sheriff intervened, however, the Mexican soldiers conducted a firefight instead. The United States required Mexico to pay the princely sum of $7,000 in gold to resolve the matter. Deputy Sheriff White, who had lost the use of his right hand during the violence, had only requested $775 . National honor, but also opportunity, explained the order of magnitude in difference. Across the continent, transnational justice remained imperfect. While extradition could result in impressive displays of federal power, the system struggled to keep pace with the flow of people. Justice remained inconsistent and unwieldy, hampered by the jurisdictional divisions created by international lines.[123]

***

In the aftermath of the Civil War and Canadian Confederation, the United States and Canada reimagined who belonged within their respective nation-states. Cultural practices, residency, tribal belonging, and a perceived ability to create families served as important strands that politicians wove together into a tapestry of belonging. The threads built on one another, but they also tangled. Prone to exaggeration and legal sleights of hand, the architects of national belonging wished for a simplicity that rarely manifested itself in the world around them. They drafted new laws across the Great Lakes aiming at creating an uneven set of barriers that shifted according to geography, status, family, and gender.

If Reconstruction and Confederation heralded a new path for the border, the practical world that local administrators faced still contained an abundance of uncertainty and frustration. Persistent power, marked with a bureaucratic regularity, remained limited. So long as Indigenous people maintained their economic independence, neither government had much success convincing them to take up European cultural practices or territorial systems. The problem went beyond ham-fisted approaches to governance. Indigenous independence represented a persistent threat to the broad claims of territorial ownership that Canada and the United States made. Erasure remained a key component of border creation. As a result, suffering, which amplified indirect forms of control, never remained far afield. At the same moment, the ways the border created legal sanctuary provided a reminder of its capacity to create odd bedfellows. Policies that had once given sanctuary to fugitive slaves soon applied to their former masters.

Crisis, at least in the beginning, provided the encouragement necessary for each country to invest in the legal, administrative, and philosophical work necessary to create a functional border. The process had a monumental tone to it. It aimed to draw abstract lines of nationality and then fit the better part of a continent within that framework. Unsurprisingly, that process never proceeded smoothly. In the Great Lakes, regional concerns over slavery, gender, wage work, and the home gave this process its distinct flair. The very nature of the region—filled with large transportation corridors across the Great Lakes and heavy concentrations of settlers on both sides of the border—encouraged a legislative, administrative, and cooperative approach. Still, despite a growth in federal power from the 1860s until the 1880s, neither country possessed the capacity to force unpopular policies in the Great Lakes. In other regions, which possessed fewer administrators, federal control remained even more anemic. Across the Prairies and the Pacific Coast regional concerns and limitations forced a very different set of approaches, which left their own distinct legacy on how the border would operate.

4

Borders of Stones, Guns, and Grass

In Winnipeg, news of the sale of Rupert's Land to the newly formed Canadian state met with a mixed reception. The majority of the village saw the purchase as a major victory and hoisted a flag with the word Canada across it in front of the North West Company's office. The flag bothered Governor McTavish and nearly all the Americans living in Winnipeg. On July 1, 1869, a group of settlers removed the Canadian flag and replaced it with a Fenian one. The Fenian flag remained only momentarily, but it made its point. For the Americans at Winnipeg the sale signaled an annoyance and a matter worth protesting. For the Métis, who hoisted no flag, the purchase signaled war.[1]

The Canada–US border was born in blood. Violence served as both a motivation and a tool for federal control. During the 1860s and 1870s, the Dakota War (1862), Red River Resistance (1869), Fenian raids (1866–1871), the continuation of the whiskey trade, and the Cypress Hills Massacre (1873) provided an ongoing series of humiliating reminders to the limited control both countries maintained along their shared border. Canada and the United States could not prevent the Dakota or the Métis from crossing the border to avoid military engagements or oppressive Indian policies. They failed to convict the participants of the Cypress Hills Massacre and struggled to prosecute those responsible for the Fenian Raid at Pembina.

While violence occurred across all portions of the border, its concentration in the Prairies created a very different regional environment there. Violence in the 1860s and 1870s motivated the creation of a new federal organization unique to the region (the North-West Mounted Police) and an ambitious boundary survey project designed to gather information on land neither country knew well. Violence also provided an inescapable reminder that the nation-building projects Canada and the United States embarked on competed not just with historic boundaries but with projected ones as well. As the Métis Resistance and Fenian movements suggested, many other groups intended to use land along the border to further their own stories of self-determination and expansion.

A Line of Blood and Dirt. Benjamin Hoy, Oxford University Press (2021). © Oxford University Press.
DOI: 10.1093/oso/9780197528693.003.0005

By the mid-1870s, the inability of both countries to stop transnational violence motivated them to rethink their approaches to border control across the Plains. The nations finished surveying their border from the Lake of the Woods to the Rocky Mountains and stationed police officers and soldiers nearby. At least on paper, the border stretched from the Atlantic to the Pacific Ocean. Canadian and American ignorance of pre-existing Indigenous boundaries became harder to maintain as time passed. So long as the Lakota, Cree, Métis, and Siksikaitsiitapi (Blackfoot) controlled bison herds and maintained a strong military presence, the border Canada and the United States created remained only one of the hundreds of important borders that divided the Plains.

Fenian Raids

Although neither country had much success preventing transnational movement during the Civil War, the peace that followed created new possibilities and challenges for border management. After the Civil War, the United States reduced its army from more than a million active soldiers to sixty thousand in 1866. By the 1870s, it maintained less than thirty thousand.[2] The move eliminated concerns that the Union army would press north into British territory, but war left behind a clear message: Britain could not compete on the continent with an American military that could enlist hundreds of thousands of soldiers in such short order. Britain allowed Canada to separate into its own Confederacy in 1867 and withdrew its military forces from the continent between 1869 and 1871.[3]

If the United States' decision to demilitarize offered relief for concerned Britons, it also created opportunities for militancy that neither country had anticipated. Well-trained and out-of-work soldiers could attach themselves to any goal, providing those who could organize them with a formidable fighting force. For the Fenian movement, Irish American Civil War veterans provided an attractive set of recruits.[4] In practice, the Fenian movement contained two approaches. The first, led by John O'Mahony, aimed to support an uprising in Ireland; the second aimed to liberate Ireland by spreading British power thin. William Roberts and Thomas Sweeny, who advocated the latter approach, hoped to use Irish American Civil War veterans to turn Canada into the battleground for Irish liberation.[5]

The Fenians' tactics linked unrest in Ireland to border security concerns in North America. In 1865 Timothy McNeff, a lieutenant in Ohio's volunteer infantry, and John Fanning decided to visit their friends and family in Ireland. At Killeshandra, Ireland, constables demanded travel passes from the two

Americans visitors. They accused the two men of being suspicious foreigners and searched their baggage. During the search, the constables uncovered McNeff's old revolver and pocket diary, which contained the name of a man accused of being a Fenian. The constables took McNeff into custody. While he awaited trail, his captors forced him "to break stones and to wear the prisoners' garb, with thieves, murders, &c., and they used to exhibit me to all the nobs of the country when they would come."[6] McNeff made bail after the US consul intervened, but he expressed significant resentment for his treatment at the hands of the British.

Similar complaints flooded into the American consul's office, accusing Britain of interfering with American citizens living abroad.[7] When Britain captured 200 Fenian suspects in Dublin, some of whom were American citizens, upward of 100,000 New Yorkers protested the action. Although separated by 3,000 miles of ocean, Irish Americans felt significant affinities with Irish living under British rule. As Fenian agitation grew in North America, conflicts that began an ocean away became less and less distant.[8]

In 1866 Fenian organizers launched a series of raids, from the United States into New Brunswick, Canada West (later Ontario), and Canada East (Quebec), hoping to use Canada as a hostage to secure Ireland's release. In early June, John O'Neill assembled approximately 1,000 men (estimates at the time ranged from 650 to 1,500 men) and crossed the Niagara River into Canada West under the cover of darkness.[9] Fenian forces defeated British Colonel Alfred Booker and 900 militiamen at the village of Ridgeway but did not press forward. O'Neill failed to capture territory, but he generated significant fear.[10] Attacks like these prompted the Canadian Parliament to grant police officers unusual powers enabling them to hold prisoners suspected of high treason or warlike behaviors in police custody for months without bail.[11]

O'Neill's hit-and-run strategy took advantage of the power he associated with the border. In his eyes, the border stopped British and Canadian troops but allowed the free movement of militants. In practice, he overestimated the warmth of the welcome he would receive from the US government on his return. The American steamer *Michigan* intercepted and arrested Fenian stragglers as they crossed back into the United States, imprisoning the officers and requiring the rank and file men to post bonds. The *Michigan's* actions, while not affecting the outcome of the battle, made clear that the Fenians could not expect aid from the United States. They would have to put their hope in either American neglect or incompetence.[12]

Attacks across the border continued throughout the year, creating instability and uncertainty on both sides of the Great Lakes. Local soldiers struggled to separate Fenian raiders from peaceful residents. When the US consul came out of his house to investigate the noise generated by the Fenian raid at Fort Erie, a passing patrolman thought he was a militant and shot at him.[13] Irish Americans suffered arrest for their feared association with the Fenian movement, sometimes spending many months in prison before being released on lack of evidence.[14] Lines of loyalty remained unclear. British citizens and sympathizers living in cities such as Chicago volunteered their military services to the Canadian cause, blurring divisions between national spaces as much as the raiders did themselves.[15]

While Canada and the United States failed to stop raids across the border, they succeeded in punishing violators of neutrality when possible. British and American jails filled with Fenian supporters. At Cornwall, Sheriff Daniel McIntyre complained that Fenian prisoners filled up not just the rooms reserved for criminals but had already spilled out into the areas reserved for debtors. The problem became so severe that he mixed military prisoners, debtors, lunatics, and criminals together to save space and converted the day room into temporary quarters. Short of mixing male and female inmates together to free up additional cells, he could think of no other solutions for the problem.[16] For those caught in the Canadian justice system the punishment for the breaches of neutrality varied, but ranged from as little as a few weeks to a few years. Of the 104 prisoners listed by the Department of Justice as imprisoned in Ontario, 82 had been discharged by 1871. By 1872 Canada had released the bulk of these prisoners, convinced that the Fenian movement had run its course.[17]

In the end, the Fenian raids had limited strategic success, but drove home the necessity of cooperation between federal governments. Border skirmishes highlighted the uncertain lines of loyalty, jurisdictional complications wrought by transnational violence, and the unease these kinds of events created between British and American politicians. Balancing public opinion, political expedience, and peace required adept decision-making and international cooperation. Without adequate damage control, Fenian militancy threatened to gain momentum, dragging the United States into an unwanted diplomatic conflict with Britain at a time when it was attempting to rebuild itself following the Civil War. Suppressing transnational militants could not be done by cracking down on dissent within a single nation's boundaries. It required the cooperation from neighboring countries if it had any hope of success.

At a regional level, transnational violence flared up and dissipated. At a national level, however, the locations of violence changed, but its presence remained a persistent headache throughout the 1860s and early 1870s. Transnational violence occurred within the gaps in federal power, but also occurred as a direct result of attempts by Canada and the United States to expand their authority into new regions. Three years after Fenian leaders led thousands of soldiersnorth into Canada West with the dream of freeing Ireland, the Métis launched their own campaign for self-determination in the face of an expanding Canadian state.

Red River

In 1869, the newly formed Dominion of Canada purchased Rupert's Land from the Hudson's Bay Company. The territory was enormous. It consisted of portions of present-day Manitoba, Alberta, Saskatchewan, Ontario, Quebec, Nunavut, Minnesota, Montana, North Dakota, and South Dakota. John A. Macdonald, Canada's first prime minister, believed that the purchase of Rupert's Land would help prevent American encirclement. With the United States' acquisition of Alaska from Russia in 1867, Macdonald feared that if Canada failed to expand, it would soon cede territory to the United States. He intended to meet American expansion in kind.[18]

The land under debate, of course, was not empty. The Indigenous and Métis residents, who controlled most of the land in question, were neither consulted nor compensated during the transfer of control. The sale sparked fears among Indigenous and Métis communities in the region that the Dominion government intended to destroy their way of life. Canada's plan to treat the acquisition of Rupert's Land as "a simple real estate transaction" sputtered as Red River Métis organized against it.[19]

The Métis descended from European men and Indigenous women (often Cree, Assiniboine, Dene, and Ojibwa) who worked together in the fur trade in the Great Lakes and on the Plains. Over the late eighteenth and early nineteenth centuries, intermarriage, trade relationships, and interpersonal alliances among settler, Indigenous, and mixed heritage individuals resulted in the development of a distinct Métis identity.[20] Many Métis served as cultural and diplomatic brokers, but saw their economic opportunities diminish after a merger between the Hudson's Bay Company and the North West Fur Company in 1821. Faced with a changing set of economic circumstances and westward push of the fur trade, the Métis and their ancestors migrated to the Prairies. There they grew crops, hunted buffalo, worked as freighters, and provisioned the Hudson's Bay Company. By the middle of the nineteenth century, the Métis maintained a significant economic presence in the northern plains launching buffalo hunts that contained upward of 1,200 carts and over 1,600 participants. Intermarriage and shared ancestry provided the Plains Métis with access to distant hunting territories, although these privileges came with reciprocal obligations.[21]

By the time of Canadian Confederation, the Métis had established themselves as a distinct cultural and political group. They developed different sociocultural and residency than those of their parents' and learned to navigate Cree, Dene, and European territorial borders. They had developed methods for acculturating strangers, forging personal and economic connections, and maintaining their independence from both the Roman Catholic Church and the Hudson's Bay Company.[22]

They had also developed complex sanctions against those who violated wahkootowin, a Cree (Nêhiyawak) and Métis worldview predicated upon the "relatedness with all beings, human and non-human, living and dead, physical and spiritual."[23] Wahkootowin structured cultural protocols, land management, and spiritual observation. It organized families and served as the basis of interpersonal and diplomatic relationships.[24] For the Métis in the Northwest, family represented their most important relationship. It not only connected humans to one another, but it also bound them to the creator. In practice, hardship and human frailty prevented wahkootowin from being adhered to at all times, in all places, and in all ways. Still, the principles of wahkootowin served as an important set of guiding principles to the Métis in the Prairies.[25]

In the Northwest, kinship structured Métis conceptions of their homeland and territory during the nineteenth century. They understood their homeland both in terms of where they resided (the location of their specific communities) but also in terms of their use of the land (hunting grounds). Strategic marriages built across multiple generations created large, often matrilocal, family networks across a wide territory. In 1887, for example, Raphaël Morin expressed his interest in living in the lands of his mother to scrip commissioners who had come to Green Lake in 1887 to extinguish Métis title to land. He showed little interest, by contrast, in the lands where he or his father had been raised, emphasizing the importance of maternal connections to Métis understandings of identity. In practice, kinship ties ensured that even on distant travels Métis could draw on the support of their extended family. Territory in this sense had both a specific dimension (distinct communities) and an imprecise aspect defined by broad patterns of kinship.[26]

The Hudson's Bay Company's attempted sale of Rupert's Land to the Dominion of Canada threatened the Métis' cultural and political autonomy. Opposition to the sale grew, and the Métis, led by Louis Riel, took up arms in 1869. They declared a provisional government, seized Fort Gary, and executed Thomas Scott for counterrevolutionary activities. They demanded that the Canadian government recognize their rights to land, language, religion, and self-governance. They added provisions for their continued free trade with the United States. Borders might one day be more substantial and, if they were, such a provision would ensure the continuation of Métis livelihoods.[27]

Like many other conflicts, the Red River Resistance spilled out across multiple borders, disrupting trade, fostering resentment, and creating uncertainty. Walter J. S. Traill, a Hudson's Bay Company employee, wrote to his mother on

January 15, 1870 that he feared the rebels would destroy trade networks and leave hundreds of people without food.[28] The resistance angered Traill, who described the rebels as the worst of sorts, "real cabbage heads," completely devoid of intelligence, "ignorant animals whose minds don't carry them to anything beyond 3 pounds of Pemmican per day."[29]

Escaping the violence, however, remained tricky. It required crossing colonial and Indigenous borders. Robert Campbell, another Hudson's Bay Company employee, sent his family from Fort Ellice across the Plains to St. Paul, Minnesota, fearing for both his livelihood and his loved ones' lives. The border, he hoped, would shield them from the violence of the resistance. He called upon the Hudson's Bay Company office in Montreal to have supplies and money ready for them should they require it on their trip. The journey proved a risky one, requiring taking a train of seventy carts carrying furs through "Sioux Country" across a route he knew little about. His family and the merchandise arrived safely, but the action displeased his superiors and cost him his job.[30]

Indigenous people looking to escape the violence faced a similar set of dilemmas. Sitting Bear (maxkwa hapit) descended from a Cree mother and an Assiniboine (Nakoda) and Saulteaux father. When the Resistance began he made a similar journey south to the Turtle Mountain area, choosing to go where his father Standing Ready (wewutci kapu) lived. Amidst this dangerous environment, settler, Indigenous, and Métis families relocated to the United States to seek refuge.[31]

The Red River Resistance, though short lived, succeeded in a number of its aims. The Manitoba Act, commencing on July 15, 1870, created the Province of Manitoba and offered some protections for the French language and Catholicism. Thomas Scott's execution during the conflict soured the English-speaking population's opinion of Riel and prompted the Dominion to send a military expedition under Garnet Wolseley to enforce order. Riel, fearing retribution, fled to the United States.[32]

Following the resistance, Riel spent much of his time in the United States building a political network on both sides of the line. The constituents of Provencher, Manitoba, elected Riel three times as a member of Parliament despite an outstanding warrant for his arrest. Riel established political connections with leading Americans and remained hopeful that he could force Canada to honor the promises it had made to the Métis.[33]

In 1875, Riel drafted a letter to President Ulysses S. Grant in which he proposed to take Manitoba by force. He believed that 68,000 souls (27,000 Métis, 3,000–4,000 adventurers, and 38,000 Indigenous) would support the venture against no more than 10,000 Canadian supporters.[34] Riel hoped to receive "from the [U]nited States, all the [F]rench Canadian and Irish [A]merican

THE VACANT CHAIR.
A *RIEL* BOND OF UNION.

Figure 4.1 A noted taped to a vacant chair reads "Notice: Louis Riel, MP is requested to step this way. No questions will be asked." John A. Macdonald and a compatriot carry swords and warrants for Riel's arrest. The two men speak in unison: "Louis Riel is a murderer and an Outlaw and he out to be hanged." In the middle a bird speaks: "Bravo! Gentleman! Unanimous for once!" J. W. Bengough, *A Caricature History of Canadian Politics Events from the Union of 1841 As Illustrated by Cartoons from "Grip" and Various Other Sources, Vol. 1* (Toronto: The Grip Printing and Publishing Co., 1886). Images from reprint (Toronto: Peter Martin Associates, 1974). Special thanks to Brittany Schmidt from University of Saskatchewan Libraries.

citizens who would be willing to share our fortune."[35] He believed he could also rally four hundred Irish along the frontier at a few days' notice to join his cause. According to Riel, the Irish, like the Métis, longed "for a province of their own."[36] Riel argued that should the president support his plan, the Irish in the United States would "throw themselves into the arms of the republican party."[37] Supporting his cause then was not only good for the United States but good politics for the president's party too.

Riel's calculations, although optimistic to a fault, indicated that he had not given up hope for returning to Canada. On February 12, 1875, Parliament granted Riel amnesty on the condition that he remain in exile for five years.

Between 1876 and 1878, however, he had begun to change. He spent time in insane asylums in Quebec City and Montreal. Soon after, he left again for the United States. His attachment to Canada diminished. He wrote to his mother in 1878 assuring her that he had no intentions of returning to Red River. His home thereafter would be the United States.[38]

A CASE OF RIEL DISTRESS!

Figure 4.2 In the political cartoon "A Case of Riel Distress" the conservative government declares: "I wish I could catch the scoundrel—I do so help me G—rits!!" Riel meanwhile stands behind the official carrying a declaration of amnesty the government had secretly agreed to grant him. A police officer declares "Mercy! But I'd like fine to arrest them both." J. W. Bengough, *A Caricature History of Canadian Politics Events from the Union of 1841 As Illustrated by Cartoons from "Grip" and Various Other Sources, Vol. 2* (Toronto: The Grip Printing and Publishing Co., 1886). Images from reprint (Toronto: Peter Martin Associates, 1974). Special thanks to Brittany Schmidt from University of Saskatchewan Libraries.

The Fenian Raid at Pembina

Peace remained short-lived. By the fall of 1871 Canadian officials noticed Fenian leaders congregating at Pembina, near the modern intersection of North Dakota, Minnesota, and Manitoba. Fearing an attack, Governor Adam G. Archibald requested troops from Ottawa. Archibald also issued a proclamation to the general public in October calling for all the "loving subjects [of Manitoba], irrespective of race or religion or of past local differences to Rally Round the flag!"[39] A Fenian attack on Manitoba worried Archibald because he could not predict how the residents of the area would respond. Canadian and American officials speculated that the Métis might use the Fenian invasion as a pretext to renew their own resistance. The US consul at Winnipeg wrote to the acting Secretary of State explaining that a month before the invasion the Fenians had hired Joseph Poitras, a Métis at St. Josephs, to them supply with hay and other provisions.[40] The movement's exact support base, however, remained very much in question. The US consul speculated that the Métis under Riel would help the Canadian government in defeating the Fenians. Other Indigenous groups, such as the Swampy Cree from Lake Winnipeg, indicated they might assist Canada or at least stay neutral. Loyalty remained a delicate and uncertain issue.[41]

While Archibald had made an open request for volunteers to put down Fenian raiders, the Canadian government had a narrow sense of who should participate. D. T. Bradley, a Canadian customs official, enlisted a number of Ojibwe living in lands disputed by Canada and the United States to help fight the Fenians. The practice ended almost as quickly as it had begun. Enlisting soldiers with ties to another country created questions about violations of neutrality, but the distain toward Bradley's actions went deeper.[42]

Bradley admitted to signing five or six "semi-civilized Indians in the employment of the Hudson's Bay Company" but considered his actions within the bounds of the proclamation Archibald had sent out. Archibald's proclamation, after all, had called for loyalty irrespective of race.[43] Governor Archibald soon qualified his statements. If he demanded loyalty from all, action remained the domain of a select few. Indigenous people would "form no part of the force required for the defense of the frontier,"[44] nor would they have a place in Manitoba's militia system.[45] The United States, concerned about the stability of the region, assisted Canada in defusing the Fenian threat. As Governor Archibald sent out his proclamation, J. W. Taylor, the US consul at Winnipeg, made a request of his own. He beseeched General William Tecumseh Sherman to send five hundred regular troops to help maintain the country's neutrality. Such a force would discourage violence and allow the United States to pursue belligerents across "the Manitoba frontier."[46]

Both governments understood the seriousness of the situation they faced. The Fenians aimed to provide a seed from which general discontent could grow. The Fenians and the Métis shared a common bond through Roman Catholicism, a desire for a sovereign homeland, and a distrust of British rule. If the attacks gained momentum, a civil war in Manitoba could break out.[47] On October 5, 1871, forty to eighty Fenians, including a number of Pembina Métis, crossed the line. William O'Donoghue, who had previously served as the treasurer of Riel's provisional government during the Red River uprising, was among the first to cross. O'Donoghue desired the United States' annexation of Rupert's Land and petitioned country to support of the Métis cause. He represented the kind of bridge figure both governments feared. He supported both the Métis and Irish bid for independence and the United States' violation of Canadian territorial claims. For O'Donoghue, imperial conflicts provided a window of opportunity for subjected people to carve out sovereign spaces of their own.[48]

Once across the line, the Fenians attacked a small Canadian trading post that sat on territory disputed by Canada and the United States. The US Army responded quickly. Colonel Lloyd Wheaton arrested many of the Fenians raiders and freed the post. US troops captured John O'Neil, Thomas Curley, and J. J. Donnelly, 7,000–12,000 rounds of ammunition, and as many as 150 rifles.[49] O'Donoghue fled toward American soil. According to the *Manitoban,* O'Donoghue attacked one of his compatriots while fleeing the battle and stole his horse. The theft did not sit well with O'Donoghue's companion who, along with a French Métis, captured O'Donoghue and turned him over to the Canadian customs agent D. T. Bradley.[50]

In a strange turn of events, Bradley turned O'Donoghue over to the US troops. Bradley feared he could neither safely hold O'Donoghue nor escort him to Fort Garry in the face of Fenian agitation. Colonel Wheaton, in turn, gave O'Donoghue to the American civil authorities.[51] The civil authorities quickly discharged the Fenian prisoners, including O'Donoghue, due to "want of jurisdiction."[52] The courts argued that the crimes the men had been accused of committing had occurred in Canada, not the United States. The question of jurisdiction proved thorny. The boundary commission had not yet surveyed the border near the fort, so the territory remained in dispute. Even within the United States, different branches of authority could not agree on who owned the territory. The US military claimed jurisdiction over the region, while the civilian courts denied it. As a result, American soldiers defused the situation, but the perpetrators walked free and soon scattered.[53] O'Neill and Curley went for St. Paul. Donnelly and O'Donoghue remained in the area temporarily.[54]

The initial attack failed, but Canadian officials suspected the Fenians would strike again. On October 8, three days after the initial attack, Governor Archibald met with Louis Riel and one hundred of his followers. Riel pledged his support and an army of two hundred men to help put down the Fenian invasion. Archibald accepted. The meeting was a dangerous one. The Canadian government still considered Riel a wanted man for the murder of Thomas Scott. The meeting also countermanded Archibald's previous statements that he would not use Indigenous people or Métis to police the boundary line. The second Fenian raid never materialized, and Archibald's backroom dealings alienated him from the English-speaking population of Manitoba.[55]

The Winnipeg *Liberal* attacked Governor Archibald's handling of the Fenian invasion, accusing him of acting unprofessionally and blowing matters out of proportion. Only a handful of Fenians had actually attacked Canada, and the governor had called the entire province into arms. The Mounted Police seemed more than capable of handling such an invasion. The paper also attacked the loyalty of the French and Métis accusing the French of intentionally waiting to see the results of the battle before mustering.[56] The *Liberal* published an affidavit by Francois Chareete calling into question the loyalty of the Métis as well. Chareete's affidavit stated that Riel had told the Métis that "our friend O'Donoghue is taken prisoner at Pembina. He has always been our friend, and we should fight for him and try and get him released."[57] The *Liberal* demanded the French and Métis demonstrate their loyalty, "sincere and outspoken, or let them raise the flag of rebellion and piracy at once."[58]

The Fenian Raid at Pembina, which federal officials might have dismissed as regional security concerns, took on a broader significance in the borderlands. Canadian newspapers demanded that international arbitrators hold the US government responsible for damages caused by the Fenian raid, citing the *Alabama* dispute as precedent.[59] The raid also unsettled relations between the Métis and the Canadian government. Unlike the Irish Fenians, who escaped punishment by crossing the border back into the United States, the Red River Métis who participated in the Fenian raid at Pembina faced arrest and persecution. The Canadian government arrested Andre Jerome St. Matte, Isadore Villeneuve, and Louison "Oiseau" Letendre. Canadian courts acquitted Villieneuvue and remanded Jerome. Letendre was given a death sentence. The courts commuted the punishment to twenty years in prison and in 1873 to exile. Despite Riel's offer, the Canadian government still viewed the Métis with suspicion. Faced with persecution after the Fenian raids, the Métis relocated to the west as well across the border into the United States.[60]

Cypress Hills

Four years after the Red River Resistance and two years after the Fenian Raid at Pembina, the Cypress Hills Massacre provided another reminder to the limited control Canada and the United States maintained along their shared border, particularly in the Prairies. In June 1873 a party of 150 to 200 American wolf hunters, whiskey traders, and Métis haulers crossed into British territory. After crossing the line, many of their horses disappeared. The upset party went to the Farwell and Solomon trading posts, where 200 to 300 Assiniboine had camped. The traders accused the Assiniboine of stealing the horses, while the Assiniboine maintained their innocence. If anyone had taken the horses, the Assiniboine noted, it had probably been the Cree.[61] Unconvinced, and increasingly angry after a night of drinking, the wolf hunters attacked. They fired repeating rifles into the unprotected Assiniboine camp, killing approximately twenty and losing one of their own in the process. The wolfers desecrated the dead, raped a Assiniboine woman, and crossed back into the United States.[62]

The massacre outraged the Canadian government. On September 25, 1873, the Minister of Justice sent a telegraph to Gilbert McMicken at Fort Gary asking McMicken to gather information and witnesses regarding the Cypress Hills Massacre and to have extradition warrants issued to Thomas Hardwick and the others accused of participating. Capturing prisoners and removing them to Fort Garry carried numerous risks. The British War Office considered the men quite dangerous and worried that compatriots might attempt a rescue operation.[63]

McMicken seemed less concerned. He described the wolfers as "a desperate set of men" with operations that took them "some 100 miles or more within the British Lines."[64] McMicken wrote that the mounted police, which John A. MacDonald had been proposing, would be necessary to escort the prisoners safely to a fort and to prevent events such as the Cypress Hills Massacre from occurring again in the future. Canada gained custody of the wanted men, but failed to convict them.[65]

Surveying the Border Across the Plains

Occurring over a span of less than a decade, the Fenian Raids, Red River Resistance, and Cypress Hills Massacre demonstrated the risks inherent in making wide territorial claims that outstripped practical control. Unlike in the Great Lakes, where both governments could muster a bevy of administrators, judges, and militia men to enforce their sense of order, their position in the Prairies remained far more precarious. When violence broke out, both governments scrambled to prop up their police forces. Frustrated by their failures, both countries invested money in their border. They aimed to clarify their respective jurisdictions through a comprehensive boundary survey and expanded the personnel they employed to exert control along the border.

Across the Plains, the border between Canada and the United States had a long history. British and American diplomats had negotiated the boundary's path across the Prairies in 1818, but the process of actual surveying it stalled for more than fifty years.[66] The delay occurred because of the monumental difficulty of the undertaking. From the perspective of the surveyors, the task required that they traverse areas "destitute of all supplies, excepting uncertain provision of fodder, of fuel, of drinkable water, and of game."[67] Poor knowledge of the area, bad roads, long supply chains, cold winters, blistering summer heat, and swarms of mosquitoes made the undertaking even less appealing.[68]

The 1860s brought new complications to a boundary survey process already long overdue. The Northwest Boundary Survey, which had begun in 1857 to mark the international line from the Pacific Ocean to the Rocky Mountains, stalled midway through the process. While the Civil War raged in the south, the Pacific survey seemed like a luxury the Union could ill afford to pursue. The end of the war allowed the British and American Pacific survey teams to finish their work, but created new complications elsewhere. Canadian Confederation added a new political player to the mix and changed the dynamics of the process. Although Britain continued to negotiate on behalf of the new Canadian state, its principal aims focused on divesting its control over North America, maintaining peace, and tying up loose ends. It became less interested in promoting Canadian interests against American ones.[69]

In 1870 pressure to survey and demarcate the border across the Plains increased, motivated by whiskey as well as violence. In 1869, John J. Healy and Alfred B. Hamilton founded Fort Whoop-Up, a whiskey trading post that generated significant profit by providing Montana-based traders with access to northern markets.[70] Policing the transnational whiskey trade remained difficult across the Plains, in part because neither country had an exact idea of where the border lay. American engineers discovered that a Hudson's Bay Company post near Pembina, which they had previously thought was located in British territory, actually fell south of the 49th parallel. The exact ownership of this land remained in doubt a year later when the Fenian raid at Pembina created a jurisdictional nightmare for the two countries.[71] Without a clear boundary, officials on both sides of the border fumbled regularly as they attempted to fulfill their duties. As Canada committed to building a transcontinental railway and becoming a continental power, the absence of certainty about what constituted its southern limits and the persistence of violence became harder to ignore. In this environment, the benefits of surveying the final segment of the 49th parallel outweighed its costs.

Surveying the border across the Plains, some 800 miles in length, commenced in 1872. The process required surveying more than 9,000 square miles of topography. To make the border visible, the survey teams placed 388 markers (135 iron pillars, 129 stone cairns, 113 earth mounds, 3 stone and earth mounds, and 8 timber posts in the Roseau Swamps) along its length. While survey team placed these markers an average of 3 miles apart in the west, in some places, upward of 25 miles could go without markings.[72]

Commissioner Donald Roderick Cameron led the British contingent. Cameron, neither a surveyor nor an engineer, received his appointment for political reasons. Close to three hundred men, including astronomers, laborers, photographers, blacksmiths, and carpenters, rounded out the British team, filling in the expertise that Cameron lacked. This team drew workers from Britain as well as Canada, a necessity given Canada's lack of bureaucratic and professional infrastructure.[73]

Commissioner Archibald Campbell led the American contingent. Campbell had far more experience than his Canadian counterpart. An 1835 graduate of West Point, Campbell gained practical experience with the 1857 boundary commission and a host of other railway and canal surveys before being hired for the boundary survey across the Plains. The American government stocked its team with army personnel to keep its costs low, having already committed to paying these personnel regardless of where it stationed them.[74]

The British and American teams approached the surveying of the border with similar concerns, but different strategies. Both worried about the difficulty of maintaining long supply lines, acquiring accurate astronomical data, and the possible challenges Indigenous groups might pose. Prior to the boundary survey, the Cree had already prevented British surveyors and construction crews from operating within their territory, using these conflicts to put pressure on Ottawa to negotiate treaties with groups living west of Manitoba.[75]

In the United States, the Lakota had previously interfered with the Northern Pacific Railroad survey in the early 1870s. The railway surveyors failed to consult the Lakota before entering their territory, creating significant friction. More broadly, the Lakota expressed reservations about the railroad's impact on bison herds and the strategic problems the railroad created. Trains could bring material wealth, but they could also bring troops. The Lakota believed the risks posed by the railway survey exceeded the benefits they expected to gain. Unimpressed, they drove the surveyors out.[76]

Both governments expressed nervousness that the "Blackfeet and other warlike Indians" might behave in a similar fashion.[77] To combat this, the United States sent an armed escort with its boundary team. More than two hundred soldiers, including the Seventh Cavalry, accompanied the surveyors. The boundary team knew the risks. Had a European power sent a party to survey lands claimed by the United States it could create the pretext for war. Building borders across Indigenous lands carried the same risks. The Americans hoped that a strong show of force would offset the risks. If not, soldiers would provide options should violence break out.[78]

The British contingent did not receive an official military escort. Instead, they relied on American protection, transparency, and the 49th Rangers. British reliance on the American army was an uneasy one. Creating too close a bond risked inheriting the animosity the Sioux felt toward the American government. Even at a distance, however, the proximity of the American military force provided a reassurance. Should violence erupt, the British party planned to take refuge with the American one until reinforcements could arrive. There was some irony in having the vanguard of Canadian power flee to the United States for protection across the very border it had been sent to clarify. If the team realized that, they did not let on.[79]

Britain's strategy also aimed to protect its surveyors through transparency and communication. Britain sent messengers out ahead of its party to ascertain the friendliness of Indigenous communities they expected to encounter.[80] They hoped to counteract the "erroneous impressions in the Indians mind as to the object of the movements of the Joint Boundary commission."[81] Cameron noted near the British depot at Wood Mountain a chief of the Oceti Sakowin (Sioux) had made "enquiries as to the nationality of the train men, and the object of their employment. It was only after repeated assurances by Cameron's men that they were employed by the British party that the chief assumed a satisfied air."[82]

A member of the Geological Society of Canada reported similar anxiety. He received inquiries about why uniformed members of both countries appeared to be working in concert. Or perhaps more fairly, he fielded Indigenous concerns about why colonial officials were working together on lands they were not invited onto during a time of stress already marked by starvation and disease.[83] Inquiries of this nature worried boundary commissioners, who viewed them as a possible prelude to violence. Despite the risk of violence, the British took pride in their approach. They believed that peaceful relations with Indigenous people differentiated their policy from the violence and aggression that characterized American relations with Indigenous people south of the border.[84]

Still, the place of both British and American surveyors remained precarious. Alexander Morris reported that a party of Oceti Sakowin (Sioux) from the Black Hills came north to express their discontent that Canada and the United States had united against them. Despite Morris's efforts the party left the post insulted and threatened to return in the spring with two thousand warriors. Morris took the threats seriously. He believed that Ojibwe from Red Lake, Minnesota had sent tobacco to the Oceti Sakowin living on the Canadian side of the border to build a common alliance against what both groups saw as a united British and American front.[85]

While Morris saw a significant threat in a transnational alliance against the boundary survey, he believed it could be dispelled without too much difficulty. Providing these groups with information as to the "real meaning of the boundary surveys," the movements of troops, and the purpose of the railroads would dispel the ill feelings and allow the boundary survey teams to move without molestation.[86] For Morris, the boundary commission alone could not create the border. That required honoring treaty promises. It required the close involvement of the Department of Indian Affairs and the hiring of "natives of the country, familiar with the Indian dialects, and in whom they have confidence, and taken from the ranks of the English and French half-breeds" to help smooth out misunderstandings.[87]

He proposed James McKay, a Métis trader, for the position. McKay spoke Cree and Ojibwe, had served on the Council of Assiniboia in 1868, and operated a successful business as a merchant out of Red River. During the Red River Resistance, McKay had left to the United States. He refused to fight against the Métis, but he would not support their conflict with Canada either. For Morris, Mckay represented the perfect bridge figure. He retained significant respect among the Métis and gave lavish gifts, sometimes in excess of $1,500 a year. His neutrality during the Resistance made him an appealing ally for the Canadian government, eager to develop partnerships in the region that might further their aims.[88]

The 49th Rangers, a team of thirty mounted Métis led by William Hallett, comprised the final piece of Britain's plan to protect its surveyors.[89] The force cost an estimated £4,000 per year with each rank-and-file ranger receiving $1.50 per day. The Canadian government supplied rangers with a Spencer Carbine but expected them to provide their own horses. The British believed that Métis scouts would create less trouble than a regular army unit and would still dissuade attacks from the Oceti Sakowin (Sioux). The rangers reconnoitered, hunted, herded, carried letters, marked trails, and found appropriate campsites. They also communicated with other Plains communities and represented an important part of Britain's plans to avoid conflict.[90]

For all the trepidation that came with encroaching on Indigenous lands, neither party ran into any serious trouble with the Cree, Oceti Sakowin, Métis, or Assiniboine they encountered. Reports received by both governments, however, suggested that animosity remained high, especially after the Cypress Hills Massacre in 1873.[91] The massacre led to debates among Métis, Oceti Sakowin, and Assiniboine as to whether or not to stop the survey of the border. Although the Teton directed their hostility largely at the United States, they feared that the United States "had got the English with them to form a rampart against the Sioux."[92] The Tetons requested that the Métis join them to prevent the boundary survey from continuing. The British Commissioner believed that the Tetons exercised restraint because attacking only the American party would not stop the survey from being completed and the Tetons realized that attacking both parties would bring "destruction on themselves, by forcing the British, with whom they had always been at peace," into arms alongside the United States.[93]

The Tetons and Assiniboine may have also held back because they realized the value that the border could hold for them. The Dakotas crossed the line in 1863 to escape the American military and Lakota later used the border as a shield after the battle of Little Big Horn in 1876. Groups such as the Assiniboine, who had suffered at the hands of Montanan traders, saw value in distinguishing British from American territory. Their disappointment came not from the border's creation, but rather from the few piles of stones, rather than a wall, being used to mark the line.[94] The boundary markers did not prevent the Dakota, Lakota, or Assiniboine from crossing the border, but they interfered with the United States' and Canada's ability to do so without risking an international incident. The very unevenness of the border made it appealing.[95]

Although violence did not materialize, Plains communities made sure to remind surveyors who was in charge. Two hundred Piikani (Piegans), for example, helped themselves to supplies guarded by only two depot keepers at Britain's West Butte Depot. They visited a nearby American post but did not press their luck against the soldiers stationed there.[96] The British suffered from a second raid against a depot located on the east fork of the Milk River. Britain's refusal to supply food served as a point of friction. Poor manners from guests required corrective action. After British depot keepers refused food to two men, a hundred Yanktonais returned to claim half of the supplies at the depot. While raids by the Oceti Sakowin and Piikani frightened surveyors, they did little to disrupt progress, nor did they threaten the overall safety of the British survey party. Compared to the costs of maintaining a military force in the field for the length of the operation, the losses Britain suffered during these raids were manageable.[97]

In general, Indigenous people on the Plains, much like those on the Pacific Coast, assisted the surveying teams more than they obstructed them. The creation of the border required both the active and passive participation of the Oceti Sakowin, Ojibwe, Métis, and Assiniboine. Indigenous guides and laborers eliminated logistical challenges faced by the boundary commission, while provisioners ensured the commission remained well fed. Many Indigenous communities passively assisted the boundary commission by allowing its workers to pass through their territory unmolested. As debates between the Métis, Oceti Sakowin, and Assiniboine suggested, permission to survey was not a forgone conclusion. Had plains communities known how the border would later affect their lives, they may well have stopped it.[98]

Throughout the surveying process, the knowledge of the local environment and geography that Indigenous people brought to the table proved a valuable commodity. At the start of the survey, for example, both governments tried to locate a wooden shack known as the Reference Monument at the Lake of the Woods that a previous survey team had placed there in 1825. The shack denoted the northwest point of the lake and was crucial for determining the Northwest Angle between the Lake of the Woods and the 49th parallel.[99] The monument's position mattered because it determined whether the United States would retain a portion of territory "projecting into the lake" that would cut off Manitoba's "means of communication with Canada" or not.[100]

Although both the British and American teams possessed sophisticated astronomical equipment, they could not find the reference monuments their own governments had erected fifty years earlier. The difficulty was not surprising. The Lake of the Woods was a complex body of water consisting of endless bays, islands, and inlets. At 65,000 miles in length, the shoreline of the Lake of the Woods is long enough to wrap around the world two and a half times.[101] To make matters worse, fire had swept through the region between the two survey parties, and only a charred oak log "under water and imbedded in the soil" remained.[102] The team discovered the monument only with the help of an old Ojibwe man, left unnamed, whose knowledge of the area and the previous survey proved invaluable.[103]

Indigenous communities expected and received remuneration when they assisted the boundary team. They forced terms of employment that the boundary commissioners acceded to, even ones the commission found uncomfortable or irregular. Ojibwe laborers, for example, insisted on bartering for food or pay on a daily basis rather than accepting a set amount for the duration of their employment.[104] Many groups also refused to work unless the boundary team cared for their families in their absence. To appease these demands, the British survey team allowed just over a dozen families to set up their lodges near an observation camp and supplied them with flour and bacon. Samuel Anderson, the chief astronomer of the British party, considered the arrangement a small price to pay to secure Indigenous men who would carry supplies for the boundary party.[105]

For all the difficulty and expense that had gone into surveying and marking the border across the Prairies, its physical manifestation did not last long. In 1875, less than a year after the survey parties completed their task, bison destroyed or damaged many of the original markers. The loss of markers extended the already long distances between indications of where the border ran. Even if the stones had remained, they alone did not ensure peace.[106]

The North-West Mounted Police

The boundary commission helped define the scope of national control, but exerting power required soldiers, administrators, and police officers. In the east and along the Great Lakes, where large-scale settlement had already occurred, Canada and the United States focused on expanding their customs forces, refining their extradition policies, and finding creative ways to outsource aspect of transnational policing. In the west, where Indigenous people remained the demographic majority, and where both countries struggled to enforce their conceptions of geography, they focused primarily on soldiers and police officers.

In 1874, Canada established the North-West Mounted Police (NWMP) to serve as its presence in the west. The force was envisioned as a catch-all organization that would collect customs duties, patrol the border, crack down on whiskey smuggling, police Indigenous people, and enforce Canadian law. At its heart, the NWMP was a compromise. Many of the forces' original proponents, including Prime Minister John A. MacDonald, realized that a few hundred NWMP officers could not achieve all of the goals that Canada had set for them. Spread across hundreds of miles of land, these officers provided a skeleton presence at best. For a country with continental ambitions and a shoestring budget, however, even a small presence had value.[107]

Although the NWMP followed closely in the footsteps of the boundary commission, it put into practice few of the lessons the boundary survey commission had learned. During the trek west the NWMP failed to bring enough provisions, brought unnecessary field guns and mortars, and attempted to traverse difficult sections of land instead of following the paths already established by the boundary commissioners.[108]

More troubling, if the North-West Mounted Police represented the vanguard of Canadian power, it was a power underwritten by American infrastructure and Indigenous supports. The force, composed originally of three hundred men, began its trek west in 1874 from Ontario. Lacking a viable Canadian route, the men relied on the Grand Trunk to make their way to Fargo, North Dakota before crossing back into Canada on June 19, 1874. Careful to avoid creating an international dispute, the officers locked their guns up as they travelled through American territory.[109]

Until the Canadian Pacific Railroad came to Alberta in 1883, the force relied on American transportation networks for supplies and new recruits. This reliance diminished but did not disappear over time. When W. H. Cox joined the force in 1880, he travelled from Sarnia, Ontario to Duluth, Minnesota before heading toward Fort Benton, Montana, and up to Fort Walsh in land that would become Saskatchewan.[110] American merchants from Fort Benton supplied the NWMP with everything from their mail to their Christmas dinner, and communication with Ottawa passed through American telegraph lines.[111] Throughout this infrastructure, Indigenous people played important roles. Joe Tanner, a Cree transporter, for example, provided the NWMP post at Fort Walsh with its mail, which he brought north from the United States.[112]

Métis and Indigenous provisioners and guides provided other essential services. Métis guides accompanied the initial party of NWMP who went out west. In August of 1874, Commissioner French noted that soon "my sketch of the Boundary Comm[ission] r[oa]d. will give out and I shall be completely in the hands of the guides, who will, doubtless, mark marches in accordance with their ideas of a days work."[113] When fresh water was on hand, the Métis cart drivers indulged in tea breaks as many as a dozen times per day. The practice frustrated French, but he could do little more than grumble about it.[114]

Other members of the force expressed disdain for the drivers, challenging their knowledge of the local topography and their overall usefulness. In the absence of better options, the NWMP continued to employ them in spite of the delays they caused. The guides and drivers took advantage of the NWMP's dependence. They demanded pay between $2 and $5 a day, well in excess of the 75 cents received by the NWMP officers. Without any knowledge of the local topography, the NWMP continued to agree to the Métis' demands. While the march west had become part of the mythology of Canada's creation by the early twentieth century, the vanguard of Canadian power on the Plains could not have existed with Indigenous, Métis, and American support.[115]

Everyday experiences similarly failed to match later mythologizing. Canadians and Americans who looked back on the North-West Mounted Police years later saw them as a symbol of Canadian identity bedecked with clean red tunics, helmets, and dark pants with a striped accent. In the late 1870s, the men fell well short of those memories. On a day-to-day level, they were a cold, bored, sick, and unhappy bunch. They drank heavily and their forays with nearby Indigenous communities caused many to acquire and spread syphilis. Despite yearly requisitions for crucial supplies, North-West Mounted Police officers at Prince Albert had to make do with insufficient gear. They used worn out saddles, incomplete uniforms, and damaged equipment for years at a time. They also relied on hand-me-down equipment, such as harnesses, from the Boundary Commission which, by 1879, had become unsafe for use.[116]

Inadequate supplies created real health risks. At some posts, NWMP constables waited three years before receiving even a basic tunic, and long periods before receiving helmets, spurs, mitts, socks, or fur caps even as the temperature where they were stationed at dropped to -42° C degrees. With gear chronically short, the men neither dressed alike nor felt supported by their own government. Insufficient insulation at the Battleford Barracks forced soldiers to burn four to five cords of wood daily in order to bring the living conditions at the barracks from an intolerable level to an uncomfortable one.[117] Intense cold coupled with exposure to smoke created by the intense fires necessary for heating caused pneumonia and exacerbated rheumatism and other ailments. The post relied on Cree laborers to build a stockade and continued to struggle with daily life. British maps depicted a homogenous Canadian state with clear boundaries. The early experiences of North-West Mounted Police emphasized a different reality—one filled with neglect, dependence, ambiguity, and uncertainty.[118]

Borders on Top of Borders

Stationing troops and police officers along the 49th parallel made the fiction of a homogenous and clear border harder to ignore. Britain, Canada, and the United States drew their border across the land as if Cree, Lakota, Siksikaitsiitapi (Blackfoot), and Métis borders did not exist. Even the most obtuse observers recognized the challenges of maintaining this kind of willful ignorance. Indigenous borders structured the land and shaped the resources available to colonial officers.

For all the ways federal observers often downplayed the importance of Indigenous borders, they occasionally mentioned them in their recollections. The notebooks of Captain Albany Featherstonhaugh, an assistant astronomer for the British Boundary Commission, for example, points to one example of this. While Featherstonhaugh's team was surveying the border, they came across a piece of territory between the Milk River and the Three Buttes that was "a sort of neutral ground between the Indian tribes . . . the Sioux and Assinebonies [*sic*] do not appear to cross to the west bank of the stream, and the Blackfeet, who cling to the skirts of the Rocky Mountains, rarely approach the Buttes."[119] For Featherstonhaugh, the neutral ground was noteworthy because it provided a refuge for buffalo, which were a much needed source of fresh meat for the surveyors. His observation, however, also revealed a deeper understanding of the implications of the project his men engaged in. Britain and the United States were not just creating borders; they were creating them on top of ones that already existed.[120]

Both countries could only ignore Indigenous borders for so long. As they began to negotiate land cessions and exert practical control in the west, their ambitious claims to land clashed with the practical realities on the ground. On paper, the border that the 1874 boundary commission created split the approximately three thousand Turtle Mountain Ojibwe—who lived in North Dakota, Montana, Minnesota, and in the British possessions—into two communities. In practice, the border created more difficulties for federal administrators than it did for the Turtle Mountain community.[121] The Ojibwe lived on both sides of the line and maintained their own territorial agreements. When Indian agents attempted to take a census of Turtle Mountain in 1893, they found the task before them impossible. Drawing borders on colonial maps was easy. Drawing them across everyday life offered a far more daunting task.[122]

Throughout the 1870s the arrival of settlers, soldiers, and police to the Cypress Hills, Fort Qu'Appelle, and File Hills regions shaped intertribal relationships, but did not reorder them. Both Cree and the Kainah (Blood) leaders saw NWMP agents as useful intermediaries for resolve existing territorial conflicts. The Kainah, for example, agreed to meet with the Cree during the 1870s to discuss a peace "on the condition that they be met and escorted by the white soldiers and the interpreter."[123] The NWMP were not, however, essential players in the kinds of processes that kept Indigenous boundaries in operation.

While Chief Black Bear utilized the NWMP to secure the initial meeting with the Kainah, the NWMP played little part in the actual peace agreement that the Kainah and Cree reached. According to Black Bear's son Pieciwhathamo (Sing Like Thunder), Black Bear made separate peace agreements with the "Peigan, Rapids, Blood, Sarcee, Blackfeet, Crow, and Flat Head" without the presence of white soldiers or police officers.[124] While the Cree might use colonial officials to assist in difficult peace negotiations, many of the region's geopolitical agreements continued to occur without colonial input. The Cree had years of success maintaining these kinds of diplomatic, military, and economic relationships. They traded porcupine quillwork for Siksikaitsiitapi (Blackfoot) and Tsuut'ina (Sarcee) blankets and clothing. They exchanged dogs for animal hides with the Ojibwe and purchased medicine from the East Saulteaux (mamihknahka-winiwuk). Strategic marriages among the Cree, Stoney Nakota, and Saulteaux transferred horses between the various communities and created flexible military ties.[125]

Oral histories provide far more detail on the ways Cree, Oceti Sakowin (Sioux), and Siksikaitsiitapi (Blackfoot) communities maintained control over enormous amounts of land. In 1934 Feather described the territorial expansiveness of the Opwasimauk, who were "originally outcasts from the Sioux."[126] Feather, roughly in his mid-eighties, recalled that the Opwasimauk inhabited land stretching from Wood Mountain to Moose Mountain and their travels brought them as far south as perhaps the Missouri River. The Opwasimauk fought against both the Oceti Sakowin and Cree and pushed the Siksikaitsiitapi out of contested territory, a success that Feather attributed to their superior numbers and tactics.[127] Over time, however, Feather believed that the Opwasimauk's ability to maintain their territorial base diminished, and "they finally landed in Canada because of their malicious exploits in the States."[128]

As Canada and the United States attempted to sign treaties and acquire land cession, they paid more attention to the overlapping and contested boundaries that they found around themselves. Adjudicating disputed lands forced treaty commissioners to define what they believed constituted Indigenous ownership, a decision they found neither clear-cut nor simple. In 1882, for example, American commissioners faced a dispute between the Sisseton and Wahpeton and the Turtle Mountain and Pembina Bands Ojibwe over land in Dakota Territory.[129] Located between Devil's Lake and the international border—a distance of about a hundred kilometers—the territory had remained in dispute for decades. In looking at this case, American commissioners prioritized long-term occupancy over broader patterns of use. The commission recognized that the Sisseton and Wahpeton had launched hunting expeditions into this region and had a territorial breadth that extended into these regions and into lands north of the international border. It argued, however, that the Sisseton and Wahpeton never "successfully disputed" the Turtle Mountain Ojibwe, who had maintained control over the region for longer.[130] The ability for American officials to decide the outcome of a territorial dispute between members of the Oceti Sakowin and the Ojibwe signaled a change in the nature of power along the border brought on by starvation and disease.[131]

***

By 1874, stone cairns and iron posts marked the US border with Canada from the Atlantic to the Pacific Ocean. Surveying the final section of this border across the Plains came almost sixty years after Britain and the United States had agreed upon the boundary's path. The embarrassment and uncertainty caused by the Dakota War, Red River Resistance, Fenian Raids, the whiskey trade, and the Cypress Hills massacre made palpable the disconnect between federal claims and practical realities. Apathy became action only because of violence and fear.

For all the importance that the Canada–US border and the NWMP would later have on life in the Plains, their initial presence came as a whimper. The border existed as only one of many boundaries across the Plains, and the NWMP spent as much of their time scraping by as they did exerting any real influence. Initially, the NWMP remained on the Plains only at the convenience of their neighbors. Without American transportation networks and Indigenous provisioners and laborers, the NWMP would have found themselves without regular access to food or communication with Ottawa. Even with those boons, many constables found their living situation unpleasant and, at times, unbearable.

While Canada and the United States expanded their knowledge of and control across the Prairies throughout the 1870s, Indigenous boundaries remained the dominant organizing principle on the Plains. For all the power that Canada and the United States gained as they stationed troops, signed treaties, and encouraged settlement, they struggled to disrupt or erase Indigenous boundaries. Their power to do that came only with starvation and disease. It came only when everything went wrong.

5

Where It All Went Wrong

After his parents died, Last Feather moved from Minnesota onto the Plains under the care of his brother. The two Ojibwe men resided in Grand Forks (ND), Pembina (ND), and Winnipeg (Man.), before relocating to Montana in the 1860s.[1] Initially, the border seemed to matter very little to the ways Last Feather moved. By the end of the 1870s, however, something had changed. By that point, Last Feather had joined the Cowessess band, a Plains Cree (nêhiyawak) and Saulteaux community with whom he shared a maternal connection. In 1874 the band took part in the Treaty 4 negotiations with Canada. Within five years, starvation had forced them onto a reserve.[2]

The treaty process and the reserve created a moral dilemma for Last Feather. According to his son, J. B. Sparvey, Last Feather believed that "he would be stealing if he took Canadian money and settled down on a reserve in Canada, since he was a United States Indian."[3] The Cowessess band disagreed with Last Feather's interpretation and convinced him to seek the advice from Father Sainte Germaine, who agreed that "if the Canadian government would give the money, he should take it."[4] The border had left a lasting impact on how Last Feather interpreted his own identity and his place of belonging. Across the broader Plains, that kind of transition came as a result of monumental set of changes.

In the 1870s, Canada and the United States had drawn a new border across the Plains but, as with other regions, the line they had created ran on top of hundreds of Indigenous boundaries and buffers zone maintained by the Cree, Métis, Siksikaitsiitapi (Blackfoot Confederacy), Dakota, Lakota, Saulteaux, and others. Canadian and American conceptions of territory required more than Indigenous groups simply recognizing the new national border they had drawn. It required the erasure of all other pre-existing forms of territorial organization and the confinement of Indigenous people to reserves and reservations. That transition only became possible because of violence, disease, and famine.

On the Plains, the disappearance of the bison coupled with the devastation wrought by disease redrew the geopolitics of thousands of miles of territory in

A Line of Blood and Dirt. Benjamin Hoy, Oxford University Press (2021). © Oxford University Press.
DOI: 10.1093/oso/9780197528693.003.0006

the span of only a few decades. Indigenous groups who relied on the buffalo for subsistence faced three major choices: find another food source, rely on the federal government, or relocate to the few remaining herds. Some groups chose to follow the buffalo into Montana; others sold land in exchange for annuities, farming implements, and reservations. Still others responded by raiding or engaging in wage labor.[5]

Violence provided the final factor that redrew the lives and territories of Plains communities. Over the 1870s and 1880s, Canada and the United States fought with the Métis, Oceti Sakowin (Sioux), and Nimiipuu (Nez Perce) forcing each community to relocate—or attempt to relocate—across the international lines. Together the Great Sioux War, Flight of the Nez Perce, and 1885 Resistance provide unmistakable examples of how much power dynamics across the Plains had changed. Together with disease and famine, violence also ushered in a crippling set of changes, as many Indigenous communities found themselves confined to reserves and reservations. For the Cree, being home meant "to be a nation, to have access to land, to be able to raise your own children, and to have political control."[6] The Cree words to describe reserves—"askîhkân ('fake land') and iskonikan ('left-overs')"—emphasized the monumental changes that disease, hunger, and violence unleashed.[7] For the Cree, 1885, the year of their military defeat at the hands of Canadian forces, became known as ê-mâyahkamikahk or the year "where it went wrong."[8]

As the Cree, Lakota, Dakota, Métis, and Siksikaitsiitapi adjusted to the decline of the buffalo, movement across traditional territories and across the borderlands became harder to maintain. In this context, the growth of a meaningful international border had as much to do with bison, violence, and disease as it did with clerks, border guards, and boundary stones. The speed at which the border transitioned from its initial survey to the time when it mattered to everyday life occurred much more rapidly on the Plains than it had in the Great Lakes or along the Pacific Coast. The speed of that transition was not an accident. The border across the interior grew quickly because it traced its path through the graveyards of the continent.

Hunger and Treaties

The bison had served as a cornerstone for Plains Indigenous life for more than 10,000 years, forming the "longest-sustained human lifeway in North American history."[9] Indigenous people killed bison on foot and used buffalo jumps, corrals, and pounds to kill bison en masse. The reintroduction of horses to the Plains allowed for a new equestrian style of hunting that changed the orientation of entire communities. It did not change, however, the underlying truth of the region: bison were a source of life.[10] As historian Ted Binnema notes, their disappearance was the "single most important turning point in the human history of the North American Great Plains."[11]

Like all monumental transitions in human history, the bison's destruction had a complicated genesis. Overhunting, habitant degradation, exotic bovine diseases, and competition for grazing and watering sites all played significant roles. Signs of a decline appeared in the Kiowa robe calendars as early as 1846, and a devastating drought from 1855 to 1866 made matters worse. By the mid-1860s, pressures on bison herds on the southern Plains had caused their numbers to drop to five million heads or less. For every two bison that had grazed the southern Plains during the eighteenth century, one or less remained.[12]

Indigenous groups felt the change immediately. Starvation set in during the 1850s and grew worse over time. During the 1870s and 1880s, hide hunters, many of them white settlers, killed most of the remaining 3.5 million bison on the southern Plains in their quest to create leather belts for factories and machinery. The complete loss of bison, coupled with devastating outbreaks of disease, forced the Cheyenne (Tsistsistas), Arapahoe (Hinono'ei), Comanche (Nimini), and Kiowa onto reservations by the end of the 1870s.[13]

In the northern Plains, comprised of present-day Alberta, Saskatchewan, Manitoba, Montana, and North Dakota, the disappearance occurred more slowly, but led to the same result. By the 1860s, only a third of the bison that had roamed the northern Plains in the early nineteenth century remained. The arrival of more than a thousand Dakota refugees from the war in Minnesota put pressure on the nearby herds.[14] Hide hunters, much like in the southern Plains, reduced an already weakened population to the brink of extinction by the end of the 1870s. The precipitous fall outpaced even the most pessimistic projections at the time. In thirty years, the bison had gone from being one of the most dominant species the Plains had ever seen to little more than a memory.[15]

Many groups, including the Lakota and the Siksikaitsiitapi, blamed white settlers for the disappearance.[16] The Lakota believed that the bison took issue with foreign smells (coffee, gunpowder, and bacon) and noises (steamboat whistles and firearms). Offended by the disrespect they had experienced, the bison had retreated "back into the earth."[17] For Lone Horn and Bull Owl, who reflected on the disappearance of the bison in 1868, the task of convincing the bison to return required addressing these slights. That meant conducting proper rituals and prohibiting whites from entering or crossing Lakota territory. Gut Fat (Hunkpapa) and Gray Hair (Itazipco) believed that if settlers had the power to make the buffalo disappear, they must in turn have the ability to bring them back. Both explanations made a great deal of sense within the Lakota's cosmology. Oral traditions made note of previous episodes in which the bison disappeared, but they always returned when the people corrected their hubris. This time, however, the bison did not return no matter what the Lakota did.[18]

As bison populations declined, protecting food meant policing land. Facing the threat of starvation, the Cree developed a harder interpretation of their own territorial boundaries. Instead of viewing the bison as a common resource, groups of Cree-Assiniboine, like the Young Dog band, sent out patrols during the 1860s to keep competing groups away. When that failed, Cree families began killing dogs and horses for food.[19] As buffalo became scarce, members of the Oceti Sakowin (Sioux) travelled north in an attempt to raid horses among the Cree, Métis, and Saulteaux. The raids became desperate. Oceti Sakowin raiders followed through with their attacks even after learning that the Cree expected them. Raiding parties not only risked death at the hands of their enemies, but also capture by Canadian and American police officers, who grew in number over time.[20]

During a Cree raid on an encampment of Oceti Sakowin (Sioux) in the 1870s, the defenders shot Owl in the leg and Day Thunder in the stomach. A Métis freighter stumbled upon Owl and turned him over to the North-West Mounted Police at Wood Mountain. Owl's capture tested the geopolitics of the region. When the Oceti Sakowin learned that the NWMP had gained custody of Owl, they demanded the officers surrender him into their custody. They believed he had killed one of their chiefs and insisted that justice should come from Sioux hands. According to Fine Day, a Cree from the Sweet Grass Reserve, "the police were afraid of the Sioux and promised to give Owl up," but an interpreter thwarted the plan by helping Owl escape to a Saulteaux camp.[21]

As the bison disappeared from Canada, the Cree shifted strategies. Intensifying their control over areas only worked so long as bison remained to protect. As they disappeared completely from Cree lands, the Cree looked to move into the Montana and into Siksikaitsiitapi (Blackfoot) territory, a practice that Ottawa did little to discourage. In crossing these borders to hunt, the Cree took significant risks.[22] Journeying south during the winter, especially while weak from hunger, cost people their lives as they fell victim to exposure or attacks by competing groups.[23] Outbreaks of violence between the Cree, the Siksikaitsiitapi, and others stretched from the Cypress Hills to Moose Jaw, serving as reminders that in times of hunger, territorial boundaries extended only as far as military strength. The Siksikaitsiitapi's defeat at the hands of the Cree at Vermillion Hills left stretches of bleach-boned skeletons.[24]

Despite these setbacks, the Siksikaitsiitapi remained strong. Battles with the American settlers and soldiers in 1869 and 1870 weakened the Siksikaitsiitapi's hold on its territory but did not destroy it. In 1870, a large party of Cree launched an attack against the Piikani (Piegan) and Kainah (Blood) encampment near present-day Lethbridge. The Siksikaitsiitapi, armed with repeating rifles, rebuffed the attack and inflicted two or three hundred casualties on the Cree party.[25] Shortly after the Cree's failed attack at the Old Man River, smallpox struck, killing more than a thousand Cree. While the Cree and Siksikaitsiitapi negotiated a peace agreement in 1872 after much bloodshed, horrific suffering continued. During the winter of 1873–74, the Cree at the Victoria Mission ate their snowshoes and moccasins in an attempt to satiate their hunger. They died shortly after. Elsewhere the Cree ate badgers, gophers, and prairie dogs to survive.[26]

The reorientation of territorial control on the Plains intensified problems with new powers as well as old ones. On November 2, 1871, American soldiers raided a camp of Métis and Santee Dakota near Frenchman's Creek, destroying houses, personal goods, and supplies in their quest to stamp out the liquor trade. Three years later, United States Deputy Marshal Charles Hard raided another Métis camp at the same location, capturing $9,000 in furs, robes, and supplies. The Métis asserted they had been on Canadian soil. Despite this ambiguity, Métis and French Canadian traders like Francois Ouelette, Antoine Ouelette, and Jean Louis Legaré received no restitution for the goods that they lost.[27] Remaining south of the line presented significant risks.

The decline of the bison and outbreaks of smallpox in 1869 and 1870 created a power vacuum that Canada and the United States exploited.[28] Facing starvation, dozens of Indigenous groups near the 49th parallel signed treaties (known as the numbered treaties) with the British Crown between 1871 and 1877. Under the British understanding of the treaty system, Indigenous people ceded vast amounts of land and agreed to relocate to small reserves or enclaves, which the Canadian state would administer. Military conflicts in the West cost the United States twenty million in 1872, roughly the size of Canada's annual budget that year. Anemia, not benevolence, pushed Canada to pursue a treaty process.[29]

For the Cree, Siksikaitsiitapi, and Stoney Nakota signatories, these agreements promised something quite different. Siksikaitsiitapi and Stoney Nakota elders in the Treaty 7 area emphasize that many of their communities saw the treaty process along the Alberta–Montana border as a peace agreement rather than a land transfer agreement. The elders who mentioned land emphasized that their people only agreed to let settlers use the surface of the earth, often described as the first six inches to a foot of soil.[30] Similar descriptions of surface rights appeared in the Treaty 6 and Treaty 8 areas in present-day northern Alberta and Saskatchewan. If Indigenous understandings of the treaty process emphasized its limited scope, colonial officials never seemed to question how deep their borders ran.[31]

For all the treaty process's problems, the Cree hoped it would offer a way to restructure their economies to take advantage of a world increasingly devoid of bison. In Treaty 6, for example, the Plains Cree demanded agricultural assistance, famine relief, and access to European medicine. Under these agreements, the Queen promised to provide for the Cree in times of need.[32] Oral histories passed down to Isabel Smallboy emphasized that treaty commissioners explained to the Cree that the Queen's "tits are very big and you will never eat them all, that's how rich they are." If the Cree grew hungry, she would feed them, "just as long as the river runs . . . the treaty will run."[33]

Although the treaty process between Canada and the Indigenous peoples living north of the line charted a different path than the one taken by the United States, the results often seemed just as grim. In its approach to the treaty process, the Canadian government aimed to undercut Indigenous control, maximize land cessions, and minimize its own costs. These choices resulted in treaty negotiations that lacked relevant parties and created suffering on a staggering scale.[34] While Canada and the United States did not create all of the conditions necessary for the bison's demise, they made no apologies for the ways they exploited the circumstances. As Plains communities grew weaker, both governments ignored the treaty promises they had made only a few years earlier. Starvation served as a tool for control, one that neither government shied from using.[35]

Little Big Horn

Persistent hunger, coupled with decades of broken treaty promises, graft, incursions, and disrespect, made the boundaries across the Prairies volatile and attempts to control them a persistent risk. Hunger had fostered a Canadian treaty process filled with misunderstandings and suffering. In the United States, the American treaty process often resulted in war. In 1868, the United States signed the Treaty of Fort Laramie with the Lakota Nation, which recognized the Lakota's exclusive rights to land west of the Missouri river including the Black Hills and recognized their right to hunt on unceded land. The treaty stipulated that that no one, other than the Sioux or authorized government employees would be allowed "to pass over, settle upon, or reside in the territory" composing the reservation.[36] Peace with the United States opened up opportunities elsewhere, allowing the Lakota to launch offensives against the Pawnee (Chatiks si chatiks), Crows (Apsáalooke), and Sahnish (Arikaras). The window of opportunity did not last long. The discovery of gold in the Black Hills in the early 1870s resulted in a flood of American gold miners into the region. While American soldiers evicted miners, the federal government used the discovery of gold to push for a new treaty and the relocation of the Lakota.[37]

The offer of a treaty so soon after the last one inspired little confidence in the process. Skirmishes, land encroachment, and a plan to create a railway through

Lakota lands caused further animosity. In practice, the United States sent soldiers to force the Lakota and Cheyenne out of Yellowstone River Valley, irrespective of treaty rights. General William Tecumseh Sherman later justified this action by arguing that both groups had hostile intentions, threatened steamer traffic on the Missouri River, and impeded the construction of the railway.[38]

The Great Sioux War, which lasted from 1876 to 1877, marked one of the last dramatic victories for Indigenous troops when the Lakota and Cheyenne defeated General Custer at the battle of Little Bighorn. Custer died as did five companies of the Seventh Cavalry.[39] The military defeat shocked the American public and resulted in swift calls for retribution. Major General Philip H. Sheridan stated that the army would "make the punishment of the Sioux for their present hostility one never to be forgotten."[40] By the mid-1870s, however, the American military could afford to lose battles during the summer. It won its wars with the coming of the cold. American soldiers drove the Lakota out of their winter camps, exposing those who resisted to starvation and the unforgiving elements.[41]

From the start of the conflict, American and Canadian officials suspected the Lakota might move north if the war went poorly. Alexander Morris worried that if the Lakota entered Canada it would cause "serious complications with the United States."[42] Their arrival also threatened to create "internal difficulties of a grave character" with the Métis, Cree, and Siksikaitsiitapi.[43] It was a messy situation from all angles. Morris recommended the North-West Mounted Police send scouts along the border to monitor the situation. Canada's limited military presence, however, prevented it from fielding a force large enough to prevent the Lakota from crossing the line into Canadian territory. For the time being, Canada could only watch as events played out.

The Lakota began to enter Canada before their war with the United States had ended. By December 1876, hundreds of lodges of the Oceti Sakowin (Sioux) led by Little Knife, Long Dog, Black Moon, and the Man Who Crawls appeared in Canada. In total, Inspector Walsh estimated at least 500 hundred men, 2,500 women and children, and 3,500 horses had crossed the line.[44] Refugees continued to come. By the spring of 1877, the Lakota had all but lost the war. Contemporary estimates of the events placed the number of refugees fleeing to Canada at between 5,000 and 10,000. Modern estimates place the number closer to 3,000.[45]

Whatever their exact number, the Lakota migrants created immediate concern. The United States feared the Lakota would use Canada as a base of operations to continue the war. The Canadian government had its own concerns regarding the financial, military, and diplomatic implications of having thousands of potentially hostile Lakota in territory it claimed. The United States and Canada had successfully marked their border on the land, but they had not resolved the complicated diplomatic, jurisdictional, and military complications borderland identities presented.[46]

The Lakota attempted to make peace with both the Canadian government and the Indigenous residents in the area. As the Dakota had done before them, the Lakota emphasized their historic ties with Britain. They brandished medals given to them by England and spoke of how they had always considered themselves to be British subjects.[47] The Canadian government had few options. Evicting the Lakota would be a costly and bloody endeavor, and Canadian military personnel could not provide assurances of victory either. Inviting the American military or British troops into Canada would bolster the strength of the Canadian forces, but threatened to undermine the legitimacy of Canada as a sovereign nation.[48]

Allowing the Lakota to stay carried its own complications. Granting refuge to the Lakota strained relations with the United States, encouraged other groups to seek refuge in Canada, increased the costs of the Canadian government, and created potential problems with the Siksikaitsiitapi (Blackfoot) and Cree who had not been on good terms with the Lakota for many years. It also emphasized the continued fluidity of the borderlands. Canada and the United States could refer to groups like the Lakota as American or Canadian Indians, but these national labels meant little if Indigenous peoples continued to move between the two countries with relative ease.[49]

The Dominion government decided to grant the Lakota asylum on three conditions. First, they had to remain peaceful. Second, they could not return to the United States unless they remained there permanently. They would not be allowed to cross at their own leisure or engage in semipermanent migrations. Should the Lakota attack the United States, the "wall [border] . . . will be broken down and the Americans may be permitted to cross the line."[50] Third, the Canadian government would not provide the Lakota with any official recognition or assistance. The Lakota could remain in Canadian territory, but they would not enjoy the rights afforded to Indigenous groups designated as Canadian Indians.[51]

In the meantime, Canada tried to limit the kinds of allies the Lakota could rely on. According to Useless Good Runner, the great-grandson of a Treaty 7 signatory, Sitting Bull's flight across the border prompted Canada to negotiate Treaty 7 in order to prevent the Siksikaitsiitapi "from joining forces with Sitting Bull's people."[52] In this context, treaties served not only as a long-term solution for opening Indigenous lands to settlement, but also as a short-term approach to crisis management in the borderlands.

None of the stipulations Canada spelled out satisfied the American government. American officials stated that international law dictated that "a belligerent or hostile party," which gained protection in a "foreign territory is compelled to lay down arms and [be] removed from the border to a sufficient distance to ensure the prevention of further hostilities."[53] The Lakota remained near the border and kept their weapons. The Canadian government did not try to confiscate their arms; they only attempted to restrict the amount of ammunition local traders had on hand. The Lakota could get ammunition for hunting, but Canadian officials tried to restrict purchases to the bare necessity. To the consternation of American officials, the Canadian government ignored Lakota parties that crossed into the United States to hunt.[54]

In addition to strengthening their ties to Britain, the Lakota also attempted to reinforce their alliances with other Indigenous groups. They had existing trading ties with the Métis at Wood Mountain. They looked to make new alliances, but failed to secure a lasting peace with the A'aninin (Gros Ventre) and Crow who controlled the areas where buffalo remained.[55] As buffalo herds declined, the Lakota found themselves hunting in the United States to stave off starvation. By 1879, extreme hunger forced them to consider wintering south of the line, despite the dangers that brought. As they did so, they suffered raids from the A'aninin, Crow, and Cheyenne and remained in constant fear of the American military.[56]

Even when the Lakota remained in Canada, they did not operate outside the sphere of American influence. In this sense, their experience was similar to with the Dakota who proceeded them. The international line curtailed the movement of American soldiers, but not the broader influence of the United States. In 1879, for example, General Miles detained one thousand Métis and their eight hundred carts because he suspected them of assisting the Lakota. Traders continued to sell munitions and arms to the Lakota, but Miles's actions raised the stakes.[57] Being a friend of the Lakota had become a liability.

In addition to interfering with the Lakota's ability to get supplies, the United States also sent commissioners into Canada to try to induce them to return south. Both Canada and the United States stood to gain from their return. While the Lakota remained, Canada had to provide rations, station NWMP officers nearby, and worry about conflicts between the Lakota and other groups. For the United States, convincing the Lakota to return would limit army expenditures and the Lakota's ability to use the border defensively should hostilities resume.[58] As the Lakota and United States government negotiated a possible surrender, news of the conflict between the Nimiipuu and the United States reached Lakota camps. The conflict was a long time coming. Years of broken promises, fraudulent agreements, encroachment, and disrespect created a volatile environment. American demands that the Nimiipuu relocate to reservations only made matters worse.[59]

The Nimiipuu War

In early June 1877, six hundred nontreaty Nimiipuu (Nez Perce) gathered at Split Rocks not far from the Salmon River (in today's northwestern Idaho). During a tel-lik-leen ceremony, where men commemorated past battles, a member of the crowd taunted Shore Crossing (Wahlitits) that he did not deserve his place of honor because he had let his father's death go unpunished.[60] The heckling hit home. Soon after Shore Crossing, Red Moccasin Tops, and Swan Necklace set off to kill Larry Otts, who had killed Shore Crossing's father in 1875 during a dispute over a fence. When they failed to find Otts, the men turned on other settlers in the area against whom they had grievances. They started by killing Richard Devine, a prospector known for attacking Indians. By the end of the day they had shot four others. The party returned to Split Rocks to recount their deeds.[61]

The killings created a fissure in leadership. Would war prevail or would the Nimiipuu surrender the men to American courts? Before the political leaders could weigh the options, sixteen more warriors launched a series of follow up raids that killed eighteen and badly injured six settlers. The parties raped at least one, but by some accounts as many as four, women. Not since the Dakota War had American civilians faced such devastating violence. A military reaction came swiftly, but underwhelmed.[62] American defeats at White Bird Canyon provided the Nimiipuu with valuable supplies, while American treachery during peace negotiations with the Alpowai band added additional warriors to the cause.[63] In practice, American bungling bought time for the Nimiipuu, but did little to change the overall orientation of the war. Faced with few prospects of victory, the Nimiipuu decided to relocate to Crow territory. In doing so, they sacrificed their connection to their homeland for a chance at maintaining their way of life.[64]

The Nimiipuu believed relocating would put them beyond the power of the United States government, a mistake they soon came to realize. The United States army, utilizing telegraphs and railways, operated on a different scale than any enemy the Nimiipuu had previously fought. Over the coming months the American army lost most of the battles, but in the end it mattered little. Starvation, deprivation, harassment, and displacement lacked the glamour of military victories. As the Great Sioux War had demonstrated, however, that kind of military attrition offered a crushing victory all the same.

As the Nimiipuu attempted to find freedom through relocation, they found little room to breathe. The Crow rejected the Nimiipuu's request for sanctuary and provided scouts to the American forces at Canyon Creek in exchange for the right to keep the ammunition and horses they captured in the field. Betrayed, the Nimiipuu turned their sights north, where they hoped to join up with the Sioux.[65] The Lakota and Nimiipuu had fought one another in the past, but their mutual disdain for the American government was stronger than their hatred of one another.[66] After trekking twelve hundred miles and surviving over a dozen encounters with the American military, the Nimiipuu arrived at the Bear Paw Mountains. They were forty miles from the Canadian border.[67]

American troops led by Nelson A. Miles attacked Chief Joseph on September 30, 1877. Miles's first two assaults failed, despite being almost total surprises. Nimiipuu warriors kept the cavalry at bay, and sharpshooters took a heavy toll on Miles's officers. The initial success by the Nimiipuu bought time for many of the women and children to escape and head north. Cheyenne scouts, along with a portion of the American army, however, succeeded in capturing many of the Nimiipuu's horses. The loss of the horses eliminated the Nimiipuu's ability to escape and soon they considered peace. They maintained hope, however, that if they held out long enough, the Lakota might cross the line to their aid.[68]

On October 3, dozens of Nimiipuu who had escape the battle arrived at a Lakota camp at Frenchman's Creek. They requested that the Lakota send men to help in their fight against the United States. The Lakota misunderstood the request, thinking the battle was occurring at the Missouri River rather than at the Snake Creek. They refused to send aid, thinking the distance too far. Two days later, Peopeo Tholekt corrected the miscommunication. By one account, the Lakota then sent a party out to assist the Nimiipuu but they were too late. Along their journey, they encountered refugees who informed them that the Nimiipuu had surrendered and the Lakota turned back. Whatever the case, the Lakota did not appear and the Nimiipuu lost hope.[69]

Chief Joseph surrendered to Colonel Miles and General Howard on October 5. Two hundred and thirty-three Nimiipuu, approximately a third of the party who made it to the Bear Paw Mountains, had succeeded in evading American forces and making it into Canada. The rest were captured.[70] Across the entire trek, the Nimiipuu lost between 94 and 145 individuals, many of them women and children. In return, they killed at least 115 soldiers, injured another 142, and cost the United States government just shy of two million dollars.[71] Peace, however, proved worse than war. Looking back on the events twenty years later, Chief Joseph expressed his disgust at the America's failure to honor "the promises made to me on the battle field by General Miles in 1877."[72] By 1885 close to half of the captured Nimiipuu had died of malnutrition or other ailments.[73] Nearing the end of his life, Joseph mourned the loss of land and his inability to die "where all my people have died before me."[74]

The flight of the Nimiipuu stalled negotiations between the Lakota and the American government. The Lakota argued that the Americans had no business negotiating for the return of the Lakota after they had just driven the Nimiipuu from the United States. The Lakota blamed them for starting the conflicts, cheating Indigenous people out of annuity money, and failing to keep treaty promises. They accused Indian agents of living lavishly off treaty money.[75]

Sitting Bull's Surrender

On October 17, 1877, Sitting Bull, Spotted Eagle, Little Knife, and others met again with the American commissioners. The United States offered a full pardon for the war and stated that the United States would receive the Lakota peacefully if they returned and refrain from hostilities. By this point, only a few groups of Lakota remained in Canada. Hungry and tired, the remainder had surrendered and returned to their agencies. The American commissioners argued that the United States had not punished anyone who had returned home. The Lakota would have to give up their weapons and horses but in return they would receive money or livestock as compensation. The commissioners remained adamant: no guns and no horses.[76]

Sitting Bull's rebuttal attacked his treatment at the hands of the Americans and reaffirmed his British identity. He stated that "on this side of the line [Canada] I first learned to shoot; for that reason I come again."[77] He accused the American government of stealing his land and mistreating him for sixty-four years. The Canadians did not mistreat him, and he was happy to remain there. The Americans refused to change their terms and the Lakota refused to leave. Remaining in Canada, however, became more challenging as access to bison diminished.

Controlling the few remaining buffalo herds operated as a delicate balance of diplomacy and military control that intertwined federal dreams of meaningful borders with the practical necessities of hunger. The Siksikaitsiitapi, Crow, Assiniboine, and A'aninin living south of the border policed their own territorial boundaries.[78] Indigenous communities living south of the line attempted to turn American troops into their auxiliaries by pushing the United States to enforce its own border. American troops might not be dependable, but they showed a willingness to evict or fight groups like the Lakota who vied for the few remaining herds. Faced with a desperate situation, even undependable allies held some value.[79]

The buffalo, for their own part, neither cared about nor understood colonial borders. They did not need to. They understood fire just fine. In July 1879, Indigenous people at Milk River burned grass near the border in an attempt to keep the buffalo in the United States. The fire and the presence of the American army along the border steered the buffalo herds south of the Missouri River again. If the Lakota wished to gain access to the herds, they would have to risk encounters with American soldiers as well as Indigenous ones.[80]

Faced with few herds remaining in Canada, the Lakota attempted to co-opt Canadian diplomatic channels to gain access to the food. In July 1879, J. M. Walsh spoke with General Miles about the possibility of Lakota refugees in Canada hunting south of the line. Miles responded to the Canadian NWMP officer that "the country south of the border was an Indian reservation and he would not allow any man either white, Halfbreed or Indian to come."[81] If the Lakota wanted to hunt, they would have to surrender. The US government reiterated that Canada must work harder to prevent Indigenous people from Canada from entering the United States.

Canada, faced with starving populations and few bison north of the line, prioritized low expenditures over clean borders. Between 1879 and 1881, the Department of Indian Affairs encouraged Indigenous communities living in Canada to cross into the United States to hunt. Canada's blessing removed a few of the hurdles for transnational hunting parties, but did not eliminate conflicts with competing tribes or with the American army. In the summer of 1879, Nelson A. Miles captured and evicted 829 Métis and Cree he considered Canadian Indians.[82] By October 1879, however, Canadian protests had convinced the US Secretary of State William Evarts to reconsider the government's position.[83] The agreement did little to change the realities of life on the Plains. It came when few buffalo remained and did nothing to create peace between the various groups that fought for control over the remaining herds.[84]

The agreement, even had it come earlier, could not turn back time. As bison herds fell precipitously, groups on both sides of the border faced dire circumstances. The Lakota, faced with years of weariness, privation, and conflict with competing Indigenous groups, began to consider reestablishing peace with the United States. In the winter of 1879–80, Louis Riel tried his hand at brokering the deal. Riel hoped to use his role in the Lakota's surrender to curry favor with the American army, take the attention off the Métis in Montana whom US authorities at Fort Belknap were trying to evict, and decrease the number of hunters competing with the Métis for buffalo.[85] Riel's attempt to gain influence as a mediator failed, a shortcoming he blamed on the underhanded tactics of the NWMP. Officially, the NWMP aimed to have the Sioux surrender peacefully to the American government. Unofficially, Riel believed that a number of the police officers had married or begun relationships with the Lakota, creating a conflict of interests in an already complicated region.[86]

By that point, it was clear to everyone that Canadian power lay in hunger, not in guns. In June of 1881, Edgar Dewdney wrote a letter that summarized Canada's border policy in a bluntness few could muster. "I feel certain," the Canadian Indian Commissioner wrote, "that the surrender can only be brought about by actual starvation."[87] Forced to eat ducks, eggs, roots, and berries, the Lakota would return to the United States or starve to death. The next month

Sitting Bull and the few of his followers who had not deserted him made a separate surrender to the American authorities. Weariness and privation had taken their toll.

In his surrender, Sitting Bull thanked Jean-Louis Légaré for provisioning the Lakota during their exile and requested that the American or Canadian government reimburse him for his costs, which Légaré estimated at close to $50,000.[88] The surrender included a moment of nostalgia. Sitting Bull spoke of a time when the Lakota lived without the Canada–US border and when they could hunt and trade wherever they pleased. The same line that had protected the Lakota from the American army had became a burden to their movements. It served as a reminder of the changes that had occurred on the Prairies and the possibilities that had closed.[89]

In granting amnesty to the Lakota throughout reservations in North and South Dakota, the United States created a series of complications it did not

Figure 5.1 Armed Indigenous people are handed plows, shovels, and other farming implements labeled "Work or Starve." Thomas Nast, "Root, Hog, or Die—Christopher Bennett Has Discovered the True Indian Policy," *Harper's Weekly*, November 8, 1879. Library of Congress Prints and Photographs Division, LC-USZ62-78255.

anticipate. The amnesty gave guidelines, but no sense of what they would mean in practice. Brave Bear (Matoopileke) soon put the practical implications of the amnesty to the test.[90] In 1879, a few years after many of the Lakota had left for Canada, Brave Bear, a Yanktonai Nakota, visited his family at the Devil's Lake Agency. He informed them that he was leaving the area to join Sitting Bull in Canada. His friends at the agency worried about the precariousness of his position. The Seventh Calvary had previously arrested him for murdering a family near Fort Pembina. He had escaped punishment and remained mobile. His return to the Devil's Lake Agency with a horse, rifle, fine boots, cashmere pants, and spending money prompted uneasy questions.[91]

When the naked and decomposing body of Joseph Johnson, a post trader and former soldier, turned up a month later with a bullet in the back of his head, many suspected Brave Bear of committing the murder. By this point, however, Brave Bear had made his way to Canada where he remained until Sitting Bull and his followers surrendered during the spring of 1881. The surrender brought Brave Bear back into the jurisdiction of the United States.[92]

During Brave Bear's trip home, Edward Allison, a scout for General Terry, alleged that Brave Bear had confessed his crimes. He had offered Allison $200 if he would help him acquire the $900 he had taken off Johnson's body and stashed east of the Missouri River before his flight to Canada. On this information, the sheriff at Bismarck captured Brave Bear. After a short trial, which included testimony by both Allison and Brave Bear's cousin Louisa Clifford, the judge sentenced Brave Bear to death.[93]

While James McLaughlin, the Indian agent at the Devil's Lake Agency, believed that Brave Bear had likely murdered Johnson he struggled to reconcile his desire for justice with the amnesty granted to Sitting Bull's followers by the US government. The residents of the Devil's Lake Agency understood the amnesty to encompass all past acts of violence committed by Sitting Bull's followers against individuals and the United States government. McLaughlin expressed a similar understanding but shied away from the logical implications of his stance.[94] He advocated for a commuted sentence, instead of freedom, believing that the execution would cause tremendous unrest at the Standing Rock reservation. If the United States hung Brave Bear, the residents of his agency would consider the amnesty worthless, which he believed would lead to future conflicts.[95]

Pleas on Brave Bear's behalf resulted in a temporary reprieve, but no presidential pardon.[96] On a cold and cloudless November morning, Father Willard and two sisters of mercy performed Brave Bear's last rites in a language he barely understood. Brave Bear smoked, ate, laughed, and shook the hands of those present. He did his best to remain calm. Just after noon, in the presence of a hundred people, an officer signaled for his execution. In spite of the amnesty and the pleas of McLaughlin, Brave Bear's body hung from a scaffold for fifteen minutes before the attending physician pronounced him dead.[97]

McLaughlin failed to save Brave Bear's life. In 1890, his penchant for misreading situations would add Big Bear and a dozen others to the long list of avoidable casualties when he called in police officers to put down the Ghost Dance movement at the Standing Rock Agency. Peace and amnesty had a hollow ring by the end of the nineteenth century. With few other options, the Lakota remained on the reservation. Hunger controlled movement far better than border guards ever could.[98]

1885

North of the line, the situation facing Indigenous people looked little better. By 1883 chronic malnutrition, starvation, and disease had forced all but a handful of communities onto reserves. Survival, as in the south, came at the cost of independence. Cree chiefs at Edmonton sent desperate pleas to Ottawa. In the absence of adequate food, their young women had become prostitutes in order to survive. The Canadian government reduced food expenditures from $607,235 in 1882 to $530,982 a year later. The intentional policy of malnutrition created a breeding ground for tuberculosis. It provided federal government with the ability to enforce order it only dreamt of a decade earlier.[99]

Food provided the Canadian government with power, but it also served a reminder of its own continued weakness· Unable to supply either the North-West Mounted Police and its treaty obligations with Indigenous communities on its own, the Canadian government turned to American merchants like I. G. Baker and Company in Montana for logistical support. The decision proved disastrous. As historian James Daschuck has demonstrated, I. G. Baker and Company "abused its privileged position, supplying inferior or contaminated food to the hungry to maximize its profit, often with the complicity of government officials."[100] Spoiled food caused as many as a hundred deaths among Piapot's band in 1883–84. Food shortages plagued many other areas.[101] Even when rations arrived, in sufficient quality and quantity, they did not necessarily alleviate hunger. In 1884 the Cree of the Sakimay Reserve forced their way into the reserve storehouse. They recovered thousands of pounds of bacon and flour that Indian Agent Hilton Keith had withheld while those on the reserve starved. The use of food to create conditions that would bring about the physical destruction of Plains communities was one of many genocides the continent would witness.[102]

In 1884 the Saskatchewan Métis invited Louis Riel to return to Canada, hoping he could replicate his earlier success against the Canadian government.

By this time, Riel had tied himself deeply to the United States. Over the past five years, he had attempted to secure land grants for the Métis in Montana. He married, helped negotiate hunting rights, and tried to negotiate with the Oceti Sakowin on behalf of the Métis.[103] On March 16, 1883, Riel became an American citizen. The process required he swore to "absolutely and entirely renounce and abjure all allegiance and fidelity to every foreign Prince, Potentate, State or Sovereignty whatsoever, and particularly to Victoria, Queen of Great Britain."[104] Such an oath did not matter under British law for much of the nineteenth century, as the law considered British subjects bound in perpetuity. By 1881 Canada, the United States, and Britain all recognized that citizenship should be a "privilege to be sought out rather than a burden to be evaded."[105] How these new rights of expatriation would apply to Indigenous and Métis communities, however, remained unclear.

Riel accepted the invitation to return north and set up a provisional government in March 1885. Métis leaders hoped that this government would pressure Canada into respecting Métis rights as it had during the 1869 Resistance.[106] The situation that had led to their previous victory, however, had changed. The partial completion of the Canadian Pacific Railway allowed Canada to bring troops into the area quickly. Fissures within the Métis, exacerbated by Riel's religious extremism, sapped its strength. Riel "pronounced that Rome had fallen," believing that his newly created council, the Exovedate, would help "transfer a revitalized Catholic Church to the New World."[107] Many English settlers and Métis in Saskatchewan opposed Riel's message and refused to take part.[108]

The battle lines revealed the complex social situation along the border. Most Plains communities—Indigenous and Métis alike—remained wary of the conflict. When given the option, they refused to take part.[109] Staying out of the conflict, however, remained difficult. When the Dakota who had fled to present-day Saskatchewan learned of the violence from travelers coming from as far south as Montana, they considered their options. On the advice of Tarasota, two dozen families left Prince Albert for the bush, believing that the risk of being caught in another war outweighed the pains of relocation.[110] Many Cree relocated across the Canada–US border in a similar bid to escape the violence. The Whitecap Dakota and the Willow Cree, who did not evacuate the warzone, faced impressment into Riel's forces.[111]

Those that took part in the violence did not operate as a single cohesive group. In practice, the resistance consisted of both isolated episodes of violence in addition to two separate campaigns launched by the Métis and Cree. Participants specifically targeted officials who had reputations for cruelty and misconduct or who had mismanaged rations.[112] Cree participants operated independently from the Métis ones. The violence also split communities internally. Jean-Louis Légaré and forty Métis men from Willow Bunch, for example, joined the North-West Mounted Police as scouts where they patrolled the Canada–US border for militants. Decisions like these created rifts within Willow Bunch, where others had joined the opposing side.[113]

On May 9–12, 1885, Canadian forces defeated the provisional government at Batoche, forcing Riel to surrender. The resistance lasted two months and only a few hundred Métis took part. They fought against close to 8,000 soldiers, militia, and police officers. The resistance, however, was a costly one. Riel's force lost close to one hundred during the conflict. Putting down the resistance cost the Canadian government more than five million dollars, including $483,000 in damages to personal property of Métis and settlers who remained out of the conflict.[114]

In the aftermath of the violence Canada tried more than eighty, including One Arrow, Poundmaker, and Big Bear. Many received jail sentences, up to seven years, in a series of cases that at times were little more than shams. The Minister of Justice demanded convictions, and lawyers, confused by Cree names, failed to keep track of who was on trial. In the end, Canadian courts gave preference to expediency and political pressure over justice. A person's presence, rather than his actions, served as sufficient evidence of his guilt.[115]

In the end, the Canadian government executed eight participants convicted of killing unarmed civilians. Many others, including Big Bear, One Arrow, and Poundmaker, faced jail time that proved little better than the gallows. Riel received no such mercy. His execution on November 16, 1885 bore a grim kind of irony.[116] As historian J. M. Bumsted rightly observes, "the most prominent individual ever executed for treason against the Canadian State—Louis Riel—was at the time of his execution an American citizen."[117] By the time of his death Riel had worked, married, and advocated for Métis rights south of the line. The United States provided a safe haven for Riel, but it was also his home. The Canada–US border, surveyed across the Prairies only a decade before Riel's execution, had not displaced the many ways Indigenous and Métis people conceptualized land. Riel could move across colonial borders without leaving the homeland of the Métis or the Cree.[118]

The Crees' experience during the Northwest Rebellion differed from that of the Métis. Unlike Riel, Big Bear (Mistahimaskwa) promoted a policy of peace. Big Bear's control over his people, however, had waned by the middle of the 1880s. On April 2, 1885, Wandering Spirit and members from Big Bear's Band attacked a church at Frog Lake. Wandering Spirit's party killed the majority of the churchgoers and took others captive.[119] The attack was unrelated to the fighting Riel was engaged in at the time, but the Canadian government lumped the Cree and Métis together as allies in the rebellion. In the aftermath of the war, Little Bear (Imasees) and Little Poplar took two hundred Cree to the United States, a trip that entailed great hardship. They travelled four hundred miles while lacking both adequate provisions and horses. For Canada, the resistance demonstrated that the nation could maintain control over its expansive territory without the aid of Britain. For the Cree and Métis, the rebellion's failure highlighted the shift in the power dynamics on the Prairies.[120]

After the 1885 Resistance, thousands of Métis and Cree fled to the United States, where they drew on their family members for support.[121] Métis women drove teams across the Prairies to Montana while armed Métis men on horseback travelled a few miles away. The decision to relocate took a significant psychological toll, especially on those who had lost contact with family members during the violence. Near to the boundary line, William John Letarde felt unable to continue south. He told the party he was travelling with that "I got enough ammunition and everything . . . I'm going to go with my family."[122] Letarde turned around, disarmed a party of Mounties, and freed his wife (Louis Riel's niece).

Letarde's life exemplified the kind of borderland identities Canada and the United States sought to destroy. Letarde had worked for the North-West Mounted Police in Fort Qu'Appelle. After the war, he resided just five miles south of the line where he helped the American government catch bank robbers, until he received amnesty from the Canadian government. By the mid-1880s, Letarde had helped enforce law on both sides of the line and used the border himself to escape capture. Returning to Canada did not end Letarde's transnational life nor the transnational lives of his family.[123] His son, William Letarde- supported the federal government during the 1885 resistance, and later worked for the North-West Mounted Police himself until 1895. He spent time in the United States rounding up cattle. By the 1905 he had relocated to Lethbridge, Alberta. For both father and son, the border limited the legal scope of the kinds of duties they could do as catchers of bank robbers and employees of the NWMP, but seemed to have little impact on their ability or willingness to find work on both sides of the line.[124]

The border provided a legal shield for William John Letarde after the Resistance. His son took a different path. William Letarde choose to avoid the draft during World War I by changing his name and relocating but did not rely on the border to avoid capture as his father had. In this sense, the border provided the Letarde family with an additional set of options for evading capture, but it was only one approach. Others, like Gabriel Dumont, who served as a general during the violence, succeeded in translating his transnational relocation into a broader global journey. Dumont relocated to the United States, joined Buffalo Bill's Wild West Show, and performed in the United States and France.[125]

The 1885 Resistance had long-term consequences for the Cree across the Plains, regardless of whether the specific community took part in the violence, withheld its support, or left for the United States when the violence began. Cree from the Little Pine community who did not want to take part in the 1885 Resistance, for example, left for the United States soon after the violence began. They travelled at night and slept in the bush to avoid detection. After the conclusion of violence, some returned home, while others chose to remake their lives south of the line. Those who remained in Canada faced a shrinking reserve base and frequent federal impositions.[126] Soldiers confiscated knives and axes as well as guns. A few people managed to conceal knives, but after the violence, the few remaining knives had to be "borrowed around all over the neighborhood. One knife would serve a whole, three or four families."[127] Faced with difficult conditions, many Cree from Little Pine relocated to the north or to the United States, where they could live with fewer restrictions.

Transnational migrations created opportunities, but also exacerbated problems as families separated and the sudden dislocation of so many people strained existing social networks. Josie Cuthand's mother abandoned him when he was three. After the resistance, Cuthand relocated to the United States with other members of his community, hoping to find his mother and the Blackfoot man she had run away with. Failing to find her, he ended up at Rocky Boy, where American soldiers in the area fed and clothed him and he served as the unofficial mascot for them. Cuthand's father survived with the help of the Catholic Church before returning to the Little Pine reserve when he was much older.[128]

Groups that had participated in the violence suffered retaliatory policies by the Canadian state, while those who had remained loyal experienced broken treaty promises and deteriorating conditions. Disease, malnourishment, mistreatment, unhappiness, and assimilationist polices created tremendous suffering. Four years after the rebellion, only about half the populations of the Crooked Lake and File Hills reserves remained.[129] The Cree at Thunderchild reserve faced an estimated morality rate of 235.5 per thousand. Starvation continued while undistributed rations rotted.[130] High mortality rates coupled with individuals renouncing their status or relocating across the international boundary altered the basic make up of Indigenous communities on the Plains.

***

From the 1860s until the 1880s, violence and hunger reshaped territorial organization on the Plains. Canada and the United States agreed on many of the same principles regarding how to reorder belonging and territory, but their relative administrative and military capacities pushed them in different directions. As historians John Herd Thompson and Stephen J. Randall note, in the three decades that followed the Civil War, "the U.S. Army fought 943 military engagements with Native peoples; Canadian troops fought 7, all but one of them a battle of the 1885 North-West Rebellion."[131] The difference was a matter of budgets, not a matter of benevolence.

In most other ways, Indian policy in Canada and the United States looked similar. Both governments used treaties, land surrenders, annuities, and coercion to exert their control and make their borders matter. Both relied on hunger and neither government kept their promises. Canadians would later romanticize their treatment of Indigenous people, but little of this history deserves praise. Canada took in Indigenous refugees from American aggression but created refugees of its own. The Cree and Métis who fled Canada after 1885 had no illusions of the kind of treatment that awaited them south of the line. Still, they viewed it as preferable to what they faced north of the line.[132]

The importance of the Canada–US border on the northern Plains grew with an unusual speed and intensity. In 1874, Canada and the United States had just finished surveying and placing boundary markers in a region across which they had little knowledge. Less than two decades later, the Canada–US border had become one of the most significant territorial divisions in the region. Persistent transnational violence had motivated both countries to take interest in their shared border, but interest did not create ability. Both countries success in displacing the Lakota, Cree, Siksikaitsiitapi, and Métis as the dominant military powers in the region required hunger and sickness. In this sense, the Cree faced not only new enemies, in the form of settlers, but old ones as well, as faminecreated fierce competition for the little remaining food.

For all the changes that occurred across the Plains, the border remained poorly guarded on a day-to-day level throughout the 1880s. Both countries increased their presence in the region, drawing on soldiers, NWMP, and Indian agents for control. Still, they could only manage a crude kind of control. They punished horse raiders and whisky traders when they could and used military forces to put down resistance. They could not stop individuals from crossing the boundary line with any regularity but they did not have to.

By the 1880s, both countries had forced Indigenous people onto reserves and reservations and guarded those boundaries with military and civilian personnel. In doing so, they gained a tremendous capacity to control movement in indirect ways. Indigenous people continued to leave reserves and reservations to cross the international line, but both governments ensured that those who did suffered tremendous deprivation. They cut off access to food and created a specter of uncertainty that stretched hundreds of miles past the boundary line. They interfered with life regardless of residency, creating an environment of fear that reached groups like the Dakota, who had relocated to Prince Albert. As Brave Bear discovered, colonial governments had long memories and tremendous patience. The kind of border Canada and the United States had created was capable of punishing specific kinds of mobility hundreds of miles from the boundary line and often years after a crossing had taken place. That kind of border was far more powerful than the thin and singular line that stretched across colonial maps.

6

Borders of Salt and Rock

Louis Paul, a young boy from the Colville Reservation, jumped into the Columbia River near Kettle Falls to escape his pursuers. Violence had erupted among the Colville and white settlers and fur traders, plunging the area into disarray. Paul struggled with the fast currents but avoided capture. He headed north into Canada, a journey that took several months to complete. Although Louis Paul lived to be over a hundred years old, he never returned to the United States.[1]

His son, Baptiste Paul, however, crossed the border regularly. For both men, the border offered significant albeit different opportunities. For Louis, the border offered a chance to escape violence and to begin his life anew. For his son, it offered a cornerstone for the region's economy. Throughout his life Baptiste Paul worked on pack trains that transported goods throughout British Columbia, Alberta, Oregon country, Washington, and Idaho.[2]

Violence, as Louis Paul's experience as a child in the late nineteenth century suggested, percolated throughout the Pacific Northwest. For all the personal suffering violence created in the region, it did not define the speed at which colonial borders became important. On the Prairies, Canada and the United States went from their initial survey of the border to exercising significant control in the span of little more than a decade. Environmental catastrophe, hunger, and persistent violence underwrote the transition in power.

On the Pacific Coast, the transition from boundary survey to day-to-day control took half a century instead, a reminder of the situational authority each government wielded. Violence along the coast motivated federal interest and made expansive settlement possible. On its own, however, it did not justify the costs of border administration. Nor did starvation or military campaigns provide either government with the kind of coercive power they wielded on the Plains. Dependency, at least at first, worked in the opposite direction. Canada and the United States found that their own dependence on Indigenous labor limited the restrictions they could initially implement.

A Line of Blood and Dirt. Benjamin Hoy, Oxford University Press (2021). © Oxford University Press.
DOI: 10.1093/oso/9780197528693.003.0007

By the mid-1880s, however, the development of new technologies and the immigration of hundreds of thousands of settlers shifted the balance of power. Both governments became less dependent on Indigenous people. They drove the Coast Salish out of the work force and imposed a new geographic order on top of existing Indigenous ones. At the same time, Chinese immigration drove grassroots pressure to reform federal border controls. In the wake of riots, protest, and vigilante justice, the United States passed the Chinese Restriction Act of 1882 and the Exclusion Act of 1888.[3] Canada, in turn, developed head taxes for much the same purpose. By the turn of the century, neither Chinese nor Indigenous communities could ignore the border as they had three decades earlier. As impetus (Chinese immigration) and power (settler immigration) coalesced across the Pacific Coast, Canada and the United States created a race-based system of federal immigration control. The system, which was developed to solve regional problems, soon expanded beyond the Pacific Coast and encompassed other groups. As it did so, it shifted the very nature of border control along the 49th parallel.

Violence and Treaty

By the beginning of the 1860s, Britain and the United States had staked their claims to lands along the Pacific Coast. The Oregon Treaty, signed in 1846, established the 49th parallel as the division between British and American territory west of the Rocky Mountains. Eleven years later boundary surveyors embarked on a campaign to mark that line on the land itself. Having established territorial agreements with one another, Britain and the United States set out to develop treaties with the Indigenous residents who remained in control of the region.

On Vancouver Island, the treaty process fell under the jurisdiction of James Douglas. Douglas had been born in 1803 in Demarara (British Guiana) to a Scottish father and a Barbadian Creole mother.[4] As a young man he had travelled to British North America, where he worked for the North West Company and Hudson's Bay Company. He did clerical work, established trading partnerships with the Nimiipuu (Nez Perce) and Fort Nelson (Secanni), and led overland brigades. By the time he had become the governor of the Colony of Vancouver Island in 1851, he had married Amelia Connolly, an Indigenous woman of mixed heritage from Rupert's Land, and had years of experience working with Indigenous people.[5]

Douglas began his work as governor establishing treaty agreements with the Indigenous communities who lived near Victoria, Nanaimo, and Fort Rupert. The treaty process, however, ended almost as soon as it began. Douglas signed fourteen treaties in rapid succession. Ninety-seven percent of Vancouver

Island remained outside the agreements. So too did the mainland. After 1854, Douglas allowed settlers to purchase unceded land. He provided no rationale for the change, although historians have speculated that logistics, finances, and Douglas's personal views toward assimilation played a role in ending treaty-making. Neither Douglas nor his successors would employ the treaty process on the rest of Vancouver Island or on mainland British Columbia. They started a process that remains to this day incomplete, creating a very different legal environment than elsewhere in Canada.[6]

Although Britain did not sign treaties with many of the Salish communities on the lower mainland of British Columbia, Indian policy there followed many of the same patterns. British officials confined Indigenous people to small plots of land. They attacked the potlatch, the winter dance, and the other cultural and spiritual practices that drew the region together. During Potlatch ceremonies hosts transferred hereditary rights across generations through ceremonies that involved redistributing wealth to large gatherings of people.[7] In the 1870s the number of invited guests at large potlatches sometimes ran into the thousands. At these gatherings, families gave away as much as $15,000 worth of goods (more than $350,000 in 2018 dollars). To the horror of European observers, families gave that kind of wealth away with little hesitation and appeared to ask little in return.[8]

In practice, potlatches served important social functions. Hosting potlatches secured a person's status within society and could be used to acquire honorary titles or mark the transfer of property. Potlatch ceremonies linked communities and clarified responsibility.[9] They also ran counter to the ways Europeans conceptualized the world. When British Columbia joined the confederation in 1871, Canada inherited a tangled mess of competing land claims, Indigenous management regimes, and settler resistance to Aboriginal land ownership and cultural practices.[10]

In the United States, the alienation of Indigenous land in the Pacific Northwest resulted in a much more extensive, but no less problematic, treaty process. Following the Treaty of Oregon, the United States signed a series of land agreements extinguishing, in its mind, Indigenous title to sixty-four million acres of land. Like many of the treaties the United States had signed in the past, the treaties it made throughout the Pacific Coast contained broken promises, mismanaged resources, and inconsistencies.[11] In 1855, during the treaty council held on the Spokane River, Governor Isaac Stevens reassured the Sqilxw (Okanogan) and Colville tribes that "your rights are your rights and . . . your lands will not be taken from you."[12] Less than two decades later, the Executive Act of April 8, 1872 created the Colville Reservation. Without treaty and without war, the United States claimed ownership of Sqilxw and Colville land.[13]

If the treaties and reservations created by the United States in Washington carried a common kind of disrespect and disregard, they also included an uncommon set of provisions. The treaties signed in Washington prohibited Indigenous people from crossing the border to trade. The stipulation, although unenforceable, emphasized American's fears that annuity money would find its way north of the border, as well as concerns that transnational mobility might encourage violence.[14]

British and American Indian Commissioners, with a few exceptions, took little interest in Indigenous systems of identity or territory. The treaty and reserve/reservation system they created along the Pacific Coast emphasized expediency and clear boundaries. British commissioners attempted to freeze Coast Salish identity at a single moment where it seemed clearest—the winter villages. The approach, which had seen use on the Prairies, mixed clumsy with cavalier. Families, not villages, controlled the most important resource sites and ceremonial rights. Moreover, winter villages served as only one of many different kinds of residency patterns a community would organize under during a single year.[15]

Considered as a whole, the treaty process on both sides of the border yielded only marginal success. In both instances Britain and the United States assigned Indigenous people to reserves/reservations, pressured them to cede at least some land, and recognized their rights to traditional subsistence sites. The shortcomings of the treaty process, however, remained glaring. Britain did not extinguish Indigenous title to more than a sliver of land, and the United States' attempts to eliminate Indigenous land rights had led to a rolling series of violent conflicts. Ignorance of the ways the Coast Salish conceptualized territory and belonging did not render the systems any less important.

Coast Salish Belonging and Territory

During the nineteenth century the Coast Salish maintained a complicated system of belonging, identity, and territory across the Pacific Northwest. Transformer stories, which told of how the world became like it is today, as well as genealogy and property provided a fabric of identity. Intermarriage, ceremony, political alliances, and mutual aid provided the thread. When fashioned together, the result was a social network that encouraged overlapping boundaries and situational ownership. The important structures that organized a person's belonging—family, status, hereditary names, household, village, and tribe—shifted over the course of a lifetime and sometimes over the course of a season. Simultaneous belonging served as a natural output of the flexible system.[16] Community belonging did not necessarily constitute the most important aspect of a person's life. Gender and class shaped relationships, creating bonds of familiarity and respect between upper class women in neighboring tribes that they did not share with the slaves and commoners from their own winter villages.[17]

The system worked because property ownership, hereditary titles, ancestral names, history, and culture provided a sense of belonging tied to place. Exogamous marriages, in turn, provided access to a wide array of seasonal resources. The Coast Salish aimed to build social cohesion and spiritual harmony using mobility and kinship to turn potential risks into sources of collective strength.[18] Lummi marriage connections prior to 1880, for example, linked communities together near present-day Seattle, Victoria, and Vancouver. The Squamish, Musqueam, and Nooksack established powerful kinship networks of their own.[19] Federal control over these networks remained limited. In 1886, for example, American Indian Agent W. L. Powell noted that despite "inflicting severe punishment," he could not get the tribes in the Neah Bay Agency to adopt "the proper view of marital relations" because the practitioners could escape discipline by "crossing the straits into British Columbia."[20]

Marriage provided a well-tested means to incorporate new people into existing Coast Salish communities. A single household of five people, for example, might trace its lineage to the Twana, Squaxin, Skagit, Samish, Dwamish, Snoqualmie, Nisqually, Skykomish (Skehwhamish), and to Europe. This kind of intermixing created problems for colonial officials who attempted to classify people. Trying to assign a single tribal or national identity to such a household required a selective blindness that ignored the complicated realities that existed along the Pacific Coast.[21]

While residency remained fluid, property ownership and belonging were less so. Ancestral names bestowed individuals with specific rights to resources sites. Moreover, while an individual's residence changed multiple times over the course of his or her life, their village of birth remained important. Marriage granted Coast Salish women access to a new community, while the death of their husbands removed their right to remain unless they remarried.[22] As anthropologist Dorothy Kennedy has noted, "so persistent was an individual's membership in his or her home village that, if death occurred some distance away, Coast Salish families commonly hired an undertaker to retrieve the body for interment at their own site."[23] This style of belonging created significant challenges for colonial officials who arrived in the region looking to secure land cessions, build international borders, and establish a reservation system predicated on the idea that each person had only one place he belonged.[24]

By the time European settlers arrived, the Coast Salish had centuries of experience managing territory and resolving disputes.[25] Their system of territorial management separated areas of common ownership from areas that belonged to a specific community or family. They viewed the Pacific Ocean, Fraser River,

Strait of Georgia, Puget Sound, and the Strait of Juan de Fuca as free of territorial restrictions. Most rivers, by contrast, belonged to the communities that resided on their banks and that enforced their territorial rights with fervor.[26]

The system worked during moments of peace as well as during moments of rupture. In the mid-nineteenth century, epidemics and landslides forced the Ts'elxwéyeqw (Chilliwack), for example, to relocate from the Skagit watershed. On their arrival in the lower Fraser River, the Ts'elxwéyeqw attempted to cement their authority in the region by adopting the Halq'eméylem language and establishing marital alliances with the existing Stó:lō residents. They supplemented this relational and linguistic strategy with a hard interpretation of their new territorial extent. Stó:lō trespassers, who found themselves within the newly claimed area without Ts'elxwéyeqw permission, faced execution.[27]

Coast Salish conceptions of belonging and territory mapped poorly onto European ones. By the mid-nineteenth century, Britain and the United States increasingly saw national boundaries as exclusive and nonoverlapping. European powers used diplomatic agreements, treaties, and military force to stake their claim to land. The Coast Salish created different boundaries and different justifications. For the Coast Salish, territory consisted of overlapping interests in land and resources that decreased as social and geographic distance increased. Even when the Coast Salish adopted firmer boundaries, they justified their control in different ways. The Ts'elxwéyeqw under Wileliq the Sixth, for example, adopted a more exclusive and well-defined set of territorial boundaries during the early nineteenth century. Ancestral rights and potlatches, however, still clarified territory and justified the transfer of property ownership.[28]

The physical proximity that mattered so much to European observers and cartographers did not explain the social closeness maintained by Indigenous communities. For the Stó:lō living in the lower watershed of the Fraser River, mystical tunnels created spatial connections between locations that appeared distant on European maps. Tunnel travel was instantaneous. Tunnels connected Hope to Burrard Inlet (124 km), Harrison Hot Springs (26 km), and Cultus Lake (54 km). Six tunnels converging at Tsawwassen and Point Roberts connected the area to Mission, Pitt Lake, the Orca Islands, Seschelt, Matsqui, and an unknown location near Harrison Mills. The tunnels spanned reserve boundaries and crossed the international line.[29] While the risks associated with tunnel travel prevented their regular use, they served as a basic organizational principle that bound the region together. As historian Keith Carlson argues, it was "enough that believers know [the tunnels] are there, just as their ancestors did" for the tunnels to create social affiliations between communities.[30]

By bending time and space, the tunnels challenged the rigid boundary lines created by European maps and the reserve systems, which privileged geographic rather than social distance. Geographically adjacent communities saw themselves as having little in common with one another, while communities located sometimes a hundred kilometers away considered themselves neighbors.[31] The Ts'elxwéyeqw, for example, had lived near Cultus Lake since at least the early nineteenth century, when they had entered the area to escape a landslide. When the Canadian government established reserves, it confined both the Ts'elxwéyeqw and Swí:lhcha on a common reserve at Soowahlie. Well into the twentieth century, the two communities refused to speak to one another or even share a common water source, despite the logistical difficulties this created on an everyday basis.[32]

As Canada and the United States contested Indigenous territorial systems, they attacked the cultural practices, origin stories, and histories that bound people to place. The process of erasure required making well-travelled areas appear new again. It required ignoring both the continued presence and histories of Indigenous residents. For the Stó:lō, the land itself served as an archive that provided tangible reminders of important stories, histories, and happenings that linked the human and nonhuman world together. For the Coast Salish more broadly, an individual family's history and lineage, as well as the stories surrounding it, cemented their claims to rights to resources across the Pacific Coast.[33]

As larger numbers of European settlers arrived on Coast Salish lands during the nineteenth century, the Stó:lō expanded their networks to incorporate the newcomers. The frequent movement of people had long-lasting implications for the Soowahlie community. Bruce Sam, a Stó:lō elder, noted that many Spanish and American people had lived in Soowahlie territory since the 1830s and 1840s and their influence on the region continued well after the United States' joint occupation of the Pacific Northwest ended in 1846.[34]

Like many of their European contemporaries, the Stó:lō stratified humanity. They differentiated the Smelá:lh ("worthy people") from Skw'iyéth (slaves) and St'éxem ("stupid people"). The Smelá:lh encompassed high status individuals, Skw'iyéth the lowest orders—not fully human. The St'éxem still carried a stigma. They had lost their history and without it, they had no access to hereditary resources sites.[35] The Stó:lō soon expanded their classification system to incorporate settlers. They described the newcomers as Xwelítem or the "hungry people" in the Halqeméylem language. The Xwelítem had an insatiable appetite for land and resources, but offered nothing in return.[36]

Labor and Commerce

Geographic mobility compounded the problems facing Canadian and American administrators tasked with establishing a new territorial system in the region where many already existed. Marriage patterns and the nature of the costal geography encouraged north to south connections. Canadian miners and loggers sold coal and lumber to American merchants in San Francisco.[37] The tax rolls of the Colony of Vancouver Island in 1863 suggested the strength of these connection. The colony imported $2,341,029 worth of goods from the United States, including ale, barley, shingles, salt, ship chandlery, stoves, sugar, boots, and sewing machines. By contrast, it imported only $1,296,003 worth of goods from Britain. The official records, however, underestimate the extent of the trade between Washington and British Columbia. The limited number of customs agents and complex geography around Puget Sound came at an immediate cost. Merchants could avoid customs collectors if they wanted to, except when moving cumbersome goods.[38]

Prior to the 1880s, Indigenous people had carved out a spot in the economies of the Pacific Northwest as an essential labor force. Indigenous laborers cleared farms, picked fruit, piloted ships, started businesses, freighted supplies, cut wood, sold fish, and worked in canneries, lumberyards, hopsfields, and sawmills. They helped create cities like Seattle and assisted in public works and nation-building projects. They built roads, transported US mail, guided boundary surveyors, and worked on the Canadian Pacific Railway.[39]

Native American women served as essential workers of the nascent cannery industry and labored heavily in the hops fields. They also worked as domestics, laundresses, and prostitutes. Indigenous laborers, much like their European counterparts, exploited markets on both sides of the border to secure better wages. In doing so, they reinforced north–south connections across national boundaries and undermined the kinds of east-west connections both countries tried to create.[40]

The nature of many of the industries on the Pacific Coast made them particularly receptive to drawing on Indigenous and transnational labor. The canning and hops industries required a large amount of labor at specific sites for only a short amount of the time. They needed workers when salmon ran and crops ripened.[41] The inconsistency of employment, low pay, and manual nature of the work held little appeal for many of the settlers. Canneries turned to Indigenous, and later Chinese, workers to meet their labor demands. By 1868, every member over the age of five from the Snoqualmie community near Lake Sammamish worked in the hops fields. Seasonal migration for work on the Pacific Coast pulled Indigenous children out of school and took Indigenous men away from the crops Indian agents encouraged them to cultivate.[42] For the Coast Salish, seasonal employment held a particular appeal. Swinomish and Tulalip communities worked in the canneries during July and August and in the hops fields in September. During the rest of the year, they gathered food for the winter and took advantage of other economic opportunities.[43]

Figure 6.1 Three Siwash Indian hop pickers posed with hops, Snoqualmie, Washington, c. 1906. Library of Congress Prints and Photographs Division, LC-USZ62-67675.

Companies not only accepted Indigenous laborers, but modified their business practices to attract them. When the Coast Salish participated in the canning industries, for example, they did so as families and communities rather than as individuals. In the canning industry, men fished and women made nets and filled cans. Children cleaned oil off the cans and helped with the labeling. Failure to hire one section of the family could result in the loss of the rest of the family's labor. The protocol was not one merchants could afford to ignore. The need for women to process fish was so substantial that canneries hired excess numbers of fishermen in order to secure access to the labor of the female members of those families.[44]

The reliance of British Columbia and Washington on Indigenous labor ensured that the border remained open and, at least for a time, that nascent industries paid attention to Coast Salish worldviews. Although Indigenous and Europeans worked alongside each other in the wage labor markets, they disagreed about fundamental questions regarding the ownership of natural resources. For settlers, the salmon were one of many resources that could be exploited. For many coastal communities, the salmon had a spiritual significance. Failure to follow the appropriate protocol could result in bad catches and discourage the salmon from returning.[45]

While the United States, Britain, and later Canada divided fishing territories around national borders, Haida, Nuu-chah-nulth, and Tsimshian divided it by lineage. In places that required large amounts of energy to harvest resources, the Coast Salish and northern Indigenous communities placed a strong emphasis on family ownership. Ownership, however, was complicated. While individuals possessed exclusive rights over fishing sites, their status and prestige came from sharing that wealth rather than hoarding it. As a result, exclusivity existed in a context of expected generosity. This helped ensure that community members, and at times even outsiders, could utilize exclusive locations so long as they established the right kind of relationships. Often they forfeited a certain portion of the catch to the site's owners and had to follow the restrictions placed on the site by those who controlled it.[46]

Understanding Indigenous cultural practices and systems of management were important goals for businesses, but did little for British, Canadian, and American administrators who desired to build nation-states across Indigenous lands. Federal administrators living in the Pacific invested few resources into understanding how or why Indigenous practices worked. Instead they aimed simply to replace earlier economic and social behaviors with ones they understood. In making this decision, each federal government invested in technology and immigration, two engines of change they believed held the key to remaking the Pacific World into the western edge of each nation.

Demography and Technology

Across the Pacific Coast, geological features presented formidable obstacles to nation-building. The Rocky Mountains separated British Columbia from the eastern provinces of Canada and created a similar barrier in trade and communication between Washington State and American population centers. To complicate matters further, the Pacific Ocean encouraged trade along the coast, blurring the national divisions both countries had committed to creating. In this context, building a border along the Pacific required more than boundary markers and surveyors. It required that both governments find ways to overcome the natural thoroughfares and barriers that already existed in the region.

Telegraphs and railways offered two important tools in each government's quest to reorder the landscape. Settlers and politicians measured distance in kilometer and miles, but more often understood it in terms of its practical effects—the time, effort, and cost associated with travel. By shaping the practical costs of travel, telegraphs and railways shifted the possibilities of governance and the incentives underpinning local social and economic interaction. In the 1860s, transmitting a message and a response between London and

British Columbia took months to complete. In the 1890s, telegraph machines had reduced such communications to a matter of days. By compressing space, railways and telegraphs allowed for direct federal input at the local and regional levels.[47] Although travelling by rail remained expensive and time consuming in the 1880s, the Northern Pacific Railroad (1883), Canadian Pacific Railway (1885), and the Great Northern Railway (1893) created new possibilities for east-west integration that had not previously existed.[48]

Railroads and telegraphs expanded federal control, but they remained at best mercenaries of governance. The same railroad systems that linked distant provinces together also undermined the boundaries of nations. In the middle of the nineteenth century, railway lines connected Soowahlie lands in British Columbia with Bellingham and Seattle in Washington. The ability of railroads and telegraphs to transport information, goods, and passenger traffic provided only opportunities. Power required people.[49]

During the 1880s, three demographic developments changed both the incentives for border control along the Pacific Coast and each government's capacity to enact it. First, Europeans migrants flooded to the West Coast, becoming the dominant population in both British Columbia and Washington. Second, Chinese immigrants began to enter the borderland in larger numbers during the 1870s and 1880s, seeking work in the mines and on the railways. Finally, Indigenous people declined both in terms of aggregate number and in respect to the growing immigrant populations on the West Coast. Outbreaks of measles (1848), smallpox (1853, 1862–63, 1876), tuberculosis, venereal diseases, and warfare all took their toll.[50]

Although disease had devastated Indigenous populations in British Columbia and Washington since contact, it took on an additional significance in the late nineteenth century as other groups grew in prominence. Over the span of fifty years, Indigenous people went from comprising almost the entire population of what would become British Columbia and Washington State to representing only a small minority.[51] In Washington, the population of European immigrants grew exponentially throughout the mid-nineteenth century. The population of white settlers recorded by the national census doubled between 1860 and 1870, tripled between 1870 and 1880, and increased fivefold again between 1880 and 1890. By 1910, the white population was a hundred times what it had been in 1860.[52]

Problems with colonial demographic records, however, limit understanding of this monumental transition. The American national census included only "Civilized Indians" in its counts of the population in the middle of the nineteenth century, and the Office of Indian Affairs struggled to get consistent information on Native Americans who lived beyond the reservation system.[53] What "civilized" meant was never clear. It sometimes referred to a level of education, religious upbringing, material wealth, or adoption of European cultural practices, but census officials used the term without having a clear definition. Even after taking into consideration these inaccuracies and challenges, Indigenous communities appear to have shrunk or at best remained stable in each decade of the nineteenth century from the 1860s onward. More importantly, Indigenous people declined in relation to the number of white settlers living in Washington. Between 1860 and 1880, Indigenous people dropped from three-quarters of Washington State's population to little more than a fifth. This demographic reversal reduced the power of Indigenous people. It concurrently decreased American and Canadian reliance on Indigenous labor and allowed both governments to implement aggressive policies with fewer concerns about retribution.[54]

In British Columbia change came slower than it did in Washington but yielded the same results. In 1855, only 774 settlers resided in the colony of Vancouver Island. Those colonists represented a few drops in a sea of the thirty-four thousand Indigenous inhabitants on the island and the tens of thousands more who resided on the mainland.[55] By 1891, however, Indigenous people comprised somewhere between a quarter and a third of British Columbia's population.[56] Their demographic superiority had evaporated. Immigration underwrote the demographic transformation that gave both governments power, and it soon provided the direction that border control efforts would take.

Chinese Exclusion

In Washington State and British Columbia, Chinese immigration had a small impact on the region's demography but an enormous one on how each country approached its border. In 1880 the national censuses recorded 3,186 Chinese residents in Washington Territory. A year later census takers found 4,350 Chinese and Japanese (populations they did not consider worth separating) in British Columbia. Although Chinese immigrants represented only 5 to 10 percent of the population in each location, they drew an uncommon ire. California, where the Chinese population represented a quarter of the work force, helped push concerns north along the border.[57] The Republican Party denounced a lack of restrictions on Chinese immigration as "an evil of great magnitude," while newspapers in Vancouver, Washington, described Chinese immigration as an invasion of servile laborers.[58] Sinophobes argued that Chinese immigrants could not assimilate and, if allowed into the country, would reduce white workers to slavery.[59] If Chinese immigration offered only a light breeze in the sails of the demographic change, settlers perceived it nonetheless as a gale force storm.[60]

In 1875, the United States passed the Page Law designed to protect the American home from unwanted immigrants. Contract laborers and women from Asia, as well as felons, served as the initial targets. The attack soon spread. Grassroots nativism encouraged the United States to adopt the 1882 Chinese Restriction Act, which made it illegal for Chinese laborers to enter the United States for ten years and prevented Chinese immigrants from becoming citizens.[61] The restrictions were the product of a long tradition. In the eighteenth century, New York and Massachusetts created inspection systems and head taxes to prevent criminals and indigents from immigrating into their states.[62]

Chinese Restriction took old practices and charted new territory. It created wide-reaching prohibitions against a single racial group for the first time and used the customs agency to police citizenship and race in ways that it had not in the past. In a wry flourish, officials on the coast justified the need to exclude Chinese immigrants as a matter of compassion to Indigenous people. Debased and dishonest Chinese laborers would influence impressionable Indians and disrupt their path to civilization.[63] Indian Superintendent I. W. Powell worried that Chinese, as well as unprincipled whites, demoralized Indigenous communities. Indian agents blamed the Chinese for introducing opium, increasing rates of intoxication, assaulting Indigenous constables, and driving down employment opportunities for Indigenous communities.[64]

If the policies that followed had not been so disastrous, Chinese immigrants and Indigenous laborers may have found a grim humor in the ways that border restrictions manifested themselves. The unrestrained flow of settlers onto Indigenous lands had made federal border policies possible. Newcomers used Social Darwinism, treaties, and what they saw as the natural order of the world to justify their rights across a region they had only recently entered. Without hesitation, they banned undesirable streams of immigration from Asia in part because they feared they could not compete with such a massive population. The policies exposed the precariousness of the British, Canadian, and American position. Immigration had made the world Americans and Canadians imagined, but it seemed poised to undo that work as well.[65]

Together American and Canadian racial anxieties toward Indigenous and Chinese people led to a border closure process that occurred from two different angles. The governments designed Chinese Restriction to keep an unwanted and inassimilable population out of the country. They created Indian policy, by contrast, to assist in the assimilation process and to clarify land cessions. Doing so required creating a border that kept Indigenous people within a single country. During the late eighteenth and early nineteenth centuries, Britain had prohibited the expatriation rights of skilled workers. By the late nineteenth century,

Figure 6.2 Print from *Frank Lesley's Illustrated Newspaper* from 1882 emphasizing the uneven restrictions facing Chinese immigrants when compared with Communists, Fenians, Nihilists, and hoodlums. "The Only One Barred Out [Caricature of Chinese Man Seated Outside Golden Gate of Liberty," *Frank Lesley's Illustrated Newspaper*, April 1, 1882. Library of Congress Prints and Photographs, LC-DIG-ds-11861.

however, United States, Britain, and Canada all recognized the rights of subjects and citizens to cross borders. Indians, as an anomalous legal category, received no such protections.[66]

By linking racial exclusion to immigration, Chinese Restriction allowed federal administrators to generalize racial control as a national border policy. They repurposed old ideas for new places and new challenges.[67] Federal restrictions to Cree, Métis, and Oceti Sakowin (Sioux) mobility on the Prairies shared many similarities to Chinese restriction. Both polices relied on perceptions of racial inferiority and advocated for the separate legal identities of the group they removed or excluded from the national identity. Just as importantly, both strategies, for all their differences, aimed to control opportunity and wealth. Both countries sought to keep Indigenous people out of productive areas and prevent Chinese migrants from fully engaging in local economies. From the mindset of settler colonialism, the approaches shared much in common. Key resources—whether land, labor, or capital—would fall into the hands of settlers. Everyone else would participate with a handicap.

For all the similarities, the approaches differed in fundamental ways. British and American claims to land rested on Indigenous people's own historic connection to territory. Broader intellectual traditions in each country emphasized a responsibility that each federal government maintained as a result of that connection. That responsibility existed even in places like British Columbia, where Canada and Britain signed few treaties, or in Washington where the United States established them slowly. In contrast, Canada and the United States could dismiss the Chinese as unwanted, incapable, and unassimilable without impacting their own claims to land.[68]

These distinctions separated the forever-foreign (the Chinese) from wards (Indians) who were just as different, but perhaps not forever so. They help explain why Chinese Restriction later served as the basis for future border polices and Indian policy often did not. The Chinese became a stand-in for a generic kind of foreignness from which federal agents could extrapolate. Indian policy, centered around historic ties to land, seemed far harder to graft onto border control when considered on a far greater scale. As a result, Chinese Restriction provided the mold for racialized border control, translating the lessons the federal government had learned over the better part of a century into a more generalizable formula.

Despite the ideological significance of the Chinese Restriction Act, the act had an uneveneffect in practice. Merchants caught bringing Chinese into the country could receive up to a year in prison and a fine. Chinese found unlawfully in the country faced deportation.[69] The wording of the act created confusion because it left individual states to appoint their own inspectors, determine which Chinese were illegal, and establish how those found guilty would be deported. The Restriction Act disrupted the ability of labor contractors to bring Chinese into the country, but left many loopholes. The main limitation of the Chinese Restriction Act, however, was financial. The US government had given the customs service the mandate to stop Chinese immigration but did not allocate enough funds to hire the additional customs agents required to enforce the policy.[70]

Concern over Chinese immigration increased in 1883 when the Canadian Pacific Railway began to lay off workers. The US government sent Special Agent J. C. Horr to investigate the threat of Chinese immigration into Washington Territory. Horr believed customs agents could watch the five most significant trails that connected British Columbia to Washington Territory without too much difficulty. The winter snows and spring rains made many paths unusable for a large portion of the year, reducing the necessity to guard the entire line. Horr remained more concerned about policing the water, but believed that while a maritime avenue of entry existed, Chinese laborers would need the good will of the people to cross the boundary line.[71]

Horr correctly recognized the importance of local populations to federal border control efforts, but overestimated the extent of anti-Chinese sentiments. Chinese migrants did not have to look far to find borderland residents, both Indigenous and settler, who would assist them in crossing for the right price. The Coast Salish charged as little as two dollars a head to smuggle people from Canada into the United States. White smugglers received as much as $125 a head by the end of the decade.[72]

Chinese entered the United States from Canada, despite Horr's confidence in the customs service's ability to police the border. If British Columbia offered a backdoor to Washington, it was often an unwelcoming place to be Chinese. Armed provincial tax collectors pursued Chinese laborers while they remained north of the line. Calls for special Chinese taxes, including taxes on rice, proliferated north of the line. Indigenous communities, which would participate in vigilante violence against the Chinese, helped to collect the taxes that made life for Chinese migrants living in BC less appealing.[73]

The situation grew worse after 1885, when Canada imposed a fifty-dollar head tax on Chinese immigrants entering the country. On the surface, the tax—roughly two months' wages for an unskilled laborer—appeared to be a positive step toward restricting Chinese immigration. In reality, the tax had unexpected consequences and did little to prevent migration. The American Restriction Act required that the United States deport Chinese laborers back "to the country from whence he came."[74] After 1885 that kind of deportation required the American government to pay the Canadian tax to do so. Complaints soon proliferated. Canada turned a profit, while it left the United States to deal with immigrants neither country desired.[75]

The Canadian policy created a conundrum for American officials. The United States had little interest in paying the head tax to return Chinese laborers to British Columbia because it provided no long-term solution to Chinese immigration. Deported laborers could recross the border at their convenience, forcing the United States to pay the fee multiple times. By the 1890s, US marshals had captured Ah Jack enough times to recognize him on sight. During Ah Jack's fifth arrest, the marshal at Port Townsend could not help but express his frustration. There seemed "no use to send him back to Victoria, he thinks it is a nice thing to come here and be sent back at the expense of the U.S. Government."[76] The US commission sent Ah Jack to the penitentiary on McNeil's Island while it attempted to figure out a more permanent solution.

The head tax and inability to prevent Chinese from recrossing the line left the customs agents with a handful of options. They could sneak the laborers back into Canada in order to avoid the Canadian tax, becoming smugglers themselves in the process. Similarly, they could shift the destination or financial burden. American officers deported Chinese laborers back to China against the policies their own government had created. They also pressured deportees to pay their own head tax when they deported them to Canada. Finally, customs inspectors imprisoned Chinese laborers like Ah Jack at the penitentiary on McNeil Island. Together these approaches provided a variety of options that customs agents tailored to their circumstances.[77]

Eng Hong, who attempted to enter the United States in September of 1890, for example, experienced more than one type of control. When British Columbia refused to allow his entry following his attempted deportation, American marshals confined him to a penitentiary before deporting him directly to China.[78] Opting to rely on deportation, coercion, smuggling or incarceration did not close other avenues for control. Even when customs agents chose a singular approach (deportation), they often varied its specifics (destination) over the course of a case to maximize their chance of success.

In the fall of 1890, the Inspector of Customs for Puget Sound investigated a sloop travelling around Hadlock Bay. As the customs vessel drew near, the unmarked ship beached itself and its crew fled into the woods. William Jackling discovered twenty Chinese migrants, including Wong Sing, on board the abandoned ship.[79] After a failed deportation to British Columbia, American officials came to the conclusion that Wong Sing must have entered the United States from China, not Canada. The dubious shift in his point of departure created a renewed opportunity to deport him "from whence he came."[80] Customs agents and district judges stretched the law to fit their local needs. Beset with problems and limitations, they also turned to the public for support.[81]

Regional animosity and local circumstances created fertile—if unstable—ground for assistance. First Nations, European immigrants, and Chinese laborers informed and assisted the customs department, but also helped smugglers. Personal grudges and financial opportunities dictated whether a family or community supported the customs officials or the lawbreakers. This choice was not a one-time decision. As circumstances shifted, so did the loyalty of the local population.

In 1883 Indigenous informants sent word to C. B. Bash, the customs collector at Port Townsend, that six Chinese had crossed the border near the Gulf of Georgia. Bash did not mention where his informants were from or what tribe they belonged to, but he took the information they provided seriously. He hired an Indigenous messenger to inform temporary special Inspector Aleck Macaulay, who was then on his way to Fort Colville, to apprehend the Chinese immigrants if possible. The messenger returned shortly with good news: Macaulay had detained ten people.[82]

Less than a year later, a Chinese laundryman from Sehome approached Arthur L. Blake suggesting that for $5 a person, he would show Blake three Chinese immigrants who had arrived from British Columbia. The deputy customs inspector remained uncertain of his own ability to "distinguish a newcomer from an old resident."[83] He was no more confident about his ability to assess the veracity of the laundryman's claims. Unsure of how to proceed, he forwarded the offer on to his superior. Less than two months later he sent another letter filled with concern. Blake voiced his trepidation that Chinese immigrants must "be caught before they reach Whatcom or not at all."[84] The structural problems facing enforcement had eaten away whatever confidence Blake might have once had.

If border enforcement provided an ongoing frustration, the customs service's ability to draw support from the general public explained some of its success. Nearby settlers provided information on the movement of illicit goods and people. They carried messages between agents and monitored suspicious ships. The customs force occasionally brought these individuals on as temporary agents, but more often paid them on a case-by-case basis for their time. Limited compensation and long delays in payment limited the appeal of the incentives to only those already disposed to help. Still, the compensation system gave the customs service hundreds of eyes and hands it could not otherwise rely upon.[85]

The same racial anxieties that animated settlers into providing information to the Customs Service also encouraged them to operate on their own initiative. Blake received frequent inquiries whether "a private citizen [had] the right to arrest Chinese entering this country across the Border line."[86] The vagueness of the Chinese Restriction Act left no easy answer. Blake interpreted the law to imply that only customs officials had the right to make the arrests. Bash, Blake's superior, ruled differently. He supported a citizen's ability to detain suspected violators of immigration laws. The conviction of six Chinese immigrants, captured by a party of settlers in the winter of 1883, supported Bash's interpretation. The broader questions of legality, however, remained murky.[87]

As frustrations mounted over the inability of Canada and the United States to prevent Chinese immigration, settlers became violent. In Washington Territory, white settlers and Indigenous hops workers attacked a Chinese work camp at Squak Valley and killed a handful. Shortly thereafter settlers drove Chinese miners out of the Coal Creek, Black Diamond, and Franklin mines. Vigilantes drove hundreds of Chinese out of Tacoma in November of 1885 and out of Seattle in February of 1886. They broke windows, looted houses, and beat Chinese laborers and merchants. The violence strained America's relationship with China and embarrassed the United States internationally. In 1886 Congress agreed to compensate the Chinese government $275,000 for damages suffered by its citizens during anti-Chinese riots.[88]

In British Columbia, the Knights of Labor passed resolutions to boycott Chinese merchants and storekeepers that sold to them. When the boycotts failed, several hundred workers attacked Chinese railway workers in Vancouver.

They set their work camp on fire before expelling an additional eighty-six Chinese fishermen from False Creek. While some Canadians distanced themselves from the violence, blaming it on the work of American agitators, the social situation suggested a less flattering picture. Workers, many of whom made their living crisscrossing the border, attacked Chinese laborers and merchants on both sides of the line. In that context, scapegoating American instigators missed the remaining fluidity of national identities in the region.[89]

By 1888, President Grover Cleveland expressed the hopelessness of controlling the movement of Chinese under the present policy. Chinese migration caused internal conflicts, rioting, and vigilantism, but the United States could not stem the movements of Chinese into the country and seemed unwilling to punish white and Indigenous workers who engaged in unsavory activities. Cleveland concluded that the "mercenary greed of parties" trading in the labor of Chinese was "too strong for the execution of the law."[90] Chinese restriction had failed. The United States moved toward a more comprehensive policy of exclusion.

In 1888, the United States introduced the Scott Act (Chinese Exclusion Act) and Congress appropriated $50,000 "to defray the expenses which may be incurred in the enforcement" of Chinese exclusion.[91] Future appropriations ranged from $30,000 to $100,000, split between the salaries of additional customs agents and the costs of deporting Chinese migrants. Along the Canada–US border, the additional funding led to the hiring of five Chinese inspectors to expand both the geography and intensity of the Customs Service's patrols. The additional men helped, but the Customs Service remained short staffed.[92]

The 1888 Exclusion Act changed the nature of illegal immigration to the United States. The act nullified the return passes of thousands of Chinese migrants, eliminated one of the main avenues (fraudulent return certificates) through which illegal immigrants entered the country, and gave even greater encouragement for Chinese immigrants to migrate across the Canada–US border rather than through American ports. The 1888 Exclusion Act succeeded in limiting the immigration of Chinese to the United States far more than its predecessor, but it did not eliminate Chinese immigration overnight. The 1890s brought hard labor and new residency documents for Chinese residents into the repertoire of border guards.[93]

The Unevenness of Control

For all the ways that Chinese Restriction and Exclusion transformed border control efforts in the west, the border remained an inconsistent, uneven, and unpredictable barrier. Laws that lay dormant in one region of the Pacific created practical barriers in others. Chinese migrants experienced this unevenness through the whims of the agents in charge, who variably subjected them to confinement, deportation, and coercion. Indigenous communities experienced the same kind of unpredictability, but often for different reasons. A customs agent's legal understanding of Indian status, tolerance of frustration, and willingness to dedicate resources to the task all shaped whether he attempted to control Indigenous movements or gave them a wide berth. Customs inspectors, for example, pressured the Tsimshian at Metlakahtla to pay at least $5,000 in customs duties a year and collected $374 for goods and oils from the Neah Bay.[94] By the 1880s, Indian agents had informed the Kootenay that they would have "pay the customs duty in the same way as the whites."[95] More often, however, government agents failed to monitor the cargos Indigenous people transported. That applied to canoes filled with dogfish oil that had crossed the border since the 1850s, as well as canoes that contained Chinese laborers.[96]

On April 2, 1883, A. L. Blake reported that he had seen a large canoe off the coast of Washington near Semiahmoo. Through his looking glass Blake saw only a single paddler. The other two passengers appeared to "wear the loose blouses of Chinamen."[97] Already pressed from so many angles, Blake decided not to pursue the matter. Even in cases where federal agents captured schooners manned by Indigenous smugglers, they rarely pursued the matter. When American officers arrested a pair of Indigenous travelers in 1905, the Superintendent of Indian Affairs in British Columbia advocated clemency on the grounds that the law "was broken through ignorance."[98] The petition occurred decades after the customs service had established a presence in the Pacific, highlighting the uneven speed at which federal control manifested itself across groups and geographies.

While the Customs Service put only minimal pressure on Indigenous mobility, other federal and nongovernmental organizations supplemented the effort. The enlargement of the Office and Department of Indian Affairs allowed Canada and the United States to exercise more direct and nuanced control over the lives of Indigenous people. In 1884, revisions to the Canadian Indian Act made participation in potlatches a misdemeanor that could carry a two- to six-month prison term. The United States followed suit shortly thereafter, cracking down on potlatches south of the border.[99]

Prohibitions against potlatches and other cultural practices that missionaries and Indian agents found offensive drove the practices underground, but did not destroy them. Restrictions against winter dancing, for example, forced the Stó:lō to limit the size of their social gatherings and post sentries to watch out for provincial policemen. When Aleck was fourteen or fifteen, he served as a lookout. While the dancers were singing in an underground pithouse, Aleck sat at the edge of the reserve. A string connected to a bell enabled him to warn the participants about police activity in their vicinity. Federal attacks against culture had economic as well as social implications. Potlatch ceremonies structured the transfer of ancestral names and productive resource sites.[100]

A century after the potlach ban went into effect, Robert Jimmie, a former Stó:lō Chief, reflected on the long-term damage caused by Canadian interference with Stó:lō social and cultural practices. By the late twentieth century, no one knew who controlled what locations anymore and "everybody [is] fighting over fishing spots."[101] Band leadership, ancestral rights, personal claims, and federal and state regulations overlapped and conflicted with one another, creating few easy answers.[102]

The shift in demographic dominance created opportunities for coercive control. It also encouraged settlers to ignore treaty promises and drive the Coast Salish out of key industries along the Pacific. In the canning and fishing industries, new technologies, alternative sources of labor, and racist fishing laws made it difficult for Indigenous nations to maintain older subsistence and commercial practices. During the 1870s, First Nations composed the majority of individuals catching fish and canning them. This monopoly disappeared in the 1880s.[103]

Chinese, and later Japanese, laborers encroached on cannery jobs, removing a dependable source of employment for Indigenous women. In 1884, a fishery officer estimated that white laborers constituted about a tenth of the canneries' workforce in British Columbia. Chinese and Indigenous laborers—numbering roughly 1,200 each—comprised the remainder. Japanese and European fishermen soon added additional hiring and strike breaking options.[104]

Thirty years later, the B. C. Packer's Association surveyed fifteen canneries, finding seven Indigenous workers, roughly 5 percent of those employed. More than four out of every five workers had Japanese heritage. Information gathered by American packers' associations suggested a similar trend in the United States. By the turn of the century, Indigenous communities could no longer rely on the canning industry as they had in the 1870s.[105]

As new labor sources challenged the dominance of Indigenous fishermen, technological innovations put pressure on Indigenous fishing sites and territorial management. Fish traps, in particular, changed the ways Pacific fisherman collected their catches. Lead nets, which reached hundreds of meters in length, guided fish into a pound where fishermen removed them at their leisure. The traps, which inundated the waterways of Washington State by the turn of the twentieth century, often overlapped with reef net sites maintained by the Coast Salish. Trap owners hired armed guards to protect their investments, leading to a militarization of the fishing sites.[106]

In a pattern that would be repeated in other industries, federal and state intervention propped up the claims of white businessmen. Treaty promises carried little weight. British Columbia instituted a system of licensing that provided higher wages to white fisherman and forced Indigenous fisherman to choose between commercial (as laborers) and subsistence fishing. Canneries, in turn, imposed race-based quota systems. In the United States, state regulators tied fishing licenses to citizenship, excluding Native Americans by definition. American authorities seized eight sealing schooners crewed by Indigenous people in 1886. In 1889, the US revenue cutter *Rush* seized more vessels, reducing profits.[107]

Confiscations and seizures turned expeditions that would have been profitable into financial disasters. Crossing the border no longer enriched economic opportunities in the ways it had in the past. The Lummi actively took the Alaska Packers' Association to court to protect their fisheries, but to little avail. Once the United States and Canada no longer required Indigenous labor to maintain Pacific economies, neither country had much interest maintaining Indigenous rights. Demographic changes made it possible to unseat Indigenous people as the dominant fishing population on the West Coast. Racist fishing laws and new technology served as the implement of choice.[108]

The same patterns that drove Indigenous laborers from the canning and fishing industries also undermined their place in the hops trade. During the 1870s and 1880s, the hops industry relied on the annual migrations of thousands of Indigenous laborers from both sides of the border. The emergence of the hops louse in the early 1890s across Puget Sound devastated harvests. What opportunities the louse did not destroy, market fluctuations, government regulation, and labor competition ate away at. Major streams of revenue grew shallow. By the end the century, they had become unpredictable trickles. Indigenous laborers continued to pick hops but they had become only one part of a large and expendable labor pool.[109]

***

On the surface, the border separating Canada from the United States in the early twentieth century looked similar to the one that existed in the 1880s. Europeans and Indigenous people still crossed the line in large numbers, establishing economic, social, and kinship ties that transcended the border. Direct control remained fleeting. A lot, however, had changed. Settlers flocked to the Pacific Coast, undermining the systems of territorial organization that Indigenous people maintained. Canada and the United States, no longer forced to respect the power of Indigenous laborers, began a more intensive campaign to disrupt Indigenous cultures, resource management, and landholding. At the same moment, fear of Chinese immigration encouraged both countries to begin to police the movement of people, not simply goods.

Between 1882 and 1900, the border separating British Columbia and Washington tightened. The multiple angles of pressure ensured the border never treated communities or ethnic groups in quite the same way. Chinese laborers felt the crackdown first and the hardest. The border tightened for Indigenous people at about the same time, albeit to a lesser degree and for very different reasons. Only later in the twentieth century did either government begin to control the movement of European bodies across the line. The result was a mosaic of border enforcement policies in which race dictated who could cross the line, under what circumstances, and with what impediments. That process did not occur by accident but was intertwined with the very blood and bone of border control itself.

7

Blood and Bones

James Morrow Walsh knew the Canada–US border better than almost anyone else. Born in Upper Canada in 1840, Walsh served as a superintendent of the North-West Mounted Police, a role that saw him lead part of the force's initial expedition west. Once in the Cypress Hills, he oversaw operations at Fort Walsh, where he policed transnational movements and developed personal as well as sexual relationships with members of the Siksikaitsiitapi (Blackfoot) confederacy and Oceti Sakowin (Sioux) who moved back and forth across the line. Walsh understood the ethereal nature of borders even as he oversold their importance.[1] For Walsh, Indigenous people "fear to touch it [the border] less their rashness bring grief to them and their people. That imaginary wall is higher than sight can reach [and] thicker than shot can pierce."[2] The border never became the colossus Walsh imagined, but his vision reflected the broader ideas that motivated Canada and the United States to increase their presence along it. When borders worked, they appeared as natural, devastating, and impassible.

In practice, the border Walsh imagined behaved less like a static line and more like a living creature. Boundary markers provide the skeletal structure and organization of the body but provided no force of their own. By 1874, Canada and the United States had surveyed land and placed boundary stones over 6,000 kilometers of territory. They had established a cohesive skeleton for the border in every major region except the Arctic.

In order for the border to inspire fear, affect everyday life, and extend upward into the heavens, as Walsh imagined it, the border needed more than just bones. It required blood and muscle: revenue and personnel. In the late nineteenth century, Canada and the United States sought to scaffold a body onto the skeleton they had built. Violence in the Prairies, immigration along the Pacific Coast, and fears of transnational crime, sexual immorality, and racial degeneration motivated this transformation. The two nations enlisted thousands of administrators to guard their shared border, expanding their presence in the east

A Line of Blood and Dirt. Benjamin Hoy, Oxford University Press (2021). © Oxford University Press.
DOI: 10.1093/oso/9780197528693.003.0008

and establishing new outposts in the west. Prior the Civil War, local governments oversaw much of the day-to-day operations of the country. Over the next three decades, as the federal government grew, it subsumed the power and duties local communities had once controlled.[3]

Growing the bureaucracy required expanding the circulatory system that supported it. In the nineteenth century, the Customs Bureau served as the government's heart. Its wide network of posts collected vast amounts of revenue. Fee-based approaches to governance stretched revenue in creative ways. Under a fee-based system, federal agents gathered a lot of their own wages as they completed their duties. Postal workers received a portion of the stamps they sold. Customs agents took a cut of the illicit cargo they captured. Political machines distributed these appointments and, in return, expected that officer holders donated a percentage of their income back to the machine. The process entrenched both patronage and a self-interested bureaucracy as basic features of American governance.[4]

After the Civil War and Confederation, both Canada and the United States possessed the crude kind of power that could win wars, but they lacked the necessary bureaucracies to handle the day-to-day operations throughout much of the territory they claimed. They outsourced where they could and floundered where they could not. Change required money, but it could also generate it as well. Customs officers, for example, returned more money to the federal government than their salaries consumed, making it relatively simple to expand their numbers.[5]

Increasing other departments came at an immediate cost. The salaries of immigration agents, NWMP officers, soldiers, and Indian agents consumed the funds each government could have spent on lighthouses, courts, naval yards, and other nation-building projects. Worries of federal bloat and corruption also tempered enthusiasm. Despite these concerns, both governments pressed forward. They created and expanded a mishmash of organizations and departments that wholly (customs and immigration) or partially (army, NWMP, Indian Affairs) helped each country maintain the border.[6]

While soldiers, NWMP officers, customs agents, and immigrations employees could make the border meaningful through patrols and inspections, borderland residents often experienced the power of the federal government in subtle ways. Power came in two forms. Direct power aimed to control people as they crossed the border itself. Indirect power attempted to stop movements before they began by undercutting the motivations that led to undesired crossings. For those who experienced the border firsthand, its impact remained an uncertain proposition. The personal characteristics of the crosser, region, agency encountered, style of surveillance, and rules of enforcement all shaped the way the border behaved and how it performed. The border had acquired more flesh and bone by the late nineteenth century, but it had never settled on a single face.

Customs

Often unheralded, the customs services in Canada and the United States made each country's federal government possible. At the expense of $6,494,847, the American customs service collected $181,471,939 in revenue for the federal government in 1885.[7] The practical value of that income is difficult to assess in practice. Federal accounting is complicated, and each bureau offset expenditures in a variety of ways. Still, if the expenditures recorded by the Treasury Department are any indication, that revenue well exceeded what was necessary to maintain the United States' Army ($42,670,578) and Navy ($16,021,079). If the Office of Indian Affairs ($6,552,494), Judiciary ($3,945,691), Interior Department ($62,654,762), Customs, Light-houses, Public Buildings ($27,125,972), and the entire branch of government devoted to diplomacy and foreign intercourse ($5,439,609) were added together, it would still leave more than ten million dollars left over to help pay the interest on public debt or to contribute to pensions.[8] With the exception of an income tax enacted in the United States from 1861 to 1870 to help pay off the Civil War, customs fees generated most of the government's revenue during the nineteenth century.[9]

A similar system operated north of the border. In 1866–67, the Canadian customs force collected 7 million dollars in fees. That amount increased to over 135 million dollars in collections and 123 million in import excise taxes by 1924–25.[10] Collections mattered. Until 1917, when Canada introduced an income tax, "three-quarters of the revenue of the Canadian government, and of the several preceding colonial governments, came from customs and excise duties."[11] At least in an economic sense, neither country could afford to ignore its border. Enforcing customs laws went far beyond border security; it involved protecting a source of income that funded entire branches of government.[12]

The customs service, for all its importance, faced an enormous task. Even in tiny ports, the amount of goods crossing the border ran into the hundreds of thousands of dollars. In just three months in 1869, Fort Erie Ontario exported $159,605 worth of goods from the United States.[13] A city of less than a thousand people, Fort Erie served as a crossing point for 440 tons of ash, 210,698 bushels of barley, and 17,380 pounds of bone in a single year.[14] Policing the staggering flow of goods across the length of an entire country required an enormous bureaucratic backbone. John S. McCalmont, the Commissioner of Customs, noted in 1885 that his office alone received 17,800 letters and wrote 9,986 letter in response. It administered 1,394 oaths, issued 2,391 requisitions, and examined

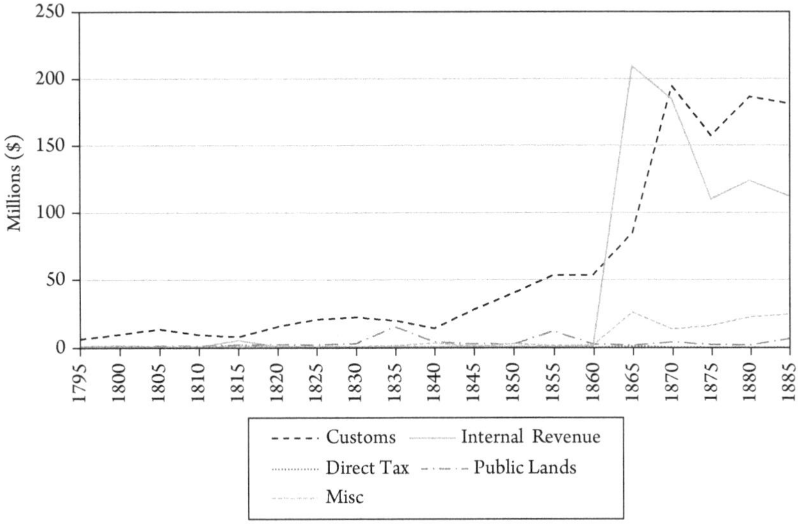

Figure 7.1 Department of Treasury—Statement of Receipts of the United States in 5-Year Intervals, 1795–1885. *Annual Report of the Secretary of the Treasury on the State of the Finances, 1886, Volume I: Finance* (Washington, DC: Government Printing Office, 1886), xc–xciii. The digitized datasets used to create these maps are available at www.buildingborders.com and http://hdl.handle.net/10388/12153.

217,217 stubs. Possessing on average 30 clerks, the office struggled to keep pace with its most basic duties and failed to create the kinds of statistical reports often desired by other agencies.[15]

Over time, the customs services in both countries grew larger. In 1879–80, for example, the customs collection in Manitoba cost the federal government $12,960.12 and provided $298,929.15 in revenue. In 1919–20 the federal government paid $288,607.80 to collect $12,160,214.32 in customs revenue. Considered over a forty-year period, customs revenue in the province grew by close to 3,968 percent, while the proportionate cost of collecting fell from 4.3 percent to 2.4 percent of the total collected.[16]

As the customs service grew, it also changed shape. In 1870, the US customs service had a strong presence along the Atlantic Coast and Gulf of Mexico, with a heavy concentration of employees in Boston, New York, and New Orleans.[17] New York alone maintained a force of 1,300 customs employees in 1877, making the department the second largest federal employer in the state after the postal service.[18] Its presence elsewhere remained far slimmer. The Customs Service maintained over two hundred personnel at San Francisco, but possessed only three Pacific posts outside of Alaska in 1870. That same year, the United States stationed only two people in Idaho and Montana. In the south, customs posts at Brazos De Santiago and Paso Del Norte in Texas provided its only presence.

Temporary employees supplemented these numbers but did not change the basic distribution of power.[19]

By 1890, customs posts dotted the perimeter of each nation, but offered different levels of control depending on the region. The US Customs Service maintained a strong presence along the Atlantic Coast as well as in the Great Lakes and Gulf of Mexico. In the south, only about a hundred customs employees (2 percent of the force) guarded the US–Mexico border. In the north, the situation looked even worse. A single American customs collector at Fort Benton monitored transnational commerce between Duluth, on western edge of the Great Lakes, and Port Townsend, on the Pacific Coast.[20] The Canadian Department of Customs relied on a similar kind of distribution but operated on a smaller scale. Canada stationed its customs force in areas of high population density and along the Atlantic seaboard. It supplied only a small force to guard the Pacific Ocean and, like the United States, all but ignored the Prairies.[21]

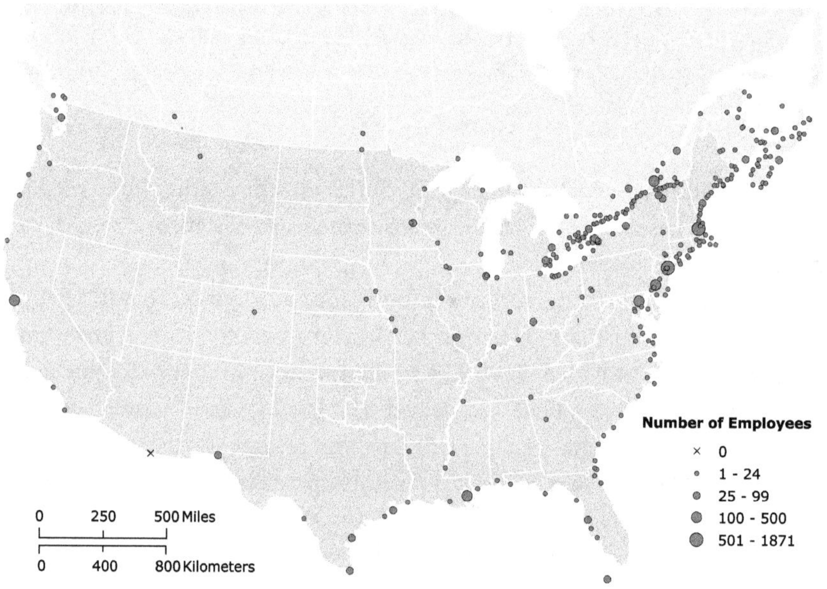

Figure 7.2 Customs Employees in Canada and the United States 1889–90. Canada, *The Civil Service List of Canada 1889* (Ottawa: Brown Chamberlin, 1890), 41–78; United States, Treasury Department, *Annual Report of the Secretary of the Treasury on the State of the Finances, 1890* (Washington, DC: Government Printing Office, 1890), 760–76. The digitized datasets used to create these maps are available at www.buildingborders.com and http://hdl.handle.net/10388/12153. GIS territorial boundary datasets: Manson, Steven, Jonathan Schroeder, David Van Riper, and Tracy Kugler. *IPUMS National Historical Geographic Information System: Version 15.0 [Dataset]*. Minneapolis, MN: IPUMS, 2020. http://doi.org/10.18128/D050.V15.0., and Nicholson, Norman L., Charles F. J. Whebell, Robert Galois, and Michael Stavely. *Territorial Evolution, 1670-2001: Version 1 [Dataset]*, 2020.

Once established, the geographic variation was hard to shake. Changing patterns of trade did not always result in shifts of personnel. In 1872, customs officers at Port Townsend handled approximately 750 annual entrances and clearances, which increased to 1,748 by 1884. Despite the more than doubled traffic, the customs force remained around 19 or 20 employees.[22] The customs agents working these sites did not apply policies consistently. By the 1880s the United States had begun to collect customs duties on Indigenous merchandise that crossed the border, but failed to apply duties to the handiwork created by the communities at Walpole Island and Sarnia until well into the twentieth century. As a result, the border grew, but it rarely looked the same.[23]

Immigration

In the late nineteenth century the Customs Service gained a sister. Born in 1891 as a federal agency, the Office of Immigration found its way onto the administrative landscape as power shifted from state to federal hands and battles raged over Chinese exclusion and undesirability.[24] From the very outset, customs and immigration shared a common heritage and a linked fate through their mutual connection to the Department of Treasury. Like many siblings, the two organizations emphasized their differences rather than their commonalities. Federal policy only made the matter worse. Asked to manage two of the most important border control organizations, the Department of Treasury blurred the lines between them. Customs agents would help monitor people, and immigration agents would do so for goods. The blurring of unequals created ample room for dissatisfaction and resentment. With over five thousand employees in 1890, the Customs Service had a bureaucratic reach well beyond anything the Bureau of Immigration could imagine. In 1895, four years after its formation, the Bureau of Immigration still possessed only 249 employees. Even those new to the civil service could see that conflict from a distance.[25]

Terence V. Powderly had grown up among the shifting bureaucratic landscape that had created the Office of Immigration. Born to an immigrant family in Pennsylvania's coal country in 1849, Powderly saw the highs and lows of an economy in flux. By 1890 he had worked on the railroads, organized protests, lost jobs, and suffered amidst a rolling series of economic depressions. He saw no contradiction between working as the mayor of Scranton, Pennsylvania, and his later role as the head of the Knights of Labor. Unions and governments fought, but they could both improve the lives of workers.[26]

Powderly knew workplace conflicts and he knew large-scale organization. Appointed by President William McKinley as the Commissioner General of Immigration in 1897, he saw a kind of discontent he knew firsthand. Federal policy had stitched together two organizations that disliked one another. Customs agents feared an increased workload as they carried the slack of the nascent immigration service. Immigration agents in turn complained of a lack of autonomy.[27] Powderly wondered openly about the logic of combining two bureaus that possessed "nothing in common."[28] Despite Powderly's concern, and the power that came with his rank, the Bureau of Immigration retained its uncomfortable relationship to its older sibling until 1903. As immigration moved under the jurisdiction of the Department of Commerce and Labor, the ties that had once bound it to the customs service began to dissipate.[29]

The emergence of an independent Office of Immigration amplified the changes already caused by the earlier jurisdictional transfers. As late as 1881, Michigan lacked any commission or board to supervise immigration.[30] By 1895, the United States recorded the entries of non-Canadians who entered the country from the north. Head taxes, set at $1 per person in 1896, did not make the office self-sufficient, but they diminished the economic burden the department placed on the American government.[31]

As concerns around immigration broadened and intensified, Congress passed laws that excluded entry to prospective immigrants on the basis of race, mental capacity, morality, poverty, and health. Moral turpitude provisions allowed inspectors to bar the entries of those suspected of adultery, bigamy, prostitution, and sodomy.[32] At Seattle, immigration inspectors rejected every single migrant from India who sought entry into the United States in 1910, using a combination of laws surrounding polygamy, public charge, labor, and disease. They justified this comprehensive ban as a necessity because of the South Asian population's physical weakness, clannishness, lower standard of living, unsanitary practices, and ethnic loyalty. They feared that the numerical superiority of South Asians would overwhelm American citizens if allowed to locate to the continent. For the Commissioner in Seattle, the official reasons for excluding each immigrant mattered less than the comprehensive ban itself. So long as the United States prohibited the population's entry wholesale, he remained happy.[33]

In Canada, the Department of Immigration saw a slow and uninspiring start. Following 1867, the federal government managed immigration jointly with individual provinces, a form of oversight that also applied to public works and agriculture.[34] Over the next few decades, control over immigration shifted and changed. If there was one consistency, it was the Department's small size. Nineteen immigration employees in 1896 grew to 35 in 1905. By 1915, the paylists of the Department of Immigration had mushroomed to 127. Despite an increase of over 550 percent in twenty years, the Department of Immigration possessed half as many employees as its American equivalent had mustered twenty years earlier. Put simply, Canada shared similar goals with United States and had just as much territory to guard. What it lacked was people.[35]

If 127 federal employees seemed inadequate to guard hundreds of thousands of kilometers of coastline and border, the number looked worse in practice than it did on paper. A bevy of 75 clerks flanked by statisticians, sorters, registrars of correspondence, messengers, and accountants ate up the bulk of the payroll. Those tasked with actually exerting federal power at ports of entry found themselves in the minority: just 5 immigration agents, 7 immigration inspectors, 3 interpreters, and a handful of medical inspectors.[36]

If the Civil Service payrolls even approximated the federal government's commitment to border security, immigration control remained more of a dream than a reality. Faced with chronic shortages of personnel, the Canadian government prioritized gaining control over oceanic travel more than continental movements. The 49th parallel would have to wait. In 1915, the Canadian government stationed men at Montreal and St. John in the East and placed men at Chemainus, Powell River, Union Bay, Vancouver, and Victoria in the west. The number of federal immigration personnel in the interior could be counted on one hand. From the edge of the Great Lakes to the coast of British Columbia, the Commissioner of Immigration John Bruce Walker, his assistant, and their accountant consisted the entire Canadian contingent.[37]

The importance of Canadian immigration agents as recruiters, not simply gatekeepers, helps to explain the geographic and occupational oddity of the department. Canada competed with the United States, Australia, and New Zealand as a potential destination for immigrants. By 1910 it had immigration agents in North America as well as in Belfast, Glasgow, Birmingham, and London. Foreign agents served as proselytizers and travelling salesmen. Canada, they argued, was a much nicer place to live than its bracing winters suggested. Auxiliaries, temporary employees, and civil servants from other areas of government could help Canada police immigration. Still, guards seemed less necessary when recruitment of white residents remained such a focus.[38]

Although small in size, the bureaucracies that controlled immigration in Canada and the United States possessed an uncommon power. The Department of Immigration operated with little oversight, and immigration agents had tremendous latitude in the ways they executed their duties. In 1893 the US Supreme Court ruled that administrative agencies, not the courts, had full domain over deportations. By drawing a distinction between criminal proceedings and deportations—both of which included arrests, trials, and punishments—the courts removed common protections from those held by the state. Presumed innocence? Gone. Judicial regulations for a fair trial? Not applicable. Canada followed the United States' example. In doing so, it distinguished itself with respect to deportations from much of the rest of the British world.[39]

As the courts stepped back, the immigration systems in both countries entrenched creativity and brazen dishonesty as core components of immigration regulation. Federal employees twisted words and fabricated statistics. They invented charges and detained people illegally. By 1919, Canadian immigration agents had found ways to strip immigrants of their naturalized citizenship as a precursor for their later deportations.[40] In the United States, the limited time allocated to each inspection encouraged questionable shortcuts. At Ellis Island, for example, a physician used the luster of women's hair to justify holding them for later inspection, believing that a dullness offered evidence of an otherwise undetectable pregnancy.[41]

In theory at least, immigration agents in both countries had a mandate to apply the laws that best applied to the cases in front of them. Reality painted a bleaker picture. Immigration agents often chose their desired outcome first and then applied, from a wide selection, the legal policy that they believed would achieve that end with as little effort as possible. Subjective interpretations flourished.

In an environment that privileged expediency, moralizing, and creative applications of policies, dishonest bookkeeping held a seductive appeal. Between 1926 and 1931, Canada deported 528 British women who had entered the country under the Empire Settlement Aftercare program for becoming a public charge. Of these, unemployment or medical conditions accounted for only half (247) of the justifications. Having an illegitimate child, poor conduct, and cohabitating while unmarried provided the justification for 244 of the remaining cases. Bureaucratic categories like "being at risk of public charge" stretched beyond recognition, but the administrators went even further.[42] As historian Barbara Roberts has noted, "immigrants who had been assured that they would be deported were asked if they looked forward to seeing their families and friends; if they agreed, the response was counted as a request to be deported or a desire to go home."[43]

Deceit occurred at all levels. Like most good bosses, the Canadian Minister of Immigration made a point of leading by example. Wesley Gordon, for instance, refused to abide by clear orders made by the Department of Justice that he review all deportation cases personally as required by law.[44] For men like Gordon conflict with the Department of Justice served as a reminder of the value of discretion, not a signal for the need for reform.[45]

The real power of these agencies, however, came from retroactive punishments and predictive approaches to policing. Older policies had assessed an immigrant's suitability at the moment of entry. Single women, Asian men, and labor agitators all received additional scrutiny. They paid for their breach of expectation with time, cost, and humiliation.[46] After 1906, Canada allowed for the deportation of individuals within two years of their arrival; by 1910 that had increased to three.[47] By the end of World War I, the United States had expanded the period of deportation to three years after arrival for "likely public charge" cases and removed the statute of limitations on other deportable offenses.[48]

Immigrants, living deep in the interior of each nation, could no longer shed the gaze of the federal state. They had crossed the border, but the border followed them home. When the power of the state remained small, that was a manageable inconvenience. As it grew, that imposition became harder to shake off.[49] Immigration agencies had sloughed off judicial oversight and expanded their control in hundreds of creative ways. Still, a lack of personnel remained at the heart of their challenges. Conscription soon provided an answer.

In 1893 and 1894, the United States brokered agreements with the Canadian government as well as Canadian railway and steamship companies. Under the agreements, transportation companies would help funnel immigrants into designated areas.[50] Under the arrangements, Canada allowed the United States to station immigration inspectors at Canadian ports in order to minimize the potential back doors into the United States. Both countries forced transportation companies to assist by using the threat of crippling delays at the border to force compliance.[51]

The genius of the agreements lay in their audacity and simplicity. In a practical sense, the policies shortened the border and changed its shape. Immigration agents did not need to guard every inch of the border so long as they controlled all of the avenues of entry. By 1911, the Canadian Pacific Railway funneled Chinese immigrants to Vancouver for processing. The company bore the cost of the detention as well as some of the expenses that immigration agents paid as part of their daily jobs. For overseas migrants, the border appeared first as a series of discrete dots—port cities—long before it appeared as a continuous line.[52]

Outsourcing immigration control to transportation companies had a distinctive American flair to it. It also came at a cost. Short on detention space, the Canadian Pacific Railway company detained Chinese migrants in common jails while they awaited decisions in their cases. Their only crime was a desire to enter the United States.[53]

Immigration policy, at the turn of the century, failed to achieve many of its lofty goals. Immigrants declared Canada as their final destination and continued to test interior ports of entry where the Bureau of Immigration lacked sufficient personnel. This was easy across the interior of the continent, where monitoring of even the simplest of border crossings remained difficult.[54]

Nor was Canada the only gateway to the United States. Mexico did not exclude Chinese immigrants and opposed American involvement in its national affairs. American officials in the south responded with patrols, raids, and deportation to combat Chinese immigration.[55] Local practices continued to differ from official policy. Mexican officials, much like Canadian ones, allowed US inspectors to travel across the line. Neighboring administrators and men of the law created informal agreements when formal ones failed to manifest.[56]

The results, much like those in the north, however, were humbling. The Mexican government estimated one to two thousand Chinese laborers crossed the border each year, a paltry amount compared to the 1.4 million Mexican citizens who entered the United States between 1900 and 1930. The exact numbers were anyone's guess. Without any real way to assess race, Chinese migrants passed for Indigenous and Mexican in order to avoid additional scrutiny.[57]

Soldiers and NWMP

If customs and immigration officials struggled under the complexity of border control, the simultaneous efforts of a diverse bureaucratic cast did little to simplify their problems. Customs and immigration focused exclusively on border control. For many other federal agencies—the War Department, North-West Mounted Police, Department of Marine and Fisheries, and Indian Affairs—border control was a byproduct of a broader set of mandates. Asked to monitor and control a complicated situation, these agencies found that their duties overlapped. The results created a decentralized, uneven, and amorphous border that even seasoned administrators struggled to comprehend.

From the very beginning, soldiers and naval vessels had served as an early nucleus of national authority. Military men claimed territory, surveyed borders, and expelled those they believed did not belong. Throughout the late nineteenth century, the United States kept regular troops to a bare minimum. The 30,000 soldiers of the standing American military exceeded what Canada could field, but was tiny compared to Germany's half-million men at arms.[58] Voluntary militia expanded the military presence of the United States, but the government reported that it often acted "without the authority or assent of the general government, and even in opposition to the wishes of its officers."[59] By the 1860s, auditors within the Department of Treasury had already expressed doubts about the functionality of a system in which the national treasury had become an "involuntary debtor" who ultimately paid the bill for actions it neither authorized nor desired.[60]

Regular troops inspired little more confidence. Like volunteers, they disobeyed orders and picked fights with officers. When Sergeant Edward Allebaugh ordered Private Porter E. Laflan to change his position in the squad room, Laflan responded that the officer should "come outside and fight, no God damned Son of a bitch with narrow strips I'm afraid of."[61] Laflan received two months' hard labor and a twenty-dollar fine. Fines, imprisonments, hard labor, and even threats of execution, however, did little to dissuade these kinds of behaviors.[62]

They did little to curb theft or desertion either. For deserters, Indigenous territory offered opportunities to evade capture in much the same ways that international borders did. Neither boundary provided perfect protection, but as both oral histories and federal documents attest, Indigenous lands continued to enable men to go beyond the immediate reach of either governments. Andrew Gordon of the Qu'Appelle agency, for example, noted that his father Jordan had deserted the United States cavalry and fled north, where he married a Saulteaux woman. Although the anthropologist taking down Gordon's family history recorded few details about the desertion, Gordon's own economic success suggested the long-term viability of his father's decision. Asked to guard the edges of power, soldiers often took the opportunity to exploit those limits rather than remedy them.[63]

Across nineteenth century, the United States used its soldiers to control the boundaries between settlers and Indigenous communities more often than the borders between nation-states. A frontier line did not stretch north to south and federal authority did not simply increase over time. In the west, soldiers dotted the landscape, more like clumps of oil suspended in water than an unbreakable or surging force. Garrisons amalgamated, broke apart, and relocated. Soldiers provided each government with vision but their sight did not expand in all directions. It latched onto pre-existing boundaries and cast shadows as it went. If maps like these clarify crude patterns of power, they obscure day-to-day life and instances of illness, absence, and extended patrols, which took soldiers away for long periods. In that sense, they show where soldiers received their pay better than they illustrate the practical control of either government maintained.

Between 1870 and 1896, the United States stationed between a fifth and a third of its soldiers within 200 kilometers of its borders with either Canada or Mexico. From the perspective of boots on the ground, the nation invested only slightly more in the south than it did in the north. Of the soldiers it stationed within 200 kilometers of either border, 55 percent (3,236) remained near Mexico, while 45 percent (2,650) resided near Canada. In practice, however, the approach created vastly different outcomes. Those in the north guarded a border twice as long as those in the south.[64] Nor did patterns stay the same over time. Texas, which fielded an impressive military in the 1870s, saw its federal troops decline over time. New York lost soldiers throughout the 1870s, only to see them rebound in the 1890s.[65]

Shifting territorial boundaries, patterns of deployment, legal developments, and the practical decisions of Indigenous communities further muddled the simple picture provided by troop deployment maps. In 1878 the United States signed the Posse Comitatus Act, which prevented the American military from enforcing civilian laws except "under such circumstances as such employment of said force may be expressly authorized by the Constitution or by Act of

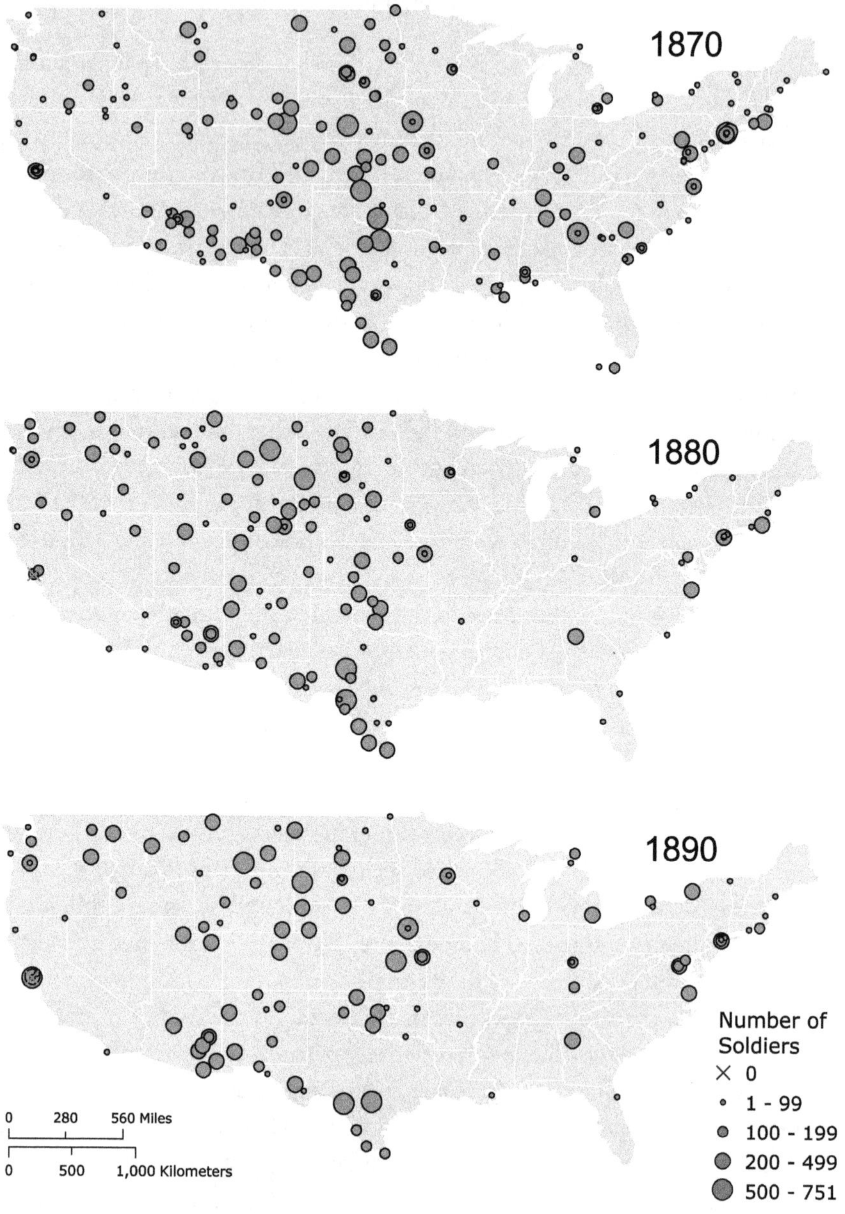

Figure 7.3 US Soldiers and Commissioned Officers Present at Post, 1870–1890. United States, Secretary of War, *Annual Report of the Secretary of War for the Year 1880*, Vol. 1 (Washington, DC: Government Printing Office, 1880), 10–23; United States, Secretary of War, *Annual Report of the Secretary of War Being Part of the Message and Documents Communicated to the Two Houses of Congress at the Beginning of the Third Session of the Forty-First Congress, Volume 1* (Washington, DC: Government Printing Office, 1870), 66–87; "The Executive Documents of the House of Representatives for the Second Session of the Fifty-First Congress, 1890–1891," H.R. Doc. No. 445, 51st Cong., 2d Sess., 1891, 70–83. The digitized datasets used to create these maps are available at www.buildingborders.com and http://hdl.handle.net/10388/12153. GIS territorial boundary dataset: Manson, Steven, Jonathan Schroeder, David Van Riper, and Tracy Kugler. *IPUMS National Historical Geographic Information System: Version 15.0 [Dataset]*. Minneapolis, MN: IPUMS, 2020. http://doi.org/10.18128/D050.V15.0.

Congress."[66] Civilian organizations, like customs and immigration, ascended. The military, it seemed, should fall away.

In reality, race-based policies created an uneven border. After the 1870s, soldiers became a less common participant in the policing of transnational smuggling operations among settler communities. For Indigenous people, however, the changes made little difference. Soldiers detained and evicted Lakota, Métis, and Cree (Nêhiyawak) found on the wrong side of the line into the 1890s. Indian policy ensured the military never fully abandoned its connection to border control. They maintained one border for Indigenous people and a separate border for everyone else.[67]

While tiny in comparison to the American army, the North-West Mounted Police served many of the same functions that American soldiers fulfilled. They captured smugglers and curtailed the mobility of the Cree, Siksikaitsiitapi, Dakota, and Métis. The limited presence of other Canadian agencies on the Prairies meant that the NWMP faced additional pressures on their time. They served as de facto customs agents, police officers, diplomats, and justices of the peace.[68]

The NWMP grew over time, but experienced wide fluctuations in both its numbers and geographic coverage. Numerically, 299 men in 1880 became 1,039 by 1885; 841 men in 1895 became 649 by 1910. Even on a short timescale, visible changes occurred. Between the summer and winter months of 1906 alone, the size of the force fluctuated by as much as 7 percent. The geography of the force's deployment also shifted with the weather. Small summer posts along the border disappeared as the cold winter winds encouraged consolidation.[69]

Maps of federal power often conceal as much as they expose. On the map of NWMP personnel, James Walker, the superintendent of the NWMP at Battleford, appears as a dot with a fixed location. In reality, Walker's duties forced him to travel more than 650 miles in 1879 alone.[70] Rank-and-file constables experienced extensive mobility as well. In 1896, the subdistrict of Estevan possessed only 15 constables and 25 horses. Despite its small size, it still sent out fortnightly patrols along the border near Buffalo Head and daily patrols between Wood End, North Portal, and Souris Valley. Biweekly and triweekly patrols expanded the complicated sets of interconnected movement across the summer months.[71]

For all the ways that annual reports distort the day-to-day allocation of federal personnel, their overall conclusion is clear: the NWMP cared at least as much about controlling movement around Indigenous reserves as they cared about movement across the international line. Like American soldiers, its police found themselves guarding not one border but many. They faced an impossible task of exerting Canadian power while living amidst a sea of nations.

If Canada's vision in the interior of the continent remained spotty, its reach along the Pacific Coast proved no more reassuring. In the middle of the nineteenth century, British gunboats had surveyed coastal waters and protected

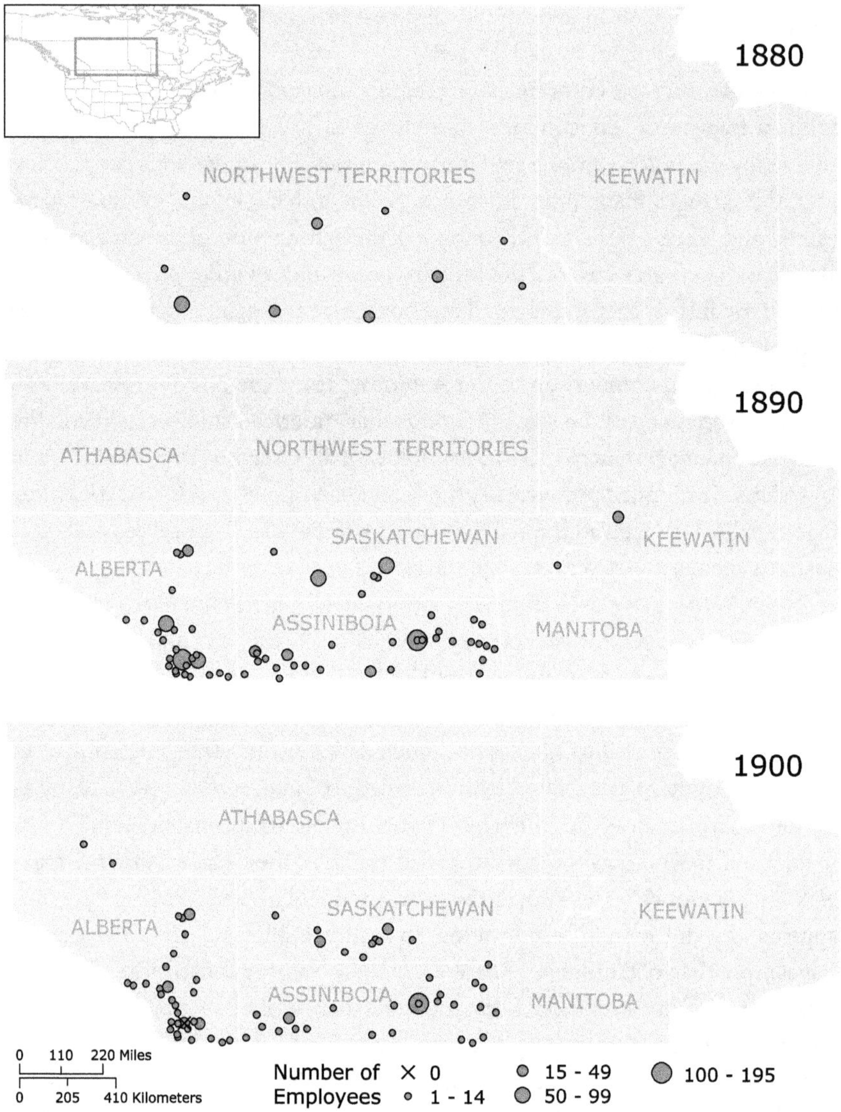

Figure 7.4 North-West Mounted Police Personnel in Alberta, Saskatchewan, and Manitoba as Described in Federal Employment Lists, 1880–1900. Canada, Parliament, "Part II North-West Mounted Police Report Commissioner's Report 1880," in *Sessional Papers, 1880–1881*, Vol. 3, 3rd session of the 4th Parliament (Ottawa: Maclean, Roger, & Co, 1881), 5; Canada, Parliament, *Sessional Papers, 1901*, Paper No 28, Vol. 35, "Report of the North-West Mounted Police, Part II Strength and Distribution of North West Mounted Police, Schedule A, 1901," 3–4; Canada, Parliament, *Sessional Papers, 1891*, "Report of the Commissioner of the North-West Mounted Police Force 1890," Paper No 19, Vol. 15, 1891, Appendix N, 137–38. The digitized datasets used to create these maps are available at www.buildingborders.com and http://hdl.handle.net/10388/12153. GIS territorial boundary datasets: Nicholson, Norman L., Charles F. J. Whebell, Robert Galois, and Michael Stavely. *Territorial Evolution, 1670-2001: Version 1 [Dataset]*, 2020.

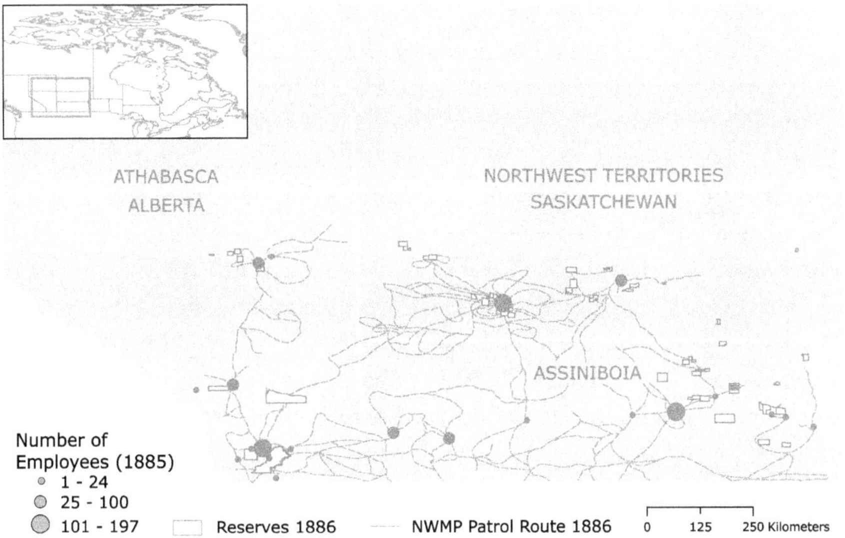

Figure 7.5 NWMP Patrol Routes and Personnel, 1885–86. Department of the Interior and J. Johnston, *Map Shewing Mounted Police Stations & Patrols throughout the North-West Territories during the Year 1886* (Ottawa: Department of the Interior, 1886), Peel's Prairie Province, Map 571, University of Alberta Library, http://peel.library.ualberta.ca/maps/M000571.html?view=big; Canada, Parliament, *Sessional Papers, 1886*, "Report of the Commissioner of the North-West Mounted Police Force 1885," Vol. 6, 4th Session, 5th Parliament, No. 8, 1886, 13. The digitized datasets used to create these maps are available at www.buildingborders.com and http://hdl.handle.net/10388/12153. GIS territorial boundary datasets: Nicholson, Norman L., Charles F. J. Whebell, Robert Galois, and Michael Stavely. *Territorial Evolution, 1670-2001: Version 1 [Dataset]*, 2020.

Canadian commercial and missionary activities. The withdrawal of Royal Naval Vessels from Canada by 1890 created gaps in coastal power that Canada was slow to fill. Power sputtered, retreated, surged, and regrouped. It had a geography as well as an intensity.[72]

Indian Agents

For all the power that soldiers, North-West Mounted Police officers, immigration agents, and customs employees brought to the Canada–US border, they had only limited control over the Indigenous people whose land the border ran through. Faced with frequent confusion, they turned to Indian Affairs to assist in the policing of national spaces. In the nineteenth century, the Department of Indian Affairs (Canada) and Office of Indian Affairs (United States) managed each government's relationships with Indigenous people. Like soldiers and NWMP officers, Indian agents found themselves working primarily in the west. Reconstructing their exact geography, however, remains as much of an art as it does a science.

In 1865, for example, Indian Agent Edwin Clark noted that he returned "from a visit to the Indians of this agency located at Leech lake, Cass lake, Red lake, and Ottertail lake, having travelled a distance of nearly five hundred miles on the round trip."[73] In 1861, Superintendent W. W. Miller noted that Indian agents often resided "in towns from seventy-five to one hundred miles distant from their agencies," leaving their subordinates to execute their duties.[74] When the agents did travel from their homes to the agency, they charged their travelling expenses to the government. In Miller's eyes, such a practice stood "utterly averse to the plainest dictates of duty."[75] He recommended new regulations to curb the practice, while attacking what he saw as an extravagance of expenses at local agencies. With only simple accounts, he could not fathom why Indian agents required dedicated clerks to help them with their paperwork.

Even when Indian agents did their job and remained relatively stationary, mapping the geographic extent of the Department and Office of Indian Affairs remains a struggle. Both organizations had a wide array of employees, making it hard to separate individuals who may have participated in border control efforts from those who did not. Should maps only include the Indian agents, scouts, and Indian police who played key roles in the process, or should they count every school matron, janitor, dining room girl, bridge-builder, and chore boy? All gave the federal government at least some vision, but many individuals who appear on the federal paylists do not seem to have participated in the enforcement of international boundaries.[76]

Like the records themselves, the resulting map is variable, ugly, and crude. It excludes the hundreds of American employees who worked in the Indian school system after 1882 when it became possible to separate them. These people likely played an insignificant role in policing of the international line. In Canada, where the federal records do not allow for easy disaggregation, and in the United States prior to 1882, members of the school system remain. Mix back in the mobility, dereliction of duty, and inconsistent record keeping between countries and across time, and a sense of limitations of the map-making become apparent.

Still, the map holds some value. It shows a heavy focus of Indian Affairs agents in key locations in both countries. Canada's preference for dozens of tiny reserves is visible, as is the clustering of agents near the border. In the United States, Oklahoma, Washington, South Dakota, Arizona, and Washington, DC loom large, as does the Canada–US border. With so many agents stationed within one hundred miles of the international line, border control became an inevitable part of the duties of Indian agents. The exact way they would participate, however, remained far from uniform.[77]

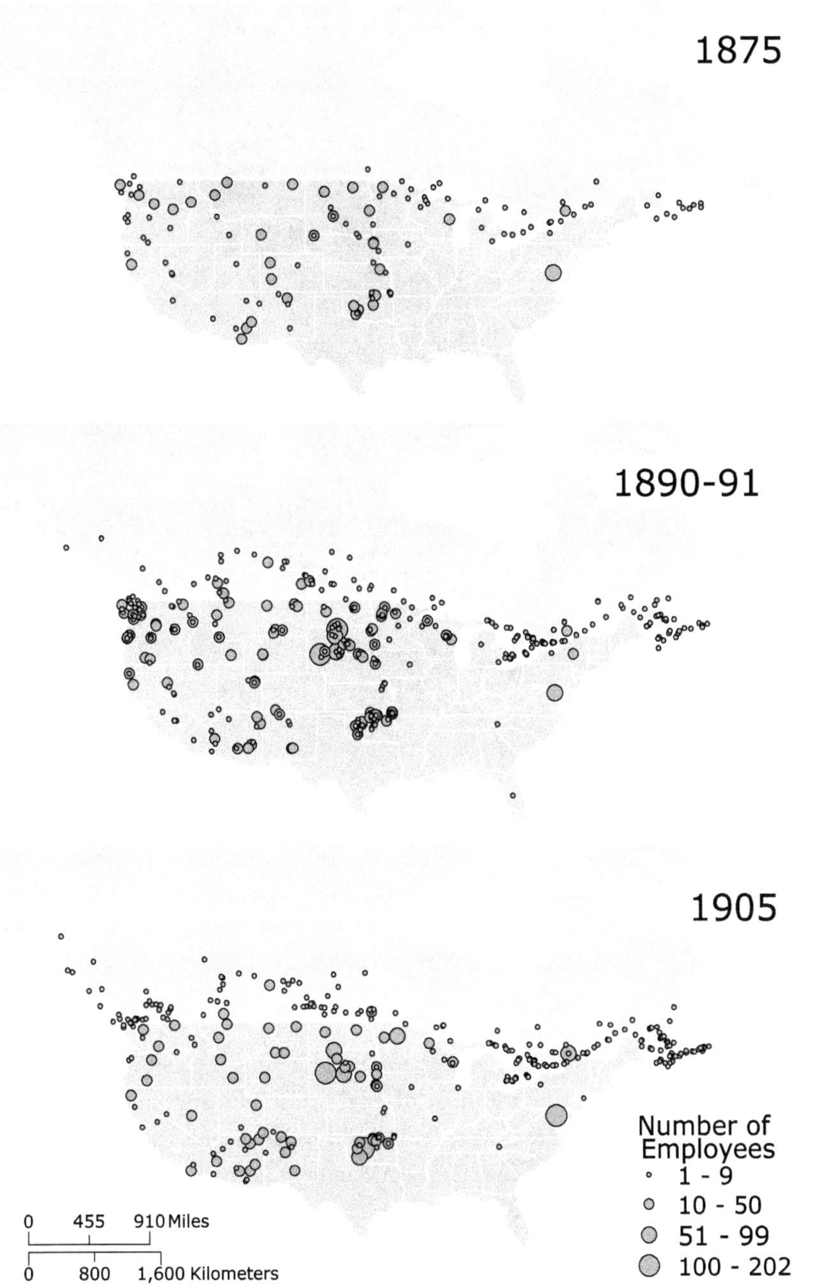

Figure 7.6 Indian Affairs Employees (Excluding School Service in United States), 1875–1905. United States, Department of the Interior, "Register of Officers and Agents, Civil, Military, and Naval, in the Service of the United States, on the Thirtieth September, 1875" (Washington, DC: Government Printing Office, 1876), 358–71; United States, Department of the Interior, "Official Register of the United States, Containing a List of the Officers and Employees in the Civil, Military, and Naval Service on the First of July, 1891 Together with a List of Vessels Belonging to the United States," Vol. 1 (Washington, DC: Government Printing Office, 1892), 697–739. GIS territorial boundary datasets: Manson, Steven, Jonathan Schroeder, David Van Riper, and Tracy Kugler. *IPUMS National Historical Geographic Information System: Version 15.0 [Dataset]*. Minneapolis, MN: IPUMS, 2020. http://doi.org/10.18128/D050.V15.0., and Nicholson, Norman L., Charles F. J. Whebell, Robert Galois, and Michael Stavely. *Territorial Evolution, 1670-2001: Version 1 [Dataset]*, 2020.

Figure 7.7 An overweight Indian agent dressed in fine clothes carries three bags labeled "profits," which are overstuffed with money. Beside him stands a lean Indigenous man who carries a package labeled "starvation rations." The caption reads: "The reason of the Indian outbreak General Miles declares that the Indians are starved into rebellion." *Judge*, December 20, 1890. Library of Congress Prints and Photographs Division, LC-USZC4-4101.

Controlling Indigenous mobility required overcoming the unique legal status of Indigenous people, their knowledge of local landscapes, and their diplomatic and kinship ties. Years of experience had taught Indian agents that power came from dependence. Faced with such an environment, Indian agents turned to a grinding kind of attrition. By controlling food, status, and annuities, they made deprivation and Indigenous suffering the tools with which to remake the geography of the continent.[78]

After the 1885 Resistance, Little Bear and hundreds of his Cree followers fled to the United States. American Indian agents, members of Congress and the general public branded Little Bear's Cree as British Indians who had no rights south of the line. Few considered that the Cree's movements fell within their broader homeland. No one suggested that the Cree, even if British, possessed a right to immigrate.[79] Their status as foreigners in their own lands soon served as a pretext for their removal.

In 1896, American soldiers deported Little Bear, Lucky Man, and more than five hundred individuals believed to be Little Bear's followers from Montana. Within a few years, most had returned. Direct control remained ineffective in the face of persistence. The American government set aside a fifty-six-thousand-acre reservation at Fort Assiniboine in 1916. Little Bear's followers, who had amalgamated with Rocky Boy's Chippewa in their bid to secure recognition in the United States, finally had a permanent home. By that point, the American policy had forced the Cree to endure cold winds, starvation, and dislocation for three decades.[80]

For the Dakota who fled in the opposite direction, the players shifted sides but the story stayed the same. Decades after their relocation from present-day Minnesota to the Canadian prairies in 1862, the Dakota continued to battle the federal government for recognition of their land and treaty rights. If the Cree and Dakota felt this kind of coercion the hardest, they certainly were not alone.[81] Status and recognition marked a form of belonging, but they also served as cudgels to punish undesired activities.

Following the 1885 Resistance, Canada supplemented their broader system of denial and deprivation with a pass system designed to restrict the movements of individual people. With passes required to hunt and to visit family, the system added hassle and risk to trips that years earlier had occurred without issue.[82] The Cree, Dakota, and Siksikaitsiitapi who found themselves living their lives under this form of surveillance did not measure the border in kilometers or dollars. They measured it in missed opportunities, loneliness, disrespect, and frustration. Antoine Lonesinger recounted that the local Indian agent refused to grant his father a permit for travel to Blackfoot country in 1899 to purchase much needed horses. Robert Goodvoice, a Wahpeton Dakota elder, blamed the pass system for interfering with the Dakota's attempts to visit Ottawa.[83]

Those caught defying the pass system faced jail time and humiliation. Elderly men received no more sympathy than young ones. When Yellow Boy and Yellow Feather violated the pass system to visit their family, they found themselves imprisoned on cold cell floors without blankets. Discomfort and disrespect served as subtler tools than fines and jail time. In both cases, the punishments left their marks on whole communities rather than merely the minds and bodies of individuals.[84]

By 1911, the Department of Indian Affairs had expanded the pass system to monitor transnational movements in a more comprehensive way. Indigenous people wishing to cross the border would have to apply to Canadian Superintendents located near the boundary line before entering the United States. American Indian agents for their part agreed to do all within their power to turn "back all visitors not provided with [Canadian] passes and [to use] any other available means to effect the desired ends."[85]

The policy focused on controlling the desired outcome instead of policing the border in its abstract sense. Neither government could stop Ojibwe travelers from Canada from crossing the border on their way to visit friends and family at Leech Lake, Minnesota. The Ojibwe knew the watersheds better than federal agents did. Instead of fighting a losing battle, Indian agents in both countries used food and family to shift the battlegrounds from the international border to the reserve and reservations, where they were far more equipped to fight.

Over the proceeding century, military defeats, declining options for subsistence, and demographic upheavals caused by disease and immigration had created continent-wide changes that had entrenched reservations and reserves as a basic building block of Indigenous life. For those living on reservations, Indian agents wielded a kind of coercive power that few other federal agents possessed. In Minnesota, Indian agents at Leech Lake denied employment, rations, and supplies to Ojibwe men and women who painted their faces, participated in ceremonies, or resisted the whims of the federal government. Indian agents could not force adults to adopt a western cosmology in their hearts, but they starved out those who publicly rejected it.[86]

The international pass system drew on this powerful network of coercion, reservations, and surveillance, but like most federal enterprises never worked exactly as planned. Superintendents sometimes received information about sanctioned travel after the trip had concluded, making the logistics of the entire system difficult to map onto the real world. Still, Indian agents wielded significant power. They deprived those who lived outside of the reservation system or who travelled without permission of food and annuities. They evicted undesired visitors and intervened on behalf of their counterparts on the other side of the border. The system did not need to be perfect in order to have real impacts on the lives of Indigenous communities who lived near the border. By increasing the risks of mobility and constricting its advantages, the approach gave both governments an expansive source of indirect power.[87]

Auxiliaries

Throughout the late nineteenth century, Canada and the United States expanded existing federal agencies and created new ones in an attempt gain control at the edges of their nations. The enormity of the task, limited personnel, and a desire for limited expenditures encouraged both governments to supplement their permanent personnel with auxiliaries. Transportation companies, local sheriffs, and provincial police officers all found themselves enlisted. Still short staffed, both countries outsourced border control to the broader public and to private organizations. Enlisting members of the public to act as spies and temporary inspectors increased the democracy of border control and reduced its costs. Opportunistic informants allowed federal agencies to draw on hundreds of sets of eyes along the border, which they only paid for when they yielded results.[88]

In 1886, for example, E. Ornom, a well-known smuggler, crossed the border into Canada with one hundred gallons of liquor. During his trip two of his horses could not continue. Ornom stashed the liquor and went to buy two fresh horses from the Kainah (Blood) who had camped nearby. Lacking cash, he offered liquor instead. The Kainah turned Ornom in, receiving half of the $300 fine he received.[89] In other instances, individuals like Indian Quilt received as much as $200 for assisting British Columbia's Provincial Police with the capture and conviction of Indian Emia. Informants, both Indigenous and settler, expected remuneration for the information they provided. Often this amounted to little more than what was necessary to cover their lost wages and expenses, but it could amount to significant windfalls.[90]

By relying on public support—compensated with rewards or short-term employment—Canada and the United States committed to a kind of border security that gave some power back to local communities. Indigenous nations supported these kinds of policies when it served their interests and undermined them when they did not. In the south, Apache Kid helped the United States track Geronimo and Apache (Nadiisha-dena) raiders, only to participate in the same kinds of transnational raids he had just helped the United States punish.[91] In the north, Indigenous scouts tracked belligerents who tried to flee across the border and soldiers who deserted their posts. Kainah, Métis, and Sioux men gathered animals on the wrong side of the border and worked as de facto border guards.[92]

While this system worked well when parts of the local community supported federal policies, it floundered when either government attempted to implement an unpopular idea. The NWMP complained that almost everyone in Saskatchewan knew how, when, and where smugglers brought wheat across the border. Still, the police could do little to destroy the practice because no one volunteered information.[93] Smuggling might be illegal, but for most people, it was "a venal offence."[94]

Mobilizing the public carried limitations, but it also came with a more explicit dark side. Both a lack and an excess of public support created problems. The same conditions that prompted federal agents to rely on auxiliaries also encouraged vigilantes and local police officers to take matters into their own hands. Canada and the United States conceptualized border control as a federal enterprise, but it remained local in its implementation. Homegrown agreements, abductions, and extralegal prisoner exchanges flourished along the border.[95]

The combination of the public's unreliability, jurisdictional headaches, and the cost of professional administrators ensured that private security forces maintained a significant place in border control efforts early on. In Canada, the Pinkerton National Detective Agency helped to expand the policing capacity of provinces like British Columbia, where bureaucratic capacity lagged. In the United States, where no national system of law enforcement existed, the Pinkertons found their niche across fragmented agencies. In either case, the Pinkerton's power came from the scale of their operations. By the 1880s the Pinkertons boasted a daily force of 2,000 men, with tens of thousands more in reserve. Even if those numbers are inflated, the Pinkertons possessed a better-resourced agency than most police departments.[96]

The Pinkerton Agency added its greatest value to each government during transborder affairs. Until the creation of the Federal Bureau of Investigation in 1908, neither country possessed any reliable means to capture criminals found in foreign lands. As a private agency, the Pinkertons could span the border in a way that no national agency could.[97] Government personnel drew diplomatic concerns as they moved across nations. When the Pinkertons crossed, they drew only salaries. US Marshals captured fugitives in foreign lands, but confined most of their efforts to borderland regions. The Pinkertons captured criminals across much the world.[98]

The mercenary nature of private detective agencies offered many boons, but created difficult questions about loyalty. In 1897, the Canadian government hired the Pinkerton agency to gather evidence against the United States after it seized Canadian sealing vessels in the Behring Strait. By the turn of the century, Britain, Canada, and the United States had accepted a blurring of allegiances. Still, the case laid bare the unease that came with borderland policing. An American company collected information for a foreign power for use against the United States. In other contexts, such work bordered on treason.[99]

***

Canada and the United States had set out to centralize border control in federal hands, but soon discovered that such a project required frequent concessions. Auxiliaries and members of the public supported more than a dozen federal agencies in giving the border its heft. The result was an awkward bureaucratic homunculus. Limbs spilled out in all directions as jurisdictions overlapped. The creature tangled on itself, but still managed to produce considerable force.

The growth of federal border control throughout the late nineteenth and early twentieth century created a decentralized and uneven kind of authority. Region dictated how many personnel each government had on hand as well as the mandates such personnel fulfilled. Customs and immigration focused their efforts on the coasts and in areas of heavy settlement. Military, NWMP, and Indian Affairs operated mostly in the interior. This variation ensured that the border never manifested itself the same way twice. Cross in a different place, encounter a different administrator, or possess a different set of characteristics, and the border crosser faced a different experience. Season and geography mattered. So too did race, gender, class, and nationality. The border was a kaleidoscope of control—a wall with many heights.

To add to the complexity, federal administrators guarded not one border but many. Cartographers ensured that the borders with Mexico and Canada appeared as clean lines on colonial maps. The borders between colonial powers and Indigenous nations never got such professional treatment. Instead, they appeared in oral histories, cultural ceremonies, and in lived practice. They appeared in patrol routes, frustrated letters back to Ottawa and Washington, and the placement of personnel. Measured in those ways, Indigenous border remained a far more persistent form of territoriality than either government cared to admit.

By pulling federal personnel in specific ways, settler–Indigenous borders changed the experiences of everyone living near international lines—native and newcomer alike. Canada and the United States had set out to build borders on Indigenous lands and erase the boundaries that already existed. Immigration, disease, and violence undermined Indigenous territorial control and created new possibilities for federal intervention. Bureaucrats entered the breach. Measured per capita, twice as many administrators filled the ranks of the US government in 1891 as they had thirty years earlier. Big government and federal control had become part of American life, especially in the West.[100]

As civil servants came to control the border, they shifted both its purpose and its dimension. Immigration officers expressed their desire to force criminals to escape prosecution on a day-to-day basis, rather than only at the moment of crossing. There would be no "haven of rest."[101] Breaking smuggling rings required a focus "in the interior as well as on the boundaries."[102] In adopting this approach, Immigration and customs officials aimed to make the border everywhere. By extending their jurisdiction into the center of each country, civil servants gave up on the idea that the border would ever be a wall. Instead, it would operate as a specter of fear that hovered across the entire country. The approach created everyday power. It also created problems. There was, after all, a certain chaos to control.

8

The Chaos of Control

If the American Secretary of the Treasury was taken at his word in 1885, Customs laws were "a chaos rather than a system."[1] By 1875, customs inspectors had to navigate thirteen tariff schedules covering more than 3,000 different kinds of articles when separating what required a duty from what did not.[2] Policies that worked fine in isolation had become an unmanageable tangle when considered collectively. With 260 acts of Congress pertaining to customs stitched together over ninety years, not much else could be expected. Merchants sometimes paid a percentage of a good's value and in other cases paid based on quantity or weight. Hybrids assessments complicated a system that was already more thorn than fruit.[3]

Border control, for all the resources poured into it, was never an easy endeavor. The length of the border, ambiguity of nationality, and need for transnational cooperation posed fundamental challenges that did not dissipate over time. Mix in an unhappy and overextended workforce. Add a heaping serving of bureaucratic complexity, a pinch of noncompliance, and a handful of irregularity, and the resulting powder keg of frustration was best measured at a distance.

For all the difficulty that swirled around border enforcement, the borderlands did not possess a monopoly on lawlessness or administrative bungling. Those were features common across North America. The border simply incubated these challenges in different ways. It gave them a new expression. Transposed to the edges of the nation, common challenges became international dilemmas. Common solutions became unworkable disasters. Pressed with so many persistent issues, Canada and the United States added civil servants. Dozens of them became hundreds, and hundreds soon became thousands. Boots on the ground created new opportunities for control, but no guarantees.

In reality, power and personnel did not exist in a one-to-one relationship. Administrative disorganization mired attempts at cooperation. Poor working conditions bred apathy and neglect. Ottawa and Washington bankrolled the agencies that guarded the international line, but never controlled what happened

A Line of Blood and Dirt. Benjamin Hoy, Oxford University Press (2021). © Oxford University Press.
DOI: 10.1093/oso/9780197528693.003.0009

day to day. Local agents created their own policies and sought their own enrichment. As they did so, they undermined or at least changed the federal project. Simply hiring more people did little to solve these broader structural problems. All the hiring did was ensure that chaos expanded just as rapidly as control.

Even when federal personnel followed the plans laid out by officials in Ottawa and Washington, they faced real logistical challenges. Where was the border? Who had jurisdiction? Which one of a thousand rules applied? The questions defied easy answers, but mattered all the same. In a world filled with ambiguity, individual agents became key arbiters of how the border felt for surrounding communities. Fortunes rested on their decisions. So too did the horrors of dislocation and suffering.

The Troubles of Recruitment

In the late nineteenth century, Canada and the United States invested ever greater amounts into their civil services, creating persistent concerns about recruitment and retention. Unless each government found a consistent way to secure qualified and motivated personnel, their attempts to hire more civil servants risked amplifying old problems rather than resolving them. The problem came from the work itself. For the men who policed the border, day-to-day life consisted of nine part's monotony for every one part of suffering. When the suffering came, it was hard to ignore. Customs agents dealt with verbal and physical abuse from smugglers who berated, intimidated, and shot at them. NWMP officers and American soldiers suffered from nutritional deficiencies, venereal diseases, burns, fractures, and other ailments. They lost fingers and toes to the cold and remained on edge about the dangers created by the elements.[4]

In 1881, deep snows forced Colonel Irvine and his NWMP party to subsist on only tea and tobacco for two straight days before receiving relief. A year later, while a party of NWMP men travelled between Maple Creek and Fort Walsh, one man froze to death on the sleigh, his body still warm when rescuers arrived. Two more died near a coulee they had tried to flee to for warmth. Louis Hagis, a Métis man, survived the ordeal but the deaths of three men exacerbated conditions that had already led to a mutiny.[5]

Annoyances and internal dangers added to the discomforts that soldiers and police officers faced. Rank-and-file soldiers entered the American military poor and left in the same condition. They ate rancid food and lived in uncomfortable housing.[6] Soldiers and police officers found camaraderie in each other's company, but not always safety. In 1882, W. H. Cox reported that many of the old hands in the NWMP feared new recruits more than they did Indigenous people.

The lack of familiarity that recruits had with their weapons ensured "rifles were popping in all directions," creating a very real risk of accidental deaths.[7]

While Constable Murray was laying down in his bed, a recruit got a hold of his pistol and discharged it. When Cox met Murray years later, Murray could "still feel the slug in his back" near his kidneys. It served as a reminder of the dangers of sensitive weapons in untrained hands.[8] American soldiers, notoriously undertrained, provided little better compatriots than the ones Murray had worked with.[9]

The bureaucrats who worked in offices faced less immediate risks, but complained just as often. In 1898 Charles E. Monteith, the US consul at Chatham, Ontario, conveyed his personal humiliation by the threadbare oilcloth rugs, shoddily constructed desks, and worn-down chairs that furnished the consulate at which he worked. He wrote to the Assistant Secretary of State to ask the government to intervene. For as little as a hundred dollars, Monteith believed, the United States could address the situation and replace all of the furniture in question. Montieth's outburst over furnishings, while petty, hit on a common refrain.[10]

Soldiers, border patrols, and customs officers faced frequent humiliation and discouragement. The unpopularity of their positions hung over those who filled them, adding a psychological burden that undermined recruitment and retention.[11] Public disdain forced customs collectors to look beyond their cities of residence when hiring assistants. They hoped the stigma that locals associated with their organization would dissipate with distance.[12]

Recruitment efforts at frontier posts looked no better.[13] While the Customs and Immigration agencies demanded "young, active, strong, and robust men" to work frontier posts, they made concessions based on who applied.[14] In some cases, the residency requirements of work had unexpected implications. Following the Canada Agreement in 1893, the United States stationed immigration agents in Canada. The policy required these men "forego the privileges of citizenship in their own country."[15] Relocation separated them from family and required that they endure "living accommodations unworthy [of] the name."[16] In effect, the very agents who served as the gatekeepers of the United States sometimes had to live beyond the barriers they built and maintained.

The physical and psychological burdens of employment ensured that attempts to amplify federal power sometimes had the opposite effect. Mismanaged personnel drained energy rather than adding to it.[17] In 1875, two Indigenous scouts expressed their dissatisfaction with their feet. Unhappy with their treatment at Fort Yates in the Dakota Territory, they deserted their positions, taking their horses and federal property with them. Lieutenant Colonel W. P. Carlin posted a reward for their capture, but worried their social connections at the Fort Totten Indian Reservation would allow them to disappear. The post had hired the scouts to help amplify the military's presence in the region. Prosecuting their disappearance took the very resources—time, labor, and expertise—that the post had hoped the scouts would contribute.[18]

The disappearance of regular soldiers created the same kinds of concerns. Between 1867 and 1891, a third of the new military recruits in the United States deserted their posts.[19] The regular army could be used as the "iron fist of an armed democracy," but it was also the "American democracy's least democratic place outside of a prison."[20] Given the opportunity, many soldiers chose to leave at the first opportunity.

Stress and insufficient personnel worsened the difficulties already present in recruitment and retention efforts. In Vermont, Collector of Customs William Wells had to maintain a district that shared 100 miles of border with Canada. While this section of frontier was much smaller than other agents had to maintain, Wells had to contend with 52 highways, five railways, and two lakes that provided a bevy of options for smuggling. In 1885, Wells possessed only 53 employees to guard the border around the clock. The duties stretched his men thin, leaving little room for illness or injury.[21]

At busy ports like Detroit an even worse situation existed. Sixty-three customs agents guarded boats that arrived or departed from Canada every five minutes from dawn until midnight. They searched goods and people loaded onto wagons or that crossed the line as part of the thundering array of railway traffic. Asked to work from seven in the morning until after dark, many customs officers expressed discontent.[22]

The frustrations and burnout of employees in the north had direct corollaries in the south. In Corpus Christi, Texas, just two mounted inspectors patrolled sixty to eighty miles of the Rio Grande River. A lack of personnel forced the deputy collector to balance his time between keeping up the clerical records and patrolling the ferry landing near his office. Asked to do double duty, the deputy inspector came up short on both fronts. Local festivals and bullfights in Mexico encouraged large amounts of transnational traffic. Celebrations for the public became moments of dismay for the officers, who in some cases already worked eighty hours or more per week.[23]

The need for transnational cooperation compounded the difficulties already created by insufficient personnel, a demoralized workforce, and an expansive border. In October 1887, the Department of Indian Affairs received word that the United States had sent approximately 180 destitute Cree across the border near Maple Creek. The United States requested that the Canadian government meet them at the line with supplies to escort the Cree back to their respective reserves in Canada.[24] The meeting, however, ran into complications when the US escort refused to wait for the Canadian one. The American contingent took the Cree to the border and set them free. When the Canadian escort arrived, all but thirty-five Cree had disappeared.[25]

Inspector Sanders, with the assistance of some nearby A'aninins (Gros Ventres), succeeded in tracking down seventy-five Cree led by Natoose but to little avail. The Cree refused to listen. Many wished to go to Maple Creek to join Front Man instead of returning to their respective reserves.[26] Sanders pressed the issue, but the Cree had already crossed back into the United States. He resorted to wiring a notice to Lethbridge to arrest any Cree coming from the south or from the east. Beyond that, Sanders had few options. He could not use the Canadian military to force the Cree, once in the United States, to return to Canada. Beseeching the American military for support might prove useful, but had already shown its limitations.[27]

When federal agents managed to monitor and stop unwanted movements across the line, the traffic simply shifted. Smugglers moved their operations as federal agents cracked down on well-travelled smuggling routes. Migrants tested the areas of the border they believed to be the weakest.[28] In 1903, the American Commissioner of Immigration reported that fifty-four aliens had traveled from Europe to Canada. The party soon pushed westward to Winnipeg. The decision required that the group travel more than a thousand kilometers past their intended destination before heading back an equal distance to Caro, Michigan. Two thousand miles of unnecessary travel was a lot to pay for access to a lightly guarded border crossing. Immigration officials stopped this party, but the sophistication and organization with which they moved suggested that this kind of activity had found success before.[29]

The Coordination of Efforts

As both countries invested more resources into monitoring the border, the value of cooperation became harder to ignore. The failed attempt in 1887 to convey the Cree between governments taught a simple lesson, one repeated in hundreds of other settings. Uncoordinated efforts offered slightly better outcomes than no effort at all. In an attempt to build bridges with potential allies, police officers from both countries socialized with one another, volunteered information, and returned stolen property without regard to its origin.[30]

Personal and professional relationships forged a homegrown system of justice, in which prisoner exchanges and extralegal practices could exist in parallel with formal extradition hearings.[31] In 1902 Jerry Murphy, a city detective in Butte, Montana, captured Tom La Mack, a Cree man accused of murder in Canada. Murphy contacted the North West Mounted Police and, with the help of Captain Everts, arranged to transfer La Mack back to Canada for trial. For his services, Murphy received a $200 reward.[32] Police officers in Washington State similarly turned Marion "Peg Leg" Brown over to officers in Victoria so he could stand trial. The police suspected that Brown, a man of mixed Indigenous and black heritage, had shot a police officer in London, Ontario. After arresting wooden-legged tramps across the entire province in search of Michael Twohey's killer, Canadian police turned their attention south of the border. Brown's capture and transfer back to Canada allowed for his execution despite petitions for a commuted sentence.[33]

When local officers could not reach informal exchanges, both states tacitly, and sometimes openly, supported transnational abductions. Hand-slapping kept the illusion of the border in place while allowing the police officers in both countries to extend their reach across national lines. Bradley Miller's compilation of 77 abduction cases along the Canada–US border reveals the underlying support of the practice. Abductors—many of them police officers—faced punishments in only 13 percent of the cases. Despite the irregular ways that the abducted men had crossed the line, the government retained control over those abducted at least 39 percent of the time. Cooperation had a dark side to it. The border encouraged officers of the state to break one country's laws in order to uphold the other's.[34]

For local, provincial, and state police officers who attempted to remain within the laws set out by both countries, divergent record keeping practices proved a constant annoyance. In 1875 Edward Young, the chief of the US Bureau of the Statistics, compared import/export records from Canada and the United States. He soon expressed his frustration. Stuck with legislation dating back to the 1820s, American customs officers found it "impracticable, if not impossible, to obtain full returns of merchandise exported to the provinces of Ontario and Quebec."[35] With counts differing by as much as $15.6 million, Young's frustration seemed warranted. The problems, however, went further.[36]

The need for a cooperative approach to policing went beyond any interest in clarifying statistics, aligning laws, or amplifying enforcement. The very logistics of border control depended on it. American railroads, bull trains, mule teams, and steamships transported NWMP recruits to the Prairies. Fort Benton (Montana) supplied the NWMP with everything from their mail to their Christmas dinner. American infrastructure, in short, underwrote Canada's presence in the west.[37]

The use of American transportation and information networks, while cost effective, created an understandable anxiety. What kind of sovereignty did Canada possess if it required American infrastructure? Would American telegraph operators listen in on private correspondence between Ottawa and its agents in the west? Encrypted telegrams might help, but they offered only a temporary patch for a much larger problem. The completion of the Canadian Pacific Railway in 1885 provided an all-Canadian network of transportation and communication, but no easy answers. American alternatives remained appealing and Canada never fully shook concerns that its power rested at least in part on American approval.[38]

Uncertain Belonging

Building railways, improving working conditions, and finding new ways to co-operate solved some of the immediate problems facing federal agents along the border. Deeper logistical problems, however, remained. Canada and the United States had spent hundreds of thousands of dollars surveying their border and marking on the land. Despite this effort, the border remained surprisingly hard to see.

In 1909, the Secretary of State complained that competing claims over the Pacific islands near the Dixon Entrance risked creating maritime borders that matched awkwardly with those on the land. He feared that he could not "readily conceive the meaning of a 'boundary line' under such conditions."[39] Bad weather, overgrown boundary markers, inaccurate navigation equipment, and heavy seas challenged the ability of fishermen and customs agents alike to determine their nautical positions. These kinds of territorial uncertainties made it difficult to separate those who had lost their way from those who intentionally violated international law.[40]

In 1898, H. O. Knudsen set out from the cannery on West Holm Island after fishing near the Fraser River. Knudsen, an American citizen who resided in New Whatcom, Washington, worked for the British-American Company using a Canadian vessel. Lost in the fog and changing tides, Knudsen's boat drifted into American waters. As dawn broke across the Pacific Ocean, an American revenue boat seized his vessel.[41]

The situation seemed simple. Knudsen was an American citizen found in American waters. The nature of his vessel and his association with a company north of the line, however, put him at risk for seizure. The transgression threatened to cost him dearly. The British-American Company withheld his pay for a season's work while the legal outcome was pending. Knudsen did not claim ignorance of the law, only his own position. He begged the customs agency for leniency.[42]

In other cases, offenders appealed to tradition rather than law or location. Caught harvesting lumber in Canada in 1889, lumbermen from Dakota Territory lobbied their consul for a reprieve. They knew the border existed, but cited their ignorance of its practical importance. To their knowledge no one had enforced the border in that particular area before.[43]

As Knudsen's and the lumberman's petitions suggested, border enforcement required an understanding of history and belonging that went beyond simple geographic position. Scientific instruments provided latitude and longitude, but no means to separate those who belonged—a concept tied up in residency, ownership, allegiance, nationality, livelihood, history, and birthplace—from those that did not. Uncertainty created ample room for dispute and contestation. Ideas about belonging structured livelihoods even as it remained a contested concept.[44]

In 1899, the movement of Sockeye salmon forced both countries to reexamine the fixed ways they approached where the boundary line ran and who belonged on either side. The salmon spent parts of their lives on both sides of the border, and fishermen from both countries depended on the fish for their economic survival. When the salmon failed to cross north of the border in 1899 in the kind of numbers they had in the past, Canadian fisherman went south into American waters to meet them.[45] That year American customs patrols captured at least twenty-one ships from British Columbia, leading the US consul at Victoria to muse "the class of men fishing do not understand or care for [the] boundary line."[46] The actual situation was even more simple. When captured, Peter Peterson justified his work south of the line by noting that the other Canadian vessels he competed with "did not regard [the] boundary line, so I went." American vessels similarly fished "north of the line." For Peterson, who was only midway through his first year in the area, popular practice justified his actions.[47]

Faced with pressure from the British Embassy over the outpouring of seizures, American authorities opted to allow boats from British Columbia to operate just south of the line. They hoped the gesture would prevent a violent confrontation and help align popular understandings of the border with federal patterns of enforcement. Practical considerations overcame abstract ones. The border did not change its position on any map, but for the fisherman that year it moved temporarily south to keep pace with the salmon.[48]

Assigning a single national identity to people created the same problems that came from assigning one to land or animals. Nationality was not a natural part of the human body any more than it was a part of the soil or a school of fish. In place of hard evidence, border guards attempted to read national belonging from the material objects and diction that accompanied human migrants. Dick Kamawo and Joe Wekanay travelled from Wikwemikong (Manitoulin Island) to the United States, where they attempted to blend in without success. Alfred Mishibinijima believed that the immigration officers discovered the men's identity "by their clothes, by the way it was sewn or somehow."[49] That kind of discovery had significant consequences. Kamawo and Wekenay spent a month in jail for the kind of crossing the Anishinaabe had done in the past without hindrance.[50] In most cases, however, neither clothing nor the human body itself gave much away about an individual's national identity.[51]

To make matters worse, policymakers conflated race and nationality in their heads, but not always in their polices. When nationality and race did not align, border guards struggled to rectify the two. Inspector Folger wondered, for example, whether a Chinese person "who has become a naturalized British subject, [should] be admitted to the United States, from a foreign port without a certificate."[52] Others worried about how federal personnel would distinguish a Chinese migrant from a Mongolian one. Agents, often with minimal familiarity with the groups in question, painted racial categories with thick brushes. Chinese Exclusion rested on the ability of federal agents to distinguish the "physical characteristics of the Mongolians" and "different standards of morality . . . their mental acuteness and ingenuity" from those of the Chinese.[53]

Debates about the nationality of Indigenous people remained a particular challenge. George Swanaset possessed family ties that connected him to the Samish, Cowichan, Sumas, Tsawwassen, and settlers along the coast. He was baptized in British Columbia, fished on the Fraser River, enrolled in schools in Washington and British Columbia, and attended weddings with Indigenous and white people from both sides of the line. Although Canada and the United States could stamp a single national identity on men like Swanaset, doing so required ignoring the realities of their life.[54]

The long history of ambiguity along the border, moreover, made future attempts to clarify nationality more difficult. Chief Paw-a-was-aug grew up on Oak Island along the Northwest Angle. During his childhood, the island fell under the claims of the British crown. As British and American officials resurveyed the region, however, they discovered a mistake. The island fell within the boundaries of the United States, not Canada. The shift brought Paw-a-was-aug's status in both countries into question. Unsure of how to handle this situation, the Canadian government left Paw-a-wass-aug to determine his own allegiance.[55]

Members of Paw-a-was-aug's family demonstrated the continued fluidity of the border in their own ways. In 1895, a faction of headmen at Leech Lake sent a request to the Department of Indian Affairs to have Flat Mouth recognized as their head chief. Flat Mouth, the son-in law of Paw-a-was-aug, had lived at Lake of the Woods for the past decade. He had served as a British chief and received annuities from the British government. The petitioners wished to bring him back across the line. In doing so, they ensured that local politics at Leech Lake, Minnesota, extended well past the international line.[56]

Creating a comprehensive system of border control required more than simply laws and government officials to enforce them. A clearly laid out border helped, but remained insufficient. Border control required an accurate system of identification. That system could be etched onto either paper or skin. While branding was possible for livestock, it had substantial limitations. Merchants and farmers altered brands and applied them to cattle they did not own. Furthermore, the brand only distinguished animals up until they arrived in the slaughterhouses.

Once animals were processed, their meat looked identical regardless of their national origin. Seasonal variations in the length of an animal's coat hid brands even on live animals. For nondomesticated animals, such as fish, and for natural resources, such as lumber, branding offered no clear options.[57]

The idea of physically marking nationality on human bodies carried even less appeal in the United States and Canada. The process would have been time consuming and painful. Liberal and natural law opposed the idea on a theoretical level. Even if they had not, both countries' reliance on immigration for their national growth made such a policy counterproductive. If national belonging could change through immigration and naturalization, the system used to track it had to remain dynamic to keep pace.[58]

Unable to mark identities on human and animal bodies, Canada and the United States turned instead of an intricate system of bureaucratic identification. They aimed to make nationality visible on paper in a way it could never be made visible on the body itself. To do so both countries created passports, immigration records, and other systems of paperwork to stabilize identities in ways that could be tracked and recorded. In doing so, they monopolized "the *authority* to restrict movement vis-a-vis other potential claimants, such as private, economic or religious entities."[59] Their implementation of identification lagged well behind their lofty visions, but it represented an attempt to reorder people's relationship to the natural world in a fundamental way. National boundaries, not geographical proximity or physical barriers, would determine the ease of movement.

Even if Canada and the United States had managed to develop a clean method of determining belonging, tracking the movement of people remained a daunting task. Immigration agents distrusted their own estimates. In 1900, the Bureau of Immigration noted that it was "impossible under existing conditions even to approximately estimate" the number of migrants who entered the United States from Canada and Mexico.[60] Incremental improvements did little to change the underlying problem. Of the at least eight million border crossers from Canada in 1909, immigration inspectors examined just over 90,000, many for only short periods of time. Whatever system of identification they employed had to work in a hurried situation and with limited personnel.[61]

Disorganization and Irregularity

Troubles with recruitment, coordination, and belonging created a volatile environment filled with irregularity and uncertainty. The diversity of personnel, which included federal employees, private citizens, local officers, and private detectives, only added to the disorganization. Chaotic and haphazard enforcement reigned even in the east, where the United States stationed the majority of its federal personnel. At least a thousand immigrants who appeared on ship manifests entering New York between April and September of 1890 did not appear in the immigration registry books. Many seem to have just wandered off into the city after their arrival.[62]

The struggle that New York City faced offered a bad omen for the rest of the border. The city possessed 35 percent (1,871 of 5,302) of the Customs Service's employees in 1890. Five years later, the newly formed Bureau of Immigration stationed 60 percent (149 of 249) of its employees at Ellis Island.[63] If New York struggled to control mobility, other posts fell well short of its example.

In 1901, Special Immigration Inspector Robert Watchorn took control of the immigration inspectors who worked the area from Sault Ste. Marie, Michigan to Eastport, Maine. He found little in his jurisdiction to be proud of. Immigration agents, beyond their consistent failure to enforce the full gamut of immigration laws, shared little in common. Each inspector understood and enforced the law differently, creating an uneven and unpredictable border. A migrant debarred by one agent might slip by another one without issue. The United States had expanded its enforcement into Canadian ports following the Canada Agreement, but the push mattered little for immigrants who declared Canada as their final destination and relied on smugglers or guides to get them across the border.[64]

Watchhorn reckoned that more undesirable and diseased immigrants entered the United States through Canada than from all ocean ports combined. He described those who slipped through the net as the most hopeless and forlorn people he had ever encountered. He blamed Canada for the resulting problems. Canada spent hundreds of thousands of dollars encouraging immigration from Europe. It kept the desirable arrivals and pushed the dregs into the United States.[65] For Watchorn, reinforcing the United States' border patrols provided the only answer. As the "contaminated stream" of people pooled north of the line, Canada would become more selective about who it encouraged to make the transatlantic journey.[66] The United States could not force Canada to change its laws, but it could force it to live with those it admitted.

Personal Profit

Men like Watchhorn blamed irregularity and chaos on differences in policy. Others blamed confusion or neglect. Chaos, however, was a lucrative industry and federal personnel stood as much to gain from it as anyone else. When smugglers could not rely on public ambivalence or subterfuge, they employed federal agents to assist them in shepherding goods or people across the line. Participation in these kinds of schemes offered fortunes to the well connected.[67] C. J. Mulkey, a special agent for the Treasury, received an estimated $1,200 a month for participating in a smuggling ring that ferried as many as 1,500 Chinese immigrants from Victoria to Portland before it was shut down. That kind of monthly salary exceeded what average laborers made in three or four years. Even for a well-paid customs agent, such a monthly payment represented the better part of a year's salary. Mulkey received a year in prison and a $5,000 fine for his role in the ring. He was one of fifty-eight eventually indicted.[68]

Federal employees did not have to adopt such a brazen approach in order to see significant windfalls. By classifying goods in specific ways, customs officers and appraisers could save importers vast amounts of money, for which they expected a cut. Charles C. Browne, an examiner for the New York customs office, took part in such an endeavor to undervalue Japanese silk imports worth over a million dollars. Concerns about undervaluation proliferated, forcing the Department of Treasury in 1879 to reappraise 556 cargoes at the Port of New York alone. At stake was millions of dollars.[69]

The brilliance of undervaluation rested in its simplicity. Merchants declared their cargo, and customs officers recorded it. Discretion opened up other avenues for graft. When peas and beans crossed the border, customs inspectors could interpret them as consumables, garden seeds, or nongarden seeds. As consumables, peas and beans received half the duty (10 percent) as those imported as garden seeds (20 percent). When they crossed as nongarden seeds, however, they received no duty at all. Confusion reigned.[70]

Honest appraisers struggled, and dishonest ones grew rich. Did an apron become a luxury good after being hemmed or dyed? If so, did the same occur once a flower was added to a hat? Were olives a form of pickles? At stake were taxes of up to 30 percent. The minutiae of categorization was as boring then as it is now, but there was money to be made in categories just as there was money to be made in confusion.[71]

The perishable nature of food added an additional layer to the reams of contrasting policies that governed the transit of goods. In 1885, M. Seisses of Minneapolis and his partner attempted to import 1,500 pounds of fish from Canada. Whether through a misunderstanding or through an intentional ploy to skip out on duties, the shippers processed the fish mid-journey to prevent them from spoiling. As they salted the fish, however, they transformed the fresh fish, which bore no duty, into a dutiable good. When the fish arrived in Minnesota, the customs inspectors noticed the change and imposed a duty, creating significant concern for the merchants who had not budgeted for the change.[72]

Customs officials made money by breaking the law and by bending it, but also by overenforcing it. Under the moiety system, government officials received half of the penalty assessed on undervalued goods imported into the country. The Collector of Customs at New York might receive between $6,400 and $12,000 in salary throughout the early 1870s, but once fees were included he took home

Figure 8.1 "The Customs-House Code of Morals Under Our Beautiful Tariff System" portrays clergymen, musicians, congressmen, tourists, and doctors slipping bribes to customs agents in a variety of ways. In the final frame, the customs-house inspector returns home "after a hard day's work" carrying a wealth of spoils on his back. A dollar bill tied around his face obscures his vision. *Puck*, October 14, 1885. Library of Congress Prints and Photographs Division, LC-DIG-ppmsca-28135.

UNDER OUR BEAUTIFUL TARIFF SYSTEM.

as much as $50,000 in annual compensation.[73] The Secretary and Solicitor who ruled on disputes between the government and importers expressed apprehension on accepting statements from government employees who had a direct financial interest in securing convictions rather than to fairness or compromise.[74]

When merchants derided the Customs Service "as an agency of personal profit" and a bureaucratic "parasite, unlawfully living upon themselves," they were not wrong, at least not completely.[75] In 1872, the American customs service assessed the Phelps Dodge and Company with a $271,000 penalty for undervaluing a cargo worth $1.75 million by roughly $6,000. The case resulted in the end of the moiety system in 1874 and new provisions. The government thereafter had to prove importers had intentionally defrauded the government before seizing merchandise.[76]

Revenue dropped immediately. The Collector of Customs at New York noted that in 1877 his post only seized $120,131.09 compared to $773,310.09 in 1873. He believed that the removal of many of the inducements to informers and detectives had cost the government millions of dollars in lost revenue.[77] Others in the force echoed the sentiment. For all the good intentions, the end of the moieties system did not end eliminate customs agent's overzealous prosecution or the abuse within the system. Agents simply found other ways to make money.

In states like New York, where as much as two-thirds of the United States' custom business occurred, courts struggled to keep up with the number of cases. As of July 1, 1881, New York courts alone had 2,376 outstanding suits against customs collectors.[78] Courts offered redress to merchants when they could prove overzealous collections, but often only after three or four years of delays. The result created hardship for merchants and embarrassment for the government.[79] The situation did not improve quickly. Five years later, importers still launched more than a thousand suits annually in New York alone against collectors who they believed imposed more than four million dollars in illegal duties. While this was far less than the seven million in claims the previous year, the excess duties claimed still amounted to what the United States appropriated each year for the Indian Service—schools, treaty payments, and salaries included.[80]

Even when customs laws aligned with one another and did not create obvious loopholes, the historic practices at each port created opportunities for abuse. In their roughest form, transit privileges existed to allow merchants from one country to ship goods through another country without paying duties. Grain producers in Manitoba, for example, sent their wheat in sealed cars to Sarnia, Ontario, using American railways to reduce their costs. When the wheat entered the United States, American customs officers kept one copy of the cargo manifest and sent another copy to the port of departure. In theory, these policies minimized the opportunities for anyone to tamper with the cargo while it was en route and ensured that goods that entered the United States duty free actually left the country through the port they were supposed to.[81]

At Duluth, however, local policies created opportunities for merchants to use through traffic regulations in creative ways. As Canadian grain made its way to Duluth, laborers transferred it between railway cars, elevators, and ships. The slow speed at which this transfer occurred and the leniency of the local customs agents allowed Canadian shippers to redirect their goods mid-journey. When merchants learned about this oversight, they exploited it. They stored 150,000 bushels of wheat in Duluth's elevators over the winter and changed the destination of their cargo mid-journey.[82] Goods that should have been treated as imports remained classified as "in-transit."[83] Canadian customs officers, rather than American ones, sealed the bonded elevators. In doing so, they contravened American customs law and limited the vision the American government had of the trade.

The practice lasted for seven years before the Department of the Treasury caught on. By that point, three-quarters of the wheat travelling through Duluth on its way to Canadian destinations was ending up in European markets.[84] Duluth had become a de facto distribution center for Canadian grain. When questioned as to how this practice could have continued for so long, the local inspector stated he had simply continued the practices set by his predecessor.[85]

Irregularities at Duluth extended beyond grain to the handling of the ships themselves. To reduce the imposition on foreign merchants, the Customs Service allowed foreign vessels travelling between Duluth and West Superior to move between the two nearby ports as if they were American vessels. Foreign vessels could pick up and drop off cargo at the adjacent American ports so long as they completed their customs clearance at the first port they entered. The customs collector at Duluth justified the policy as necessary to ensure expediency. The deputy collector at Superior, however, refused to take part.

The disagreement created a bureaucratic nightmare. Vessels granted clearance at Duluth still had to gain clearance at Superior, forcing these ships to enter the United States twice while crossing the border only once.[86] Ghost ships appeared but never arrived. They came but never departed. Merchants found good reason for resentment when forced to navigate divergent sets of policies and regulations that even customs officers could not agree on. The world created in the ledger books of bureaucrats resembled the real world, but never mirrored it exactly.[87]

If customs agents made significant amounts of money navigating this bureaucratic labyrinth, they were not alone. Informal industries grew up to exploit loopholes and confusion. Chinese immigrants hired coaches to get them into the United States. Strangers became family for a price.[88] A federal judged mused that "every Chinese woman who was in the United States twenty-five years ago

Figure 8.2 A political cartoon pokes fun at the breadth of disguises that Chinese migrants used to circumvent the border restrictions. In the various pictures, a Chinese man poses as an anarchist, boat racer, "humble Irishman, "an English wife-hunter," and a "peaceful, law-abiding Sicilian" who brandished both a pistol and knife in hand. The picture's caption reads "How John may dodge the exclusion act." *Puck*, July 12, 1905 Library of Congress Prints and Photographs Division, LC-DIG-ppmsca-25972.

must have had at least 500 children" to make the number of American births before the courts plausible.[89]

Merchants on both sides of the line gained competitive advantages by knowing the rules and exploiting them with precision. In order to avoid paying consul fees, merchants divided their shipments into tiny parcels to stay under a favorable fee structure. In 1880, for example, a merchant sent thirty-nine horses from Fort Erie (Ontario) to Buffalo (New York). Instead of classifying the horses as part of a single shipment, the merchant divided them into thirty unique ones, creating a large amount of additional paperwork. Consular and customs agents corrected these kinds of inconsistencies when they caught them, but the opportunity for this kind of sleight-of-hand revealed the existence of deep structural problems. Dozens of strategies existed that skirted the margins of the laws rather than openly defying them.[90]

***

If Canada and the United States bumbled through border control, the problems were as much with the fabric as with the weaver. Any attempt to impose a binary

(American or Canadian) on a spectrum (lived experience) resulted in rough edges. National belonging came in many forms: birthplace, residence, employment, history, investments, culture, loyalty, and family. When those featured aligned, it made stratifying by nationality simple. When they did not, federal agents deferred to paper identities—passports and other forms of bureaucratic identification—to make sense of a confusing world.

Disconnects between lived experience and paper identities ensured that as state power grew, confusion did too. If the chaos that surrounded control was unavoidable to some extent, neither government did itself any favors. The haphazard sets of rules and the lack of oversight created wide variation in on-the-ground practices. Personal incentives within customs policy only made matters worse. Both countries had set out to create a border that treated potential migrants differently based on their race, gender, and legal status. In reality, hundreds of other factors shaped the border's practical form. Season, port of entry, individual inspector, type of good, and local history all left their mark. Federal maps portrayed the border as an unbroken line, but in reality thousands of overlapping policies and personnel dictated its shape, creating a patchwork from one end of the continent to the other.

9

Higher Than Sight Can Reach

In March of 1903 the *Phoenix Pioneer*, a Canadian newspaper, published an account it hoped would demonstrate the breadth of goodwill that existed between Britain and the United States. An American sailor had landed in Chile and, while horsing around with his friends, got into a fight with a local police officer. After being struck by the officer, the sailor returned in kind. Chilean authorities arrested the American and within a day had sentenced him to death.[1] Pleas by the American consul fell on deaf ears. Fearing the execution would take place, the English consul, with British and American flags in hand, fought his way to the prisoner. He covered the man with both flags yelling, "shoot, if you dare . . . through the heart of England and America." The sailor was spared.[2] Likely apocryphal, the story conveyed real yearnings and expectations. It bore some truth even 10,000 kilometers away.

In 1900, American citizens in British Columbia built a float for Dominion Day. They covered the display with bunting and topped it with two uniformed men, one British and one American. Each carried the flags of his respective country. The men's "right hands were joined" to symbolize the friendship between the nations.[3] The Peace Arch, unveiled two decades later along the border between British Columbia and Washington, echoed a similar sentiment. Canada and the United States shared a common mother and linked destiny. Those perceptions allowed for a cooperative approach to the border not possible between the United States and Mexico.[4]

Brotherhood, however, did not mean an absence of conflict. Four months after the *Phoenix Pioneer* published its story about the sailor in Chile, a more unsettling story emerged in Fernie, British Columbia. Located only 70 kilometers from the border, the town was small but prosperous. It possessed six hotels, two wholesale houses, and residences for three thousand people. The buildings alone were worth more than half a million dollars.[5] In early July, the residents of Fernie awoke to find the flag above the American consulate had been taken down over

A Line of Blood and Dirt. Benjamin Hoy, Oxford University Press (2021). © Oxford University Press.
DOI: 10.1093/oso/9780197528693.003.0010

night. Outraged by the disrespect, the town promised a $500 reward for any information that led to a conviction.[6]

While the citizenry of Fernie worked to bring the unknown assailant to justice, the American consul attempted to bring the matter to a quiet resolution. He wrote to the mayor of the city expressing his hope to have the reward withdrawn. Better to let the police handle the matter, he believed, than to place it in the hands of the broader public.[7] Within a week, the local authorities had captured the assailant. The perpetrator had made little effort hide his intentions. Prior to the flag's disappearance he had "threatened that if nobody else would pull it down he would do so."[8] It seemed he had made good on his promise. The man's status in the community, however, gave pause. He was neither a degenerate nor a criminal. He was a young Canadian policeman who was angry and upset.[9]

As the Fernie flag controversy suggested, national identity along the border remained a complicated matter. International cooperation served as a point of pride for some, but a risk for others. Police officers both supported federal border control efforts and undermined them. In this sense, the twentieth century shared much in common with the century proceeding it. Important changes, however, had occurred. As the consul's comments suggested, federal administrators increasingly attempted to monopolize power and sought to limit the public's input into border control. Piecemeal attempts to expand, centralize, and professionalize border enforcement had born fruit.

By the 1920s, the Canada–US border had reached its adolescence. It possessed much of its adult strength, but it remained clumsy in practice. Both countries had surveyed the last major section of their shared border and used steel and stone to make it visible. Professional administrators exerted power once retained by local communities and military organizations. The gaps in enforcement that had typified nineteenth-century border control efforts began to disappear.[10] Moralizing, whether around liquor, deviancy, sexuality, civility, or race, became bolder and more ambitious. As battles with Indigenous border crossers and rum runners attested, however, ambition and personnel never substituted for the strength offered by popular support or legal clarity. Canada had taken the lessons learned on the Prairies, Great Lakes, and West Coast and applied them across the border's entire length. Only one section of border remained.

The Arctic Survey

In 1896, the discovery of gold in the Yukon encouraged Canada and the United States to survey the last major section of land separating the two countries. The survey was a long time coming. In 1825, the Anglo-Russian treaty established a boundary between Britain and Russia along the Pacific Coast. The division would follow mountain summits and pass no more than ten leagues from the coast. Vague provisions reflected limited knowledge. Diplomats penned agreements over land they could not see and over people they could not control.[11]

The purchase of Alaska by the United States and the expansion of Canada's territorial boundaries changed the players but not the game. "Word for word," Moscow's border with London became the US border with Canada.[12] Each nation agreed to a general set of principles and a common kind of output. The darkness that filled their workspace, however, required trust and faith: trust in one another's workmanship, faith that the descriptions each craftsman gave corresponded to an object each could feel but none could see.[13]

Disputes over furs (1840s), gold (1870s), and fisheries (1880s) prompted correspondence and investigations. The dim light cast by surveyors, astronomers, soldiers, and geologists washed away any kind of optimism. Each country had misjudged the shape of the object it had created. They had woven uncertainty and dispute into the fabric of the treaties themselves. Did inlets count when measuring maritime league or was the general outline of the coast to be measured? What exactly constituted a summit within a broader mountain range?[14]

The Klondike Gold Rush (1896–1898) laid bare the border's uncertainty. In a moment, the rush made the border's arctic path a matter of national significance, while also making it harder to resolve. As tens of thousands of prospectors made their way north, the international line determined the jurisdiction that ships laden with gold, supplies, and people passed through.[15] Facing requests for arbitration, the United States worried that "every foreign nation [was] interested in trading directly with the British gold fields."[16] It believed that desire prejudiced any adjudicator in favor of Britain's claims to the coastal ports.

Britain, Canada, and the United States attempted to resolve the matter internally. The resulting Alaska Boundary Tribunal (1903) ruled for a compromised position. Canadian interpretations of mountain summits held firm. American understandings of inlets and coastal measurements prevailed. The decision cost British Columbia valuable Pacific ports, causing Canadian accusations to run wild. Had Lord Alverstone, the British juror, sold out Canada to improve Anglo-American relations?[17]

For all the controversy that surrounded the tribunal's work, its decision clarified the treaty language enough for a comprehensive survey to take place. Beginning in 1904, the International Boundary Commission sent out surveyors to both mark Alaska's border with Canada and to clarify earlier survey attempts. The process required a common kind of colonial confidence. National borders would need to absorb or erase the older boundaries maintained by the Eyak, Tlingit, and Dene (Athapaskan). Britain, Canada, and the United States bet that by acquiring scientific knowledge of the region they could fix a border born out of ignorance. Like many repairs, it would have been easier to start from scratch.[18]

The process of marking the border in the north, like the surveying operations elsewhere, faced a wide array of problems. Neither government looked forward to surveying a "sea of mountains" buffeted by cold winds and filled with what they believed to be hostile residents.[19] The surveyors would have to overcome an unknown geography in addition to torrential rains, mosquitos, and collapsing glaciers. Unexpected problems soon added to the challenges of the work.[20]

In other regions, surveyors had drawn on Indigenous knowledge and labor during the surveying process. In the north, disease made such a work force unpredictable. An outbreak of smallpox at Rampant House in 1911, for example, deprived commissioners of a much needed labor force. Unable to rely on Indigenous packers and laborers at that location, every member of the survey party, from its officers to cooks, helped unload three hundred tons of freight. The work, while necessary, created bottlenecks in the supply chain. Only a portion of the supplies made it past Rampant House. Boundary survey officers—who were stuck unloading cargo by hand—could not head north to "study the situation for next year," creating further anxiety and delays.[21]

At the same moment that the Boundary Commission worked to bring clarity to the last major divide between Canada and the United States, nations and their borders came into question across the globe. Violence a continent away shifted the relationships in North America. An assassination in Sarajevo sparked a world at war. Domestic dissatisfaction, fueled in part by Britain's betrayal over the Alaska Boundary and the upheavals caused by World War I, pushed Canada further along its long road to independence. Power—measured in dollars, laws, gunboats, and influence—changed hands.

Canada's Long Road to Independence

Canada had begun its path to independence in 1867. Almost a century later, Britain remained in the process of divestment. Britain withdrew its few remaining garrisons at Halifax and Esquimalt in 1906. By 1909, Canada had created its own Department of External Affairs. It signed its first independent treaty in 1923, established independent diplomatic connections with the United States in 1927, and gained legislative independence from Britain in 1931.[22] Canada would declare its 1939 entry into World War II as its own country rather than as a colony and separated its citizenship from Britain in 1947. By that point, the last vestiges of British authority on the continent had all but disappeared.[23]

Economic data provides a different timeline for Britain's retreat from the continent, but emphasize the same overall trend. Between 1886 and 1926, the percentage of Canadian imports (by value) coming from the United States increased from 44 percent to 66 percent, while imports from the United Kingdom fell from 41 percent to 17 percent.[24] Over the span of forty years, Britain ceased to be a dominant source of external goods for Canadian markets. Canada's economic dependence remained; its suppliers simply became more continental.

The movement of laborers reinforced the continental bridges already forming as a result of political and economic developments. As World War I eliminated older streams of overseas immigration, the United States turned to both Mexico and Canada for support. Between 1915 and 1918, Canadians accounted for 31 percent of all immigrants to the United States. Strengthening borders and encouraging mobility were not always opposing activities. Each government coveted the ability to monitor movements, even ones it did not necessarily wish to prohibit. Power included the ability remain idle if one desired.[25]

Shifts in transnational economics, politics, and labor impacted everyday life in complex ways. In 1906, for example, *The Ladysmith Daily Ledger* noted that in Vancouver, British Columbia "at least two-thirds of the silver in circulation" was American.[26] Silver was not necessarily equal either. The *Ledger* complained that "it is a matter of history that some counterfeiters have put more silver into their coin than does the United States Mint, and still they have made money."[27] Everyday Canadians attempting to redeem a foreign currency faced devaluation. Currency had a locality that borders played with in frustrating ways.

As political cartoons at the turn of the century suggested, the relationship between Canada and the United States had long elicited concern. Was Uncle Sam's relationship to Miss Canada a troubled love affair or a form of imperialism? In 1888 *Puck* magazine attempted to visualize the connection. It depicted Uncle Sam, banjo in hand, singing "O come and joine the Federal U. / I'll freeze to you if you'll freeze too / Canada, my Canada!" Miss Canada responds simply, "Not this evening! Some other evening, may be!"[28]

More concerning, however, were images of annexation. In 1897, *Puck* released a cartoon titled "Patient Waiters are no Losers." In the image, Uncle Sam stands next to a basket of apples labeled "Louisiana," "Alaska," "California," "Texas," and "Florida." On the branches above him apples labeled "Canada," "Central America," "Cuba," and Hawaii" remain attached to the tree in various states of ripening. Sam muses "I ain't in a hurry;—it'll drop into my basket when it gets ripe."[29] While few believed economic integration posed any risk to American independence, Canada received no such reassurance. The population disparity between the two countries ensured that integration, in whatever form it took, would occur on American terms.[30] With Britain increasingly out of the picture, the future of the Confederacy never seemed fully secure.

Economic integration, colonial divestment, and administrative reorganization allowed a new kind of border to emerge. Britain's slow withdraw from the

Figure 9.1 Uncle Sam attempts to woe Miss Canada, as an eagle and beaver watch on. "Miss Canada," *Puck*, December 26, 1888. Library of Congress Prints and Photographs Division, LC-USZ62-58804.

continent allowed the two players with the most at stake in creating a lasting border to interact with one another more directly. As that became possible, both countries pushed for a permanent organization that would care for and maintain boundary markers and vistas. In creating the International Boundary Commission, Canada and the United States accepted that borders required constant maintenance and clarification.[31]

Permanent organizations replaced ad hoc arrangements in other ways as well. The Arbitral Tribunal served as the flagship of the new kind of order. Created in August 18, 1910 by Britain, the United States, and Canada, the Arbitral

Figure 9.2 Patient Waiters are No Losers. January 13, 1897. Library of Congress Prints and Photographs Division, LC-USZC4-4133.

Tribunal consisted of a cooperative attempt to resolve the legal disputes created by everyday life along the border.[32] Saddled with a backlog of old cases in North America, the organization ran into problems from the start. Still, the tribunal succeeded in standardizing and centralizing how both countries handled border disputes.

In May of 1914, the tribunal reviewed a collision between the Canadian steamship *Canadienne* and American steamship *Yantic,* which had occurred on October 29, 1897. After reviewing separate investigations made by the Canadian maritime authorities and United States Naval Authorities, it ruled that both ships were at fault and expected to pay "half the loss of the other."[33] The decision demonstrated both the frustrations inherent in border enforcement and the new potentials the tribunal created. The two decades that elapsed between the collision and the tribunal's ruling prevented a full investigation. The witnesses, ship papers, and engineering logs were no longer available for consultation.[34]

For all the problems the tribunal experienced, it provided opportunities for restitution that had not existed previously. The tribunal's mandate included claims related to violence, resource depletion, fisheries, breaches of contract, and the destruction of property, which it ruled on through a mutually agreed upon process.[35] It also provided a venue for handling infractions made by customs, military, or naval personnel of either country.[36] By centralizing this authority into a single organization, Canada and the United States increased the consistency of border resolutions and created a venue for resolving decades-old disputes.

As power shifted hands and Canada and the United States committed to a permanent and professional form of border control, they revived older ideas of surveillance and identification. Following World War I, passports became a permanent part of the American and Canadian government's arsenal to track overseas migrants. As earlier attempts had demonstrated, however, documenting nationality on paper or on flesh contained inherent problems. Like an ill-fitting suit, federal categories created awkward lumps when applied to human models.[37]

Nora Soney, for example, left Squirrel Island in Ontario around the age of eight to attend the Indian industrial boarding school at Mount Pleasant, Michigan because the local Canadian school was too far away. While Soney was in the eighth grade, the American government discovered her Canadian birth and sent Soney, along with four classmates, home. Indigenous parents who lied or did not disclose their families' birthplaces, kept their children enrolled. The reliance of school staff on the truthfulness of the parents' statements underscored the difficulties that federal administrators encountered along the border even into the 1920s. People's skins did not carry the marks of nationality.[38]

Practical considerations ensured that border guards and administrators often made decisions based on incomplete information. In 1929, as many as 4,000 cars crossed the Ambassador Bridge between Detroit and Windsor each hour.[39] Without an administration capable of cataloguing and disseminating minute details about millions of people, federal officials had to make do with a system that valued expediency over accuracy. Pressed for time, the Immigration and Naturalization Service invested in heuristics. Suspicious border guards asked immigrants to recite the alphabet to see how travelers pronounced the letter "z." They used the process to separate those who said "Zed" (the British or Canadian pronunciation) from those who said "Zee" (the American pronunciation). The approach had obvious flaws but gave border guards, who spent only minutes or seconds interacting with those crossing the line, a glimpse of identity.[40]

The Ambitious and Dissatisfied

If the geopolitical and administrative changes of the early twentieth century created a more consistent and professional border administration, they did little to erase the basic problems that vexed both governments. Transiency, racial fears, and ambiguity all left their mark. Close to forty thousand Americans residing in Canada returned to the United States in 1912. Twenty thousand Canadians moved in the opposite direction.[41] The Commissioner General of Immigration believed that this movement "represent the aspirations of the ambitious and dissatisfied."[42] Circular migrations undermined the idea of a national sense of belonging. Transnational identities remained commonplace.

On December 4, 1907, five residents of Blind River, Ontario, attempted to cross into Michigan with the hopes of visiting Sault Ste. Marie for a few hours during their holiday. The party was no stranger to the United States. John Allen was an American citizen, while the remaining members of the party had worked in Michigan during the preceding year.[43] When the five men attempted to cross into the United States, immigration officials waved Allen through but refused entry to the other four men. They suspected James Ryan of being an alien contract laborer and classified the other men as members of a taxable class of immigrants. If they wished to enter, they would have to pay four dollars each and submit to a medical examination. Allen and the rest of the party rejected the conditions and returned to Canada.[44]

In defiance, the five men found a boat on the Canadian side of the border and rowed across the river hoping to avoid the checkpoint altogether. The plan failed. American officers apprehended the party and imprisoned them. Four members of the party posted bonds for their release on the condition they would return to testify in a trial against John Allen. Allen himself remained in prison after his admission that he had led the botched expedition. The four men soon denied Allen's leadership role and began to petition Canadian officials to investigate their case.[45] The case came before Albert Edward Dyment, a Canadian Member of Parliament, who took issue with the treatment of the five men. While penniless immigrants from Michigan flooded into Ontario, the United States had prevented Canadian men of relative wealth from entering the United States. Dyment recommended that Canada appoint two additional officers to guard the Canadian side of the river. If the United States wished to harass travelers Canada could too.[46]

For all the frustrations that remained, the Canada–US border had changed in notable ways between the 1880s and 1930s. Medical tests and literacy exams, while contentious, became more common. Federal personnel proliferated. The American Bureau of Immigration hired female inspectors with skills in foreign languages to travel to distant ports. Once there, they mingled with female passengers and assessed their motives for entry. Border protection had expanded into the interior of each country in the nineteenth century and crossed oceans as well.[47]

Amidst these changes, concerns about sexual morality remained a touchstone of power.[48] Sikh immigrants, who seemed to blur the lines of gender, faced censure. North Americans attacked Sikh women for wearing trousers and sharing lodging spaces with both genders. They condemned Sikh men as sodomites and child molesters. Immigration and miscegenation laws, which prohibited Sikhs from creating permanent families, later justified Sikhs' exclusion from the continent.[49] On a broader scale, diplomats added a host of crimes against the family to extradition agreements. The border no longer offered as clear a refuge for child abandoners and bigamists as it once had.[50]

Battles over women's suffrage and citizenship revealed the complexity of identity and belonging. Federal attempts to subsume a woman's citizenship within her husband's sputtered under sustained resistance from women's organizations, temperance unions, and trade leagues. The 1922 Cable Act separated a wife's citizenship from her husband's. The protections the Cable Act provided, however, only applied to the respectable. Women who married men ineligible for American citizenship still lost their status. The restriction served as a visible sanction against those who married across racial lines.[51]

Residency provisions within the Cable Act added an additional wrinkle. Living abroad with a foreign husband still cost American women their citizenship. The approach had a half a century of history tied up in it. Since the late nineteenth century, Canadian Indian agents had used residency provisions to strip Indigenous men and women of their status. By 1922, American Immigration officers had committed to applying a similar set of principles in their bid to control American women as well.[52]

Racial concerns mixed with gendered ones, adding new legislation and personnel to the boundary line. In 1923 Canada passed a Chinese exclusion act, ending its system of head tax in favor of an outright ban on the immigration of Chinese laborers into the country. In the United States, the National Origins Acts reiterated long-standing restrictions against Asian immigration and created new ones for eastern and southern Europeans. In order to prevent undesirable immigrants from using Canada and Mexico as a back door to the United States, as the Chinese had done after 1882, the National Origins Act was accompanied by one million dollars for personnel and a new organization designed to catch unauthorized travelers.[53]

The Border Patrol, created in 1924, operated along the US borders with Mexico and Canada. By 1930, 805 Border Patrols monitored a line already guarded by immigration officers and customs patrols. Their mandate stretched into the interior. It included anyone who crossed the border, but who had not reached their destination. Just as importantly, the 1924 Act eliminated the statute of limitation for migrants who entered the United States without inspection. Deportation programs expanded rapidly. In 1920 the United States deported 2,762 aliens. Nine years later it deported 38,796.[54]

Deskahah and Diabo

For the Haudenosaunee (Six Nations), the National Origins Acts would been unremarkable had the United States not signed the Indian Citizenship Act that very same year. While the National Origins Act attempted to shore up the US borders against overseas immigration, the Indian Citizenship Act made all "non-citizen Indians born within the territorial limits of the United States . . . citizens."[55] It replaced a jumbled mess. Prior to 1924, a wide array of different processes governed Indigenous people's access to citizenship. Treaty provisions, allotments, fee simple patents, educational provisions, inheritance, military service, marriage, and special acts of Congress all offered viable means.[56] The Indian Citizenship Act centralized the older processes, creating one overarching rule with a far expanded scope.

Ham-fisted and unapologetic, the Indian Citizenship Act drew from the same backhanded benevolence that the United States and Canada had cultivated for years. It aimed to recognize the contributions Indigenous people made during World War I. For the Haudenosaunee, military service represented a renewal of historical alliances, not a bid for inclusion. In that context, the Haudenosaunee viewed the act as an assault on their treaty rights and a form of assimilation.[57]

On their own, neither the Indian Citizenship Act nor the National Origins Act remade the ways Indigenous people crossed the border. Together, however, they created something new. Immigration agents had a long history of stretching policies to their breaking point. In their hands, the two acts interacted in peculiar ways. Under the Indian Citizenship Act, Indigenous people born "within the territorial limits of the United States" qualified for citizenship.[58] Those born in Canada did not. Immigration agents concluded that Indigenous people from Canada were ineligible for citizenship. That meant that under the National Origins Act, they were ineligible for entry. On the surface, it was simple and clean.[59]

Benevolence, unwanted and misguided, had quickly become another tool for federal control. The result ignored more than a century of treaty law and practice. Since the 1880s, Mohawk construction workers from Canada had made their living building bridges in New York, New Jersey, and Pennsylvania. Mohawk churchgoers from St. Regis (New York) crossed the border weekly to attend church services in Canada.[60] The Indian Citizenship Act's intentions came as no surprise to the Haudenosaunee. The Cayuga had been fighting Canada and Britain over similar issues for years.[61]

In 1921, the Six Nations Council sent Deskaheh (Levi General), a Cayuga chief born on the Six Nations Reserve in Garden River (Ontario), to England.[62] Travelling on a Haudenosaunee passport, Deskaheh argued that the Haudenosaunee had a fundamental right to self-governance.[63] They did not want or need enfranchisement within the Canadian system of governance; "we have our own franchises, men, and women, too, and are quite satisfied on that score."[64]

Deskaheh returned to Europe in 1923 to lobby the Haudenosaunee's case before the League of Nations. Prevented from doing so by Britain and Canada, Deskaheh instead spoke in front of thousands of people in Geneva. His access to the centers of power, however, remained limited. Britain and Canada undermined his diplomatic efforts and the long battle for recognition soon took its toll on Deskaheh's well-being. Domestic problems only added to the strain.[65]

In 1925, Deskaheh returned home to find himself in a precarious position. In his absence, the Canadian government had dissolved the Six Nations Council at Grand River and replaced it with an elected council more likely to support the federal government's agenda. The annulment of the council removed the Canadian government's need to recognize Deskaheh's political office, even as the council continued to operate. Deskaheh's personal wealth also came under attack. In his absence, the Brant County Sheriff had attempted to auction off all of his property to pay for a judgment regarding Haudenosaunee lands.[66]

Denied entry to his home, Deskaheh turned to his friends south of the border for support. He found work and lodgings with Clinton Rickard, a Tuscarora, in New York. The combination of two notable activists in a single location worried officials in both countries. Immigration agents prevented visitors, family members, and medicine men from crossing the line to see Deskaheh, hoping that tight border enforcement would limit his influence.[67]

On March 10, 1925, Deskaheh made his last speech. He condemned Canada and the United States for failing to keep treaty promises, false accounting, abusive Indian policy, and an insatiable demand for land. He accused both countries of forming a "silent partnership of policy . . . to dominate every acre of [the Redman's] territory." He chastised them for hiding their imperialism behind the rule of law rather than doing away with the pretenses and "subjugat[ing] us to your will."[68] Deskaheh's speech ended with a plea for the future and a reflection on the past. He hoped the Haudenosaunee would remain together, resist assimilation, and thwart colonial attempts to grant them citizenship. Should they fail to do so, their communities would be torn apart and they would be forced to drift to the cities. The Haudenosaunee would be no more.[69]

At the same moment, he asked Americans and Canadians to reflect upon their own history. If the Haudenosaunee had not helped the British during the Seven Years' War, France would have succeeded in driving the English from the continent. Deskaheh experience in Geneva tempered his optimism. Still, he hoped that his speech and his broader work would one day find those who had not been listening.[70]

Deskaheh died June 27, 1925 of pleurisy and pneumonia. The Garden River and Tuscarora communities viewed his death as an avoidable tragedy. Had federal officials allowed their medicine men to visit him, he may have lived. The crackdown did not end with Deskaheh's death.[71] As the Tuscarora prepared for their annual national picnic in mid-August, Rickard sent another round of complaints to the Department of Labor that immigration officers classified "us Indians as the Yellow race" in order to block their entry into the country.[72]

While Deskaheh had crossed oceans in his fight for Haudenosaunee independence, many of his compatriots turned their attention inward. Prolonged campaigns by Canada and the United States to curtail Indigenous mobility, for example, convinced Clinton Rickard to create the Six Nations Defense League on December 1, 1926. Later expanded into the Indian Defense League of America (IDLA), the organization attempted to foster pan-Indigenous resistance to the new border restrictions. For Rickard, the categories of "Canadian Indians" and "American Indians" made little sense.[73] The IDLA reflected his belief that "all Indians are one people. We were here long before there was any border to make an artificial division of our people."[74]

Even within the Tuscarora community, however, divergent views toward the border created instability and conflict. J. Warren Brayley, president of the Chiefs Council, and Chief Lucius Williams accused Rickard of being a liar and misrepresenting the Tuscarora's interests. Brayley suggested that tighter border controls benefited the Tuscarora and would prevent Indigenous people from Canada from competing with the Tuscarora on the American job market, squatting on the Tuscarora's reservation, and exploiting natural resources south of the line. Brayley advocated for temporary passes and literacy tests. He hoped the United States would limit visits from Canada to only thirty days.[75]

Conflicts over mobility manifested themselves in personal ways. Rickard's son suffered permanent chest and lung damage from schoolyard bullies, who beat him for his father's political stance. Personal mixed with national. National mixed with global. The 1924 acts did not create the problems; they only made them worse.[76]

Deskaheh's attempts to raise awareness for Indigenous sovereignty and Rickard's attempts to foster pan-Indigenous resistance to border laws soon found legal expression. On March 8, 1926 the United States took Paul K. Diabo, a Mohawk ironworker, and his wife Louise Kawennes Nolan into custody for violating American immigration laws. According to the American government, the couple lacked passports, avoided check points, and possessed insufficient financial support to enter the country.[77]

Born in Kahnawake, Quebec, Diabo and Nolan had relocated to the United States after the turn of the century for work. Until their arrest, the couple had travelled regularly between their home in the United States and Kahnawake, where they both had family. During their travel across the border they avoided immigration checkpoints.[78] The United States saw the couple's actions as a violation of federal law. The Diabos saw it as an exercise of their sovereign rights. In June of 1926, the assistant secretary of labor ruled in favor of the Diabos' deportation. The couple, supported by fellow ironworkers, the community at Kahnawake, and the Haudenosaunee community at Grand River, fought the decision. They hired Philadelphia attorneys William N. Nitzberg and Adrian Bonnelly to defend them.[79]

Demonstrating that the Diabos did not fall under public charge provisions required little effort. At the time of Paul Diabo's arrest he worked on the Delaware River Bridge in Pennsylvania where he made seventy dollars a week. The Diabos' challenge to the other two charges required more work.[80] The resulting case, *Diabo v McCandless,* rested on two major questions. First, had the War of 1812 abrogated the provisions of the Jay Treaty that granted Indigenous peoples the rights to cross the border without molestation? Second, should the United States treat Indigenous communities as potential aliens who fell under existing immigration laws or did their unique historical and legal ties to land on both sides of the border require separate provisions?[81]

As the Diabo case unfolded, federal officials considered modifying the immigration acts to soften the hardships it created. The American Senate considered a bill that would ensure "that nothing contained in this [National Origins Act] or any other Act shall be construed to impair the right of American aborigines in crossing the Great Lakes or the waters thereof so heretofore recognized or declared in treaties of the United States."[82] At the same time, Immigration and labor officials encouraged Indigenous migrants to cross the border on temporary permits, a style of movement they argued the National Origins Act did not affect. Encouraging short-term movements helped. It did not eliminate the uncertainty that hung over mobility.[83]

While immigration inspectors waited for the courts to clarify the matter, lawyers, immigration agents, and Indigenous tribes all put forward different interpretations of the act's applicability.[84] William E. Lockner, an attorney from New York, for example, opposed the unrestricted movement of Indigenous people across the border. Lockner believed that there existed "no reason under heaven why these rebellious Six Nations of the Iroquois should not before long be compelled to give up their roving lives and settle down like white people. . . . The time for coddling with them is past."[85] Indigenous people would receive all of the benefits and responsibilities of "civilized" life, against their will if necessary.

Lockner's opposition to an amendment to the Indian Citizenship Act mirrored the kinds of complaints American politicians and Indian agents had made for over a century. Unrestrained mobility prevented assimilation and control. For Lockner, the matter became a simple dichotomy. Support for the Indian Citizenship Act promised to transform Indigenous people from a savage state into cheerful American citizens. A rejection of threatened to confine groups like the Haudenosaunee to five hundred years of coddling, tax exemption, and savagery. They would remain "a thorn in the flesh and a menace to the peace and safety of our people who live roundabout them."[86]

Supporters of Indigenous rights must have found grim humor in the entire affair. The United Stated seemed poised to create a category of "alien" Indians who had no rights to enter the United States. And yet the United States' own claims to the land rested upon treaties signed with those people's ancestors. Could someone become an alien on their traditional lands? Excluding Chinese had required no conceptual gymnastics. Excluding the Haudenosaunee would require an impressive display.

The Diabos and their supporters found success in American courts. District Judge Oliver B. Dickinson ruled that the United States had not extinguished the Haudenosaunee's rights to cross the border. The Immigration Service could not believe the outcome. Surely the rights codified in the Jay Treaty protected only temporary commercial border crossings and did not supersede immigration legislation.[87] Opponents of the court's decision launched an appeal. When that failed, they contended that the case only applied to the Haudenosaunee. If so, that left the border restrictions in place for all other groups. In 1928, Congress ruled that all Canadian-born Indians had a right to cross into the United States. The Immigration Service had lost.[88]

Yet uncertainty remained. With little guidance, federal agents wondered if the provisions that barred the entries of criminals, deviants, public charges, and the diseased also applied to Indigenous migrants.[89] The problems went deeper. While the 1928 Act had clarified the rights of Indigenous people, it did little to clarify who fulfilled that criteria. Did mixed race or nonstatus people count as Indian for the purpose of immigration law? Deportations and control rested on such distinctions. When immigration agents attempted to deport a twenty-year-old woman who cohabitated with a white horse trader, she used her racial identity as a shield. The woman claimed Indigenous heritage. Immigration agents sought support but found little. The Indian Superintendent of the Consolidated Chippewa Agency and the District Director of Immigration ruled that "a person having any Indian blood would be exempt from the restrictions under the Immigration Act."[90]

The joint decision only ruffled feathers. The Superintendent of Indian Affairs at the Turtle Mountain Agency could not hide his displeasure, nor could J. Henry Scattergood, the Assistant Commissioner of Immigration. Scattergood believed that such a policy would "create a refuge in the United States for undesirable Indians, many of whom are not of pure Indian blood."[91] He sent his concerns up the chain of command. Harry Hull, Commissioner General of Immigration in 1925, had previously dealt with tense political situations in his work as an alderman, mayor, postmaster, and Congressman.[92] If the situation that Scattergood sent him demanded nuance, Hull saw it as an opportunity for simplicity and brevity instead. For mixed race individuals, Hull stated, "no particular degree of Indian blood decides the question."[93]

As the complaints and Hull's terse response suggested, the Department of Immigration's defeat over the interpretation of the Indian Citizenship Act narrowed the kinds of direct border-control strategies Canada and the United States could pursue. By that point, however, they had a wealth of indirect approaches to draw from. In Hyde's case he could deprive the woman of her access to those living on the reservation. In other instances, status, rations, marriage, inheritance, and annuities all provided coercive opportunities to punish unwanted movements. With the balance of power on the continent fully in its favor, the United States could adopt a more patient and indirect approach to control.[94]

The decisions around Indigenous citizenship emphasized that for all that had changed, federal power remained inconsistent when applied to everyday life. Federal organizations contradicted and undercut one another. Failure remained an ever-present feeling that grew from the gaps between expectation and reality. Inability created a sense of failure, but as both governments discovered, so too did ambition.

Prohibition and Depression

In 1920, the US Congress began an ambitious campaign to prohibit the manufacturing and sale of alcohol. Optimism in the venture soon faded. Wayne Wheeler, a leader of the Anti-Saloon League, estimated in 1920 that enforcing prohibition would require only five million dollars. Three years later, he increased his estimate twenty-eight million dollars.[95] The failures of prohibition drove home the importance of old lessons. The United States might have emerged as a world power following World War I, but it was unable to implement policies without popular support. In areas of high transnational mobility,

Figure 9.3 A prohibition poster denouncing the social damage caused by saloon owners. A man (labeled "license voter") dangles a young boy over the mouth of a crocodile labeled "Saloon for the Revenue." "He Wants the Revenue—Is the Game Worth the Bait?," American Issue Publishing Company, c. 1915–1919. Library of Congress Prints and Photographs Division, LC-USZ62-118171.

domestic control still required international cooperation. Borders, like dancing, worked far better when all parties agreed on both the style and the steps.

American prohibitionists faced resistance at home and abroad. In Detroit alone, fifty thousand men and women took part in the illegal trade in alcohol, making it a staple of the city's economy, second only to the automotive industry in size. Canada did little to help. Although Ontario prohibited the consumption of alcohol after 1916, it left open both production and exportation.[96] As historian

Holly Karibo notes, the result was that by "1921, 'dry' Ontario had forty-four breweries, a dozen native wine plants, and nine distilleries."[97] Canadian distillers sent large shipments of liquor across the border, where they fetched eight times more than they did north of the line. As with Chinese Exclusion, the Canadian government benefitted from the asymmetry of national spaces. It saw no qualms in collecting an export tax on alcohol it knew full well would end up in the United States.[98]

Controlling alcohol required controlling borders. American attempts to catch smugglers drew from a dedicated unit of prohibition agents as well as from the Coast Guard, customs, and immigration agencies. The US Coast Guard patrolled up to three miles off the coast and by the mid-1920s maintained over three hundred vessels of various sizes. Although the United States seized hundreds of ships, the division of national spaces complicated its efforts. It could not seize British smuggling ships in international waters, so large merchant vessels would anchor three miles (later increased to twelve miles) off the American coast, while smaller boats ferried their illicit cargo to the mainland. This approach kept the bulk of the cargo and the most expensive vessels safe from seizure.[99]

As with previous attempts at a bureaucratic solution to border control, chaos exploded alongside control. The exclusion of prohibition agents from civil service requirements resulted in patronage and graft. According to Peter Andreas, a professor of International Studies, the United States fired "one out of twelve Prohibition agents" between 1920 and 1926 on "corruption-related charges."[100] In Detroit alone, smugglers spent an estimated two million dollars in bribes.[101]

The creation of new infrastructure across the border, such as the Ambassador Bridge between Detroit and Windsor, encouraged far more cross-border traffic than federal officials could hope to monitor. Alcohol moved south, and American citizens moved north in search of it. By 1929, the American tourist trade contributed an estimated $300 million to the Canadian economy, making it twice as lucrative as Canada's worldwide wheat exports. This movement helped balance Canada's trade deficit and served as a reminder of the limits of any form of border control not met with cooperation by both parties. For all its problems, prohibition limped on until the Great Depression sounded its death knell. By that point, the one-time source of pride had become a painful reminder of the limits of federal power.[102]

As the economic future of the continent came into question, interest in increasing border restrictions increased and changed. Prohibition had provided incentives to controlling cross-border trade. The fears it generated, however, paled in comparison to what immigration and economic uncertainty could create. Policy shifted to keep pace. In the early twentieth century, Canadian deportation hovered around 1 or 2 percent. During the Great Depression, "for every 100 immigrants entering . . . between 27 and 36 were officially deported."[103]

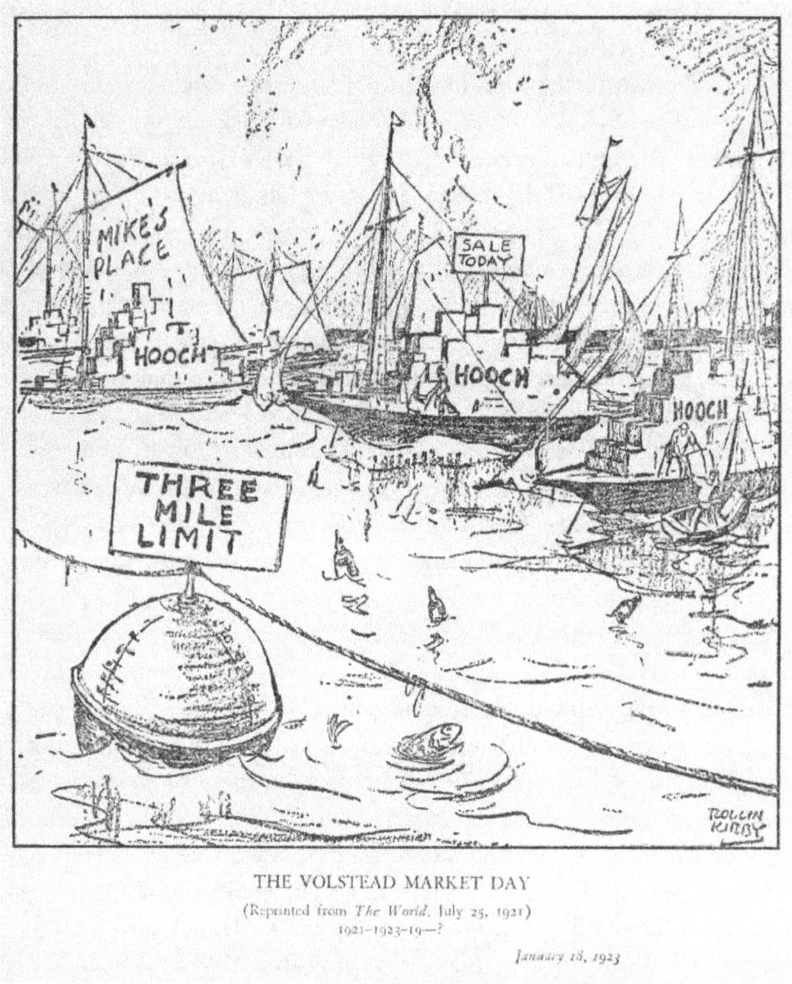

Figure 9.4 Cartoonist Rollin Kirby emphasizes the competition between merchant vessels from Canada and the Bahamas who hovered around the three-mile limit as they peddled alcohol through a fleet of smaller motorboats. "The Volstead Market Day," *The World*, July 25, 1921. From Rollin Kirby, *Highlights: A Cartoon History of the Nineteen Twenties* (New York: William Farquhar Payson, 1931), 30–31. Internet Archive, uploaded by the Whitney Museum of American Art.

At Sault Ste. Marie and Winnipeg, officials required immigrants to sign deportation requests before receiving relief. Mass deportations allowed Canada and the United States to profit off the bodies of immigrants during periods of economic growth, only to discard them when they required economic aid.[104]

Exploiting hunger and suffering offered powerful tools for indirect control. Canada and the United States had learned first-hand the coercive value of food from their treatment of Indigenous people on the Plains. By the twentieth century, they had expanded that policy elsewhere. Neither country needed to monitor the entire border in order to exclude or expel undesired people. During an economic depression, controlling breadlines often worked just as well. The practice required redefining failure. When native-born Canadians lost jobs and required relief, it became a sign of a systemic problem. When immigrants failed, it remained a shortcoming of individual character.

The Width of Borders

On July 11, 1939, the Royal Canadian Mounted Police loaded thirty-two-year-old Myron Bradford Pratt onto a train headed for the United States. Pratt travelled from Saskatoon, Saskatchewan to Quincy, Massachusetts. The 3,500-kilometer journey was continental in dimension. Across a similar distance, a traveler could journey from the heart of Mexico to the doorstep of Canada. For Pratt, such a long journey was between two homes: his wife and children in Saskatoon and his hometown and new residence in Quincy. He left behind his twenty-six-year-old wife, Ada Pratt, and his two Canadian-born children.[105]

It was the second time Canadian officials had deported Pratt. In 1931, he had volunteered to be deported. He hoped such action would let him to find work as a carpenter in the United States. He soon found out that such an approach had unexpected complications. His wife, a Canadian citizen, could not enter the United States without a visible means of support. He scrambled to stay the proceedings but failed.[106] Myron Pratt's deportation back to the United States in 1931 created significant emotional strain. His wife gave birth in Canada during his absence, but the infant became ill and died before Pratt ever set eyes on it. The baby's death prompted Pratt's return to Canada.[107]

Upon his return, Pratt found relief work building the Arena Rink in Saskatoon. In passing, he let slip to a friend that he was an American. The next day he was unemployed again. Destitute, he turned to relief regularly over the better part of a decade.[108] In times of struggles, men like Pratt measured borders in food and precarious working conditions. He understood why his coworkers "didn't like seeing an American work here while Canadians were out of jobs."[109] Still, that kind of policy put a deep strain on his family.

By the time city officials and RCMP officers began to plan Pratt's second deportation in 1939, he knew all he needed to about the damage that deportations caused. Shortly before his scheduled removal, Pratt disappeared.[110] While he hid out, his friends began to gather petitions of support for him. Hundreds of residents of the city lent their signatures, revealing both the racial and gendered ways that everyday people conceptualized the border and belonging. The United States would allow Pratt, an American citizen, to enter the country. It still refused

Figure 9.5 Ada Pratt (nee Hersikon) and her children. City of Saskatoon Archives, City Commissioners series, file #1200-0177-001.

to allow his Canadian family to follow with him. Until he had demonstrated his ability to support dependents, American immigration officials would not let them enter.[111]

For many Saskatoon residents, such a policy ran counter to the proper ordering of society. The family, not the individual, composed the basic building block of the nation. They believed that breaking that unit across borders set a dangerous principle. Saskatoon's mayor declared that "whether the man should be deported was a matter of law." Still, he argued that "the wife and children should be permitted to remain with the man, regardless of the country in which he was required to live."[112]

Pratt's supporters disagreed on the exact reason for their support but they came to the same overall conclusion. Either he should remain in Canada or federal officials should let his family follow with him. George Graves, a welder, noted that "I am a taxpayer and I know what relief" costs. Still, Graves supported Pratt's petition because Graves had "two kiddies myself, and I can understand the predicament of this family."[113] Sympathy contained a gendered dimension, but it was a sympathy that came in shades of whiteness. One citizen argued that "if it was necessary to deport relief recipients, a beginning might be made with unmarried men of oriental race instead of singling out an American citizen and breaking up his home here."[114]

Despite the popularity of Myron's petition, his dream of remaining in Saskatoon faded. So too did his hope that his family could follow him to Quincy. Brought into police custody, Pratt waited for his second deportation in isolation, deprived by the police of speaking with his friends. They denied requests for interviews made by reporters from the *Star Phoenix*. At the train station, his wife—flanked by police officers and immigrations agents—said her tearful goodbyes.[115]

Five months after his second deportation, Pratt wrote to Ada hoping to allay her frustrations. He had little good news to report. He had gained work and lost it. He had new leads on a carpentry job, but nothing that would provide more than piecemeal employment. The periodic work provided enough for him to live on, but prevented him from saving the fifty dollars required to send for Ada and their children. He condemned Saskatoon for its shortsighted sympathy. It continued to provide for his wife and children through public relief, but failed to act on recommendations to use relief funds to pay for her transportation across the line. He hoped to "find a builder with money instead of the shoestring bums I've met so far." As soon as that happened, he promised to send for his family.[116]

Myron Pratt's account suggests the breadth of changes that had occurred within Canada since turn of the century. Saskatoon—located almost 400 kilometers north of the United States and more than a thousand of kilometers from either the Pacific or Atlantic Coast—was about as far from any of Canada's borders as any major Canadian city could be. And yet borders mattered. Even in Saskatoon, deportations had come to act as a viable way to solve domestic concerns about charity, civic expense, and morality. They served as center points for answering questions about the rights of families and the impacts of nationality during precarious economic times. Considered across these dimensions, Pratt's case suggested just how deep the border's influence ran. It shaped the lives of individuals and families. By the 1930s, it had grown to shape the day-to-day operations of cities deep within the interior of each nation as well.

***

For all the horrors experienced by families like the Pratts, their outcome represented only one of many possibilities that existed in the 1930s. Federal power had grown, but power was both inconsistent and irritable. It changed by time and place. It appeared irrepressible in one context, only to seem anemic in others.

By the twentieth century Canada and the United States had expanded their administrations, reformed their immigration policies, and eliminated some of the most glaring gaps in their systems of enforcement. The impact of these changes, however, remained uneven. Haudenosaunee legal victories in the 1920s expanded their ability to circumvent existing immigration structures. The victory, however, had occurred as much on paper as it had in practice. Immigration agents continued to test the exact boundaries of the law. Practical harassment extended long after legal clarifications emerged. Indirect forms of control continued to undermine the economic, familial, and social connections that drew Indigenous people across the line.

For other communities, the twentieth century witnessed an increase in exclusions and racial stratification. Chinese migrants felt the sting of immigration restrictions in the 1880s. Sikhs, Japanese, southern Europeans, eastern Europeans, and dozens of other communities experienced a similar rejection after the turn of the century. By the 1920s, even desirable migrants could not escape the expansion of federal control. Both countries had succeeded in putting the burden of proof on border crossers and had reduced the easiest forms of entry across the line.[117]

For all that changed, border enforcement remained a cooperative venture across nations and within local communities. Both governments believed that the growing sophistication of their agencies would allow them to implement unpopular policies over local disdain. Prohibition suggested the folly of such an approach. Federal administrators might not need the eyes and ears of local men and women to the same extent they had in the nineteenth century, but unpopular policies still created dangerous currents that neither government could navigate safely. As a result, cooperation remained critical to the border's development.

Over the preceding century, the border had grown from its infancy to its adolescence. By the end of the 1930s it had started to reach its adulthood. World War I, the Great Depression, Prohibition, fears of immigration, and bureaucratic growth entrenched how the border looked, who it targeted, and how it behaved. Adulthood, however, did not mean the border ceased to grow or change.

The limitations, frustrations, and flaws the border had acquired during its childhood continued to shape its later life. Like the men and women who guarded it, the border never became a finished product. Adulthood centralized border policies and ensured that permanent organizations governed its operations. Adulthood, however, did not make the border any less permeable or illusory. Administrators continued to redefine the border's goals and struggled to actualize their dreams for it. They could not to account for the complexities of everyday life, a lesson that applied to the Canada–US border in its adulthood as much as in its infancy.

10

The Borders of Everyday Life

Mildred Redmond was born on Walpole Island in 1917. The island, located near Wallaceburg, Ontario, looked out onto Lake St. Clair, not far from Detroit, Michigan. The Potawatomi who made the island their home had lived transnational lives for more than a century. Redmond and her family carried on that tradition. As Redmond grew up, her family moved back and forth across the border to sell goods.[1]

When Redmond's parents, grandmother, and aunt died unexpectedly, Mildred and her siblings moved to an orphanage in Oakville. Despite the drastic change of setting, connections across nations continued to permeate their lives. Of the six Redmond children, one married an American, two lived in the United States, two married Canadians, and one married a member of the Walpole reserve.[2]

The children who they grew up with at the orphanage also built lives that spanned the international line. When the orphanage held a reunion in Oakville, Ontario, two of the attendants returned from the United States (Florida and California), while the remaining five came from Toronto.[3] The connections created by Redmond's kin and the orphanage extended both short (Ontario–Indiana) and long (Ontario–California) distances. Many grew up, married, and lived their lives in close proximity to their birth. Even those who remained close to home found themselves intertwined in the borderlands themselves. Their friends and family created links across the border line that extended well past their own individual residency.

By the 1930s, the border between Canada and the United States resembled a young adult. Boundary surveyors and diplomats had laid the groundwork of the border from the Atlantic to the Pacific Oceans. The muscles, while still growing, were strong. Thousands of administrators guarded the line. Tribunals had replaced ad hoc measures. Administrators not only used the border to control movement, butas the story of Myron and Ada Pratt suggested, used it as a means to solve domestic concerns.

A Line of Blood and Dirt. Benjamin Hoy, Oxford University Press (2021). © Oxford University Press.
DOI: 10.1093/oso/9780197528693.003.0011

Power, however, remained a fickle beast. Federal administrators measured their presence along the border in terms of personnel, confiscations, treaties, deportations, and tribunals. They made such measurements alone. Local communities continued to tell very different stories about the border, even as the balance of power shifted. Few diaries bothered to record border crossings. Those who reflected on mobility, however, measured the border in picnics and medicine bundles. They saw its presence through marriages, insults, and headaches. Everyday power required everyday impacts. In that context, the Canada–US border continued to have a far less certain legacy than the reams of administrators who guarded its length would suggest.

A Border for Everyday Life

Gratia A. Countryman was an unusual woman. Born in Hastings, Minnesota, in 1866, she received her education at the University of Minnesota at a time when few women entered higher education. Well-educated and determined, she worked as a cataloger for the Minneapolis Public Library before becoming its head librarian in 1904.

Countryman travelled throughout her life, visiting parts of France, Spain, England, the United States, and Canada. She moved for pleasure and for work. In 1934, she set out from Wisconsin to explore Montreal and Prince Edward Island with some of her friends, including the Canadian-born Marie Geneviera. The women purchased fur coats, dined at fine restaurants, and enjoyed hot baths at local resorts. They attended events with the Hon. John Macdonald and the Chief Justice of Prince Edward Island. Illness, dust, cold, and minor car accidents dampened the women's spirits, but did not overshadow an otherwise positive experience.[4]

As the women travelled east, friendships rather than international lines dictated the direction of travel. The border offered little barrier between their lunch at St. John's, Michigan, and a visit to one of Marie Geneviera's friends in Exeter, Ontario, later that night. Social stops at Exeter, Port Hope, and Greenwood Towers to visit friends punctuated long stretches of driving.[5]

While many of Countryman's contemporaries kept records of their travels, few took the time to note uneventful border crossings. Countryman was different. She gave voice to the mundane and the forgettable, including a rare glimpse into border crossings gone well, at least as experienced by a woman of wealth and education. At Port Huron, for example, Countryman noted, "we had no trouble with the customs, and started right toward London [Ontario]."[6] Their crossing along the St. Croix River twenty-two days later brought a minor snag.

Immigration and customs officers insisted Countryman "pay duty on the hooked rugs which I bought in Quebec, but it was only $1.00 and I was willing." Still the border crossing "delayed us a good deal, and it was dark when we started out."[7]

The delay at the border forced the women to abandon their earlier plans to reach a camp eleven miles away. They choose instead to spend the night at the Freling Farm, "a large delightful old place filled with old furniture and two delightful hostesses."[8] By the time the women awoke, a wonderful breakfast and the beautiful views out over Passamaquoddy Bay made the earlier inconvenience at the border feel distant. By the end of the day the roaring waves, large pine and spruce trees, fresh blueberries, fried clams, and baked mackerel rendered it forgotten.[9]

The delays Countryman's party experienced near St. Croix had no impact on the women's future travels. They continued to zig zag across the border whenever they desired. Like their earlier crossing at Port Huron, their future interactions with the border often "took a moment only."[10] For a border that had cost so much time and energy to create, it seemed insubstantial against the magnificence of Niagara Falls and the delicious of fresh fruits the women continued to enjoy.

Although unintuitive, Countryman's experience helped signal the border's growing significance rather than its chronic anemia. By the 1930s, the border had become natural for women like Countryman. Even when it acted as a trifling impediment, however, the border remained in the background, there but not absent.

Many others experienced the border as Countryman did, as a minor but present part of life. By 1927, roughly 60 percent of the 25,334 Canadians living in the Windsor area worked in Michigan.[11] Born in 1906 on the Chippewa of the Thames Reserve near London, Ontario, Carl Lewis experienced the mobility firsthand. In 1913 Lewis's family moved to Windsor. Three years later, at the age of ten, he found himself attaching lamp wicks in the Ford Motor plant in Detroit.[12] Cities like Windsor, Walkerville, and Sandwich operated as part of Detroit's greater metropolitan area more often than they did as independent cities with distinct national identities.

The scale of integration between Detroit and Windsor had few peers, but other border cities replicated the principle. Until the 1950s, the Canadian city of White Rock relied on fire prevention services from a neighboring American town in Washington State.[13] Americans who migrated to Canada maintained their connections back home. Family correspondence and newspaper subscriptions linked distant parts of the continent together. Regular trips renewed connections with friends and relatives. When prairie fires burned down the houses of American immigrants in Canada, they called upon family members living in the United States for support.[14]

Marriage patterns enhanced the connections created by economics and migration. Young men from the Lummi, for example, looked for eligible mates across the border. On September 7, 1907, Edward Warbus, a twenty-four-year-old Lummi from Washington, married Rosanna Frank, a fifteen-year-old Skagit woman from British Columbia.[15] By 1916, Joseph Jefferson, James Reid, William Moore, Clarence R Phair, Pe Hal O Can (Andrew Thomas), and Mathias Paul had all married across the Washington–British Columbia border. The marriages linked the Tulalip, Lummi, and Colville living in Washington to the Caggie, Musqueam, Stz'uminus (Chemainus), Lyackson, Kwantlen (Langley), Penelakuts, and Hatzick in British Columbia.[16]

The choices of Indigenous women intensified a situation already overburdened with complexity. The marriage of Helen Paynes of Muckleshoot to U. Kagami, a twenty-nine-year-old citizen of Japan, provided a reminder of the fictions of racial and national clarity that federal administrators attempted to enforce. Federal officials, for all their power, could not draw clean lines among race, nationality, tribal rights, and citizenship.[17]

While many transnational connections occurred in areas adjacent to the border, distance alone did not dictate the ways people moved or how they connected. By the time Sidonia Elizabeth Black was thirty-seven years old, she had lived in Missouri, where she was born, as well as in California, Manitoba, and Minnesota. She had relocated to Winnipeg with husband, Albert Black, during World War I so he could escape the draft. Once there, she found herself at home within the significant African American community. If national policy had motivated her move to Canada, sadness and family gave inspiration for her return. After a falling out with her husband, Sidonia came to Duluth, where her sister lived.[18]

The stories of Countryman, Warbus, and Black demonstrate the possibilities that coexisted with the new kind of border that Canada and the United States had created. Pleasure, travel, and opportunities for work remained. So too did connections between family members. Still, for all the personal histories that depicted the border as invisible and insignificant, many others suggested the ways it shaped their lives and movements. Social divisions echoed national lines, creating barriers that extended into the streets, offices, and playgrounds of both countries.

Day-to-day interactions embedded birthplace, mobility, and ethnicity into the fabric of society. Social slights carried national overtones. When Alf Weisshaar traveled from Iowa to Saskatchewan in 1914, he noted that "most of the big shots [in Regina] were English, and . . . considered themselves a lot above the [American] farm people."[19] Snubs to American born farmers sat poorly with men like Weisshaar, who believed that Americans represented the demographic majority in some areas of Canada. Their social standing, he inferred, should reflect the size of their population.[20] Weisshaar did not experience such insults alone.

Josephine Handy Grondahl had visited Canada twice before her family relocated there when she was a young girl. Her peers teased her upon her arrival. She used American terminology (such as "writing tablet" and "overshoes") instead of their Canadian equivalents ("scribblers" and "galoshes"). Her family's position in the community, however, shielded Grondahl from further abuse. When she complained to her grandfather about her treatment, he told her that "if any of those teachers or those kyds [*sic*] aren't nice to you, you just tell them that they can't have any water out of my Grandpa's well." She did not have trouble after that. The well, which the community relied upon, provided social protection for Grondahl as she transitioned to the new social dynamic north of the line.[21]

As Grondahl's and Weisshaar's stories suggest, everyday interactions shaped how individuals came to understand their relationship to national spaces. Insults remained fresh decades later, long after mundane border crossings were forgotten. Even positive social interactions fostered a sense of difference. The American Woman's Club, founded after World War I, drew a membership largely from Canadian citizens. The club's only admission requirement was American birth.[22]

By infiltrating into everyday life, local understandings of the border helped to curtail mobility in ways well beyond the immediate capacity of federal administrators. Indirectly, and at a distance, fear prevented journeys before they even began. So too did perceived hassle. In 1931, Mary McCall visited her family in Oregon. While there, she noticed the abundance of food vis-à-vis the sparsity she knew in Saskatchewan. Her cousin noted that much of the food in Oregon remained unsellable and went to waste. The cousin confided that "if it wasn't for that international boundary line and customs between us that we could ship carloads [of food] into your neighborhood."[23]

McCall's approach to food shortages emphasized how imposing a barrier the border could seem. Instead of finding a way to bring goods across the border from Oregon, McCall looked for parallel opportunities in Canada. She began a letter-writing campaign to British Columbia, which she believed had a similar surplus of crops.[24] In doing so, she looked to solve the problem within the nation-state rather than reaching beyond it where clear possibilities existed.

If the border presented an economic barrier to McCall's charity, it had an almost ethereal presence for others. Edward Dienst moved from Illinois to Saskatchewan in 1908 on a doctor's recommendation. Perhaps his asthma would yield in a drier climate. According to Dienst, he "started to feel better right away. . . . At the border you might say. The air seemed to be different, light and everything, and I started to improve and get better."[25]

Dienst measured the border in terms of air quality, Grondahl as childhood bullying, and McCall as an impediment to charity. Attempts to centralize the border's administration had done little to destroy the fractured ways people identified themselves with respect to national lines. Even within settler communities, the border came to mean different things for different people, a common word to describe endless possibilities.

Indigenous Borders

For Indigenous people, the border's impact on day-to-day life remained similarly unstable throughout the early twentieth century. The border served as both an imposition and an absence, a shadow cast across daily life. Oral histories by Mary Jourdain, Max Ireland, Jim Windigo, and Two Voices suggested the ways that the border structured heartache and esteem. They also point to some of the places it remained conspicuously absent.

Mary Jourdain was born in the early 1920s at Basswood Lake on the border between Minnesota and Ontario. Unknown assailants chased Jourdain's family out of the area when she was too young to remember many of their details. Jourdain's family moved to "Lac La Croix [Ontario] and then went back to Tower [Minnesota]. . . . We grew up in both places."[26]

Like many others living near Vermillion Lake, Basswood Lake, Burntside Lake, Lac La Croix, and Prairie Portage, Jourdain's family moved back and forth across the line with few impediments.[27] Her family collected wild rice at Basswood Lake seasonally. She attended Indian school at Tower, Minnesota, and lived in both La Croix (Ontario) and Vermillion Lake (Minnesota). Set amidst the backdrop of Prohibition, the Indian Citizenship Act, and the Great Depression, Jourdain's early childhood highlighted the existence of an open and less federalized border than the correspondence of administrators suggested. She was not alone.[28]

In recalling his family's history, Max Ireland noted that his parent's home served as a crossing point for the Haudenosaunee along the border. Oneida from the Wisconsin stopped by as they moved north into Canada. These visitors received information, stories, and company. Most importantly, they received food from Ireland's father, who retained a well-paying job throughout the Depression.[29] Gifts of food shaped the movement of transnational traffic. It also brought Ireland's father significant esteem.

For Two Voices (Kaniswiwitay), the border offered sadness rather than opportunity. Two Voices, an Ojibwe living in the United States, travelled to Canada on a visit. When he attempted to return to the United States, American immigration officials prohibited his reentry on account of an eye disease. At the time of his interview with D. G. Mandelbaum in 1934, Two Voices had not succeeded in returning to the United States. Estimated to be 105 years old, Two Voices faced a decision that likely prevented him from returning home for the rest of his life.[30]

Indigenous languages and territorial practices bore the marks of a world in motion. By the 1930s, Fine Day noted the Cree had developed terms for Chinese (Oce-kipatcwan, "Braided Men"), Frenchmen (Wemistigooiwuk), Americans (Kihteimo-kuma-nak, "Big Knives"), and African Americans (Kaskitowayas, "Black Flesh"), as well as generic terms for English Speakers (Akayaciu) and whites (Munias).[31] New conceptual categories helped make sense of the new social, cultural, and political borders the Cree encountered.

For the Matsqui in British Columbia, the continued arrival of outsiders required more than just new terms to describe them. It required concerted action. Joe Louis, from the Matsqui reserve, noted that when he was fifteen (c. 1910), B.C. Electric imported laborers from India who frequently passed through the reserve.[32] The Masqui "gave them Hindus a rough time." [33] While young Matsqui men did not beat up the South Asians they found on their land, they "had a lot of fun" with them. They took the pants off a trespasser "and hung it somewhere else."[34] Louis framed the harassment as both a form of amusement as well as a means of enforcing Matsqui territory. He noted that "we didn't think that they should be here, you know, working there. They had to go right through the reservation."[35] Federal agents exercised power, but so too did local communities.

If the border remained an uncertain impediment built from both federal and local power, it had significant potential to disrupt spiritual practices. In the mid-1930s, Fine Day described the ways the border interfered with the transmission of ceremonial objects between communities. Sacred bundles needed to be covered in braided sweet grass, which required annual renewal. The requirement encouraged trade between Cree communities living in the United States, where sweet grass was limited, and those living in Canada, where the grass was abundant. Cree living north of the border, by contrast, faced a shortage of pipe stone. While they could trade for it with communities west of the Rocky Mountains, they could also collect it in the United States.[36]

Other Plains communities faced similar dilemmas. The border divided Siksikaitsiitapi (Blackfoot) communities from the paint necessary for their sacred ceremonies.[37] Settlers viewed delays and interference at the border as a logistical concern. For the Cree and Siksikaitsiitapi, obstructions had spiritual implications as well.

The stories of ceremonial objects reveal the continued importance of mobility and trade across borders, as well as the increased restrictions such movements faced in the early twentieth century. George First Rider, of the Kainah (Blood) Reserve, recounted in 1969 the story of a dangerous medicine pipe. During his father's lifetime, the pipe wreaked havoc on First Rider's community before eventually making its way south. First Rider believed that the problems began when Night Wailer (Lone Caller) constructed and transferred a pipe improperly. The object became a danger to all around it. Those who received it—including Spear Chief and his family—died or became ill.[38]

Fearful that the improperly constructed medicine pipe would cause more damage, Dog Child (First Rider's father) took the pipe across the border to Browning, Montana, where it remained for a year or two. Unable to sell the pipe in the United States, Dog Child brought the pipe back to Alberta. Shortly thereafter, First Rider's mother (The Only Handsome Woman, Catching Another Horse) and father both died, as did the people they tried to transfer the pipe to. Eventually Calling Last took the pipe back to Browning, Montana where he sold it to an antique store. Calling Last died, and the community lost track of the dangerous object.[39] For the Kainah community in southern Alberta, Browning, Montana, operated as a close enough location to sell such an object but distant enough to help insulate the community from the object's immense spiritual power. Under such circumstances, prohibitions on movement either at reserve boundaries or at national ones had physical as well as spiritual implications.[40]

On the Pacific Coast, the transfer of songs revealed a similar network of culture, trade, and spirituality. The First Peoples of Alberni on Vancouver Island shared their songs with groups as far north as Alaska as well as south into the United States. Shared songs across international borders continued into the twentieth century. The songs emphasized a close connection that did not disappear over time. As George Clutesi and Annie Hayes recalled, "one of the greatest privileges you could accord another tribe was to grant or give him one of your own songs and in return receive one from them."[41]

Mobility created opportunities to acquire pipestone, sweet grass, and songs. It helped enrich and maintain spiritual activities. The opposite, however, was also true. For the Kwakuitl, mobility had assisted in protecting cultural practices and economic opportunities in the nineteenth century. The Kwakuitl conducted ceremonial events at Gilford (Gwayasdums) and secured food at Kingcome (Gwayeyee) on the Pacific Coast. The hops fields of Washington State and the nearby canneries and fisheries supplemented local incomes. Taking full advantage of these opportunities required the Kwakuitl to cross the international line.[42]

By the 1920s, the Department of Indian Affairs' suppression of cultural practices encouraged the Kwakuitl to establish a permanent village at Kingcome. They chose to sacrifice some of their mobility in order fortify their culture against federal interference. Relocation to an isolated area, they hoped, would provide a buffer against the assimilation campaigns launched by both federal governments.[43]

Cree, Siksikaitsiitapi, and Kwakuitl accounts of the early twenty century suggest some of the ways the international border influenced their lives and spiritual practices. Establishing when the border became important to everyday life, however, remains difficult. It was a kind of power that had a weight and a roughness. It had a presence even as it defied easy measurement.

Like Countryman, Jim Windigo measured the border in terms of day-to-day life, in picnics, camping, mountains, and food. Although Windigo struggled to pin down the exact moment he believed the border became significant, he knew what markers demonstrated the transition.[44] For Windigo, the Anishinaabe's inability to access camping grounds in the United States signaled the border's growing influence. Wild rice or mukluks acquired on one side of the line faced seizure or taxation when brought back across. Reciprocal gift-giving between borderland communities became less common.[45]

Windigo measured the border's influence against his own desires, but also against the past. His grandfather and grandmother came to Canada from Leech Lake on the "American side, so called *American Side,* but in those days there was no such thing as *American Indians* or *Canadian Indians,* you know."[46] Their relocation north did not prohibit later journeys to Spirit Mountain (Nana boo jo namuk ta vik). Located near Duluth, Minnesota, Spirit Mountain had significant spiritual significance for Windigo's family.[47]

Windigo grew up in a different world than his grandparents. As a young child he remembered crossing to Nett Lake, Minnesota, and "no one said anything."[48] By the time he was older, the border had changed. While Spirit Mountain did not change its geographic home, it felt increasingly distant to him. He could measure its proximity in kilometers, time, and cost. Any calculation he made needed to incorporate the border as well. That concern ensured that a mountain that Widigo's grandparents had visited felt increasingly distant to their grandson.[49]

For all the criticism Windigo levied against the border, he remained careful not to overemphasize its power. The border occupied an inconsistent place ever shaped by the circumstances that surrounded it. During the Great Depression, Windigo believed the Anishinaabeg living in Ontario near Lake Superior thrived in part because of their ability to rely on the fur trade when many other forms of employment faltered. They gathered wild rice at Nett Lake (Minnesota). Frequent canoe trips along international waterways and participation in ceremonial events linked communities otherwise split by the border.[50] Power had a history as well as a geography.

The Mille Lac Trading Post

Despite all the changes that occurred along the border throughout the early twentieth century, transnational lives continued to thrive. Oral histories pertaining to the Mille Lacs Trading Post, in Minnesota, for example, suggest the many ways that people, animals, and goods bridged borders in North America. These accounts linked the Ojibwe in Minnesota across the nearby border with Canada as well as to distant lands like Mexico.

Letitia B. Caldwell was born March 12, 1912, on the White Earth Reservation in Minnesota. Her mother was white. Her father, William Markum Dailey, was a full-blood Ojibwe. When Caldwell was four years old her parents took her to Canada. Her mother remained north of the line, while her father returned to Minnesota where he became chief and interpreter for the Mille Lacs.[51]

The geographic relocation and her parent's separation created an opportunity for a new kind of identity. While living in Canada, Caldwell noted that "I didn't know anything about Indians, didn't even know actually for sure that I was Indian because my mother always said, 'if anybody asks you what you are, you tell them you're French.' "[52] When her father died in March of 1930, his community buried him at White Earth.[53] Caldwell, nearly eighteen at the time, was attending business college in Winnipeg.

Although Caldwell wished to attend the funeral, the journey was expensive. Money from her minister allowed her to embark on the first half of the trip, but did not provide her enough for return fare. Stuck in Minnesota, she relied on her father's connections to acquire a job. For the next three years, she worked as a secretary and sales clerk for Harry and Jeannette Ayer at the Mille Lacs Trading Post. The job allowed her to learn about her Ojibwe heritage and to reconnect in small ways with her father's community. It also provided her with enough money to journey back to Canada in 1931 to visit her mother and sister in Winnipeg.[54]

The Mille Lacs Trading Post was a unique place. It gathered curios from communities from Alaska to the American Southwest and catered to a diverse set of tourists, including Haitian diplomats and Osage from Oklahoma. It also featured a parrot, named Chi-be-be (Ojibwe for "big baby"), that the Ayers family had acquired in Mexico.[55] The parrot, who the Ayers taught to speak Ojibwe, tormented patrons by whistling them as they walked to the outhouses, scaring some of the patrons away.

Caldwell's stories highlighted the ways in which people and animals continued to move across borders into the 1930s. The photograph of her on the steps of the trading post with Chi-be-be was only possible because of the fluidity of borders. It required a parrot that had been captured in Mexico to make a journey to Minnesota. Once there the parrot met Caldwell, a mixed heritage woman who had been born in the United States, grew up in Canada, and returned south on the death of her father.[56]

The transnational connections that passed through Mille Lake linked Minnesota to more than just the adjacent Canadian provinces (Manitoba and Ontario). The trading post also served as a connection point between Minnesota and the Canadian Pacific. During the late 1920s or early 1930s, for example,

Figure 10.1 Letitia Caldwell, Chi-be-be, and a man Caldwell believed may have been a millionaire from Texas at the Mille Lacs Trading Post. *Letitia Caldwell at Mille Lacs Trading Post*, 1933, Photograph, 1933, E97.1C r9, Minnesota Historical Society.

Gordon (last name unknown) passed by the Mille Lacs Trading Post on his way to homestead out west. The man "just got tired of his wife and his family and his dentist office, everything, so he just picked up and walked out . . . without a nickel in his pocket."[57] While at the trading post, the man spoke at length with Letitia B. Caldwell who gave him a dollar and her mother's address in Winnipeg. The money and support allowed Gordon to draw on Caldwell's transnational connections, which had been created by her parent's own split, to assist him in separating from his wife.[58]

Gordon homesteaded in British Columbia using Caldwell's link between Winnipeg and Mille Lacs to support his much more extensive aim. After settling down, Gordon wrote back to both Caldwell and her mother thanking them for the support they had given him. He let them know that he had named an island on his property after Letitia. Letitia Caldwell, for her own part, named her own son Gordon Paige after him.[59]

***

Federal officials measured the border in terms of imports and exports as well as in posts, seizures, and legislation. Everyday people measured it instead in songs, sweet grass, and pipes. From either perspective, the border of the nineteenth century differed from that of the twentieth century. Social, cultural, and spiritual connections remained, even as everyday life shifted.

The lives of those near the border incorporated at least a part of the border regime into their daily routines. Overseas migrants faced heavy restrictions on their movement at key port cities. The 49th parallel, by contrast, offered a much less certain kind of control. The addition of hundreds of border guards increased both countries' ability to catch smugglers and to exclude undesirables along their terrestrial border. The scope of transnational movements and the breadth of territory, however, ensured federal agents still played a losing game. Even with the most devoted and tireless agents, neither country could expect to monitor more than a fraction of the traffic across the line. In some ways, however, they did not need to.

By the middle of the twentieth century, Canada and the United States had achieved a far more subtle kind of victory. Belonging increasingly ran across national lines. Insults carried a national tone. The border closed possibilities at a distance. It restricted imagination. When this kind of border worked, it operated far better as a border of discouragement than one of debarment. The absence of a border-crossing attempt signaled the line's effectiveness far more often than did a prohibition of entry.

Border guards still mattered, but their impact extended beyond their presence. They helped project fear, uncertainty, and a commonality of belonging into the interior. They served as catalysts for a growing sense of national identity and helped to foster a more restricted sense of territory and belonging. Practical limitations on border enforcement remained, but those would require another half a century to begin to resolve.

Epilogue

In 1903, Montana Congressman Joseph M. Dixon made a formal resolution that the United States build a barbed wire fence that stretched from the Lake of the Woods, in northern Minnesota, to Point Roberts on the West Coast.[1] This fence would "be charged with electricity in such a way that when a Chinaman attempts to climb over it warning will be given at some station along the line."[2] Dixon had first come up with the idea during a chance meeting with George M. Hatch, a special immigration inspector, while the two men shared a train from Helena. Unable to patrol 400 miles of territory, Hatch's mind had turned to science fiction. He hoped an electric fence of this nature might overcome the real limits he faced in the field.[3]

While Dixon admitted that he "knew nothing about the feasibility of the project, and had really given the matter little thought," he hoped the Secretary of Commerce and Labor would investigate the fence's feasibility.[4] Such a fence promised not only to help with Chinese immigration but, in Dixon's estimation, would also help northern Montana avoid being "overrun by wandering bands of Cree Indians."[5] Dixon's proposal received widespread attention and disdain.[6] The *Helena Independent* worried that Dixon bet against the intelligence of the working class. Fervor for border reform, the paper hoped, would not outweigh the impracticality of the idea.[7]

A hundred years after Dixon's proposal, border walls continued to draw the public's interest and condemnation. In 2014, US presidential candidate Donald Trump tweeted "SECURE THE BORDER! BUILD A WALL!"[8] Over the next four years, the wall he imagined shifted. Its length decreased from 1,900 miles to only 1,000 and its height shifted from as tall as 45 feet to as short as 32. At the same time, the price tag jumped from four billion to twenty billion dollars.[9] The idea mattered more than the specifics. For Trump, "we don't have a country—if we don't have borders."[10]

Separated by more than a hundred years, the two proposals differed in terms of their geographic coverage, the technological possibilities, and the undesired

A Line of Blood and Dirt. Benjamin Hoy, Oxford University Press (2021). © Oxford University Press.
DOI: 10.1093/oso/9780197528693.003.0012

groups they wished to target. Despite these differences, they shared a confidence that technology and infrastructure would provide an answer to border control that personnel alone had not.[11] They shared a common belief that borders made nations strong and that a failure to act was worse than whatever problems such a project might create.

In the century that separated the two proposals, much about the continent's borders had changed. Men on foot and horseback guarded the Canadian, American, and Mexican borders at the end of nineteenth century. Fifty years later airplanes and FM radios expanded surveillance. In the twenty-first century satellites and drones would soon scan the US borders from the heavens.[12] The technology of border enforcement expanded, but the underlying problems remained.

North America's battle over belonging paralleled struggles worldwide. Globalization reconfigured how borders worked but it did not mend the fissures between identity and nationality. In Kenya, Somalis who have lived in the same regions for generations continued to possess an uncertain status, both Indigenous and foreign.[13] Across the Mediterranean, work created identities that spanned national lines. Residents of Ceuta slept in Morocco and worked in Spain.[14] The problem of assigning a single national identity to individuals in motion leads to creative approaches but no lasting solutions. During the Cold War, Thailand employed teachers to work as border guards. It hoped the dual-purpose positions would help instill a singular cultural identity at the edges of the nation, which matched the clear borders the state had already drawn.[15]

Even seemingly simple tasks, like clarifying the boundaries of a given state, had not become much easier. In India, more than 150 enclaves, territories of one state completely surrounded by another, remain along the Indo–Bangladesh border.[16] Borders continue to move. Throughout the 1990s, nation-states constructed an average of more than four new international borders (created or redrawn) across the globe each year and have invested billions into border control.[17] Canada and the United States have not escaped either the ambiguity or the difficulties created by these larger processes.

In the first month of 2018, 2.18 million vehicles crossed the Canada–US border. The diversity of personal and commercial traffic creates thousands of practical questions.[18] Could cigarette companies evade Canadian laws by advertising in American magazines they knew were destined for Canadian consumption?[19] Did using a Virtual Private Network (software that allows a person to change the country they appear to access the internet from) constitute an illegal kind of border crossing? If so, what responsibility did companies like Netflix have for discouraging the practice?[20] In Oregon, waste-to-energy incinerators processed cargo from Canadian hospitals. A nearby Catholic community wondered if that meant that aborted fetuses from Canada, in some small way, powered their homes.[21] Both the scale and nuance of these kinds of questions defies easy answers. Thousands of small questions create piecemeal efforts, but with no guiding force for reform.

Large scale changes, as in the nineteenth century, still came from moments of crisis. The terrorist attacks on September 11, 2001, for example, resulted in one of the largest administrative reorganizations the United States had ever seen. Twenty agencies became one as the newly created Department of Homeland Security restructured the operations of 150,000 personnel. Passports became mandatory to enter the United States, even for Canadians who had long avoided such provisions.[22] For all the ways 9/11 changed the United States' approach to borders, its relationship with Canada remained distinctive. While the United States relied on 10,000 border patrol agents to guard its border with Mexico a year after the attacks, it utilized only 600 to guard its northern reaches. The decision to militarize and fortify one border while leaving the other open highlighted a difference in mindset that had existed since at least the nineteenth century. The United States saw itself as sharing a common heritage and brotherhood with Canada. It extended no such recognition to Mexico.[23]

Cosimo Cavallaro's life and art perhaps described the relationship the best. In 2019, Cavallaro erected a 300-meter-long wall of expired cheese along California's border with Michoacán, Mexico. The project, titled "Make America Grate Again," was part of the theater of the absurd. It aimed to demonstrate the wastefulness of border walls and their perishable nature. Cavallaro's own movements exemplified the uneven ways that the borders of North America influenced life. Born in Montreal, he relocated to the United States in 1995 for work. The openness of the northern border allowed him to find financial support for his career in the United States, while the closure of the southern border gave him inspiration for his craft.[24] The repugnancy of old cheese in hot sun made for an arresting sight, but summarized a common kind of criticism. Those who stood on the wrong side—downwind—of a national border often struggled to have anything but a distasteful experience.

For Indigenous people, the problems with the Canada–US border rested not just with the policies, but with the entire project itself. Canada and the United States had spent a hundred years attempting to paper over Indigenous territorial arrangements. Despite thick paint and many passes, the older conceptions of land and belonging still showed through. Oral accounts by the Cree, Haudenosaunee, Soowahli, Ojibwe, and Dakota all emphasize a continued belief in a relatedness that spanned the continent.[25] Hybridized understandings of territory added new layers of complexity. In 1969 Solomon Wilson, a Haida born in Vancouver, railed against the settler societies that "took our land and give it a different name. Which you people didn't pay for."[26] At the same time, Wilson took pride that he did not "have to go outside of Canada to make a living. I don't have to be a foreigner." He joked, "as the songs says, [laughs] 'this land was made for us.'"[27] For Wilson, being Haida and Canadian existed together, both a reflection of the horrors of colonialism and the ways nation-states came to shape everyday conceptions of the world.

Raymond Owen, a Dakota from Minnesota, expressed a different kind of understanding of the relationship between Indigenous and colonial land systems. For Owen, those living west of the Mississippi resided in the "United States of Dakota." Those residing in "Montana and Wyoming are West Dakota, and Canada and Manitoba and Saskatchewan is Northern, Northern Dakota."[28] Like Wilson, Owens recognized the damage caused by the transition of power on the continent, even as he reaffirmed the breadth of lands the Dakota claimed. If Owens described a conception of land that looked past colonial boundaries, he was describing what he thought should have been, not what many people recognized in practice. For most of the Dakota who had crossed into Canada after 1862, the international border continued to carry a sense of stigma and loss a hundred years later. David Pasche recalled that while he was attending high school in Manitoba, the Soto he interacted with "used to call me a refugee all the time."[29] A refugee to Canada or to Soto lands? Both were possibilities.

For all the ways the experience of the Dakota emphasized the damage national borders could create, their conceptions of territory continued to push back against the basic assumptions that nation-states made.[30] Clifford Canku argued that while the Minnesota War forced many Dakota to relocate, they retained a connection in their "hearts and minds, and spirits" to Minnesota, "the birthplace of the Dakota people."[31] Military victories did not grant belonging; that came from creation itself.[32]

Border crossings proved no less complicated than territorial understandings. Paul Diabo's legal challenge to American immigration law in the 1920s had established the rights of Indigenous people to cross the Canada–US border. More than half a century later, the practical application of those rights remained contested. In 1996, Vincent Stogan of Musqueam criticized American border guards for charging "us even if it's just a gift, they charge us for it, that's why we're fighting for it now, why have that border, why do that to us."[33] The problem was only made worse by the events of 9/11. Each winter, Coast Salish Spirit Dancers travelled between Washington and British Columbia carrying ceremonial objects within sealed containers that nondancers could not search or handle.[34] On 9/11 this longstanding practice was transformed into a visible security risk. Guards disrupted the transits with greater frequency and began to police the summer canoe trips the Stó:lō made across the international line.[35]

The Coast Salish did not experience these new impositions on border crossings alone. In 2010, the United Kingdom refused entry to members of the Iroquois national lacrosse team travelling on Haudenosaunee passports, despite

Secretary of State Hillary Clinton's attempted intervention.[36] A year later the Canadian Border Service Agency denied entry to Joyce King, a member of the St. Regis Mohawk Tribe in the United States. They confiscated her Haudenosaunee passport, which they described "a fantasy document."[37] Indigenous sovereignty remained at odds with the world that nation-states had set out to create.

The outbreak of COVID-19 in 2020 brought questions about sovereignty and self-determination back to the forefront. Canada and the United States closed their border, and Indigenous communities followed suit. For grand chief Alvin Fiddler of the Nishnawbe Aski Nation, boiled water advisories and overcrowding on reserves forced Indigenous people to explore options beyond social distancing and hand washing. Protecting elders required creating checkpoints and designing other policies to limit contact between on-reserve communities and outsiders. These approaches, however, raise questions about whether the Pimicikamak Cree Nation, for example, has the legal right to close highway access points and impede the movement of Canadians attempting to enter or cross tribal lands. As battles over sovereignty and self-determination have shown, those kinds of questions have no easy answers.[38] Borders remain messy creations.

The Canada–US border still bears the guide marks of the nineteenth century. Changes in demography, technology, and political climate have altered the specifics of policy, but not always their thrust. The border's fluidity and unmanageable size remain eye-catching. Power still flows through direct and indirect means—controlling minds as much as bodies. If the border today is a more prominent impediment to movement than it was even twenty years earlier, it has not succeeded in shaking its past. It remains one border among many, a border built on Indigenous lands with all the ambiguity and complexity that such a venture creates.

Appendix

TERMINOLOGY GUIDE

This terminology guide is not comprehensive. It mentions only the nations that appear in this book and does not include all of the sub-divisions that exist for each linguistic or cultural group.

Linguistic/Cultural/Geographic Groups

Anishinaabeg (Anicinape, Neshnabé, Nishnawbe)

The term "Anishinaabeg" has been used both in a narrow sense as a synonym with Ojibwe and in a broader sense (as used in this book) to refer to the Anishinaabemowin-speaking people who originally inhabited the Great Lakes and surrounding regions. The size, geographic breadth, and complexity of Anishinaabe societies has meant that not only does the historical literature disagree on terminology, but contemporary communities often differ on the autonym they prefer. In the nineteenth century the Ojibwe, Odawa, and Potawatomi "formed a loose confederacy known as The Three Fires."[1]

- **Ojibwe** (Ojibwa, Ojibway, Chippewa, Bungi): The term "Chippewa" appears primarily in the United States. "Chippewa" is used as the primary self-designation for the non-Cree population residing at Rocky Boy.[2]
  - **Saulteaux** (Soto, Plains Ojibwe, Saulteurs): the term is often used to describe the people of the rapids who lived near Sault St. Marie and who later relocated west onto the Plains.[3]
  - **Saugeen** (Chippewas of Saugeen): the Ojibwe living around the Bruce Peninsula.[4]
- **Odawa** (Ottawa)[5]
- **Potawatomi** (Boodewaadamiig, Pedadumies)[6]

Assiniboine (Nakoda Oyadebi, Hohe Nakota)

A Siouan-speaking people who broke apart from the Oceti Sakowin (Sioux). By the nineteenth century, they occupied parts of present-day Saskatchewan, Montana, and North Dakota. The term "Assiniboine" comes from the Ojibwa word "*asinii-bwaan*" or "Stone Sioux," while they call themselves the Nakota. By the seventeenth century, the Assiniboine had joined the Iron Confederacy (*Nehiyaw-Pwat*) with the Cree. The exonyms used by other groups reflected the Assiniboine's complicated place in plains geopolitics (e.g., Tsuu T'ina: "wood-in Cree," Blackfoot: "original Cree," Hidatsa, "Sioux in the West").[7]

- **Stoney Nakota** (Stoney, Stonie): The term "Stoney" often refers to the Assiniboine who live in present-day Alberta or Saskatchewan.[8]

Coast Salish

The term "Coast Salish" has a complicated genesis. Originally, scholars used it in a strict sense to describe a language group, although the term has grown more ambiguous over time. In this sense, linguists differentiated those who belonged to the Coast Salish—located along the eastern portion of Vancouver Island, the western shores of southern British Columbia, and in Puget Sound—from the Nuu-chah-nulth, located on the northwest tip of Washington (the Makah) and the eastern half of Vancouver Island. The term "Coast Salish" today also implies a sense of cultural commonality, including the use of winter dances and transformer stories to help define belonging. It comprises more than three dozen distinct groups belonging to many different language groups.

- **Halq'eméylem Speakers**
  - **Stó:lō** (Stalo): The Stó:lō live along the Fraser River. Their name, which means "River People" in Halkomelem, emphasizes the importance of that geography to their sense of belonging. There is little consensus as to exactly which bands make up Stó:lō. Anthropological definitions and contemporary organizations like the Stó:lō Nation Canada and Stó:lō Tribal Council have overlapping or competing definitions of memberships. Groups like the Yale First Nations, who were once lumped in with the Stó:lō, have engaged in legal battles against that classification.
    - **Sumas:** Member of the Stó:lō Nation
    - **Ts'elxwéyeqw** (Chilliwack, Chillukweyuk): a group of seven tribes living in the watershed of the Chilliwack River.
- **Soowahlie** (Tsoowahlie)

- **Swí:lhcha** (Cultus Lake): a reference to Cultus Lake or alternatively the people who lived there
    - **Kwantlen** (Langley): reside near Langley
    - **Matsqui**: reside below the Sumas Mountain
  - **Cowichan**
  - **Lyackson**
  - **Musqueam**
  - **Penelakuts** (Pannalehuts)
  - **Stz'uminus** (Chemainus)
  - **Tsawwassen**
- **Nooksack Speakers**
  - **Nooksack**
- **Northern Straits Speakers**
  - **Semiahmoo**
  - **Lummi**
  - **Samish**
- **Twana Speakers**
  - **Twana** (tuwáduxq)
- **Squamish** (Swaumish)
- **Lushootseed (Puget Sound Salish) Language Speakers**
  - **Snoqualmie**
  - **Puyallup**
  - **Nisqually**
  - **Muckleshoot**
  - **Swinomish**
  - **Dwamish** (Duwamish)
  - **Skagit**
  - **Squaxin** (Squakson)
  - **Skykomish** (Skehwhamish, skai-wha-mish)[9]

Cree (Nêhiyawak)

Scholars have often used the term "Plains Cree" to distinguish those who lived on the prairies from those in the woodlands. This approach emphasizes the linguistic (pronunciation) and cultural (buffalo hunting) differences between the two groups.[10]

- **Swampy Cree** (Muskegon, Swampy Tribe of Lake Winnipeg)[11]
- **Calling River Cree** (Katepwu-cipi-wiyiniwuk): located on the Qu'Appelle River (Kâ-têpw êwi-sîpiy)[12]

- **Nêhiyaw** (Cree person)[13]
- **Nêhiyawak** (Cree people)[14]
- **Nêhiyawaskiy** (Cree territory)[15]

Haudenosaunee (Iroquois, Rotinonsionni, Six Nations)

The Haudenosaunee (people of the longhouse) formed a Confederacy that consisted of six nations who spoke interrelated languages and shared a common culture. Each nation occupied a distinct place in the Confederacy. The Seneca and Mohawk acted as Elder Brothers. The Cayuga, Oneida, and Tuscarora took the place of Younger Brothers, and the Onondaga served as fire keepers. These positions structured the duties that each nation had and the patterns of deliberation that occurred during council meetings. The Tuscarora, originally from the Carolinas, joined the Haudenosaunee Confederacy in the eighteenth century after conflict with British colonists. The Haudenosaunee understood the addition of the Tuscarora as the return of an old group, rather than the introduction of a new one.[16]

- **Mohawk** (Kanyen'kehaka)
- **Seneca** (Onondawa:ga)
- **Cayuga** (Gayo'goho:no')
- **Onondaga** (Onodagega)
- **Oneida** (Onyata'a:ka)
- **Tuscarora** (Skaru:reh)

Métis (métis, metis, Bois-Brulé, Chicot, Half-Breeds, Michif, Gens de Libre, Canadese)

Significant contention exists around the term used to describe offspring of European and Indigenous marriages.

- **Métis**: When capitalized, the term "Métis" often refers to the specific community that developed around the Red River Valley. It emphasizes the emergences of a culture, language (Michif), history, politics, and set of traditions distinct from both the French and Indigenous communities that the Métis emerged from.
- **métis**: When written without capitalization, the term "métis" refers to mixed-race communities that share European-Indigenous ancestry. This definition emphasizes the biological process (the intermixing of people) over the cultural process (the development of a unique people) and has been broadly

applied (with controversy) to individuals living in Quebec, Nova Scotia, and elsewhere.[17]

Northern Indians

The term "Northern Indians" appears in settler accounts around Puget Sound often to reference groups like the Haida, Tlingit, and Tsimshian.[18]

- **Tsimshian** (ćmsyan, Chimmesyan, chipsain): Coast Tsimshian and Southern Tsimshian use the term "ćmsyan" ("inside the Skeena River") to describe themselves. The Gitksan and Nishga use the autonyms "nisqá?a" and "kitxsan" respectively to describe themselves.[19]
- **Tlingit** (Clingats, Klinket, Kaloshes): an autonym based on the word for "human beings."[20]
- **Haida** (Haidah, Hai-dai): autonym for the occupants of Haida Gwaii (Queen Charlotte Islands).[21]

Oceti Sakowin (Sioux)

The Oceti Sakowin (Seven Council Fires) refers to a collection of nations commonly referred to as the Sioux. The seven council fires, which denote homes or hearths, consisted of the Mdewakanton, Wahpekute, Wahpeton, Sisseton, Yankton, Yanktonai, and Teton. Three major branches (often referred to as the Dakota, Nakota, and Lakota) divided the oyates (nations/peoples) within the broader Oceti Sakowin confederacy.[22]

- **Dakota Oyates (Santee, Eastern Dakota)**
    - **Mdewakanton** (Mdewakantonwan, Bdewakantowan, Bdewakanton)
    - **Wahpekute** (Wapekute)
    - **Wahpeton** (Wahpetonwan)
    - **Sisseton** (Sisitonwaŋ)
- **Nakota Oyates (Western Dakota)**
    - **Yankton** (Ihanktonwaŋ)
    - **Yanktonai** (Ihanktonwanna)
- **Lakota Oyates (Titonwan, Teton, Tetonwan, Tintantonwan, Tintanton):**
    - **Teton**: The Teton Oyate moved away from the other groups and formed their own council fire consisting of seven groups.
        - **Oglala** (Oglalahca)
        - **Mnikowoju** (Mnisa/Unkceyuta, Mniconjou)

- **Sicangu** (Brule, Burnt Thigh)
- **Oohenunpa** (Two Kettles)
- **Itazipco** (Itazico, Sans Arcs, Sanun)
- **Sihasapa** (Blackfeet)
- **Hunkpapa** (Inkpapaya)

Siksikaitsiitapi (Blackfoot) Confederacy

The Siksikaitsiitapi (Blackfoot speakers) lived on a vast section of the Great Plains bounded by the Rocky Mountains (west), North Saskatchewan (north), Sweet Grass hills (east), and Yellowstone River (south).[23] Three nations (four if both branches of the Piikani are considered) formed the core of the larger the Confederacy.

- **Piikani** (Pikuni, Piegan, Peigan)
  - **Aapatohsipiikani** (Northern Piikani)
  - **Aamsskaapipiikani** (Southern Piikani)
- **Kainah** (Blood, Apaitsitapi))
- **Siksika** (Blackfoot, Blackfeet, Kaskitiwayasituk): the Cree called the Siksika Kaskitiwayasituk (and various derivations) which translated as "person with black soles."[24]

Individual Communities or Nations

A'aninin (Gros Ventre): A nation of Algonquian speakers who inhabited the Fort Belknap agency by the nineteenth century. Not to be confused with the Hidatsa, who the French also call "Gros Ventre."[25]

Abenakis (Wabanaki, Oubenaquis, or ambiguously as Loups)[26]

Alberni (First Peoples of Alberni): The term contains ambiguity as it references a place where multiple groups live. It may describe the Tseshaht First Nation, a Nuu-chah-nulth-speaking people who lived in the Alberni Valley, or the Hupacasath people, who live near the present day location of Port Alberni.[27]

Apache (Nadiisha-dena): The Apache use various terms of self-identification. This includes Nadiisha-dena ("our people") for the broader group and "Ka-ta-kas" for the northern Apache, who maintained a plains lifestyle after the Comanche and other groups pushed the Lipan and Jicarilla Apache to the southwest.[28]

Arapahos (Hinono'ei): The term "Arapahos" is likely derived from a Crow or Pawnee exonym for the nation. Despite the uncertain origin, contemporary Hinono'ei communities continue to use the term "Arapaho" as a common self-designation. Prior to their separation in the eighteenth century, the term also encompassed the A'aninin (Gros Ventre).[29]

Bannock (Nimi, Bonnacks, Ponasht, Pannaitti): Other Indigenous communities called the Bannock, and the Northern Shoshone with whom they are closely associated, "Snakes."

The Bannocks refer to themselves as the Nimi ("the people"). They prioritize the term "Bannock" on their tribal website and in their press releases.[30]

Cheyenne (Tsistsistas, La chien): The term "Cheyenne" comes from a Sioux word for the group. Contemporary Tsistsistas communities continue to use the term "Cheyenne" as a common self-designation.[31]

Colville: A broad term used to describe the "Chelan, Chief Joseph Band of Nez Perce, Colville, Eniat, Lakes, Methow, Moses-Columbia, Nespelem, Okanogan, Palus, San Poil, Wenatchi" who became part of the Confederate Tribes of the Colville Reservation.[32]

Comanche (Nimini, Nʉmʉnʉʉ): The term "Comanche" is an ethnonym from the Ute (kimanči/kimá·čI) meaning enemy. Other Indigenous communities called them the snakes or various derivatives. The Nimini continue to use the term "Comanche" to describe their nation, despite its original meaning.[33]

Crow (apsâ·ro·ke, Absaroka, Apsáalooke): The term "Crow/Raven" comes from the various Siouan and Algonquian-speaking people who lived around the Apsáalooke, a term that has been translated variously as "sparrowhawk people," "anything that flies," and so on. Today the term "Crow" remains the widely used by the community.[34]

Dene (Athapaskan, Dinnie, Tinneh): The autonym (Dene) comes from the word "person" in various Athapaskan languages.[35]

Eyak: The Eyak live on the North Gulf Coast of present-day Alaska. The Eyak historically have used terms like "ʔi·ya·ġdalahġayu" ("inhabitants of Eyak village") and "daxʊ̨̣hyu" ("human being") for self-identification.[36]

Fort Nelson (Secanni, Sekani): The Fort Nelson First Nations live in Northern British Columbia and use the term "Fort Nelson" as their preferred designation.[37]

Kiikaapoi (Kickapoo, kiwegapaw,): The autonym kiwegapaw translates as "He stands about."[38]

Kiowa: The term used by many plains groups and Europeans to describe the Kiowa are all closely related to the autonym.[39]

Klickitat (Qwû'lh-hwai-pûm): a Sahaptin-speaking community who are closely associated with the Yakama.[40]

Ktunaxa (Kootenai, Kootenay): Ktunaxa is the self-designation while other terms are commonly used in Canada (Kootenay) and the United States (Kootenai).[41]

Kwakuitl: The Kwakuitl can refer either narrow (to a specific group) or a collection of roughly thirty autonomous communities who shared a common language and cultural practices and lived around the Queen Charlotte Strait.[42]

Muscogee (Creek): members of the Muscogee Confederacy inhabited parts of what became southeastern United States prior to their removal west in the 1830s.[43]

Nimiipuu (Nez Perce): speakers of the Nimipuutímt language use both the term "Nimiipuu" (autonym) and "Nez Perce" (the tribal designation) to describe themselves.[44]

Nlaka-pamux (Nlakapamux, Thompson, Thompson River Salish): The name Thompson appears in historical accounts the 1890s as a reference to the Thompson river, which flows through the group's land. The group refers to themselves as Nlaka-pamux.[45]

Nuu-chah-nulth: inhabitants of the western portion of Vancouver Island.[46]

Pawnee (Chatiks si chatiks): The Pawnee Nation uses both "Pawnee" (common) and "Chatiks si chatiks" (less common) in its official news publication. The term "Chatiks si chatiks" translates as "Men of Men."[47]

Passamaquoddy: The name "Passamaquoddy" references "those of the place where Pollock are plentiful."[48]

Salish (Flathead): Salish is used as the self-designation of the Salishan-speaking group who Lewis and Clark recorded as Flatheads.[49]

Sahnish (Arikaras, Ricaree, Rees, Tsa'nish): Oral histories suggest that the Pawnee gave the Sahnish the name "Arikara" to describe the way they wore their hair. The autonym Sahnish translates as "the original people from whom all other tribes sprang."[50]

Sqilxw (Okanogan, Sylix): "Sqilxw" is the self-referential term used by those who speak Nsyilxcen.[51]

Tsuut'ina (Sarcee, Sasiwuk, Sarsi): the name Sarcee is derived from the Blackfoot term "Sa arsi," meaning "not good."[52]

Wendat (Huron, Wyandot, Wyandotte): The Wendat Confederacy originally consisted of "four or five autonomous nations: the Bear Nation (Attignawantan), the Nation of the Rock (Arendaeronnon), the People of the Cord (Attigneenongnahac), the People of the Deer (Tahontaenrat), and perhaps a fifth group, the People of the Marsh (Ataronchronon)."[53] The modern Wendat Confederacy includes the Huron Wendat Nation (Quebec), the Wyandotte Nation (Oklahoma), the Wyandot of Anderdon Nation (Michigan/Ontario), and the Wyandot Nation of Kansas (Kansas).[54]

Yakama (Yakima, Eyakima): a Sahaptin-speaking group whose name derives from a Spokane term for "a growing family."[55]

NOTES

A Note on Terminology

1. United Nations, *United Nations Declaration on the Rights of Indigenous Peoples* (United Nations, 2008), http://www.un.org/esa/socdev/unpfii/documents/DRIPS_en.pdf; Kathryn Labelle, Brittany Luby, and Alison Norman, "(Re)Naming and (De)Colonizing the (I?)ndigenous People(s) of North America—Part II," *Active History*, November 8, 2016, http://activehistory.ca/2016/11/renaming-and-decolonizing-the-indigenous-peoples-of-north-america-part-i/.

Introduction

1. CIA, "CIA and Nazi Warcrim. and Col. Chap. 1–10, Draft Working Paper_0003," n.d., 2, Special Collection, Nazi War Crimes Disclosure Act, FOIA/ESDN (Crest) 519697e8993294098d50c2a3, CIA Freedom of Information Act Electronic Reading Room, https://www.cia.gov/library/readingroom/document/519697e8993294098d50c2a3; A. N. Marquis Company, *Who's Who In America with World Notables: Biographical Dictionary of Notable Living Men and Women*, vol. 35 (1968–69) (Chicago: A. N. Marquis Company, 1968), 193.
2. Andrue Berding, "Canadian Border Is Mere Symbol: Lack of Formalities Is in Striking Contrast to Europe," *Washington Post*, August 14, 1938.
3. Berding, "Canadian Border Is Mere Symbol."
4. Red Dog, File Hills Agency Interview #1 (Red Dog), interview by D. G. Mandelbaum, trans. Jimmie Tuck, June 30, 1934, O CPRC, IH-DM.08, Transcript Disc 133, University of Regina.
5. Red Dog, File Hills Agency Interview #1.
6. Zalfa Feghali, "Border Studies and Indigenous Peoples: Reconsidering Our Approach," in *Beyond the Border: Tensions across the Forty-Ninth Parallel in the Great Plains and Prairies*, ed. Kyle Conway and Timothy Pasch (Montreal: McGill-Queen's University Press, 2013), 157; William Scow, Chief William Scow Interview #2, interview by Imbert Orchard, c 1967, O CPRC, IH-BC.61, Transcript disc 178, University of Regina.
7. David Newman, "On Borders and Power: A Theoretical Framework," *Journal of Borderlands Studies* 18, no. 1 (2003): 17; Paul Nadasdy, *Hunters and Bureaucrats: Power, Knowledge and Aboriginal-State Relations in the Southwest Yukon* (Vancouver: UBC Press, 2003), 239–45.
8. Newman, "On Borders and Power," 14; Daniel S. Margolies, *Spaces of Law in American Foreign Relations: Extradition and Extraterritoriality in the Borderlands and Beyond, 1877–1898* (Athens: University of Georgia Press, 2011), 7.
9. Karl S. Hele, ed., *Lines Drawn Upon the Water: First Nations and the Great Lakes Borders and Borderlands* (Waterloo: Wilfrid Laurier University Press, 2008), xv.
10. William Rodney, "Brown, John George," in *Dictionary of Canadian Biography*, vol. 14 (Toronto: University of Toronto Press/Université Laval, 2003).

11. Benjamin H. Johnson and Andrew R. Graybill, eds., *Bridging National Borders in North America: Transnational and Comparative Histories* (Durham, NC: Duke University Press, 2010), 4, 6, 10–11; Marcus Lee Hansen, *The Mingling of Canadian and American People* (New Haven, CT: Yale University Press, 1940), 3; Samuel Truett and Elliott Young, "Making Transnational History: Nations, Regions, and Borderlands," in *Continental Crossroads: Remapping U.S. Mexico Borderlands History* (Durham, NC: Duke University Press, 2004), 3; David Thelen, "The Nation and Beyond: Transnational Perspectives on United States History," *Journal of American History* 86, no. 3 (December 1, 1999): 965, https://doi.org/10.2307/2568601.
12. Johnson and Graybill, *Bridging National Borders in North America*, 2, 4; Pekka Hämäläinen and Samuel Truett, "On Borderlands," *Journal of American History* 98, no. 2 (2011): 343; Truett and Young, "Making Transnational History," 8; James Daschuk, *Clearing the Plains: Disease, Politics of Starvation, and the Loss of Aboriginal Life* (Regina: University of Regina Press, 2013), xv.
13. Gloria E. Anzaldúa, *Borderlands: La Frontiera the New Mestiza*, 2nd ed. (San Francisco: Aunt Lute Books, 1999); Brian DeLay, *War of a Thousand Deserts: Indian Raids and the U.S.–Mexican War* (New Haven, CT: Yale University Press, 2008); Rachel St. John, *Line in the Sand: A History of the Western U.S.–Mexico Border* (Princeton, NJ: Princeton University Press, 2011); Geraldo Cadava, *Standing on Common Ground: The Making of the Sunbelt Borderland* (Cambridge, MA: Harvard University Press, 2013); Kelly Lytle Hernández, *Migra!: A History of the U.S. Border Patrol* (Berkeley: University of California Press, 2010); Newman, "On Borders and Power," 2003, 14.
14. Brandon Dimmel, "'Shutting Down the Snake Ranch': Battling Booze at the BC Border, 1910–1914," in *Beyond the Border: Tensions across the Forty-Ninth Parallel in the Great Plains and Prairies*, ed. Kyle Conway and Timothy James Pasch (Montreal: McGill-Queen's University Press, 2013), 95.
15. Edgar W. McInnis, *The Unguarded Frontier: A History of American–Canadian Relations* (Garden City, NY: Doubleday, 1942); Hansen, *The Mingling of Canadian and American People*; Edith Patterson Meyer, *The Friendly Frontier: The Story of the Canadian–American Border* (Toronto: Little, Brown, 1962); Tony Rees, *Arc of the Medicine Line: Mapping the World's Longest Undefended Border Across the Western Plains* (Lincoln: University of Nebraska Press, 2007); John J. Bukowczyk, Nora Faires, David R. Smith, and Randy William Widdis, *Permeable Border: The Great Lakes Basin as Transnational Region 1650–1990* (Pittsburgh: University of Pittsburgh Press, 2005).
16. The phrase is etched onto the Peace Arch, which separates Blaine, Washington from Surrey, British Columbia. Bruce Granville Miller, ed., *Be of Good Mind: Essays on the Coast Salish* (Vancouver: UBC Press, 2007), 55; John Herd Thompson and Stephen J. Randall, *Canada and the United States: Ambivalent Allies*, 4th ed. (Athens: University of Georgia Press, 2008).
17. Kornel S. Chang, *Pacific Connections* (Berkeley: University of California Press, 2012); Beth Lew-Williams, *The Chinese Must Go: Violence, Exclusion, and the Making of the Alien in America* (Cambridge, MA: Harvard University Press, 2018); Erika Lee, *At America's Gates: Chinese Immigration during the Exclusion Era, 1882–1943* (Chapel Hill: University of North Carolina Press, 2003).
18. Daschuk, *Clearing the Plains*; Sarah Carter, *Lost Harvests: Prairie Indian Reserve Farmers and Government Policy* (Montreal: McGill-Queen's University Press, 1990); Cathleen D. Cahill, *Federal Fathers & Mothers: A Social History of the United States Indian Service, 1869–1933* (Chapel Hill: University of North Carolina Press, 2011); Keith Thor Carlson, *The Power of Place, the Problem of Time: Aboriginal Identity and Historical Consciousness in the Cauldron of Colonialism* (Toronto: University of Toronto Press, 2010), 7.
19. Richard White, *The Middle Ground: Indians, Empires, and Republics in the Great Lakes Region, 1650–1815* (Cambridge: Cambridge University Press, 1991); David G. McCrady, *Living with Strangers: The Nineteenth-Century Sioux and the Canadian–American Borderlands* (Lincoln: University of Nebraska Press, 2006); Kathryn Magee Labelle, *Dispersed But Not Destroyed: A History of the Seventeenth-Century Wendat People* (Vancouver: UBC Press, 2013); Hele, *Lines Drawn Upon the Water*; Michel Hogue, *Metis and the Medicine Line: Creating a Border and Dividing a People* (Regina: University of Regina Press, 2015).

20. Nayan Shah, *Stranger Intimacy: Contesting Race, Sexuality, and the Law in the North American West* (Berkeley: University of California Press, 2011); Sheila McManus, *The Line Which Separates: Race, Gender, and the Making of the Alberta–Montana Borderlands* (Lincoln: University of Nebraska Press, 2005); Holly M. Karibo, *Sin City North: Sex, Drugs, and Citizenship in the Detroit–Windsor Borderland* (Chapel Hill: University of North Carolina Press, 2015); Sarah Carter and Patricia McCormack, eds., *Recollecting: Lives of Aboriginal Women of the Canadian Northwest and Borderlands* (Edmonton: Athabasca University Press, 2011).
21. Lew-Williams, *The Chinese Must Go*; Lee, *At America's Gates*.
22. Barbara Roberts, *Whence They Came: Deportation from Canada 1900–1935* (Manitoba: University of Ottawa Press, 1988); Deirdre M. Moloney, *National Insecurities: Immigrants and U.S. Deportation Policy Since 1882* (Chapel Hill: University of North Carolina Press, 2012); Mae M. Ngai, *Impossible Subjects: Illegal Aliens and the Making of Modern America* (Princeton, NJ: Princeton University Press, 2004).
23. Cahill, *Federal Fathers & Mothers*; Dave McIntosh, *The Collectors: A History of Canadian Customs and Excise* (Toronto: NC Press, 1984); Hernández, *Migra*; Andrew R. Graybill, *Policing the Great Plains: Rangers, Mounties, and the North American Frontier 1875–1910* (Lincoln: University of Nebraska Press, 2007); Katherine Unterman, *Uncle Sam's Policemen: The Pursuit of Fugitives Across Borders* (Cambridge, MA: Harvard University Press, 2015).
24. Edward Thornton to Marquis of Salisbury, March 28, 1879, RG 10, Indian Affairs, Black Series, Reel C-10114, Volume 3652, File 8589 pt 1, LAC.
25. Bill Chappell, "Cheese-Smuggling Ring Is Brought Down In Canada," *National Public Radio*, September 27, 2012, https://www.npr.org/sections/thetwo-way/2012/09/27/161917296/cheese-smuggling-ring-is-brought-down-in-canda; Simon Little, "Smuggler's Inn Owner Charged with Trying to Illegally Sneak People into Canada," *Global News*, April 9, 2019, https://globalnews.ca/news/5149248/smugglers-inn-charged-sneak-people-into-canada/.
26. "US–Mexico Border Wall: Pentagon Authorises $1bn Transfer," *BBC*, March 26, 2019, https://www.bbc.com/news/world-us-canada-47702152; Associated Press, "Separation of Parents, Kids at U.S.–Mexico Border: How the Trump Administration Got Here," *CBC News*, June 17, 2018, https://www.cbc.ca/news/world/border-children-parents-separation-trump-1.4710055; David K. Androff and Kyoko Y. Tavassoli, "Deaths in the Desert: The Human Rights Crisis on the U.S.–Mexico Border," *Social Work* 57, no. 2 (2012): 165.
27. Andrew Johnson, "Detailed Statement of Disbursements on Account of Northwest Boundary Survey, From February 14, 1857 to December 31, 1868," in *Message from the President of the United States Concerning the Northwest Boundary Commission*, 40th Congress, 3d Session, Ex. Doc. No. 86, 1869; Larry Haag and Lawrence Barkwell, *The Boundary Commission's Metis Scouts The 49th Rangers* (Winnipeg: Louis Riel Institute, 2009), 3–6, 25.
28. James W. Taylor to J. C. B. Davis, October 28, 1871, Hecht Collection, University of Washington Special Collections; Allan MacNab to Sir George, June 28, 1838, 103–19, RG 8, C Series, Vol 610, Reel C-3155, 103-119, LAC.
29. Elliott West, *The Last Indian War: The Nez Perce Story* (New York: Oxford University Press, 2009), 193, 208, 247; MacNab to Sir George, June 28, 1838.
30. Richard Barrington Nevitt, *Frontier Life in the Mounted Police: The Diary Letters of Richard Barrington Nevitt, NWMP Surgeon, 1874–78* (Calgary: Alberta Records Publication Board, Historical Society of Alberta, 2010), 185–89; R. N. Wilson, "Diary 1881–1884," n.d., 4–5, Wood Family Fonds, M9460, File 116, Glenbow Archives; J. J. Campbell to Superintendent General of Indian Affairs, July 23, 1895, 57, DIA ARO, LAC; Benjamin Hoy, "A Border without Guards: First Nations and the Enforcement of National Space," *Journal of the Canadian Historical Association* 25, no. 2 (2014): 89–115, http://dx.doi.org/10.7202/1032842ar.
31. For other places I've described this phenomenon see Hoy, "A Border without Guards."
32. Indian Commissioner for Manitoba and Northwest Territories, "Indians Enrolled in Canada and United States," May 26, 1908, 2–3, 63–68, RG 10, Vol 3573, File 142, Reel C-10188 [Online], LAC.

33. For other ways that governments exercise power at a distance see Michel Foucault, *Discipline & Punish: The Birth of the Prison*, trans. Alan Sheridan, 2nd ed. (New York: Vintage Books, 1995).
34. James Laxer, *The Border: Canada, the U.S. and Dispatches from the 49th Parallel* (Toronto: Doubleday Canada, 2003).

Chapter 1

1. Robert Goodvoice, Robert Goodvoice Interview #3, interview by Robert Goodvoice, 1977, O CPRC, IH-104-5, Transcript Disc 10 (Originals held at PAS, R-A1336), University of Regina.
2. Elliott West, "A Horse-Man's View of a Grassland Revolution," in *Bison and People on the North American Great Plains*, ed. Geoff Cunfer and Bill Waiser (College Station: Texas A&M Press, 2016), 188–89.
3. Great Britain and United States, "Definitive Treaty of Peace and Friendship between His Britannic Majesty and the United States of America [Treaty of Paris]," September 3, 1783, Early Canadiana Online; United Kingdom and United States, "The Oregon Treaty," 1846, RG 11, Perfected Treaties 1778–1945, NAI 299808, NARA; Great Britain and United States, "Convention Respecting Fisheries, Boundary, and Restoration of Slaves, Signed October 20 1818," in *Treaties and Conventions Concluded Between the United States of America and Other Powers Since July 4, 1776* (Washington, DC: Government Printing Office, 1873), 351; Paul Arthur Berkman, "The Anglo-Russian Convention Concerning the Limits of Their Respective Possessions on the Northwest Coast of America and the Navigation of the Pacific Ocean," in *Baseline of Russian Arctic Laws* (New York: Springer, 2019), 57.
4. John Herd Thompson and Stephen J. Randall, *Canada and the United States: Ambivalent Allies*, 4th ed. (Athens: University of Georgia Press, 2008), 19; Alan Taylor, *The Civil War of 1812: American Citizens, British Subjects, Irish Rebels, & Indian Allies* (New York: 2010), 22.
5. Great Britain and United States, "Treaty of Paris, 1783," 781.
6. Great Britain and United States, "Treaty of Paris, 1783," 782–83.
7. Thompson and Randall, *Canada and the United States*, 19.
8. Robin W. Winks, "Slavery, the Loyalists, and English Canada, 1760–1801," in *The History of Immigration and Racism in Canada*, ed. Barrington Walker (Toronto: Canadian Scholars' Press, 2008), 29, 35; Thompson and Randall, *Canada and the United States*, 15; Ontario, "An Act for Encouraging New Settlers in His Majesty's Colonies and Plantations in America," in *The Statutes of the Province of Upper Canada 1792–1831: Together with Such British Statutes, Ordinances of Quebec, and Proclamations, as Relate to the Said Province* (Kingston: Francis M. Hill, 1831), 12.
9. Timothy C. Winegard, *For King and Kanata: Canadian Indians and the First World War* (Winnipeg: University of Manitoba Press, 2012), 16.
10. James Mason, James Mason Interview, interview by Alex Cywink, June 7, 1983, O CPRC, IH-OT.026, Transcript Disc 105a, University of Regina; Taylor, *The Civil War of 1812*, 436–37.
11. Edith Patterson Meyer, *The Friendly Frontier: The Story of the Canadian-American Border* (Toronto: Little, Brown, 1962), 52–56; Bill Hubbard, *American Boundaries: The Nation, the States, the Rectangular Survey* (Chicago: University of Chicago Press, 2008), 57; Francis M. Carroll, *A Good and Wise Measure: The Search for the Canadian-American Boundary, 1783–1842* (Toronto: University of Toronto Press, 2001), 9, 19.
12. United States and Great Britain, "Treaty of Amity, Commerce, and Navigation, between His Britannic Majesty, and the United States of America [Jay Treaty]," November 19, 1794, article II, III, VI, Early Canadiana Online.
13. Dave McIntosh, *The Collectors: A History of Canadian Customs and Excise* (Toronto: NC Press, 1984), 66.
14. United States, "An Act Respecting Alien Enemies," July 6, 1798, The Avalon Project, Yale University Law School.
15. John Torpey, *The Invention of the Passport: Surveillance, Citizenship, and the State* (Cambridge: Cambridge University Press, 2000), 94.
16. Taylor, *The Civil War of 1812*, 4.
17. Taylor, *The Civil War of 1812*, 105.

18. Taylor, *The Civil War of 1812*, 134.
19. Taylor, *The Civil War of 1812*, 140–41, 321, 328; Elizabeth Jane Errington, *The Lion, the Eagle, and Upper Canada: A Developing Colonial Ideology* (Montreal: McGill-Queen's University Press, 1994), 64.
20. Thomas Jefferson, *The Jeffersonian Cyclopedia: A Comprehensive Collection of the Views of Thomas Jefferson*, ed. John P. Foley (New York: Funk & Wagnalls Company, 1900), 124.
21. Taylor, *The Civil War of 1812*, 417.
22. Taylor, *The Civil War of 1812*, 151, 290–91; Peter Andreas, *Smuggler Nation: How Illicit Trade Made America* (New York: Oxford University Press, 2013), 83–86; United States, "An Act to Prohibit American Vessels from Proceeding to or Trading with the Enemies of the United States, and for Other Purposes," July 6, 1812, The Avalon Project, Yale University Law School; John Irvine Little, *Loyalties in Conflict: A Canadian Borderland in War and Rebellion 1812–1840* (Toronto: University of Toronto Press, 2008), 43.
23. Little, *Loyalties in Conflict*, 45.
24. Andreas, *Smuggler Nation*, 88–89.
25. Taylor, *The Civil War of 1812*, 107, 334.
26. Taylor, *The Civil War of 1812*, 347.
27. Thompson and Randall, *Canada and the United States*, 22; Taylor, *The Civil War of 1812*, 436, 458.
28. Taylor, *The Civil War of 1812*, 428.
29. Great Britain and United States, "A Treaty of Peace and Amity between His Britannic Majesty and the United States of America [Treaty of Ghent]" (R. G. Clarke, December 24, 1814), 11, Early Canadiana Online.
30. Frederick Wm. Major, *Manitoulin: The Isle of the Ottawas Being a Handbook of Historical and Other Information on the Grand Manitoulin Island* (Gore Bay: The Recorder Press, 1934), 13.
31. Ernest Debassigae, Ernest L. Debassigae Interview #3, interview by Tony Snowsill and Christine Welsh, February 17, 1984, O CPRC, IH-OM.03B, Transcript Disc 78, University of Regina.
32. Errington, *The Lion, the Eagle, and Upper Canada*, 181–84.
33. Fred Gaffen, *Cross-Border Warriors: Canadians in American Forces, Americans in Canadian Forces From the Civil War to the Gulf* (Toronto: Dundurn Press, 1995), 13.
34. Errington, *The Lion, the Eagle, and Upper Canada*, 181.
35. Peter Marshall, "Americans in Upper Canada, 1791–1812: 'Late Loyalists' or Early Immigrants?," in *The History of Immigration and Racism in Canada*, ed. Barrington Walker (Toronto: Canadian Scholars' Press, 2008), 46.
36. Peter Burroughs, "Tackling Army Desertion in British North America," *Canadian Historical Review* 61, no. 1 (1980): 37.
37. Great Britain and United States, "Treaty of Ghent," 7; Gordon T. Stewart, *The American Response to Canada Since 1776* (East Lansing: Michigan State University Press, 1992), 35; United States, *Statement on the Part of the United States, of the Case Referred in Pursuance of the Convention of 29th September, 1827 between the Said States and Great Britain to His Majesty, the King of the Netherlands for His Decision Thereon* (Washington, DC: Office of the United States Telegraph, 1829), 5–8, 22.
38. Cole Harris, *The Resettlement of British Columbia: Essays on Colonialism and Geographical Change* (Vancouver: UBC Press, 1997), 33, 44, 48.
39. John G. Deane, "Journal of the Commission to Explore the North Eastern Boundary," September 2, 1838, 8, 16, Coll. S-6365, Misc. Box 192/2, Maine Historical Society (Maine Memory Network).
40. Great Britain, *First Statement on the Part of Great Britain, According to the Provisions of the Convention Concluded Between Great Britain and the United States, on the 29th September 1827 in Regulating the Reference to Arbitration of the Disputed Points of Boundary Under the Fifth Article of the Treaty of Ghent* (J. Harrison and Son, 1829), 123.
41. Great Britain, *First Statement on the Part of Great Britain*, 79, 129, 133, 140.
42. "Interrogations Administered to John Curry Esquire by Phineas Bruce Esquire Acting on Behalf of the United States of America," 1797, 185–87, Northeast Boundary Papers, Papers, 1790, 1796–1799, R13223-0-8-E, Reel M-9624, LAC.

43. Michel Hogue, *Metis and the Medicine Line: Creating a Border and Dividing a People* (Regina: University of Regina Press, 2015), 27.
44. Great Britain and United States, "Convention between the United States of America and Great Britain. Concluded September 29, 1827. Ratified April 2, 1828. Proclaimed May 15, 1828," in *Treaties and Conventions Concluded Between the United States of America and Other Powers Since July 4, 1776*, ed. John Chandler Bancroft Davis (Washington, DC: Government Printing Office, 1871), 367.
45. Bill Waiser, *A World We Have Lost: Saskatchewan Before 1905* (Markham, ON: Fifth House Limited, 2016), 152.
46. Tom Mutceheu (te-tapaxtoweu "Falling Noise"), Carlton Agency #2, interview by D. G. Mandelbaum, trans. Bob, July 19, 1934, O CPRC, IH-DM.25, Transcript Disc 135, University of Regina.
47. Sam (Long Horned Sitting Bull) Belanger and Kicemanito'owacis (God's Child), Round Lake Indian School Interview #2, interview by D. G. Mandelbaum, trans. Joe Bear and Joe Still, June 27, 1934, O CPRC, IH-DM.06, Transcript Disc 133, University of Regina.
48. tigisikgo-awasis ("Child of the Sky Right Above" and "migwan"), File Hills Agency #2, interview by D. G. Mandelbaum, trans. Alec Brass, July 2, 1934, O CPRC, IH-DM.09 Transcript Disc 133, University of Regina.
49. Augustine Yellow Sun and Joe Poor Eagle, Augustine Yellow Sun, Joe Poor Eagle Interview #2, interview by Allan Wolf Leg, 1974, O CPRC, IH-246A, Transcript 3, University of Regina; Lynn Hickey, Elder's Interviews: Support From Anthropological Sources, May 1974, 10, O CPRC, IH-341A, Transcript Disc 31, University of Regina.
50. Ted Binnema, "A Fur Trade Historian's View of Seasonal Bison Movements on the Northern Plains," in *Bison and People on the North American Great Plains*, ed. Geoff Cunfer and Bill Waiser (College Station: Texas A&M Press, 2016), 170–71.
51. Joe Louie, Joe Louie Interview #1, interview by Imbert Orchard, 1967, O CPRC, IH-BC.53, Transcript Disc 176, University of Regina.
52. Louie, Joe Louie Interview #1, 6.
53. Louie, Joe Louie Interview #1, 6–7.
54. Charles S. Kelly, interview by Margaret Robertson, October 20, 1986, Minnesota Environmental Issues Oral History Project: Interview with Charles S. Kelly, OH 58, AV1988.99.15, MHS.
55. Bradley Miller, *Borderline Crime: Fugitive Criminals and the Challenge of the Border, 1819–1914* (Toronto: University of Toronto Press, 2016), 19.
56. Great Britain and United States, "Treaty of Paris, 1783," 781.
57. McIntosh, *The Collectors: A History of Canadian Customs and Excise*, 190.
58. Carroll, *A Good and Wise Measure*, 196, 211–12; Meyer, *Friendly Frontier*, 88–90; Stewart, *The American Response to Canada Since 1776*, 44; Thompson and Randall, *Canada and the United States*, 30–31.
59. McIntosh, *The Collectors: A History of Canadian Customs and Excise*, 190.
60. Great Britain, *Correspondence Respecting the Operations of the Commission for Running and Tracing the Boundary Line Between Her Majesty's Possessions in North America and the United States Under the VIth Article of the Treaty Signed at Washington, August 9, 1842* (London: T. R. Harrison, 1845), 15.
61. Great Britain, *Correspondence*, 26.
62. *Narrative of the Survey by the British Commission of the Boundary Between the British Possessions in North America and the United States of America under the Treaty of Washington of 9th August, 1842* (S.l.: s.n., 1846), 2.
63. *Narrative of Survey 1842*, 8.
64. Adam Mayers, *Dixie and the Dominion: Canada, the Confederacy, and the War for the Union* (Toronto: Dundurn Group, 2003), 75–76.
65. Earl of Durham, "Report on the Affairs of British North America," 1839, 112, Early Canadiana Online; Allan Greer, "1837–38 Rebellion Reconsidered," *Canadian Historical Review* 76, no. 1 (1995): 15.
66. Carroll, *A Good and Wise Measure*, 207.
67. Great Britain, "Enclosure 1, in No. 87 Declaration by Robert Nelson," in *British North America: Copies or Extracts of Correspondence Relative to the Affairs of British North America*

(London: HMSO, 1839), 249–50; Richard Chabot, Yves Roby, and Jacques Monet, "Nelson, Robert," in *Dictionary of Canadian Biography*, vol. 10, 1972.
68. Chabot, Roby, and Monet, "Nelson, Robert."
69. William Sandom to George Arthur, August 14, 1838, 50, RG 8, Reel C-3155, C Series, Vol. 611, LAC.
70. Sandom to Arthur, 51.
71. Greer, "1837–38 Rebellion Reconsidered," 16.
72. Little, *Loyalties in Conflict*, 88.
73. Allan MacNab to Sir George, June 28, 1838, RG 8, C Series, Vol 610, Reel C-3155, 103–119, LAC.
74. Greer, "1837–38 Rebellion Reconsidered," 16; William I. Kerr to Col. Halkett, June 30, 1838, 149–51, RG 8, C Series, Vol 610, Reel C-3155, 149–151, LAC.
75. Mathieu Sossoyan, "The Kahnawake Iroquois and the Lower-Canadian Rebellions, 1837–1838" (MA thesis, McGill University, 1999), 1.
76. Sossoyan, "The Kahnawake Iroquois," 59.
77. MacNab to Sir George, June 28, 1838.
78. Great Britain, "Copy of a Despatch from Lieutenant-Governor Sir George Arthur to Lord Glenelg, 28 September 1838," in *British North America: Copies or Extracts of Correspondence Relative to the Affairs of British North America* (London: HMSO, 1839), 342.
79. Great Britain, "No. 2 Upper Canada Gazette Extraordinary By Authority—Toronto, Friday, November 16, 1838," in *British North America: Copies or Extracts of Correspondence Relative to the Affairs of British North America* (London: HMSO, 1839), 357.
80. Sossoyan, "The Kahnawake Iroquois and the Lower-Canadian Rebellions, 1837–1838," 44, 57, 60, 64.
81. Richard Bullock, "Militia General Order," June 4, 1838, 20, RG 8, C Series, Vol 609, Reel C-3155, 20, LAC; Sossoyan, "The Kahnawake Iroquois and the Lower-Canadian Rebellions, 1837–1838," 44.
82. Carroll, *A Good and Wise Measure*, 207.
83. Mayers, *Dixie and the Dominion*, 76.
84. Stewart, *The American Response to Canada Since 1776*, 72.
85. Little, *Loyalties in Conflict*, 95; Greer, "1837–38 Rebellion Reconsidered," 15–16.
86. T. Hartley Crawford to J. R. Poinsett, November 28, 1840, 246, OIA ARO, UWDC; D. P. Bushnell to Gov. J. D. Doty, September 30, 1842, 407, OIA ARO, UWDC; W. Sheridan Warrick, "The American Indian Policy in the Upper Old Northwest Following the War of 1812," *Ethnohistory* 3, no. 2 (1956): 111.
87. Warrick, "American Indian Policy in the Upper Old Northwest," 111.
88. Henry R. Schoolcraft, "Report of H. R. Schoolcraft, Agent at Mackinac, and Acting Superintendent[,] Michigan," in *Message from the President of the United States to the Two Houses of Congress at the Commencement of the Second Session of the Twenty-Sixth Congress* (Washington, DC: Blair and Rives Printer, 1840), 344.
89. Tim Alan Garrison, *The Legal Ideology of Removal: The Southern Judiciary and the Sovereignty of Native American Nations* (Athens: University of Georgia Press, 2002), 5–10.
90. James M. McClurken, "Ottawa Adaptive Strategies to Indian Removal," *Michigan Historical Review* 12, no. 1 (1986): 40–41.
91. McClurken, 40; Warrick, "American Indian Policy in the Upper Old Northwest," 119.
92. Unsigned petitioners and Andrew Gordon Chisholm to Secretary of the Interior, "[Petition of Andrew Gordon Chisholm]," August 1916, 2, "Headquarters—Correspondence, Reports, Petitions, and Memoranda Regarding the Potawatomi Claim Against the United States Government for Annuity Money Owing under Treaties", RG 10, Volume 2788, File 156, 610 pt.1., LAC.
93. Unsigned petitioners and Chisholm to Secretary of the Interior, 3.
94. Robert Stuart to T. Hartley Crawford, "No. 93," October 13, 1843, 426, OIA ARO, UWDC.
95. George Ironside to Col. S. P. Jarvis, September 16, 1843, Burton Historical Collection, George Ironside Papers, Correspondence Papers 1774–1848, Vol L5 1837–45, Detroit Public Library.
96. Frank Pedley to E. L. Newcombe, November 20, 1912, "Headquarters—Correspondence, Reports, Petitions, and Memoranda Regarding the Potawatomi Claim Against the United

States Government for Annuity Money Owing under Treaties", RG 10, Volume 2788, File 156, 610 pt.1., LAC.

97. United States Congress, *Congressional Record, V. 153, Pt. 1, January 4, 2007 to January 17, 2007* (Washington, DC: Government Printing Office, 2007), 136–38.
98. West, "A Horse-Man's View of a Grassland Revolution," 188–89.
99. Jan R. Van Meter, "Fifty-Four Forty or Fight!," in *Tippecanoe and Tyler Too* (Chicago: University of Chicago Press, 2008), 76–81; Danl. Webster and Ashburton, "A Treaty to Settle and Define the Boundaries Between the Territories of the United States and the Possessions of Her Britannic Majesty in North America [Treaty of Webster-Ashburton] Concluded August 9, 1842," in *Treaties and Conventions Concluded Between the United States of America and Other Powers Since July 4, 1776*, ed. J. C. Bancroft Davis (Washington, DC: Government Printing Office, 1873), 369–75.
100. Meter, "Fifty-Four Forty or Fight!," 80.
101. John S. Galbraith, "The Early History of the Puget's Sound Agricultural Company, 1838–43," *Oregon Historical Quarterly* 55, no. 3 (1954): 234.
102. The use of parallels created a small peninsula of American territory known as Point Roberts, under five square miles in area, connected by land only to British Columbia. Point Roberts had originally been Coast Salish territories but European fisherman began encroaching on the land as early as 1853. This area later became a haven for smuggling to the dismay of customs agents who wondered whether it was beneficial at all that the area was considered American domain. A. L. Blake to A. W. Bash, February 9, 1883, RG 36, U.S. Customs Service, Puget Sound, Box 111, Letters Received from Subports and Inspectors, File 3, NARA Seattle; Richard Clark, *Point Roberts, U.S.A. The History of a Canadian Enclave* (Bellingham, WA: Textype, 1980), 2, 7, 41.
103. United Kingdom and United States, "The Oregon Treaty."
104. Rosemary Neering, *The Pig War: The Last Canada–US Border Conflict* (Toronto: Heritage House Publishing, 2011), 128.
105. Alexandra Harmon, *Indians in the Making: Ethnic Relations and Indian Identities Around Puget Sound* (Berkeley: University of California Press, 1998), 89; J. W. Nesmith to J. W. Denver, "No. 134," September 1, 1857, 218, OIA ARO, UWDC; J. Cain to Geo. W. Manypenny, "No. 97," October 6, 1855, 192, OIA ARO, UWDC.
106. Harmon, *Indians in the Making*, 86–87; "Narrative Section X—History, Tulalip Reservation Washington, Annual Report," 1914, 142–43, University of Washington Special Collections.
107. Ezra Meeker, *Pioneer Reminiscences of Puget Sound : The Tragedy of Leschi* (Seattle: Lowman & Hanford Stationary and Printing Co., 1905), 156, 304, 420, 453.
108. Michael Phillips to Superintendent General of Indian Affairs, July 28, 1891, 127, DIA ARO, LAC.
109. Barry M Gough, *Gunboat Frontier: British Maritime Authority and Northwest Coast Indians, 1846–90* (Vancouver: UBC Press, 1984), 58–59.
110. Gough, *Gunboat Frontier*, 158.
111. Phillips to Superintendent General of Indian Affairs, July 28, 1891, 127.
112. Leland Donald, *Aboriginal Slavery on the Northwest Coast of North America* (Berkeley: University of California Press, 1997), 185–86.
113. John Sutton Lutz, *Makúk: A New History of Aboriginal-White Relations* (Vancouver: UBC Press, 2008), 257; Gough, *Gunboat Frontier*, 27.
114. Gough, *Gunboat Frontier*, 13, 30.
115. George A. Paige to W. H. Waterman, "No 10," July 8, 1865, 99, OIA ARO, UWDC; Lissa K. Wadewitz, *The Nature of Borders: Salmon, Boundaries, and Bandits on the Salish Sea* (Seattle: University of Washington Press, 2012), 68–69; M. T. Simmons to Edward R. Geary, "No. 180," July 1, 1859, 396, OIA ARO, UWDC; M. T. Simmons to J. W. Nesmith, "No. 137," July 1, 1857, 332, OIA ARO, UWDC.
116. Andrew Johnson, "Message from the President of the United States Concerning the Northwest Boundary Commission, February 13, 1869," 1869, 95, 40th Congress, 3d Session, Ex. Doc. No. 86.
117. Johnson, "Message from the President," 95.
118. Johnson, "Message from the President," 2–22.

119. Johnson, "Message from the President," 24–92.
120. Johnson, "Message from the President," 27, 31, 33–34.
121. Johnson, "Message from the President," 28, 30, 33.
122. Jno G. Parker, September 20, 1858, 5–6, Records Relating to the Northwest Boundary, 1853–1901, MicrocopyT606, Roll 1, Letters Received 1857–1870, NARA; Henry Custer, "Report of Henry Custer, Assistant of Reconnaissances Made in 1859 over the Routes in the Cascade Mountains in the Vicinity of the 49th Parallel," 1866, 5–9, 001246, Stó:lō Library and Archive.
123. Custer, "Report of Henry Custer," 8.
124. Custer, "Report of Henry Custer," 42–43.
125. Parker, September 20, 1858, 9.
126. Keith Thor Carlson, *The Power of Place, the Problem of Time: Aboriginal Identity and Historical Consciousness in the Cauldron of Colonialism* (Toronto: University of Toronto Press, 2010), 161; Gough, *Gunboat Frontier*, 13; Lutz, *Makúk*, 174–76; Clark, *Point Roberts, U.S.A.*, 13.
127. I wanted to express my gratitude to Keith Carlson and the Stó:lō Library & Archives/ Repository for their assistance locating pertinent documents to the 1857 boundary survey and clarifying terminology. Carlson, *The Power of Place the Problem of Time*, 161.
128. Carlson, *The Power of Place the Problem of Time*, 163, 166; Lutz, *Makúk*, 174–75.
129. Carlson, *The Power of Place the Problem of Time*, 167.
130. Carlson, *The Power of Place the Problem of Time*, 168.
131. Johnson, "Message from President (1869)," 95.
132. Tony Rees, *Arc of the Medicine Line: Mapping the World's Longest Undefended Border Across the Western Plains* (Lincoln: University of Nebraska Press, 2007), 25.
133. Rachel St. John, *Line in the Sand: A History of the Western U.S.–Mexico Border* (Princeton, NJ: Princeton University Press, 2011), 31.
134. Johnson, "Message from President (1869)," 24–92; Custer, "Report of Henry Custer," 3.
135. Johnson, "Message from President (1869)," 40, 47.
136. The American boundary commissions "Statement of services of Indians employed" noted that Indigenous workers supplied 1,016 days of labor in 1857, 2,754 days in 1858, 3,063 in 1859, 946 in 1860, and 94 in 1861 representing a total of 7,873 days of labor contributed. The inconsistency of their reporting, however, limits what can be surmised about this work. Indigenous workers also received an additional dollar a day for each canoe they supplied as well as money for selling paddles, pack straps, food, rope, planks, and canoes. Johnson, "Message from President (1869)," 42–54, 71.
137. Johnson, "Message from President (1869)," 39, 52.
138. Custer, "Report of Henry Custer," 5–6.
139. Keith Thor Carlson, Albert (Sonny) McHalsie, and Jan Perrier, *A Stó:Lo-Coast Salish Historical Atlas* (Vancouver: Douglas & McIntyre, 2001), 124–25.
140. Custer, "Report of Henry Custer," 7, 18, 31, 45.
141. Custer, "Report of Henry Custer," 41.
142. Custer, "Report of Henry Custer," 39.
143. Custer, "Report of Henry Custer," 3.
144. Custer, "Report of Henry Custer," 4.
145. Custer, "Report of Henry Custer," 4.
146. Custer, "Report of Henry Custer," 5.
147. The original source mentions a Somena guide, which is the Thompson term for the Sto:lo. Custer, "Report of Henry Custer," 15.
148. Custer, "Report of Henry Custer," 15.
149. Custer, "Report of Henry Custer," 57.
150. McIntosh, *The Collectors: A History of Canadian Customs and Excise*, 186.
151. Stewart, *The American Response to Canada Since 1776*, 23–34.

Chapter 2

1. John Boyko, *Blood and Daring: How Canada Fought the American Civil War and Forged a Nation* (Toronto: Knopf, 2013), 7; Robin W. Winks, *The Civil War Years: Canada and the*

United States, 4th ed. (Montreal: McGill-Queen's University Press, 1998), 13, 17, 68–70; Adam Mayers, *Dixie and the Dominion: Canada, the Confederacy, and the War for the Union* (Toronto: Dundurn Group, 2003), 34.

2. Michael Thomas Smith, "The Most Desperate Scoundrels Unhung: Bounty Jumpers and Recruitment Fraud in the Civil War North," *American Nineteenth Century History* 6, no. 2 (2005): 151; Winks, *The Civil War Years*, 52.
3. Mayers, *Dixie and the Dominion*, 53.
4. Great Britain. War Office, "British North America (Arms, &c.): Return Showing the Number of Arms, &c., Sent to British North America, from December 1861, and Ordered in Consequence of the Affair of the 'Trent'" (HMSO, 1863), Early Canadiana Online; Canada, *Report of the Commissioners Appointed to Consider the Defences of Canada, 1862* (London: G. E. Eyre and W. Spottiswoode, 1862), 5; "The Mason and Slidell Case," in *The Upper Canada Law Journal and Local Courts' Gazette*, vol. 8 (Toronto: W. C. Chewett, 1862), 63–66; John Herd Thompson and Stephen J. Randall, *Canada and the United States: Ambivalent Allies*, 4th ed. (Athens: University of Georgia Press, 2008), 37; Winks, *The Civil War Years*, 82.
5. Winks, *The Civil War Years*, 115.
6. Peter Andreas, *Smuggler Nation: How Illicit Trade Made America* (New York: Oxford University Press, 2013), 155, 162, 167; Winks, *The Civil War Years*, 115.
7. Stephen R. Wise, *Lifeline of the Confederacy: Blockade Running During the Civil War* (Columbia: University of South Carolina Press, 1988), 7.
8. Andreas, *Smuggler Nation*, 159, 167; Winks, *The Civil War Years*, 137.
9. United States, Department of the Treasury, ed., "Report of the Secretary of the Treasury on the State of the Finances for the Year 1864," *Annual Report of the Secretary of the Treasury on the State of the Finances*, 1864, 139, https://fraser.stlouisfed.org/scribd/?item_id=5508&filepath=/files/docs/publications/treasar/AR_TREASURY_1864.pdf.
10. United States, Department of the Treasury, 140.
11. Winks, *The Civil War Years*, 132, 136, 327; John Torpey, *The Invention of the Passport: Surveillance, Citizenship, and the State* (Cambridge: Cambridge University Press, 2000), 95.
12. "The Passport System," *The Toronto Globe*, December 20, 1864, 2.
13. "The Passport System to Be Rigidly Enforced—Interruption to Railway Traffic on the Frontier—How Passports Are to Be Procured," *The Toronto Globe*, January 2, 1865, 2.
14. "The Passport System to Be Rigidly Enforced," 2; Winks, *The Civil War Years*, 330.
15. John D. McDermott, "Were They Really Rogues? Desertion in the Nineteenth-Century U.S. Army," *Nebraska History* 78 (1997): 166.
16. Thompson and Randall, *Canada and the United States*, 37.
17. Linda Brown-Kubisch, *The Queen's Bush Settlement: Black Pioneers 1839–1865* (Toronto: Natural Heritage, 2004), 165.
18. Smith, "Most Desperate Scoundrels Unhung," 153–54.
19. "Sergeant's Report Book Victoria BC," 1863, March 24, 1863, GR 426, Volume 1, BCA.
20. Smith, "Most Desperate Scoundrels Unhung," 159; Fred Gaffen, *Cross-Border Warriors: Canadians in American Forces, Americans in Canadian Forces From the Civil War to the Gulf* (Toronto: Dundurn Press, 1995), 10; Winks, *The Civil War Years*, 192–93.
21. F. M. Stowell to Geo. H. Keith, February 22, 1864, RG 110 Provost Marshal General's Bureau, Minnesota, Entry 6655, Box 4, NARA Chicago.
22. S. W. Furber to Geo. H. Keith, October 4, 1863, RG 110 Provost Marshal General's Bureau, Minnesota, Entry 6655, Box 4, NARA Chicago.
23. Jno T. Averill to Geo H. Keith, "To Enlist No Indians after This Date, without the Sanction of Indian Agent," January 25, 1865, RG 110 Provost Marshal General's Bureau, Minnesota, 2d Dist., Entry 6675, Box 5, unorganized, NARA Chicago; Jno T. Averill to Geo H. Keith, "Relative to Indian + Mixed Blood Substitutes," January 27, 1865, RG 110 Provost Marshal General's Bureau, Minnesota, 2d Dist., Box 5, unorganized, NARA Chicago; H. H. Sibley to Lt. Col. J. T. Averill, September 2, 1864, RG 110 Provost Marshal General's Bureau, Minnesota, Entry 6655, Box 4, NARA Chicago; Smith, "Most Desperate Scoundrels Unhung," 152, 155; Winks, *The Civil War Years*, 184.
24. Smith, "Most Desperate Scoundrels Unhung," 149–50.

25. Stephen Kantrowitz, *More than Freedom: Fighting for Black Citizenship in a White Republic, 1829–1889* (New York: Penguin, 2012), 289, 294; Richard M. Reid, *African Canadians in Union Blue: Volunteering for the Cause in the Civil War* (Vancouver: UBC Press, 2014), 4–5; Winks, *The Civil War Years*, 184; Brown-Kubisch, *The Queen's Bush Settlement*, 170.
26. Geo. H. Keith, J. A. Thacher, and J. D. Wheelock, "Names of Men Drafted: In the Second Congressional District, Minnesota, in the Draft Commencing May 28th, 1864, And Who Have Failed To Report at These Head-Quarters, And Are Now Deserters." (St. Paul Press Print, n.d.), RG 110 Provost Marshal General's Bureau, Minnesota, 2d Dist., Entry 6675, Box 5, unorganized, NARA Chicago; Oren D. Storrs and Wm. Trescott to Provost Marshall St. Paul, November 12, 1864, RG 110 Provost Marshal General's Bureau, Minnesota, 2d Dist., Entry 6675, Box 5, unorganized, NARA Chicago; George M. Seymour to Geo. H. Keith, August 15, 1864, RG 110 Provost Marshal General's Bureau, Minnesota, Entry 6655, Box 4, NARA Chicago.
27. Albert Wieland, Jajan Gi[?], Ernst Wieland, Henry Wieland, Jakob Häugärtner , Christian Wieland, and August Wieland , July 25, 1864, RG 110 Provost Marshal General's Bureau, Minnesota, 2d Dist., Entry 6675, Box 5, unorganized, NARA Chicago.
28. Wieland et al.
29. Winks, *The Civil War Years*, 201; W. H. Billing to John Ewan, October 2, 1861, RG 22-1863, Essex County Sheriff's Correspondence and Jail Reports, AO.
30. Mayers, *Dixie and the Dominion*, 58, 81; Boyko, *Blood and Daring*, 190–91.
31. Wellington County Historical Society, "Records of The Wellington County Historical Society Vol. 3 1934" (Mount Forest: The Confederate, 1935), 12, 1979.75.5, Guelph Civic Museum Archive.
32. United States, Department of the Treasury, ed., "Report of the Secretary of the Treasury on the State of the Finances for the Year 1865," *Annual Report of the Secretary of the Treasury on the State of the Finances*, 1865, 229, https://fraser.stlouisfed.org/scribd/?item_id=5509&filepath=/files/docs/publications/treasar/AR_TREASURY_1865.pdf.
33. Winks, *The Civil War Years*, 298–301; L. N. Benjamin, ed., *The St. Albans Raid; or, Investigation into the Charges against Lieut. Bennett H. Young and Command, for Their Acts at St. Albans, Vt., on the 19th October, 1864.* (Montreal: John Lovell, 1865), 78–79, 281; Boyko, *Blood and Daring*, 179–81.
34. Winks, *The Civil War Years*, 314–16; Benjamin, *St. Albans Raid*, 96; Boyko, *Blood and Daring*, 192.
35. Winks, *The Civil War Years*, 317–19; Boyko, *Blood and Daring*, 182–84, 193.
36. Winks, *The Civil War Years*, 329–36; Boyko, *Blood and Daring*, 225; John Bartlet Brebner, *North Atlantic Triangle: The Interplay of Canada, the United States and Great Britain*, 5th ed. (New York: Columbia University Press, 1958), 164.
37. Richard White, *The Republic For Which It Stands: The United States During Reconstruction and the Gilded Age, 1865–1896* (Oxford: Oxford University Press, 2017), 28.
38. Laurence M. Hauptman, *The Iroquois in the Civil War: From Battlefield to Reservation* (Syracuse: Syracuse University Press, 1993), 3, 67; Brown-Kubisch, *The Queen's Bush Settlement*, 170; Kantrowitz, *More than Freedom*, 304–305, 312–13.
39. Carol Chomsky, "The United States-Dakota War Trials: A Study of Military Injustice," *Stanford Law Review* 43, no. 1 (November 1990): 16; Gontran Laviolette, *The Sioux Indians in Canada* (Regina: Saskatchewan Historical Society, 1944), 31; Ed LaBelle, interview by Deborah Locke, June 7, 2012, 13, DW OHP, AV2011.45.52, MHS; John D. Bessler, *Legacy of Violence: Lynch Mobs and Executions in Minnesota* (Minneapolis: University of Minnesota Press, 2003), 26–30; George H. Spencer Jr., "The Sioux War," n.d., 1, P1548, U.S. Interior Dept. Indian Division, Select Files Relating to Minn. and Northern Plains, Box 1, Entry 663: Special Files, File 1 Sioux Claims Commis. "The Sioux War," MHS.
40. Chomsky, "The United States-Dakota War Trials," 17.
41. Dean Blue, interview by Deborah Locke, April 27, 2011, 11–12, DW OHP, AV2011.45.5, MHS; Clifford Canku, interview by Deborah Locke, June 10, 2011, 15–16, DW OHP, AV2011.45.6, MHS; Spencer, "The Sioux War," n.d., 8.
42. Robert Goodvoice, Robert Goodvoice Interview #1, 1977, 5–7, O CPRC, IH-102, Transcript Disc 8 (Originals held at PAS, R-A1334), PAS.

43. Lewis J. Germain to Cyrus Aldrich, Eli R. Chase, and Alburt S. While, April 14, 1863, P1548, U.S. Interior Dept. Indian Division, Select Files Relating to Minn. and Northern Plains, Box 1, Entry 663: Special Files, File 1 Sioux Claims Commis. March-May 1863, MHS.
44. David Pashe, interview by Deborah Locke, January 19, 2012, 5, DW OHP, AV2011.45.44, MHS; John S. Bowman, *Chronology of War* (New York: Infobase Publishing, 2003), 86.
45. Michael Childs, interview by Deborah Locke, April 20, 2011, 8, DW OHP, AV2011.45.7, MHS; Frederick Juni, interview by Deborah Locke, June 1, 2011, 11, DW OHP, AV2011.45.15, MHS; Evelyn Eischen, interview by Deborah Locke, August 10, 2011, 12–13, DW OHP, AV2011.45.8, MHS.
46. Walter LaBatte, interview by Deborah Locke, April 28, 2011, 10, DW OHP, AV2011.45.18, MHS.
47. Spencer, "The Sioux War," n.d., 10.
48. Spencer, "The Sioux War," 2–4.
49. Spencer, "The Sioux War," 9–10.
50. Spencer, "The Sioux War," 11–12.
51. Spencer, "The Sioux War," 13–14.
52. Goodvoice, Robert Goodvoice Interview #1, 9; Robert Goodvoice, Robert Goodvoice Interview #8, 1977, 3, O CPRC, IH-111, Transcript Disc 11 (Originals held at PAS, R-A1343), University of Regina.
53. United States, Department of the Treasury, "Report of the Secretary of the Treasury on the State of the Finances for the Year Ending June 30, 1863" (Washington, DC: Government Printing Office, 1863), 101, Fraser.
54. Chomsky, "The United States-Dakota War Trials," 21.
55. Childs, interview, 8; Chomsky, "The United States-Dakota War Trials," 13–14, 27, 34, 40; Pamela Halverson, interview by Deborah Locke, February 23, 2011, 18, DW OHP, AV2011.45.12, MHS; Bessler, *Legacy of Violence*, 45–46.
56. Dallas Ross, interview by Deborah Locke, May 1, 2011, 10, DW OHP, AV2011.45.25, MHS; Canku, interview, 6–7; Robert Goodvoice, Robert Goodvoice Interview #3, interview by Robert Goodvoice, 1977, 5, O CPRC, IH-104-5, Transcript Disc 10 (Originals held at PAS, R-A1336), University of Regina; Elsie Noel, interview by Deborah Locke, January 18, 2012, 11, DW OHP, AV2011.45.42, MHS; David G. McCrady, *Living with Strangers: The Nineteenth-Century Sioux and the Canadian–American Borderlands* (Lincoln: University of Nebraska Press, 2006), 16.
57. Melvin Littlecrow, interview by Deborah Locke, January 18, 2012, DW OHP, AV2011.45.39, MHS.
58. LaVonne Swenson, interview by Deborah Locke, February 15, 2011, 26, DW OHP, AV2011.45.31, MHS.
59. Marina James, interview by Deborah Locke, January 18, 2012, 8, DW OHP, AV2011.45.38, MHS.
60. Goodvoice, Robert Goodvoice Interview #3, 15.
61. Goodvoice, Robert Goodvoice Interview #3, 17.
62. Goodvoice, Robert Goodvoice Interview #3, 18.
63. Goodvoice, Robert Goodvoice Interview #3, 18.
64. Goodvoice, Robert Goodvoice Interview #3, 18.
65. Goodvoice, Robert Goodvoice Interview #3.
66. Goodvoice, Robert Goodvoice Interview #3.
67. Peter Douglas Elias, *The Dakota of the Canadian Northwest: Lessons for Survival* (Regina: Canadian Plains Research Center, 2002), 21–22.
68. Bessler, *Legacy of Violence*, 65.
69. Goodvoice, Robert Goodvoice Interview #3, 13.
70. Elias, *The Dakota of the Canadian Northwest*, 19–20; Gerhard J. Ens, "The Border, the Buffalo, and the Métis of Montana," in *The Borderlands of the American and Canadian Wests: Essays on Regional History of the Forty-Ninth Parallel*, ed. Sterling Evans (Lincoln: University of Nebraska Press, 2006), 142.
71. McCrady, *Living with Strangers: The Nineteenth-Century Sioux and the Canadian–American Borderlands*, 16, 30.

72. "Notes Taken at a Meeting between the Lieut. Governor of the N.W. Territories Attended by the Officers of the Mounted Police at the Station and a Deputation of about 20 Sioux Indians Headed by a Chief Named 'White Cap at Swan River on the 29th Day of June '77," June 29, 1877, RG 10, Indian Affairs, Black Series, Reel C-10114, Volume 3651, File 8527, LAC; James Henri Howard, *The Canadian Sioux* (Lincoln: University of Nebraska Press, 1984), 28.
73. Elias, *The Dakota of the Canadian Northwest*, 22–23; Alvin C. Gluek, "The Sioux Uprising: A Problem in International Relations," *Minnesota History* 34, no. 8 (Winter 1955): 317.
74. Joseph James Hargrave, *Red River* (Montreal: John Lovell, 1871), 315–17.
75. Gluek, "The Sioux Uprising: A Problem in International Relations," 323–24.
76. Howard, *The Canadian Sioux*, 29.
77. Robert Goodvoice, Robert Goodvoice Interview #2, interview by Goodvoice Robert, 1977, 2–4, O CPRC, IH-103, Transcript Disc 9 (Originals held at PAS, R-A1335), University of Regina; Robert Goodvoice, Robert Goodvoice Interview #9, interview by Helga Reydon, September 1979, 2–3, O CPRC, IH-112/113, Transcript Disc 11 (Originals held at PAS, R-5761 to R-5763), University of Regina.
78. Goodvoice, Robert Goodvoice Interview #2, 3.
79. Goodvoice, Robert Goodvoice Interview #2, 3.
80. Goodvoice, Robert Goodvoice Interview #2, 4, 6.
81. Noel, interview, 11; Robert Goodvoice, Robert Goodvoice Interview #5, interview by Robert Goodvoice, October 13, 1977, 4, O CPRC, IH-107, Transcript Disc 10 (Originals held at PAS, R-A1339), University of Regina.
82. George Arthur Hill to Capt Ward, April 13, 1874, Alexander Morris (Lieutenant-Governor's collection) MG 12 B1, Microfilm Reel M135, No 715, AM.
83. Goodvoice, Robert Goodvoice Interview #5, 5–9.
84. Goodvoice, Robert Goodvoice Interview #5, 9.
85. Billy Heavy Runner, Useless Good Runner Interview, interview by Dila Provost and Albert Yellowhorn, 1973, 4, O CPRC, IH-234, Transcript 2, University of Regina, https://ourspace.uregina.ca/bitstream/handle/10294/546/IH-234.pdf?sequence=1&isAllowed=y; Julian Moses, Henry Cardinal, Ralph Shirt, Tom Cardinal, John Cryer, William Steinhauer, George Hunter, and Max Houle, Saddle Lake Interview, interview by Richard Lightning, trans. Richard Lightning, February 13, 1975, 12, O CPRC, IH-220, Transcript Disc 34, University of Regina, https://ourspace.uregina.ca/bitstream/handle/10294/2177/IH-220.pdf?sequence=1&isAllowed=y.
86. Goodvoice, Robert Goodvoice Interview #5, 8.
87. Goodvoice, Robert Goodvoice Interview #5, 2, 5–10; Pashe, interview, 5.
88. Pashe, interview, 5.
89. Pashe, interview.
90. J. Holt to Secretary of War, "The Case of Shakopee and Medicine Bottle Sioux Indians under Sentence of Death Is Respectfully Returned to the Secretary of War for the President," November 17, 1865, M68, Roll 1, U.S. Army Judge Advocate General Papers, Re Trials of Medicine Bottle and Little Six 1862–1865 Roll 1. Originals held at NARA, MHS; Chomsky, "The United States-Dakota War Trials," 43–44; Winks, *The Civil War Years*, 175.
91. Goodvoice, Robert Goodvoice Interview #3, 12.
92. Goodvoice, Robert Goodvoice Interview #3.
93. Goodvoice, Robert Goodvoice Interview #3, 12.
94. Goodvoice, Robert Goodvoice Interview #3, 13.
95. Goodvoice, Robert Goodvoice Interview #1.
96. Goodvoice, Robert Goodvoice Interview #5, 2.
97. Goodvoice, Robert Goodvoice Interview #3, 13.
98. Juni, interview, 7.
99. LaBatte, interview, 11–12.
100. The spelling of Tiwacktag-win's name may be incorrectly recorded here as some of the ink has blurred over time. James McLaughlin to E. A. Hayt, February 4, 1880, 555–56, McLaughlin Papers, MF 970.1 M219As Reel 19, Perdue University; Carolynn Schommer, interview by Deborah Locke, April 27, 2011, 2–3, 15, DW OHP, AV2011.45.27, MHS.
101. Elias, *The Dakota of the Canadian Northwest*, 39–40.

102. Alexander Morris to Minister of Interior, June 26, 1877, RG 10, Indian Affairs, Black Series, Reel C-10114, Volume 3650, File 8400, LAC; Elias, *The Dakota of the Canadian Northwest*, 38.
103. W. J. Christie, "Notes of an Interview with the Sioux Indian Chief 'White Cap' and Others," September 10, 1875, Alexander Morris (Lieutenant-Governor's collection) MG 12 B1, Microfilm Reel M136, No 1101, AM; "Notes Taken at a Meeting"; Elias, *The Dakota of the Canadian Northwest*, 37–41.
104. G. H. Wheatley to Frank Pedley, April 11, 1911, 79, DIA ARO, LAC.
105. Wm. Gordon to Frank Pedley, "Standing Buffalo Band," April 15, 1907, 142, DIA ARO, LAC; J. A. Markle to Superintendent General of Indian Affairs, August 16, 1900, 132, DIA ARO, LAC; Elias, *The Dakota of the Canadian Northwest*, 205.

Chapter 3

1. Richard White, *The Republic For Which It Stands: The United States During Reconstruction and the Gilded Age, 1865–1896* (New York: Oxford University Press, 2017), 1–2.
2. Martin Kitchen, "The Empire, 1900–1939," in *A Companion to Early Twentieth Century Britain*, ed. Chris Wrigley (Malden, MA: Wiley-Blackwell, 2003), 193; John Herd Thompson and Stephen J. Randall, *Canada and the United States: Ambivalent Allies*, 4th ed. (Athens: University of Georgia Press, 2008), 72; Gordon T. Stewart, *The American Response to Canada Since 1776* (East Lansing: Michigan State University Press, 1992), 4.
3. Bill Waiser, *A World We Have Lost: Saskatchewan Before 1905* (Markham, ON: Fifth House Limited, 2016), 440.
4. Sarah Carter, *Lost Harvests: Prairie Indian Reserve Farmers and Government Policy* (Montreal: McGill-Queen's University Press, 1990), 22; William Johnston, William G. P. Rawling, Richard H. Gimblett, and John MacFarlane, *The Seabound Coast: The Official History of the Royal Canadian Navy, 1867–1939*, vol. 1 (Toronto: Dundurn Press, 2010), 12; Richard A. Preston, *The Defence of the Undefended Border: Planning for War in North America 1867–1939* (Montreal: McGill-Queen's University Press, 1977), 63; Waiser, *A World We Have Lost*, 440.
5. Claire A. Smearman, "Second Wives' Club: Mapping the Impact of Polygamy in U.S. Immigration Law," *Berkeley Journal of International Law* 27, no. 2 (2009): 391–94; White, *The Republic For Which It Stands*, 5.
6. White, *The Republic For Which It Stands*, 31, 157, 605; Sheila McManus, *The Line Which Separates: Race, Gender, and the Making of the Alberta-Montana Borderlands* (Lincoln: University of Nebraska Press, 2005), 91.
7. "What Women Should Be," *The Cleveland Weekly Herald*, September 9, 1880, 4, CAHAN, LOC.
8. "A Plea for Early Marriages," *Alpena Weekly Argus*, January 6, 1874, 4, CAHAN, LOC.
9. White, *The Republic For Which It Stands*, 793.
10. White, *The Republic For Which It Stands*, 78.
11. White, *The Republic For Which It Stands*, 5, 734.
12. White, *The Republic For Which It Stands*, 5; Nancy F. Cott, *Public Vows: A History of Marriage and the Nation* (Cambridge, MA: Harvard University Press, 2000), 4.
13. Bradley Miller, *Borderline Crime: Fugitive Criminals and the Challenge of the Border, 1819–1914* (Toronto: University of Toronto Press, 2016), 5.
14. Miller, *Borderline Crime*, 5.
15. Christian G. Samito, *Becoming American Under Fire: Irish Americans, African Americans, and the Politics of Citizenship During the Civil War Era* (Ithaca, NY: Cornell University Press, 2009), 1–2; Alexander Keyssar, *The Right to Vote: The Contested History of Democracy in the United States* (New York: Basic Books, 2009), 20, 44.
16. Sheryl Lightfoot, "The International Indigenous Rights Discourse and Its Demands for Multilevel Citizenship," in *Multilevel Citizenship*, ed. Willem Maas (Philadelphia: University of Pennsylvania Press, 2013), 141.
17. Stephen Kantrowitz, *More than Freedom: Fighting for Black Citizenship in a White Republic, 1829–1889* (New York: Penguin, 2012), 312–13; Samito, *Becoming American Under Fire*, 1–3, 159, 212.

18. United States, "Naturalization; Signed in London May 13, 1870, Came into Force August 10, 1870," in *Treaties and Other International Agreements of the United States of America 1776–1949*, ed. Charles I. Bevans, vol. 12 (Washington, DC: Department of State, 1968), 158–60; Jeremy Ravi Mumford, "Why Was Louis Riel, a United States Citizen, Hanged as a Canadian Traitor in 1885?," *Canadian Historical Review* 88, no. 2 (2007): 243; Samito, *Becoming American Under Fire*, 3, 211–12.
19. H. Bernard to J. H. Pope, May 4, 1872, RG 13-A-2, Vol. 27, No. 673, LAC.
20. J. J. Elder to Joseph Pope, September 6, 1900, RG 6, Vol 97, Secretary of States Correspondence, 1900, Document 1449, "Information as to repatriation of British subjects who have become citizens of the United States," LAC.
21. Joseph Pope to J. J. Elder, September 17, 1900, RG 6, Vol 97, Secretary of States Correspondence, 1900, Document 1449, "Information as to repatriation of British subjects who have become citizens of the United States," LAC.
22. Patrick Wolfe, "Race and Citizenship," *OAH Magazine of History* 18, no. 5 (2004): 67; Joyce Green, "Canaries in the Mines of Citizenship: Indian Women in Canada," *Canadian Journal of Political Science* 34, no. 4 (2001): 724.
23. n.a., "Bulletin File 45 [Bulletin 20 (1922)] Indian Citizenship," c 1922, 45, Record 266, Box 14 Montana Governor's Office: Montana Indian Reservations Historical Jurisdiction Study, folder Crow Reservation 1916–1923, C-135, MHS.
24. Henry O'Brien, "Regina Ex Rel, Gibb v. White Chambers, March 23, 1870," in *Reports of Cases Determined in the Practice Court and Chambers* (Toronto: Roswell & Hutchison, 1872), 315.
25. O'Brien, "Regina Ex Rel, Gibb v. White Chambers," 317.
26. Michigan, "Constitution of Michigan 1835," 1835, Legislature of Michigan, http://www.legislature.mi.gov/documents/historical/miconstitution1835.htm.
27. Michigan, *The Revised Constitution of the State of Michigan* (Lansing: R. W. Ingals, 1850), 18.
28. Michigan, William Blair Lord, and David Wolfe Brown, *The Debates and Proceedings of the Constitutional Convention of the State of Michigan: Convened at the City of Lansing, Wednesday, May 15th, 1867*, vol. II (John A. Kerr & Co., 1867), 260.
29. Michigan, Lord, and Brown, *The Debates and Proceedings of the Constitutional Convention*, II:779.
30. Alexander Porter Morse, *A Treatise on Citizenship, by Birth and by Naturalization: With Reference to the Law of Nations, Roman Civil Law, Law of the United States of America, and the Law of France* (Boston: Little Brown, 1881), 161.
31. Morse, *A Treatise on Citizenship*, 248.
32. Michigan, Lord, and Brown, *Debates and Proceedings 1867, Vol 2*, II:781.
33. Michigan, Lord, and Brown, *Debates and Proceedings 1867, Vol 2*, II:781.
34. Michigan, Lord, and Brown, *Debates and Proceedings 1867, Vol 2*, II:267, 781.
35. Canada, Parliament, Senate., *Debates of the Senate of the Dominion of Canada*, vol. 2, Third Session—Fifth Parliament (Ottawa: A. S. Woodburn, 1885), 1277, 1283.
36. E. A. Heaman, *Tax, Order, and Good Government: A New Political History of Canada, 1867–1917* (Montreal: McGill-Queen's University Press, 2017), 156.
37. Canada, Parliament, Senate, *Debates of the Senate of the Dominion of Canada*, 2:1199.
38. Canada, Parliament, Senate, *Debates of the Senate of the Dominion of Canada*, 2:1202.
39. "Evidence Taken in John Crowe's Case Charged with Political Partisanship and Abuse of Office," 1896, 19, RG 10, Microfilm Reel C-11291, Vol 2884, File 180,541, Saugeen Agency—correspondence and official investigation into the charges brought against agent John Crowe of Chippewa Hill who was accused of influencing Indians voting in a federal election and issuing illegal timber licences, LAC; "Memorandum," c 1896, item 5-6, RG 10, Microfilm Reel C-11291, Vol 2884, File 180,541, Saugeen Agency—correspondence and official investigation into the charges brought against agent John Crowe of Chippewa Hill who was accused of influencing Indians voting in a federal election and issuing illegal timber licences, LAC.
40. "Evidence Taken in John Crown's Case," 28.
41. Unsigned, "1805[Illegible]," April 12, 1897, item 154, RG 10, Microfilm Reel C-11291, Vol 2884, File 180,541, Saugeen Agency—correspondence and official investigation into the charges brought against agent John Crowe of Chippewa Hill who was accused of influencing Indians voting in a federal election and issuing illegal timber licences, LAC.

42. Thos Elliott to John MacDonald, February 3, 1886, Sir John A. Macdonald Papers, Volume 423, Microfilm reel C-1774, 205461 to 205463, LAC.
43. Thos Elliott to John A. MacDonald, February 3, 1887, Sir John A. Macdonald Papers, Volume 436, Reel C-1781, 214911 to 214912, LAC; Heaman, *Tax, Order, and Good*, 335.
44. Lesley A. Jacobs, *Mapping the Legal Consciousness of First Nations Voters: Understanding Voting Rights Mobilization* (Ottawa: Elections Canada, 2009), 13–14.
45. Lightfoot, "International Indigenous Rights," 141–42; Beth Lew-Williams, *The Chinese Must Go: Violence, Exclusion, and the Making of the Alien in America* (Cambridge, MA: Harvard University Press, 2018), 114; White, *The Republic For Which It Stands*, 113, 603.
46. Michigan, Lord, and Brown, *Debates and Proceedings 1867, Vol 2*, II:781; White, *The Republic For Which It Stands*, 603; Cathleen D. Cahill, *Federal Fathers & Mothers: A Social History of the United States Indian Service, 1869–1933* (Chapel Hill: University of North Carolina Press, 2011), 34.
47. United States, "An Act to Provide for the Allotment of Lands in Severalty to Indians on the Various Reservations, and to Extend the Protection of the Laws of the United States and the Territories over the Indians, and for Other Purposes [Dawes Act]" (49th Cong., 2nd sess., 1887).
48. Emily Greenwald, *Reconfiguring the Reservation: The Nez Perces, Jicarilla Apaches, and the Dawes Act* (Albuquerque: University of New Mexico Press, 2002), 7; White, *The Republic For Which It Stands*, 605.
49. White, *The Republic For Which It Stands*, 606.
50. Kathleen S. Sullivan, "Marriage and Federal Police Power," *Studies in American Political Development* 20, no. 1 (2006): 50.
51. Cahill, *Federal Fathers & Mothers: A Social History of the United States Indian Service, 1869–1933*, 39; McManus, *The Line Which Separates*, 93.
52. Wm. H. Sims to Commissioner of Indian Affairs, May 8, 1894, RG 75 BIA, Letters received—Commissioner of Indian Affairs, Tulalip Agency, Box 9, Folder 1894, NARA Seattle.
53. Sullivan, "Marriage and Federal Police Power," 55.
54. Sarah Carter, *The Importance of Being Monogamous: Marriage and Nation Building in Western Canada in 1915* (Alberta: University of Alberta Press, 2014), 8; Canada, "An Act to Amend and Consolidate the Laws Respecting Indians Assented to 12th April, 1876," in *Acts of the Parliament of the United Kingdom of Great Britain and Ireland* (Ottawa: Brown Chamberlin, 1876), 44.
55. J. R. M. Innus to A. C. Elliot, "Indian Woman Gains 'White' Status through Marriage 1876," October 31, 1876, Attorney General Records, T 0429 Microfilm BO 9318. Box 1, File 5, 104/76, BCA; Robert A. Campbell, "Making Sober Citizens: The Legacy of Indigenous Alcohol Regulation in Canada, 1777–1985," *Journal of Canadian Studies* 42, no. 1 (2008): 108; Canada, "An Act to Amend and Consolidate the Laws Respecting Indians Assented to 12th April, 1876," 66.
56. R. H. Milroy to E. P. Smith, "No 62," October 20, 1873, 304, OIA ARO, UWDC.
57. L. Vankoughnet to John A. Macdonald, "Memorandum," March 3, 1882, "Headquarters—General Correspondence Regarding Indians Living Close to the United States Border," RG 10, Indian Affairs, Volume 2170, File 35,891, LAC.
58. Milroy to E. P. Smith, "No 62," October 20, 1873, 304.
59. William King, "Transcript of the Autobiography of Rev. William King Written at Intervals during Last Three Years of His Life," January 6, 1892, 365, MG24 J14, William King Collection, LAC; Marcus Lee Hansen, *The Mingling of Canadian and American People* (New Haven, CT: Yale University Press, 1940), v.
60. Bruno Ramirez, *Crossing the 49th Parallel: Migration from Canada to the United States, 1900–1930* (Ithaca, NY: Cornell University Press, 2001), ix, 8, 24, 31.
61. "Notes and News," *Butte Weekly Miner*, June 10, 1879, 1, CAHAN, LOC.
62. Jas M Shepard to David J. Hill, February 11, 1889, Despatches from U.S. Consuls in Hamilton, Ontario, T470, Volume 7, Reel 7, University of Calgary Library; United States, *Register of the Department of State* (Washington, DC: Government Printing Office, 1925), 188.
63. The 1901 census records Ryerson's nationality as Canadian. He appears in the 1911 census as an American citizen. Canada, "Census of Canada 1911, Ontario, Dist 131, S. Dist 4, Enum

Dist 7-8 Galt," 1911, 11, Automated Genealogy, http://automatedgenealogy.com/census11/SplitView.jsp?id=142223; Canada, "Census of Canada 1901, Ontario, Dist 121 Waterloo South, S. Dist C, Polling Sub-Div 7, Town of Galt," April 15, 1901, 12, Automated Genealogy, http://automatedgenealogy.com/census/ViewFrame.jsp?id=106819&highlight=34; Shepard to Hill, February 11, 1889; United States, *Official Register of the United States, Containing a List of Officers and Employees in the Civil, Military, and Naval Service* (Washington, DC: Government Printing Office, 1899), 40; United States, *Register of the Department of State*, 63.

64. I. L. Mahan to E. P. Smith, September 30, 1875, 371, OIA ARO, UWDC; Wm. Van Abbott to Superintendent General of Indian Affairs, September 18, 1888, 8, DIA ARO, LAC.
65. J. Ansdell Macrae to Superintendent General of Indian Affairs, October 18, 1893, 35, DIA ARO, LAC; J. Blain to Superintendent General of Indian Affairs, July 20, 1904, 46, DIA ARO, LAC; J. E. Pinsonneault to Superintendent General of Indian Affairs, December 9, 1875, 18, DIA ARO, LAC.
66. Joseph Cote to Frank Pedley, April 30, 1913, 42, DIA ARO, LAC; J. P. Donnelly to Superintendent General of Indian Affairs, August 25, 1892, 12, DIA ARO, LAC; H. Vassal to Superintendent General of Indian Affairs, November 28, 1882, 159, DIA ARO, LAC; L. A. DeBlois to Superintendent General of Indian Affairs, October 20, 1876, 22, DIA ARO, LAC.
67. Ramirez, *Crossing the 49th Parallel*, 31.
68. Shelley J. Pearen, *Exploring Manitoulin*, 3rd ed. (Toronto: University of Toronto Press, 1993), 151.
69. John J. Bukowczyk, Nora Faires, David R. Smith, and Randy William Widdis, *Permeable Border: The Great Lakes Basin as Transnational Region 1650–1990* (Pittsburgh: University of Pittsburgh Press, 2005), 105, 130.
70. King, "Autobiography of Rev. William King," 136–42; Gregory Wigmore, "Before the Railroad: From Slavery to Freedom in the Canadian–American Borderland," *Journal of American History* 98, no. 2 (2011): 438, 446; Sharon A. Roger Hepburn, *Crossing the Border: A Free Black Community in Canada* (Urbana: University of Illinois Press, 2007), 2; Kantrowitz, *More than Freedom*, 254.
71. Linda Brown-Kubisch, *The Queen's Bush Settlement: Black Pioneers 1839–1865* (Toronto: Natural Heritage, 2004), 26; Sharon A. Roger Hepburn, "Following the North Star: Canada as a Haven for Nineteenth-Century American Blacks," *Michigan Historical Review* 25, no. 2 (1999): 97–98; Thompson and Randall, *Canada and the United States*, 34.
72. United States, "Fugitive Slave Act 1850," September 18, 1850, The Avalon Project, Yale University Law School; Hepburn, *Crossing the Border*, 10; Samuel May, *The Fugitive Slave Law and Its Victims*, vol. 15, Anti-Slavery Tracts (New York: American Anti-Slavery Society, 1861), 88; John Boyko, *Blood and Daring: How Canada Fought the American Civil War and Forged a Nation* (Toronto: Knopf, 2013), 26; Michael Wayne, "The Black Population of Canada West on the Eve of the American Civil War: A Reassessment Based on the Manuscript Census of 1861," *Social History* 28, no. 56 (1995): 467.
73. Hepburn, *Crossing the Border*, 18–22; Brown-Kubisch, *The Queen's Bush Settlement*, 5, 20, 23, 91, 254.
74. Hepburn, *Crossing the Border*, 25; Wayne, "The Black Population of Canada West," 471.
75. Hepburn, *Crossing the Border*, 4; Wayne, "The Black Population of Canada West," 471.
76. White, *The Republic For Which It Stands*, 31, 34; Kantrowitz, *More than Freedom*, 358.
77. Lou Falkner Williams, *The Great South Carolina Ku Klux Klan Trials 1871–1872* (Athens: University of Georgia Press, 1996), 46–47; G. Manigault to John A. Macdonald, December 5, 1871, RG 13-A-2 Vol 26, No 1487, LAC.
78. Hansen, *The Mingling of Canadian and American People*, 149.
79. Williams, *The Great South Carolina Ku Klux Klan Trials 1871–1872*, 47; Jerry Lee West, *The Reconstruction Ku Klux Klan in York County, South Carolina, 1865–1877* (Jefferson, NC: McFarland and Company Inc., 2002), 128.
80. Hamilton Fish to Edward Thornton, November 12, 1872, RG 13-A-2, Vol. 27, No. 810, LAC; Manigault to Macdonald, December 5, 1871; United States, *Testimony Taken by the Joint Selection Committee to Inquire into the Conditions of Affairs in the Late Insurrectionary States—South Carolina*, vol. III (Washington, DC: Government Printing Office, 1872),

1297, 1725; "The Abduction Case Preliminary Examination Yesterday How Dr. Bratton Was Kidnapped: What a Little Girl Saw," *The Free Press*, June 14, 1872, Despatches from U.S. Consuls in Hamilton, Ontario, T470, Volume 3, Reel 3, University of Calgary Library; "International Outrage: A Man Kidnapped, Chloroformed and Forced to the States Charged with Embezzlement—His Return Demanded," June 8, 1872, Despatches from U.S. Consuls in Hamilton, Ontario, T470, Volume 3, Reel 3, University of Calgary Library; Williams, *The Great South Carolina Ku Klux Klan Trials 1871–1872*, 106.

81. Fish to Thornton, November 12, 1872; West, *The Reconstruction Ku Klux Klan in York County, South Carolina, 1865–1877*, 128; West, 173.
82. William Blake to Chas Hale, June 13, 1872, Despatches from U.S. Consuls in Hamilton, Ontario, T470, Volume 3, Reel 3, University of Calgary Library; "The London Outrage," June 15, 1872, Despatches from U.S. Consuls in Hamilton, Ontario, T470, Volume 3, Reel 3, University of Calgary Library.
83. "International Outrage: A Man Kidnapped, Chloroformed and Forced to the States Charged with Embezzlement—His Return Demanded"; "The Abduction Case Preliminary Examination Yesterday How Dr. Bratton Was Kidnapped: What a Little Girl Saw."
84. Williams, *The Great South Carolina Ku Klux Klan Trials 1871–1872*, 106; "International Outrage: A Man Kidnapped, Chloroformed and Forced to the States Charged with Embezzlement—His Return Demanded"; "The Kidnapping Case: Further about the Outrage on Canadian Authority: No Truth in the Reported Criminality of the Victim," *London Daily Advertiser*, n.d., Despatches from U.S. Consuls in Hamilton, Ontario, T470, Volume 3, Reel 3, University of Calgary Library.
85. Edward Thornton to Governor General, November 15, 1872, RG 13-A-2, Vol. 27, No. 810, LAC; Edward Thornton to Hamilton Fish, October 11, 1872, RG 13-A-2, Vol. 27, No. 810, LAC; John Bassett Moore, *A Treatise on Extradition and Interstate Rendition*, vol. 1 (Boston: Boston Book Company, 1891), 283; Fred Landon, "The Kidnapping of Dr. Rufus Bratton," *Journal of Negro History* 10, no. 3 (1925): 332; Geo H. Williams to D. J. Corbin, November 2, 1872, RG 13-A-2, Vol. 27, No. 810, LAC.
86. For competing accounts for how Bratton made it back to Canada see Williams, *The Great South Carolina Ku Klux Klan Trials 1871–1872*, 106; J. Michael Martinez, *Carpetbaggers, Calvary, and the Ku Klux Klan* (Lanham, MD: Rowman & Littlefield Publishers, 2007), 194; West, *The Reconstruction Ku Klux Klan in York County, South Carolina, 1865–1877*, 100, 129–30.
87. "The Colored Boy and White Girl Who Ran Away from Rochester," *Alexandria Gazette*, January 13, 1883, 2, CAHAN, LOC.
88. "Vermont News," *Vermont Phoenix*, January 12, 1883, 3, CAHAN, LOC; "Rochester," *Woodstock Spirit of the Age*, January 10, 1883, 3, CAHAN, LOC; "[Rochester's Othello]," *Woodstock Spirit of the Age*, January 17, 1883, 3, CAHAN, LOC; "A Negro Runs Away with a Girl," *Washington National Republican*, January 6, 1883, 2, CAHAN, LOC; "The Colored Boy," 2.
89. "A Negro Runs Away with a Girl," 2.
90. "Vermont News," 3; "[Rochester's Othello]," 3; "[Rochester's Othello]," 2.
91. White, *The Republic For Which It Stands*, 336, 622, 635; Kantrowitz, *More than Freedom*, 411.
92. R. Bruce Shepard, "Diplomatic Racism: Canadian Government and Black Migration from Oklahoma, 1905–1912," *Great Plains Quarterly* 1, no. 1 (Winter 1983): 13.
93. Sarah-Jane Mathieu, *North of the Color Line: Migration and Black Resistance in Canada, 1870–1955* (Chapel Hill: University of North Carolina Press, 2010), 31, 41–42; Robin W. Winks, "Slavery, the Loyalists, and English Canada, 1760–1801," in *The History of Immigration and Racism in Canada*, ed. Barrington Walker (Toronto: Canadian Scholars' Press, 2008), 29.
94. "Untitled," *The Maysville Evening Bulletin*, December 26, 1890, 4, CAHAN, LOC.
95. "Untitled," 4.
96. C. P. Luse, "[Illegible] Taken by the Indian Dep. Cash Accounts C. P. Luse U.S. Indian Agent 1st Quarter 1884," February 18, 1885, 31, RG 75, BIA, White Earth Agency, Letters Sent to the Comm. of Ind. Affairs 1885–1914, NAI 5239141, Entry 1248, Vol 2, NARA Chicago.
97. Luse, "[Illegible] Taken by the Indian Dep.," 32, 40.

98. C. P. Luse to H. Price, March 24, 1885, 92, RG 75, BIA, White Earth Agency, Letters Sent to the Comm. of Ind. Affairs 1885–1914, NAI 5239141, Entry 1248, Vol 2, NARA Chicago.
99. Luse to Price, 97.
100. Luse to Price, 97–98.
101. Luse to Price, 99.
102. T. J. Sheehan to J. D. C. Atkins, March 26, 1887, 101, RG 75, BIA, White Earth Agency, Letters Sent to the Comm. of Ind. Affairs 1885–1914, NAI 5239141, Entry 1248, Vol 3, NARA Chicago.
103. Sheehan to Atkins, 103.
104. Sheehan to Atkins, 100–108.
105. Sheehan to Atkins, 106.
106. Katherine Unterman, *Uncle Sam's Policemen: The Pursuit of Fugitives Across Borders* (Cambridge, MA: Harvard University Press, 2015), 76; Miller, *Borderline Crime*, 156.
107. Danl. Webster and Ashburton, "A Treaty to Settle and Define the Boundaries Between the Territories of the United States and the Possessions of Her Britannic Majesty in North America [Treaty of Webster-Ashburton] Concluded August 9, 1842," in *Treaties and Conventions Concluded Between the United States of America and Other Powers Since July 4, 1776*, ed. J. C. Bancroft Davis (Washington, DC: Government Printing Office, 1873), 374.
108. Miller, *Borderline Crime*, 153.
109. Miller, *Borderline Crime*, 154; Unterman, *Uncle Sam's Policemen*, 16–17, 22; Christopher H. Pyle, *Extradition, Politics, and Human Rights* (Philadelphia: Temple University Press, 2001), 75.
110. Miller, *Borderline Crime*, 144–46, 166–67; T. F. Bayard to Edward J. Phelps, "No 229," March 3, 1886, RG 59, General Records of Department of State, Extradition Papers, A-1, Entry 863, Box 1, "Correspondence Concerning the Extradition Treaty with Great Britain, 1870–1890," NARA College Park; Ulysses S. Grant, *The Papers of Ulysses S. Grant*, ed. John Y. Simon, vol. 28 November 1, 1876–September 30, 1878 (Carbondale: Southern Illinois University Press, 2005), 100–104; Daniel S. Margolies, *Spaces of Law in American Foreign Relations: Extradition and Extraterritoriality in the Borderlands and Beyond, 1877–1898* (Athens: University of Georgia Press, 2011), 222; "The Extradition Muddle," *Winnipeg Free Press*, December 29, 1876, 1.
111. "The Extradition Deadlock," *Winnipeg Free Press*, August 8, 1876, 2, Legislative Library of Manitoba.
112. "The Extradition Deadlock," 2.
113. "An Artful Dodger: The Astonishing Baggage of a Family of Montreal," *The Fairfield Herald*, September 20, 1876, 2, CAHAN, LOC.
114. "Crimes and Casualties," *The Portland Daily Press*, August 26, 1876, 2, CAHAN, LOC.
115. "An Artful Dodger: The Astonishing Baggage of a Family of Montreal," 2.
116. "Absconding Jeweler Held," *Utica Morning Herald*, September 13, 1876.
117. Margolies, *Spaces of Law in American Foreign Relations*, 222.
118. Great Britain and United States, "Extradition Convention Between the United States of America and Her Britannic Majesty, Supplementary to the Tenth Article of the Treaty, Concluded Between the Same High Contracting Parties on the Ninth Day of August, 1842. Convention Signed at Washington July 12, 1889, Ratifications Exchanged March 11, 1890, Entered into Force April 4, 1890," in *Treaties and Other International Agreements of the United States of America, 1776–1949*, vol. 12, Department of State Publication 8761 (Washington, DC: Government Printing Office, 1974), 211–14.
119. Charles I. Bevans, ed., *Treaties and Other International Agreements of the United States of America, 1776–1949*, vol. 12 (Washington, DC: Government Printing Office, 1974), 212, 257, 483.
120. Eithne Luibhéid, *Entry Denied: Controlling Sexuality at the Border* (Minneapolis: University of Minnesota Press, 2002), 9; Deirdre M. Moloney, *National Insecurities: Immigrants and U.S. Deportation Policy Since 1882* (Chapel Hill: University of North Carolina Press, 2012), 13; Nayan Shah, *Stranger Intimacy: Contesting Race, Sexuality, and the Law in the North American West* (Berkeley: University of California Press, 2011), 229.
121. Margolies, *Spaces of Law in American Foreign Relations*, 144.

122. Margolies, 9–10; Miguel Ángel González-Quiroga, "Conflict and Cooperation in the Making of Texas-Mexico Border Society, 1840–1880," in *Bridging National Borders in North America*, ed. Benjamin H. Johnson and Andrew R. Graybill (Durham, NC: Duke University Press, 2010), 38.
123. Margolies, *Spaces of Law in American Foreign Relations*, 140–45.

Chapter 4

1. Alexander McArthur, *The Causes of the Rising in the Red River Settlement 1869–1870* (Winnipeg: Manitoba Free Press, 1882), 5.
2. Richard A. Preston, *The Defence of the Undefended Border: Planning for War in North America 1867–1939* (Montreal: McGill-Queen's University Press, 1977), 57.
3. Desmond Morton, "Cavalry or Police: Keeping the Peace on Two Adjacent Frontiers, 1870–1900," *Journal of Canadian Studies* 12, no. 2 (1977): 28; Robin W. Winks, *The Civil War Years: Canada and the United States*, 4th ed. (Montreal: McGill-Queen's University Press, 1998), 2.
4. John Boyko, *Blood and Daring: How Canada Fought the American Civil War and Forged a Nation* (Toronto: Knopf, 2013), 257; David Brundage, *Irish Nationalists in America: The Politics of Exile, 1798–1998* (New York: Oxford University Press, 2016), 101–102.
5. Boyko, *Blood and Daring*, 260; Brundage, *Irish Nationalists in America*, 104–105.
6. Timothy D. McNeff to Hon. Wm. B. West, November 1865, 22, Message of the President of the United States, 40th Congress, 2nd Session, House of Representatives, Ex. Doc 157, Part 2, Trial and Conviction of American Citizens in Great Britain.
7. Wm. B. West to Patrick S. Walsh, November 22, 1865, 23, Message of the President of the United States, 40th Congress, 2nd Session, House of Representatives, Ex. Doc 157, Part 2, Trial and Conviction of American Citizens in Great Britain, 1868.
8. Boyko, *Blood and Daring*, 266; *The Fenian Raid at Fort Erie, June the First and Second, 1866: With a Map of the Niagara Peninsula, Shewing the Route of the Troops, and a Plan of the Lime Ridge Battle Ground* (Toronto: W. C. Chewett & co, 1866), 25.
9. *The Fenian Raid at Fort Erie*, 30–31; F. N. Blake to William H. Seward, June 20, 1866, Despatches from United States Consuls in Fort Erie, Ontario, T-465, Volume 1, Reel 1, NARA; Brundage, 104–105.
10. Hereward Senior, *The Last Invasion of Canada: The Fenian Raids, 1866–1870* (Toronto: Oxford; Dundurn Press in collaboration with the Canadian War Museum Canadian Museum of Civilization, 1991), 42–44; *The Fenian Raid at Fort Erie*, 49.
11. F. N. Blake to F. W. Seward, August 6, 1866, Despatches from United States Consuls in Fort Erie, Ontario, 1865–1906, T-465, Volume 1, Reel 1, March 9, 1865—December 31, 1869., NARA.
12. Boyko, *Blood and Daring*, 261; *The Fenian Raid at Fort Erie*, 66.
13. F. N. Blake to H. W. Hermans, June 5, 1866, Despatches from United States Consuls in Fort Erie, Ontario, 1865–1906, T-465, Volume 1, Reel 1, March 9, 1865—December 31, 1869., NARA.
14. F. N. Blake to F. W. Seward, February 18, 1869, Despatches from United States Consuls in Fort Erie, Ontario, 1865–1906, T-465, Volume 1, Reel 1, March 9, 1865—December 31, 1869., NARA.
15. *The Fenian Raid at Fort Erie*, 36.
16. D. E. M. McIntyre to John A. Macdonald, September 20, 1866, RG 13, Vol 15, folder 508–528 (1866), LAC.
17. Department of Justice, "Americans Imprisoned as Fenians," 1871, RG 13-A-2, Vol. 26, No 707, LAC.
18. Bill Waiser, *A World We Have Lost: Saskatchewan Before 1905* (Markham, ON: Fifth House Limited, 2016), 431, 440.
19. Waiser, *A World We Have Lost*, 440.
20. Brenda Macdougall, *One of the Family: Metis Culture in Nineteenth-Century Northwestern Saskatchewan* (Vancouver: UBC Press, 2010), 50, 60; Michel Hogue, *Metis and the Medicine Line: Creating a Border and Dividing a People* (Regina: University of Regina Press, 2015), 21–22; Chris Andersen, "From Nation to Population: The Racialisation of 'Métis' in the Canadian Census," *Nations and Nationalism* 14, no. 2 (2008): 349.

21. Macdougall, *One of the Family*, 19–21; Hogue, *Metis and the Medicine Line*, 21, 31; Gerhard J. Ens, *Homeland to Hinterland: The Changing World of the Red River Metis in the Nineteenth Century* (Toronto: University of Toronto Press, 1996), 19.
22. Andersen, "From Nation to Population," 350; Macdougall, *One of the Family*, xi, 70.
23. Macdougall, *One of the Family*, 3.
24. Macdougall, *One of the Family*, 7, 133.
25. Macdougall, *One of the Family*, 10, 44, 66.
26. Macdougall, *One of the Family*, 86–88, 98, 125.
27. Thomas Flanagan, "Louis Riel and the Dispersion of American Métis," *Minnesota History* 49, no. 5 (1985): 179.
28. Walter J. S. Traill to Mother, January 15, 1870, 1, Traill Family Fonds, M1241, Box 4, Folder 30, Glenbow Archives.
29. Traill to Mother, 4.
30. Robert Campbell to Gentleman in Charge of HBC Office Montreal, April 4, 1870, MG1 D8, P7457A, Folder 5, AM; Robert Campbell, "Part of Chief Factor Robert Campell's Diary," n.d., 38–42, Robert Campbell Collection, 4M140, E.47/7, AM.
31. Kikehgowe (Eagle Voice) et al., Moose Mountain Interview #1, interview by D. G. Mandelbaum, trans. Fred and Jack Sheepskin, June 22, 1934, O CPRC, IH-DM.02, Transcrip Disc 133, University of Regina.
32. Canada, "An Act to Amend and Continue the Act 32 and 33 Victoria, Chapter 3; and to Establish and Provide for the Government of the Province of Manitoba—Assented 12th May, 1870 [Manitoba Act]," in *Statutes of Canada Vol 2* (Ottawa: Brown Chamberlin, 1870), 20; Flanagan, "Louis Riel and the Dispersion of American Métis," 179–80; J. M. Bumsted, "Louis Riel and the United States," *American Review of Canadian Studies* 29, no. 1 (1999): 21.
33. Kevin Bruyneel, "Exiled, Executed, Exalted: Louis Riel, Homo Sacer and the Production of Canadian Sovereignty," *Canadian Journal of Political Science* 43, no. 3 (2010): 716–17; Louis Riel, "2-003 Memoir to Ulysses S. Grant [Washington] [75/12?/1015?]," in *The Collected Writings of Louis Riel/Les Ecrits Complets de Louis Riel*, ed. George F. G. Stanley and Gilles Martel, vol. II (Edmonton: University of Alberta Press, 1985), 6.
34. It is unclear whether the draft was ever sent to Grant. Riel, "Memoir to Ulysses S. Grant," 8–9.
35. Riel, "Memoir to Ulysses S. Grant," 7.
36. Riel, "Memoir to Ulysses S. Grant," 10.
37. Riel, "Memoir to Ulysses S. Grant," 13.
38. Flanagan, "Louis Riel and the Dispersion of American Métis," 181; Bumsted, "Louis Riel and the United States," 27; Gilles Martel, ed., *The Collected Writings of Louis Riel*, vol. II (Alberta: University of Alberta Press, 1985), 84–85.
39. "The Fenians: Attack on Province! Universal Enthusiasm- All Nationalities, Races and Creeds Combine," *The Manitoban*, October 7, 1871, Hecht Collection, Dispatches from United States consuls in Winnipeg 1869–1906, Roll 1, University of Washington Special Collections.
40. James W. Taylor to J. C. B. Davis, September 11, 1871, Hecht Collection, University of Washington Special Collections.
41. H. M. Robinson to J. C. B Davis, May 20, 1870, Hecht Collection, University of Washington Special Collections; James W. Taylor to General W. T. Sherman, October 3, 1871, Hecht Collection, University of Washington Special Collections.
42. James W. Taylor to J. C. B. Davis, October 11, 1871, Hecht Collection, University of Washington Special Collections; James W. Taylor to Lyod [*sic*] Wheaton, October 12, 1871, Hecht Collection, University of Washington Special Collections.
43. Adams G. Archibald to J. W. Taylor, October 10, 1871, Hecht Collection, University of Washington Special Collections.
44. Archibald to Taylor.
45. Taylor to Davis, October 11, 1871.
46. Taylor to Sherman, October 3, 1871.
47. James W. Taylor to J. C. B. Davis, November 21, 1871, Irene W. D. Hecht collection, acc. 2783-001, Microfilm reel 11, drawer 5, Despatches from the United States Consuls in Winnipeg, Volume 1, University of Washington Special Collections; Ruth Swan and Edward A. Jerome, "Unequal Justice: The Metis in O'Donoghue's Raid of 1871," *Manitoba History* 39 (Spring 2000).

48. Hogue, *Metis and the Medicine Line*, 89–90; Swan and Jerome, "Unequal Justice: The Metis in O'Donoghue's Raid of 1871."
49. Taylor to Davis, November 21, 1871; "Extracts October 11," *Winnipeg Liberal*, October 11, 1871, Hecht Collection, University of Washington Special Collections; Taylor to Wheaton, October 12, 1871.
50. "The Fenians: Attack on Province."
51. James W. Taylor to J. C. B. Davis, October 28, 1871, Hecht Collection, University of Washington Special Collections.
52. Taylor to Wheaton, October 12, 1871.
53. "The Fenians: Attack on Province"; "Captain Lloyd Wheaton," *Daily Press*, November 9, 1871, Hecht Collection, University of Washington Special Collections; John Parsons, *West on the 49th Parallel: Red River to the Rockies, 1872–1876* (New York: William Morrow and Company, 1963), 17.
54. Taylor to Wheaton, October 12, 1871; Extract: Manitoba Liberal October 25 in Taylor to Davis, October 28, 1871.
55. Taylor to Davis, October 28, 1871.
56. "Extracts October 18," *Winnipeg Liberal*, October 18, 1871, Hecht Collection, University of Washington Special Collections.
57. "Extracts October 18."
58. "Extracts October 11."
59. During the Civil War, Britain sold ships (such as the Alabama) to the Confederacy. American politicians claimed damages owed as a result of these ships to be high as two billion dollars. International arbitrators awarded the United States 15.5 million dollars in gold in compensation on July 15, 1872. The Canadian press called for similar measures to be taken with regard to the Fenians throughout the process but the Fenian question was left off the agenda. Tom Bingham, "The Alabama Claims Arbitration," *International and Comparative Law Quarterly* 54, no. 1 (2005): 1, 13.
60. Swan and Jerome, "Unequal Justice: The Metis in O'Donoghue's Raid of 1871."
61. Waiser, *A World We Have Lost*, 462; Jim Uttley, "The Cypress Hills Massacre: A Tragedy Hidden Too Long," *Indian Life* 31, no. 3 (December 2010): 2; T. Fournier to Department of Justice, April 7, 1874, Alexander Morris (Lieutenant-Governor's collection) MG 12 B1, Microfilm Reel M135, No 997, AM.
62. Waiser, *A World We Have Lost*, 462; Hogue, *Metis and the Medicine Line*, 83–84.
63. Fournier to Department of Justice, April 7, 1874, 8.
64. Fournier to Department of Justice, 9.
65. "Account of Cypress Hills Massacre Taken from the Helena Weekly Herald," June 11, 1873, 6–7, Southern Alberta Research Project, M4561, Box 4, Folder 284, Glenbow Archives; Fournier to Department of Justice, April 7, 1874, 10.
66. William Johnson Twining and Archibald Campbell, *Reports upon the Survey of the Boundary between the Territory of the United States and the Possessions of Great Britain from the Lake of the Woods to the Summit of the Rocky Mountains* (Washington, DC: Government Printing Office, 1878), 31.
67. Major D. R. Cameron, "North American Boundary Commission, from the Most North-Western Point of the Lake of the Woods to the Stony Mountains," February 8, 1876, 7, 'General Correspondence United States of America, Series II, North West Boundary, Commissioner D. R. Cameron and Generals 1876, MG 16-FO 5, Vol 1667, LAC.
68. Cameron noted that the nearest valuable markets for the boundary survey were "St. Paul, in Minnesota, and about 790 miles from the main depot of the expedition on Red River; at Windsor, Hamilton, Toronto, and Ottawa, in Ontario, respectively distant about 1,700 miles, 1,930 miles, 2,000 miles, and 2,300 miles." Cameron, 7–8; Tony Rees, *Arc of the Medicine Line: Mapping the World's Longest Undefended Border Across the Western Plains* (Lincoln: University of Nebraska Press, 2007), 133.
69. Rees, *Arc of the Medicine Line*, 2007, 25.
70. Sheila McManus, *The Line Which Separates: Race, Gender, and the Making of the Alberta-Montana Borderlands* (Lincoln: University of Nebraska Press, 2005), 76–78.
71. Twining and Campbell, *Reports upon the Survey of the Boundary*, 18.

72. Twining and Campbell, 24, 31–32; McManus, *The Line Which Separates*, 11; Parsons, *West on the 49th Parallel*, 145.
73. Capt. Featherstonhaugh, *Narrative of the Operations of the British North American Boundary Commission, 1872–1876* (Woolwich, UK: A. W. and J. P. Jackson, 1876), 25; L. F. Hewgill, "In the Days of Pioneering: Crossing the Plains in the Early 70's The Prairie Black with Buffalo," March 1, 1894, 2, MG1 B23/5, AM; Tony Rees, *Arc of the Medicine Line : Mapping the World's Longest Undefended Border Across the Western Plains* (Lincoln: University of Nebraska Press, 2007), 6.
74. Rees, *Arc of the Medicine Line*, 2007, 10–11, 110.
75. Waiser, *A World We Have Lost*, 469–70.
76. David G. McCrady, *Living with Strangers: The Nineteenth-Century Sioux and the Canadian–American Borderlands* (Toronto: University of Toronto Press, 2006), 50–51.
77. Twining and Campbell, *Reports upon the Survey of the Boundary*, 26.
78. Twining and Campbell, 69; United States, *Report of the Secretary of War Being Part of the Message and Documents Communicated to the Two Houses of Congress at the Beginning of the First Session of the Forty-Third Congress*, vol. 1 (Washington, DC: Government Printing Office, 1873), 62–63.
79. Larry Haag and Lawrence Barkwell, *The Boundary Commission's Metis Scouts The 49th Rangers* (Winnipeg: Louis Riel Institute, 2009), 4; Rees, *Arc of the Medicine Line*, 2007, 101.
80. Cameron, "North American Boundary Commission," 11; Alexander Morris to Antoine-Aimè Dorion, "Alexander Morris Telegram Book No 2, 1874–1877," May 26, 1874, Alexander Morris (Lieutenant-Governor's collection) MG 12 B2, Microfilm Reel M141, No 15, AM; David Laird to Lieut Governor of NW Territories, June 9, 1874, Alexander Morris (Lieutenant-Governor's collection) MG 12 B1, Microfilm Reel M135, No 763, AM.
81. D. R. Cameron to Alexander Morris, April 23, 1874, Alexander Morris (Lieutenant-Governor's collection) MG 12 B1, Microfilm Reel M135, No 715, AM.
82. Cameron, "North American Boundary Commission," 17.
83. James Daschuk, *Clearing the Plains: Disease, Politics of Starvation, and the Loss of Aboriginal Life* (Regina: University of Regina Press, 2013), 94–95.
84. Rees, *Arc of the Medicine Line*, 2007, 234.
85. Alex Morris to Secretary of State for the Provinces, December 13, 1872, 13, DIA ARO, LAC.
86. Morris to Secretary of State for the Provinces, 13.
87. Morris to Secretary of State for the Provinces, 13.
88. Morris to Secretary of State for the Provinces, 13. See also Scott Stephen, "Manitoba History: James McKay (1828–1879): Métis Trader, Guide, Interpreter and MLA," *Manitoba Historical Society* 58 (2008).
89. Hallett was chosen for his loyalty to the British crown during the Red River Rebellion. During the rebellion Hallett was imprisoned in an unheated jail cell and acquired an incurable form of streptococcus causing him immense pain. Larry Haag and Lawrence Barkwell have suggested that Hallett's suicide in 1873 may have been a direct result of infection. Haag and Barkwell, *The Boundary Commission's Metis Scouts The 49th Rangers*, 11–12.
90. Rees, *Arc of the Medicine Line*, 2007, 103–104, 111; Haag and Barkwell, *The Boundary Commission's Metis Scouts The 49th Rangers*, 4–5, 25; Cameron, "North American Boundary Commission," 12.
91. Featherstonhaugh, *Narrative of the Operations*, 24; Daschuk, *Clearing the Plains*, 95; David G. McCrady, *Living with Strangers: The Nineteenth-Century Sioux and the Canadian–American Borderlands* (Lincoln: University of Nebraska Press, 2006), 52.
92. Alexander Morris to Secretary of the Interior, May 27, 1874, Alexander Morris (Lieutenant-Governor's collection) MG 12 B2, Microfilm Reel M141, No 114, AM.
93. Cameron, "North American Boundary Commission," 11.
94. Rees, *Arc of the Medicine Line*, 2007, 279.
95. McCrady, *Living with Strangers*, 51.
96. Parsons, *West on the 49th Parallel*, 121; McCrady, *Living with Strangers*, 55.
97. Parsons, *West on the 49th Parallel*, 121–22; McCrady, *Living with Strangers*, 55.
98. Featherstonhaugh, *Narrative of the Operations*, 40.
99. Cameron, "North American Boundary Commission," 2.

100. Twining and Campbell, *Reports upon the Survey of the Boundary*, 23.
101. Rees, *Arc of the Medicine Line*, 2007, 48.
102. Cameron, "North American Boundary Commission," 2.
103. Twining and Campbell, *Reports upon the Survey of the Boundary*, 308–309.
104. Parsons, *West on the 49th Parallel*, 41.
105. Rees, *Arc of the Medicine Line*, 2007, 57.
106. Rees, 357.
107. McManus, *The Line Which Separates*, 78; Andrew R. Graybill, *Policing the Great Plains: Rangers, Mounties, and the North American Frontier 1875–1910* (Lincoln: University of Nebraska Press, 2007), 12–15; "Reign of Outlawry Along the Montana Border Was Ended By Mounted Police," *The Mineral Independent*, July 24, 1919, 3.
108. Waiser, *A World We Have Lost*, 465; George Arthur French, "Diary of Lieut. Col. G. A. French, Commanding Officer NWMP," 1874, George Arthur French Papers, MG6 A3, AM.
109. Fred Bagley, "The '74 Mounties,'" 1938, 11, 14, 16, Fred Bagley Fonds, Series 1, M-43, Glenbow Archives; French, "G. A. French Diary 1874"; Fred Bagley, "Fred Bagley's Diary," 1884, June 6, 1874, Fred Bagley fonds, M44, Glenbow Archives.
110. W. H. Cox, "Diary of a Mountie from 1880 to '85 [Transcribed by Innes]," 1885, A113 Innes Papers, II. (b) Manuscripts, Diary of a Mountie, PAS; James M. Francis, "Business, Enterprise, and National Policy: The Role of T. C. Power & Brother and I. G. Baker & Company in the Political and Economic Development of the Southwest Canadian Prairies and Northern Montana, 1870–1893" (MA thesis, University of British Columbia, 1978), 58, Glenbow Archives (M4498).
111. Edward Barnett, "Reminiscences of Edward Barnett," n.d., 1–2, Edward Barnett Fonds, M3876, Glenbow Archives.
112. W. H. Cox, "Diary of a Mountie from 1880 to '85 [Transcribed by Innes]."
113. French, "G. A. French Diary 1874," August 1, 1874.
114. Bagley, "The '74 Mounties,'" 78–79.
115. Joseph J. Carscadden, "Diary," 1874, 10–11, Joseph J. Carscadden Fonds, M6608, Glenbow Archives; French, "G. A. French Diary 1874," July 15, 1874; Bagley, "The '74 Mounties,'" 54.
116. Superintendent to J. F. Macleod, December 19, 1879, A113 Innes Collection, III. (a) 15. Mounted Police Barracks, Battleford, 1936–1942, PAS; Waiser, *A World We Have Lost*, 467.
117. Superintendent to Macleod, December 19, 1879, 2–3.
118. Superintendent to Macleod, 5; "Canadians Honor the North West Mounted and Royal North West Mounted Police," *Western Canada*, c 1949, 54, A113 Innes Papers, III. Canadian North West Historical Society (a) subject files Mounted Police Barracks, Battleford, 1936–1942, PAS.
119. Featherstonhaugh, *Narrative of the Operations*, 44.
120. Featherstonhaugh, *Narrative of the Operations*, 44.
121. U.S. Senate, "Turtle Mountain Band of Pembina Chippewa Indians" (55th Congress, 2d Sess. Doc 154, February 23, 1898), 3, P1548, U.S. Interior Dept. Indian Division, Select Files Relating to Minn. and Northern Plains, Box 1, Entry 662 Files 1–81, MHS.
122. U.S. Senate, 4.
123. Pieciwhathamo (Sing Like Thunder), File Hills Agency #3, interview by D. G. Mandelbaum, trans. Alec Brass, July 3, 1934, O CPRC, IH-DM.10, Transcript Disc 134, University of Regina.
124. Pieciwhathamo (Sing Like Thunder).
125. Fine Day, Fine Day Interview #11, interview by D. G. Mandelbaum, trans. Joe Tanner, August 23, 1934, 2, 9, O CPRC, IH-DM.51, Transcript Disc 139, University of Regina; Fine Day, Fine Day Interview #12, interview by D. G. Mandelbaum, trans. Joe Tanner, August 24, 1934, 3, O CPRC, IH-DM.52, Transcript Disc 139, University of Regina.
126. Feather was a member of the Peepeekisis (Pihpihkisis or Little Hawk) band. Feather (Migwan)/ tipisko-tigisikgo-awasis, File Hills Agency #2, interview by D. G. Mandelbaum, trans. Alec Brass, July 2, 1934, 2, O CPRC, IH-DM.09, Transcript Disc 133, University of Regina.
127. Feather (Migwan)/ tipisko-tigisikgo-awasis, 4.
128. Feather (Migwan)/ tipisko-tigisikgo-awasis, 2.

129. U.S. Senate, "Turtle Mountain Band of Pembina Chippewa Indians," 8, 11.
130. U.S. Senate, "Turtle Mountain Band of Pembina Chippewa Indians," 11.
131. U.S. Senate, "Turtle Mountain Band of Pembina Chippewa Indians," 5, 8, 16.

Chapter 5

1. J. B. Sparvey and Kaniswiwetag "Two Voices," J. B. Sparvey and kaniswiwetag interview, interview by D. G. Mandelbaum, trans. Norbert, June 24, 1934, 1, O CPRC, IH-DM.04, Transcript Disc 133, University of Regina.
2. Kenneth J. Tyler, "KIWISÂNCE," in *Dictionary of Canadian Biography,* vol. 11 (Toronto: University of Toronto Press/Université Laval, 2003).
3. Sparvey and Kaniswiwetag "Two Voices," J. B. Sparvey and kaniswiwetag interview, 2.
4. Sparvey and Kaniswiwetag "Two Voices," 2.
5. Coming Day, Coming Day interview, interview by D. G. Mandelbaum, August 27, 1934, 5–6, O CPRC, IH-DM.53, Transcript Disc 138, University of Regina; Arthur Ray, *I Have Lived Here Since the World Began: An Illustrated History of Canada's Native People,* 3rd ed. (Montreal: McGill-Queen's University Press, 2011), 255; Michel Hogue, "Disputing the Medicine Line: The Plains Crees and the Canadian–American Border, 1876–1885," *Montana: The Magazine of Western History* 52, no. 4 (Winter 2002): 6, 8; Peter Douglas Elias, *The Dakota of the Canadian Northwest: Lessons for Survival* (Regina: Canadian Plains Research Center, 2002), 37.
6. Neal McLeod, *Cree Narrative Memory: From Treaties to Contemporary Times* (Saskatoon: Purich Publishing Limited, 2007), 54.
7. McLeod, *Cree Narrative Memory,* 57.
8. McLeod, *Cree Narrative Memory,* 57; Michel Hogue, *Metis and the Medicine Line: Creating a Border and Dividing a People* (Regina: University of Regina Press, 2015), 175.
9. Dan Flores, "Reviewing an Iconic Story: Environmental History and the Demise of the Bison," in *Bison and People on the North American Great Plains,* ed. Geoff Cunfer and Bill Waiser (College Station: Texas A&M Press, 2016), 44.
10. Otcackiposs (Eater of Raw Liver) and Jack Kenny, Sundance, interview by D. G. Mandelbaum, trans. Ayk'ipci'M and Joe Still, June 23, 1934, 5, O CPRC, IH-DM.03, Transcript Disc 133, University of Regina; Ernest G. Walker, "An Overview of Prehistoric Communal Bison Hunting on the Great Plains," in *Bison and People on the North American Great Plains,* ed. Geoff Cunfer and Bill Waiser (College Station: Texas A&M Press, 2016), 139, 147.
11. Ted Binnema, "A Fur Trade Historian's View of Seasonal Bison Movements on the Northern Plains," in *Bison and People on the North American Great Plains,* ed. Geoff Cunfer and Bill Waiser (College Station: Texas A&M Press, 2016), 159.
12. Flores, "Reviewing an Iconic Story," 39–40; Geoff Cunfer, "Overview," in *Bison and People on the North American Great Plains,* ed. Geoff Cunfer and Bill Waiser (College Station: Texas A&M Press, 2016), 19–20.
13. Cunfer, "Overview," 21–22; Elliott West, "A Horse-Man's View of a Grassland Revolution," in *Bison and People on the North American Great Plains,* ed. Geoff Cunfer and Bill Waiser (College Station: Texas A&M Press, 2016), 194–95; Ray, *I Have Lived Here,* 170.
14. Bill Waiser, "A Legislator's View of Bison Collapse: The 1877 North-West Territories Bison Protection Ordiance," in *Bison and People on the North American Great Plains,* ed. Geoff Cunfer and Bill Waiser (College Station: Texas A&M Press, 2016), 246.
15. Bill Waiser, *A World We Have Lost: Saskatchewan Before 1905* (Markham, ON: Fifth House Limited, 2016), 500; West, "A Horse-Man's View of a Grassland Revolution," 194.
16. Dick Starlight et al., Interview with five elders of the Sarcee Reserve, interview by John Smith, March 17, 1975, 4, O CPRC, IH-247, Transcript Disc 25a, University of Regina; John Yellowhorn, John Yellowhorn (Hereditary Chief), interview by Johnny Smith and Tom Yellowhorn, trans. Johnny Smith, n.d., 4, O CPRC, IH-244, Transcript Disc 25, University of Regina; Mrs. Buffalo, Mrs. Buffalo Interview, interview by Johnny Smith, trans. Johnny Smith, March 12, 1975, 2, O CPRC, IH-228, Transcript Disc 25, University of Regina.
17. David C. Posthumus, "A Lakota View of Pté Oyáte (Buffalo Nation)," in *Bison and People on the North American Great Plains,* ed. Geoff Cunfer and Bill Waiser (College Station: Texas A&M Press, 2016), 295–96.

18. Posthumus, 295–96; John Gneisenau Neihardt, *The Sixth Grandfather: Black Elk's Teachings Given to John G. Neihardt*, ed. Raymond J. DeMaille and Hilda Neihardt Petri (Lincoln: University of Nebraska Press, 1985), 393.
19. Starlight et al., Interview with five elders of the Sarcee Reserve, 5; Fine Day, Fine Day Interview #15, interview by D. G. Mandelbaum, August 31, 1934, 6, O CPRC, IH-DM.56, Transcript Disc 138, University of Regina; Waiser, "A Legislator's View of Bison Collapse: The 1877 North-West Territories Bison Protection Ordiance," 246.
20. Fine Day, Fine Day Interview #28, interview by D. G. Mandelbaum, trans. George Poplar, July 29, 1935, 2–3, O CPRC, IH-DM.82, Transcript Disc 143, University of Regina.
21. Fine Day, Fine Day Interview #28, 2–3.
22. Waiser, "A Legislator's View of Bison Collapse: The 1877 North-West Territories Bison Protection Ordiance," 256.
23. Fine Day, Fine Day Interview #15, 6.
24. Waiser, *A World We Have Lost*, 419.
25. Waiser, *A World We Have Lost*, 468; James Daschuk, *Clearing the Plains: Disease, Politics of Starvation, and the Loss of Aboriginal Life* (Regina: University of Regina Press, 2013), 80.
26. Fine Day, Fine Day Interview #15, 6; Daschuk, *Clearing the Plains*, 83, 86, 101; Ray, *I Have Lived Here*, 210.
27. Michel Hogue, "Between Race and Nation: The Creation of a Métis Borderland on the Northern Plains," in *Bridging National Borders in North America: Transnational and Comparative Histories*, ed. Benjamin H. Johnson and Andrew R. Graybill (Durham, NC: Duke University Press, 2010), 68–70; Marie Albina Hamilton, "Jean Louis Legare," n.d., 2–4, Zachary M. Hamilton Papers MG9 A50/1, Folder 27, AM.
28. Daschuk, *Clearing the Plains*, xx; Sheila McManus, *The Line Which Separates: Race, Gender, and the Making of the Alberta-Montana Borderlands* (Lincoln: University of Nebraska Press, 2005), 73–74; Gerhard J. Ens, "The Border, the Buffalo, and the Métis of Montana," in *The Borderlands of the American and Canadian Wests: Essays on Regional History of the Forty-Ninth Parallel*, ed. Sterling Evans (Lincoln: University of Nebraska Press, 2006), 147; Elias, *The Dakota of the Canadian Northwest*, 57, 83.
29. George Arthur French, "Diary of Lieut. Col. G. A. French, Commanding Officer NWMP," 1874, George Arthur French Papers, MG6 A3, AM; Desmond Morton, "Cavalry or Police: Keeping the Peace on Two Adjacent Frontiers, 1870–1900," *Journal of Canadian Studies* 12, no. 2 (1977): 28–29; Sally Provost, Sally Provost Interview, interview by Johnny Smith, March 7, 1975, O CPRC, IH-237, Transcript 15a, University of Regina.
30. Lynn Hickey, Elder's Interviews: Support From Anthropological Sources, May 1974, 6, O CPRC, IH-341A, Transcript Disc 31, University of Regina; Jim Bottle, Jim Bottle Interview, interview by Harry Shade and Mike Devine, trans. Harry Shade, October 25, 1973, 1, O CPRC, IH-227.1, Transcript Disc 26, University of Regina; James Takes A Gun Strong, James Takes A Gun Strong, interview by Mike Devine, November 9, 1973, 2, O CPRC, IH-241, Transcript 2, University of Regina.
31. Lynn Hickey, Summary of Elders' Interview: "Land and Land Surrenders," April 1974, 2, O CPRC, IH-341.3, Transcript Disc 31, University of Regina; Lynn Hickey, Summary of Elders' Interviews Treaty 6, 1976, 2–3, O CPRC, IH-221, Transcript Disc 25a, University of Regina.
32. McLeod, *Cree Narrative Memory*, 47; Daschuk, *Clearing the Plains*, 98.
33. Isabel Smallboy, Isabel Smallboy Interview, interview by Louie Crier and Phillip Soosay, 1975, 3, 6, O CPRC, IH-208, Transcript Disc 32, University of Regina.
34. McManus, *The Line Which Separates*, 70; Daschuk, *Clearing the Plains*, 185.
35. Cecile Many Guns and Annie Buffalo, Interview with Mrs. Cecile Many Guns (Grassy Water) and Mrs. Annie Buffalo (Bear Child), interview by Dila Provost and Albert Yellowhorn, trans. Dila Provost, 1973, 3–4, O CPRC, IH-236, Transcript Disc 26, University of Regina; Flores, "Reviewing an Iconic Story," 42.
36. US Government, "Treaty of Fort Laramie," 1868, RG 11, Indian Treaties, M668, Ratified Indian Treaties, 1722–1869. T494 Documents Relating to the Negotiation of Ratified and Unratified Treaties With Various Indian Tribes, 1801–1869, NAI: 299803, NARA.
37. Richard White, *The Republic For Which It Stands: The United States During Reconstruction and the Gilded Age, 1865–1896* (Oxford: Oxford University Press, 2017), 299–301; Charles

D. Collins Jr., *Atlas of the Sioux Wars* (Fort Leavenworth: Combat Studies Institute Press, 2006), Map 13.

38. W. T. Sherman to G. W. McCrary, July 16, 1877, 36–37, Papers Relating to the Sioux, University of Waterloo; White, *The Republic For Which It Stands*, 301; Craig Howe, Lydia Whirlwind Solider, and Lanniko L. Lee, eds., *He Sapa Woihanble: Black Hills Dream* (St. Paul: Living Justice Press, 2011), 63.
39. Sherman to McCrary, July 16, 1877, 36–37; David G. McCrady, *Living with Strangers: The Nineteenth-Century Sioux and the Canadian-American Borderlands* (Toronto: University of Toronto Press, 2006), 1.
40. A. G. Irvine to Secretary of State, "The Indian War. General Sheridan to Take Command—Plan of Operation," July 24, 1876, 3, "Papers Relating to the Sioux Indians of U.S. who have Taken Refuge in Canadian Territory," December 13, 1875 to April 14, 1879, Microfilm CA1 IA H5P37, University of Waterloo.
41. White, *The Republic For Which It Stands*, 303.
42. Alexander Morris to Secretary of State, May 15, 1876, Alexander Morris (Lieutenant-Governor's collection) MG 12 B2, Microfilm Reel M141, No 177, AM.
43. Morris to Secretary of State.
44. J. M Walsh to J. F. Macleod, December 31, 1876, 9–10, Papers Relating to the Sioux, University of Waterloo.
45. McCrady, *Living with Strangers*, 73–74.
46. David Mills, "Memorandum," August 23, 1877, 42–43, Papers Relating to the Sioux, University of Waterloo.
47. Hamilton, "Jean Louis Legare," 4.
48. F. R. Plunkett to Earl of Derby, July 24, 1877, 32–33, Papers Relating to the Sioux, University of Waterloo.
49. James F. MacLeod to Alex MacKenzie, May 30, 1877, 18–19, Papers Relating to the Sioux, University of Waterloo; Plunkett to Earl of Derby, July 24, 1877, 32–33; Hamilton, "Jean Louis Legare," 4; A. G. Irvine to R. W. Scott, March 22, 1877, 16, Papers Relating to the Sioux, University of Waterloo.
50. "North-West Mounted Police Fort Walsh," October 17, 1877, 81–84, Papers Relating to the Sioux, University of Waterloo.
51. "North-West Mounted Police Fort Walsh," 81–84.
52. Billy Heavy Runner, Useless Good Runner Interview, interview by Dila Provost and Albert Yellowhorn, 1973, 2, O CPRC, IH-234, Transcript 2, University of Regina.
53. Thornton to Marquis of Salisbury, "Extract—Congressional Record," April 7, 1879.
54. Hamilton, "Jean Louis Legare," 3; A. G. Irvine to Frederick White, November 10, 1878, 125–26, Papers Relating to the Sioux, University of Waterloo.
55. J. W. Walsh to Assistant Commissioner NWMP Fort Walsh, January 25, 1879, 130, Papers Relating to the Sioux, University of Waterloo; Irvine to White, November 10, 1878, 125–26; A. G. Irvine to James F. Macleod, November 20, 1877, 99, Papers Relating to the Sioux, University of Waterloo; McCrady, *Living with Strangers*, 64.
56. A. G. Walsh to Colonel Moale, February 23, 1879, 131–32, Papers Relating to the Sioux, University of Waterloo; Hogue, *Metis and the Medicine Line*, 142; W. L. Lincoln to E. A. Hayt, June 16, 1879, RG 10, Indian Affairs, Black Series, Reel C-10114, Volume 3652, File 8589 pt 1, LAC; "Wood Mountain," July 22, 1879, RG 10, Indian Affairs, Black Series, Reel C-10114, Volume 3652, File 8589 pt 1, LAC; McCrady, *Living with Strangers*, 95–96.
57. McCrady, *Living with Strangers*, 80.
58. Sir Edward Thornton to Marquis of Salisbury, July 1, 1878, 122–23, Papers Relating to the Sioux, University of Waterloo; Hogue, "Between Race and Nation," 73.
59. Elliott West, *The Last Indian War: The Nez Perce Story* (New York: Oxford University Press, 2009), 75–80, 95; White, *The Republic For Which It Stands*, 338; Robert Ross McCoy, *Chief Joseph, Yellow Wolf, and the Creation of Nez Perce History in the Pacific Northwest* (New York: Routledge, 2004), 103–104, 107.
60. Other accounts point to an old woman who had scolded Wahlitits for his failure to avenge his father's death well before he actually set out to enact vengeance. McCoy, *Chief Joseph, Yellow Wolf, and the Creation of Nez Perce History*, 117.

61. West, *The Last Indian War*, 126–27; McCoy, *Chief Joseph, Yellow Wolf, and the Creation of Nez Perce History*, 111.
62. West, *The Last Indian War*, 128, 131.
63. West, 75–78, 123–36.
64. McCoy, *Chief Joseph, Yellow Wolf, and the Creation of Nez Perce History*, 123.
65. McCoy, *Chief Joseph, Yellow Wolf, and the Creation of Nez Perce History*, 123; West, *The Last Indian War*, 230–31.
66. West, *The Last Indian War*, 271–72.
67. White, *The Republic For Which It Stands*, 340; McCrady, *Living with Strangers*, 94; McCoy, *Chief Joseph, Yellow Wolf, and the Creation of Nez Perce History*, 124, 186; Alvin M. Josephy, *Nez Perce Country* (Lincoln: University of Nebraska Press, 2007), 134.
68. West, *The Last Indian War*, 249–53.
69. McCoy, *Chief Joseph, Yellow Wolf, and the Creation of Nez Perce History*, 255; "'Chief Joseph General Miles Overtakes Joseph and His Band—a Fierce and Bloody Battle Fought-Desperate Fighting by the Indians—Aid from Sitting Bull Expected—the Indians in the "Lava Beds" Again—List of Killed and Wounded,'" *National Republican*, October 8, 1877, 76, Papers Relating to the Sioux, University of Waterloo.
70. White, *The Republic For Which It Stands*, 340; McCrady, *Living with Strangers*, 94; Unknown to Cora, May 21, 1890, 31, J. M. Walsh Fonds, M3636, Glenbow Archives.
71. West, *The Last Indian War*, 287–88.
72. "Field Notes (Taken from Colville Reservation)," 1905, 1, Edmond S. Meany Papers, Box 84, V -344b, Folder 85-14, University of Washington Special Collections.
73. McCoy, *Chief Joseph, Yellow Wolf, and the Creation of Nez Perce History*, 127.
74. "Field Notes (Taken from Colville Reservation)," 1.
75. Macleod to David Mills, October 27, 1877, 78, Papers Relating to the Sioux, University of Waterloo.
76. "The Sitting Bull Commission," October 17, 1877, 80, Papers Relating to the Sioux, University of Waterloo.
77. "The Sitting Bull Commission," 80; "North-West Mounted Police Fort Walsh," 81–84.
78. Hogue, "Disputing the Medicine Line," 6.
79. "Wood Mountain"; McCrady, *Living with Strangers*, 96.
80. Edgar Dewdney to Commissioner of Indian Affairs, December 15, 1882, 196, DIA ARO, LAC; James Morrow Walsh, "Miscellaneous," n.d., Morton Manuscripts Collection, MSS-C550-1-22-4 (Box 35) [online], University of Saskatchewan Library Special Collections; L. N. F. Crozier to J. Johnson, December 8, 1879, RG 18, Series B3, RCMP, Volume 2232, Reel T-6573, LAC; "Wood Mountain."
81. J. M. Walsh to J. T. MacLeod, July 25, 1879, RG 10, Indian Affairs, Black Series, Reel C-10114, Volume 3652, File 8589, pt 1, LAC.
82. Hogue, "Disputing the Medicine Line," 8, 11.
83. Hogue, "Disputing the Medicine Line," 8.
84. James Macleod to J. S. Dennis, December 1, 1879, RG 10, Indian Affairs, Black Series, Reel C-10114, Volume 3652, File 8589 pt 1, LAC.
85. David G McCrady, "Louis Riel and Sitting Bull's Sioux: The Three Lost Letters," in *The Western Métis: Profile of a People*, ed. Patrick C. Douaud (Regina: Canadian Plains Research Center, 2007), 204.
86. McCrady, "Louis Riel and Sitting Bull's Sioux," 206–207.
87. Edgar Dewdney to Superintendent General of Indian Affairs, June 7, 1881, RG 10, Indian Affairs, Black Series, Reel C-10114, Volume 3652, File 8589, pt 1, LAC.
88. By 1903, Légaré claims to have only received $2,000 despite pressing the case on a number of instances. Jean Louis Legaré to Clifford Sifton, March 25, 1903, 44, S-E1, Department of the Interior, Dominion Land Branch, File 49185, PAS; unsigned, "Memorandum to Accompany the Application of Jean Louis Légaré to the Right Honorable Minister of the Interior of Canada for a Grant of Land on the Northern Slope of Wood Mountain," n.d., 28, S-E1, Department of the Interior, Dominion Land Branch, File 49185, PAS; Beth LaDow, *The Medicine Line: Life and Death on a North American Borderland* (New York: Routledge, 2001), xv.

89. LaDow, *The Medicine Line*, xv.
90. His name has multiple spellings including Mato O-be-te-ke and Mah-to-o-hit-ka. The Northern Pacific Farmer also attributes him with the name Wa-pe-pi "An Indian Hanged: Brave Bear Finally Executed at Yankton, Meeting His Fate with Great Calmness," *The Northern Pacific Farmer*, November 23, 1882, 2; James McLaughlin to H. Price, September 1, 1882, 190–92, McLaughlin Papers, MF 970.1 M219As Reel 2, Perdue University; "Brave Bear's Neck Broken," *The Benton Weekly Record*, December 7, 1882, 1; McCrady, *Living with Strangers*, xvi.
91. McLaughlin to Price, September 1, 1882, 190–92; "An Indian Hanged," 2; "United States Court," *Yankton Press and Daily Dakotaian*, January 5, 1882, 2.
92. McLaughlin to Price, September 1, 1882, 190–92; "Brave Bear's Neck Broken," 1; "An Indian Hanged," 2.
93. There are multiple variations of how Brave Bear was arrested and what he offered to Allison "United States Court," 2, 4; "An Indian Hanged," 2; "Brave Bear Hung," *Press and Daily Dakotaian*, November 15, 1882, 4, CAHAN, LOC; "United States Court," 2, 4.
94. McLaughlin to Price, September 1, 1882, 190–92.
95. McLaughlin to Price, 190–92.
96. "An Indian Hanged," 2.
97. "Brave Bear Hung," 4; "An Indian Hanged," 2.
98. Running Antelope, Standing Bear, Thunder Hawk, and Low Elkto Secretary of Interior, March 20, 1891, 419–28, McLaughlin Papers, MF 970.1 M219As Reel 2, Perdue University; E. G. Fechet to Post-Adjutant, Fort Yates, n.d., December 17, 1890, 208–209, McLaughlin Papers, MF 970.1 M219As, Reel 31, Fort Yates, Letters Sent 1886–1891, Perdue University.
99. Daschuk, *Clearing the Plains*, xxi, 124, 133–34, 153.
100. Daschuk, *Clearing the Plains*, 184.
101. Waiser, *A World We Have Lost*, 509; Daschuk, *Clearing the Plains*, 129, 143.
102. Daschuk, *Clearing the Plains*, 146; The intentional withholding of food or annuities was not unique to the Canadian prairies. It appeared in other regions (like the Great Lakes) and in the United States as well. Lewis Stowe, "Why the Millie Lacs Indians Were Not Paid," November 30, 1874, P2309, Lewis Stowe and Family Papers, 1819–1954, Box 1, Correspondence and Miscellaneous Papers and vols.1–11, Box 1, Folder 3 Cor. And Misc., 1870–1879, MHS.
103. McCrady, "Louis Riel and Sitting Bull's Sioux," 204; Louis Riel, "Letter to Messrs. James Isbister, Gabriel Dumont, Moise Ouillette, and Michael Dumais, June 4, 1884," in *Reminiscences of the North-West Rebellions: With a Record of the Raising of Her Majesty's 100th Regiment in Canada, and a Chapter on Canadian Social & Political Life*, by Charles Arkoll Boulton (Toronto: Grip printing and publishing, 1886), 170–71; Macleod to Dennis, December 1, 1879; J. A. Chapleau, "The Riel Question," n.d., Sir John A. Macdonald Papers, Volume 109, Reel C-1525, LAC; Gerhard J. Ens and Joe Sawchuk, *From New Peoples to New Nations: Aspects of Metis History and Identity from Eighteenth to Twenty-First Centuries* (Toronto: University of Toronto Press, 2016), 109.
104. J. A. Jackson to Zachary M. Hamilton, February 24, 1948, Zachary M. Hamilton Papers MG9 A50/1 Folder 21, AM.
105. Jeremy Ravi Mumford, "Why Was Louis Riel, a United States Citizen, Hanged as a Canadian Traitor in 1885?," *Canadian Historical Review* 88, no. 2 (2007): 243.
106. Hogue, *Metis and the Medicine Line*, 174.
107. Ens and Sawchuk, *From New Peoples to New Nations*, 111.
108. Thomas Flanagan, *Riel and the Rebellion: 1885 Reconsidered* (Toronto: University of Toronto Press, 2000), x,15; Ens and Sawchuk, *From New Peoples to New Nations*, 111–12.
109. Flanagan, *Riel and the Rebellion*, 3.
110. Robert Goodvoice, Robert Goodvoice Interview #8, 1977, 4, O CPRC, IH-111, Transcript Disc 11 (Originals held at PAS, R-A1343), University of Regina.
111. Waiser, *A World We Have Lost*, 536–37, 547; Widow Crane, Mrs. Widow Crane, interview by Louis Rain, September 4, 1974, 3, O CPRC, H-178, Transcript 2, University of Regina.
112. Daschuk, *Clearing the Plains*, 152.
113. Hogue, *Metis and the Medicine Line*, 176–78.

114. Waiser, *A World We Have Lost*, 574; Andrew R. Graybill, *Policing the Great Plains: Rangers, Mounties, and the North American Frontier 1875–1910* (Lincoln: University of Nebraska Press, 2007), 89; Flanagan, *Riel and the Rebellion: 1885 Reconsidered*, 3.
115. Waiser, *A World We Have Lost*, 561–63.
116. Waiser, *A World We Have Lost*, 559–62; Lauren L. Basson, "Savage Half-Breed, French Canadian or White US Citizen? Louis Riel and US Perceptions of Nation and Civilisation," *National Identities* 7, no. 4 (December 2005): 374; Flanagan, *Riel and the Rebellion: 1885 Reconsidered*, 13; Flanagan, *Riel and the Rebellion*, 16.
117. J. M. Bumsted, "Louis Riel and the United States," *American Review of Canadian Studies* 29, no. 1 (1999): 17.
118. Mumford, "Why Was Louis Riel, a United States Citizen, Hanged as a Canadian Traitor in 1885?," 239; Flanagan, *Riel and the Rebellion*, 14.
119. Waiser, *A World We Have Lost*, 541.
120. Hans Peterson, "Imasees and His Band: Canadian Refugees after the North-West Rebellion," *Western Canadian Journal of Anthropology* 8, no. 1 (1978): 27.
121. Peterson, "Imasees and His Band," 25; Hogue, *Metis and the Medicine Line*, 180.
122. Harry Tremayne, Harry Tremayne Interview, interview by Victoria Racette, March 30, 1984, 7, Gabriel Dumont Institute Archives.
123. Tremayne, Harry Tremayne Interview, 7–8.
124. Tremayne, Harry Tremayne Interview, 8–9.
125. Tremayne, Harry Tremayne Interview, 7, 15.
126. Ada Ladue and Beatrice Nightraveller, Ada Ladue and Beatrice Nightraveller Interview, interview by Christine Welsh, June 15, 1983, 14–15, O CPRC, IH-123, Transcript 6, University of Regina.
127. Ladue and Nightraveller, Ada Ladue and Beatrice Nightraveller Interview, 15.
128. Ladue and Nightraveller, Ada Ladue and Beatrice Nightraveller Interview, 15–17.
129. Daschuk, *Clearing the Plains*, 162.
130. Daschuk, *Clearing the Plains*, 164.
131. John Herd Thompson and Stephen J. Randall, *Canada and the United States: Ambivalent Allies*, 4th ed. (Athens: University of Georgia Press, 2008), 48.
132. Marian C. McKenna, "Above the Blue Line: Policing the Frontier in the Canadian and American West, 1870–1900," in *The Borderlands of the American and Canadian Wests: Essays on Regional History of the Forty-Ninth Parallel*, ed. Sterling Evans (Lincoln: University of Nebraska Press, 2006), 83; Morton, "Cavalry or Police," 27–30; Graybill, *Policing the Great Plains*, 51; Thompson and Randall, *Canada and the United States*, 48–49.

Chapter 6

1. Frank Paul, Frank Paul Interview, interview by Imbert Orchard, July 1, 1964, 2–3, O CPRC, IH-BC.58, Transcript Disc 177, University of Regina.
2. Paul, Frank Paul Interview, 3.
3. I have adopted historian Beth Lew-Williams use of the term "restriction" to describe the 1882 act and "exclusion" to denote the 1888 act to help distinguish the intentions and resources behind each policy. Beth Lew-Williams, *The Chinese Must Go: Violence, Exclusion, and the Making of the Alien in America* (Cambridge, MA: Harvard University Press, 2018), 55–56.
4. Julie H. Ferguson, *James Douglas: Father of British Columbia* (Toronto: Dundurn Press, 2009), 217.
5. Margaret A. Ormsby, "Douglas, Sir James," in *Dictionary of Canadian Biography*, vol. 10 (University of Toronto Press/Université Laval, 1972), http://www.biographi.ca/en/bio/douglas_james_10E.html.
6. Hamar Foster and Grove Alan, "'Trespassers on the Soil': United States v. Tom and A New Perspective on the Short History of Treaty Making in Nineteenth-Century British Columbia," *BC Studies* 138/139 (2003): 53–55, 62–63; Lissa K. Wadewitz, *The Nature of Borders: Salmon, Boundaries, and Bandits on the Salish Sea* (Seattle: University of Washington Press, 2012), 65; Cole Harris, *Making Native Space: Colonialism, Resistance, and Reserves in British Columbia* (Vancouver: UBC Press, 2002), 21, 71–72; John Sutton Lutz, *Makúk: A*

New History of Aboriginal-White Relations (Vancouver: UBC Press, 2008), 80; Keith Carlson, ed., *You Are Asked to Witness: The Stó:Lō in Canada's Pacific Coast History* (Chilliwack, BC: Stó:lō Heritage Trust, 1997), 65–67, 74.

7. Harry Assu, *Assu of Cape Mudge: Recollections of a Coastal Indian Chief* (Vancouver: UBC Press, 1989), 45.
8. Lutz, *Makúk*, 82–83.
9. Harry Assu, a Kwagiulth, noted that the restrictions on potlatching did not affect the Indigenous people living at Cape Mudge until 1922. Federal control continued to differ by region. Assu, *Assu of Cape Mudge:*, 1, 10, 40–42, 48 57; Lutz, *Makúk*, 80–87; Clellan S. Ford, *Smoke from Their Fires: The Life of a Kwakiutl Chief*, 2nd ed. (Hamden: Archon Books, 1968), 17–22, 218, 230.
10. Robin Fisher, "Indian Warfare and Two Frontiers: A Comparison of British Columbia and Washington Territory during the Early Years of Settlement," *Pacific Historical Review* 50, no. 1 (February 1, 1981): 41; Harris, *Making Native Space*, 57–64.
11. Inconsistencies included the Oregon Donation Land Act in 1850 that "disregarded a long-standing federal policy of obtaining consent from Indian occupants before issuing land titles" Alexandra Harmon, *Indians in the Making: Ethnic Relations and Indian Identities Around Puget Sound* (Berkeley: University of California Press, 1998), 58; For complaints regarding the treaty process see E. P. Drew to J. W. Nesmith, "No. 91," June 30, 1858, 254–55, OIA ARO, UWDC; M. T. Simmons to Edward R. Geary, "No. 180," July 1, 1859, 395, OIA ARO, UWDC; C. H. Hale to Wm. P. Dole, "Washington Superintendency," October 19, 1862, 395, OIA ARO, UWDC; John Mullan to Charles E. Mix, "No. 101," September 5, 1858, 279, OIA ARO, UWDC; Elizabeth Rose Lew-Williams, "The Chinese Must Go: Immigration, Deportation and Violence in the 19th-Century Pacific Northwest" (PhD diss., Stanford University, 2011), 55–56.
12. James M. Lynch and William S. Lewis, "Brief Statement of Certain Claims of Okanongan and Colville Indians, of the State of Washington, against the United States," n.d., Edmond S. Meany Papers, Box 85, V -344b, Folder 85-15, University of Washington Special Collections.
13. United States, President, *Executive Orders Relating to Indian Reservations: From May 14, 1855 to July 1, 1912* (Washington, DC: Government Printing Office, 1912), 194–95.
14. Wadewitz, *The Nature of Borders*, 69; J. W. Nesmith to J. W. Denver, "No. 134," September 1, 1857, 318, OIA ARO, UWDC.
15. Geo. W. Manypenny to Isaac I. Stevens, "No. 85," May 9, 1853, 219, OIA ARO, UWDC; Keith Thor Carlson, *The Power of Place, the Problem of Time: Aboriginal Identity and Historical Consciousness in the Cauldron of Colonialism* (Toronto: University of Toronto Press, 2010), 20–21; Bruce Miller, "An Ethnographic View of Legal Entanglements on the Salish Sea Borderlands," *UBC Law Review* 47, no. 3 (2014): 1007.
16. Dorothy Kennedy, "Quantifying 'Two Sides of a Coin': A Statistical Examination of the Central Coast Salish Social Network," *BC Studies*, no. 153 (2007): 5–7, 25; Carlson, *The Power of Place the Problem of Time*, 75.
17. Carlson, *The Power of Place the Problem of Time*, 30.
18. Bruce Miller, "The 'Really Real' Border and the Divided Salish Community," *BC Studies* 112 (1996): 65; Miller, "An Ethnographic View," 1007; Kennedy, "Quantifying 'Two Sides of a Coin'," " 17; Harmon, *Indians in the Making*, 445.
19. Kennedy, "Quantifying 'Two Sides of a Coin'," 29–30.
20. W. L. Powell to Commissioner of Indian Affairs, August 17, 1886, 236, OIA ARO, UWDC.
21. Alexandra Harmon, "Lines in Sand: Shifting Boundaries between Indians and Non-Indians in the Puget Sound Region," *The Western Historical Quarterly* 26, no. 4 (Winter 1995): 447.
22. Kennedy, "Quantifying 'Two Sides of a Coin'," 25–26.
23. Kennedy, "Quantifying 'Two Sides of a Coin'," 26.
24. Carlson, *The Power of Place the Problem of Time*, 50.
25. Miller, "An Ethnographic View," 996.
26. Miller, "The 'Really Real' Border and the Divided Salish Community," 998–99; Kennedy, "Quantifying 'Two Sides of a Coin'," 24; Carlson, *The Power of Place the Problem of Time*, 54–55, 127.
27. Carlson, *The Power of Place the Problem of Time*, 127–29.

28. Carlson, *The Power of Place the Problem of Time*, 226–30.
29. Carlson, *The Power of Place the Problem of Time*, 7–10.
30. Carlson, *The Power of Place the Problem of Time*, 8.
31. Carlson, *The Power of Place the Problem of Time*, 7–9.
32. Larry Commodore, interview by Anne Janhunen and Dallas Posavad, May 29, 2013, Stó:lō Library and Archive; Carlson, *The Power of Place the Problem of Time*, 117–21.
33. Bruce Sam, D1, interview by Sabina Trimble, May 29, 2013, D.1 29.05.2013, Stó:lō Library and Archive; Sabina Trimble, "Storying Swí:Lhcha: Place Making and Power at a Stó:Lō Landmark," *BC Studies* 190 (2016): 42, 51.
34. Sam, D1, 3–7 min.
35. Carlson, *The Power of Place the Problem of Time*, 136.
36. James M. Hundley, "We Are Coast Salish: Politics and Society across a Settler Colonial Border in the Post–9/11 World" (PhD diss., State University of New York–Binghamton, 2017), 16–17.
37. James Douglas to Archibald Barclay, "On the Affairs of Vancouver Island," February 16, 1853, 121, James Douglas Fond, A/C/20/Vi/2A, BCA; James Douglas to Archibald Barclay, "On the Affairs of Vancouver Island," May 16, 1853, 137, James Douglas Fond, A/C/20/Vi/2A, BCA.
38. "Colony of Vancouver Island," 1863, 263–71, Box 28, location 542502, C/AA/10.6/1, BCA.
39. George Swanaset, "George Swanaset: Narrative of a Personal Document," 1951, 9, Melville Jacobs Collection, 1693-91-13-001 Box 112, V 206, Folder 10, University of Washington Special Collections;Jean Barman, *The West Beyond the West: A History of British Columbia* (Toronto: University of Toronto Press, 1991), 55; Coll Thrush, *Native Seattle: Histories from the Crossing-Over Place* (Seattle: University of Washington Press, 2007), 47–49; Russel Lawrence Barsh, "Puget Sound Indian Demography, 1900–1920: Migration and Economic Integration," *Ethnohistory* 43, no. 1 (winter 1996): 67; Lutz, *Makúk*, 176, 192, 219–20.
40. W. H. Lomas to unknown [likely Superintendent General of Indian Affairs], August 16, 1882, 54, DIA ARO, LAC; Thrush, *Native Seattle*, 41, 47; Cole Harris, *The Resettlement of British Columbia: Essays on Colonialism and Geographical Change* (Vancouver: UBC Press, 1997), 95; Jeremiah Gorsline, ed., *Shadows of Our Ancestors: Readings in the History of Klallam-White Relations* (Port Townsend, WA: Empty Bowl, 1992), 82; Lutz, *Makúk*, 217; Paige Raibmon, "The Practice of Everyday Colonialism: Indigenous Women at Work in the Hop Fields and Tourist Industry of Puget Sound," *Labour* 3, no. 3 (2006): 31.
41. Raibmon, "The Practice of Everyday Colonialism: Indigenous Women at Work in the Hop Fields and Tourist Industry of Puget Sound," 29.
42. Kenneth D. Tollefson, "The Political Survival of Landless Puget Sound Indians," *American Indian Quarterly* 16, no. 2 (April 1, 1992): 217; Thrush, *Native Seattle*, 111; Barman, *The West Beyond the West*, 119, 133.
43. Edward Bristow to Charles M. Buchanan, July 15, 1902, RG 75, BIA, Annual Reports Tulalip Agency, Box 1 1863–1908, Folder 1902, NARA Seattle; Edward Bristow to Charles M. Buchanan, July 20, 1903, RG 75, BIA, Letters received—Tulalip Agency, Swinomish, Box 7 1899–1904, NARA Seattle; Daniel L. Boxberger, "In and out of the Labor Force: The Lummi Indians and the Development of the Commercial Salmon Fishery of North Puget Sound, 1880–1900," *Ethnohistory* 35, no. 2 (April 1, 1988): 172; A. W. Neill to Frank Pedley, June 30, 1906, 255, DIA ARO, LAC; W. H. Lomas to Superintendent General of Indian Affairs, August 7, 1885, 80, DIA ARO, LAC.
44. Henry Doyle, "British Columbia Fish and Fisheries," June 1907, 2, Henry Doyle Collection, Acc. 861, box 1, folder 1, dismantled scrapbook, University of Washington Special Collections; Lutz, *Makúk*, 93, 186–87; Chris Friday, *Organizing Asian American Labor: The Pacific Coast Canned-Salmon Industry, 1870–1942* (Philadelphia: Temple University Press, 1994), 88.
45. Wadewitz, *The Nature of Borders*, 28–29.
46. Wadewitz, *The Nature of Borders*, 22, 26.
47. Harris, *The Resettlement of British Columbia*, 162–65.
48. Kornel S. Chang, *Pacific Connections* (Berkeley: University of California Press, 2012), 20; Harris, *The Resettlement of British Columbia*, 169–70; For the problems, corruption,

and costs surrounding the transcontinental railways see Richard White, *Railroaded: The Transcontinentals and the Making of Modern America* (New York: Norton, 2011).

49. Katherine Unterman, *Uncle Sam's Policemen: The Pursuit of Fugitives Across Borders* (Cambridge, MA: Harvard University Press, 2015), 3.
50. Harris, *The Resettlement of British Columbia*, 4, 18–26, 77, 90, 120; Barman, *The West Beyond the West*, 156; Thrush, *Native Seattle*, 26, 110; Carlson, *The Power of Place the Problem of Time*, 98; Jennifer Seltz, "Epidemics, Indians, and Border Marking in the Nineteenth Century Pacific Northwest," in *Bridging National Borders in North America: Transnational and Comparative Histories*, ed. Benjamin H. Johnson and Andrew R. Graybill (Durham, NC: Duke University Press, 2010), 91.
51. Seltz, "Epidemics, Indians, and Border Marking in the Nineteenth Century Pacific Northwest," 95.
52. United States, Bureau of the Census, *Thirteenth Census of the United States 1910: Bulletin Population: United States—Color or Race, Nativity, Parentage, and Sex* (Washington, DC: Government Printing Office, 1913), 82; United States, Census Office, *Compendium of the Eleventh Census: 1890. Part 1—Population* (Washington, DC: Government Printing Office, 1892), 473.
53. Benjamin Hoy, "Uncertain Counts: The Struggle to Enumerate First Nations in Canada and the United States 1870–1911," *Ethnohistory* 62, no. 4 (2015): 730, 732.
54. United States, Census Office, *Compendium of the Eleventh Census: 1890. Part 1—Population*, 473; United States, Office of Indian Affairs, *Annual Report of the Commissioner of Indian Affairs, for the Year 1860* (Washington, DC: Government Printing Office, 1860), 21; United States, Office of Indian Affairs, *Annual Report of the Commissioner of Indian Affairs, for the Year 1870* (Washington, DC: Government Printing Office, 1870), 16; United States, Office of Indian Affairs, *Annual Report of the Commissioner of Indian Affairs for the Year 1880* (Washington, DC: Government Printing Office, 1880), iv.
55. Lutz, *Makúk*, 163.
56. Demographic changes did not affect all parts of the coast in the same way. The European population that came to British Columbia settled on the southern portion of the province near Vancouver Island giving them a disproportionate influence near the border and a relatively weak presence in the northern interior. In 1881 First Nations vastly outnumbered whites and Chinese on the Skeena and Nass rivers on the northwest coast. In the south, near Vancouver Island, by contrast, non-Natives comprised three fourths of the population in 1881. Harris, *The Resettlement of British Columbia*, 149–53; George Johnson to Minister of Agriculture and Statistics, "Dispute with Ottawa on Indian Census," 1894, GR-0429, Box 3, File 2, British Columbia, Attorney General, Correspondence Inward, B09318 69/94, BCA; "Re Census of British Columbia," 1894, GR-0429, Box 3, File 2, British Columbia, Attorney General, Correspondence Inward, 1894, BCA.
57. United States, Census Office, *Compendium of the Tenth Census of the United States*, vol. 1 (Washington, DC: Government Printing Office, 1883), 377; *The Canada Year Book 1911*, Second Series (Ottawa: C. H. Parmelee, 1912), 16; Lew-Williams, *The Chinese Must Go*, 34.
58. "Republican Position on the Chinese Question," *Seattle Daily Intelligencer*, October 27, 1880, 1, CAHAN, LOC; "Butler on the Chinese," *The Vancouver Independent*, June 24, 1880, 7, CAHAN, LOC.
59. Renisa Mawani, "Cross-Racial Encounters and Juridical Truths: (Dis)Aggregating Race in British Columbia's Contact Zone," *BC Studies*, 2007 2008, 141–71.
60. Richard White, *The Republic For Which It Stands: The United States During Reconstruction and the Gilded Age, 1865–1896* (New York: Oxford University Press, 2017), 381.
61. United States, "Chap 141—An Act Supplementary to the Acts in Relation to Immigration [Page Act], 18 Stat L., 477, March 3, 1875," in *Supplement to the Revised Statutes of the United States 1874–1891*, ed. William A Richardson, 2nd ed., vol. 1 (Washington, DC: Government Printing Office, 1891), 86–88; United States, "An Act to Execute Certain Treaty Stipulations Relating to Chinese [Chinese Restriction Act]," May 6, 1882, U. S. Statutes at Large, Vol. XXII, p. 58 ff, 22 Stat. 58; Lew-Williams, *The Chinese Must Go*, 55–56; Lucy Salyer, *Laws Harsh as Tigers: Chinese Immigration and the Shaping of Modern Immigration Law* (Chapel Hill: University of North Carolina Press, 1995), 14, 17.

62. Salyer, *Laws Harsh as Tigers*, 4. Hidetaka Hirota, *Expelling the Poor: Atlantic Seaboard States and the Nineteenth-Century Origins of American Immigration Policy* (New York: Oxford University Press, 2017), 208–209.
63. Mawani, "Cross-Racial Encounter."
64. I. W. Powell to Superintendent-General of Indian Affairs, October 31, 1883, 107, DIA ARO, LAC; Lew-Williams, *The Chinese Must Go*, 7; John A. MacDonald, "Report of the Department of Indian Affairs," January 1, 1884, lx, lxiv, DIA ARO, LAC; P. McTiernan to Superintendent General of Indian Affairs, August 15, 1884, 104, DIA ARO, LAC.
65. White, *The Republic For Which It Stands*, 156, 381; Francis A. Walker, "The Indian Question," *North American Review* 66, no. 239 (1873): 333, 336; Josiah Strong, *Our Country Its Possible Future and Its Present Crisis* (The Baker & Taylor Co.: New York, 1885), 165, 170, 178.
66. United States, "Naturalization; Signed in London May 13, 1870, Came into Force August 10, 1870," in *Treaties and Other International Agreements of the United States of America 1776–1949*, ed. Charles I. Bevans, vol. 12 (Washington, DC: Department of State, 1968), 158–60; Alfred Howell, "An Act Respecting Naturalization and Aliens, 44 Vic., c. 13 (Canada) 1881," in *Naturalization and Nationality in Canada: Expatriation and Repatriation of British Subjects: Aliens, Their Disabilities and Their Privileges in Canada* (Toronto: Carswell & co, 1884), 57; Peter Andreas, *Smuggler Nation: How Illicit Trade Made America* (New York: Oxford University Press, 2013), 103.
67. Lew-Williams, *The Chinese Must Go*, 9.
68. Salyer, *Laws Harsh as Tigers*, 16.
69. United States, "An Act to Execute Certain Treaty Stipulations Relating to Chinese [Chinese Restriction Act]."
70. Lew-Williams, "The Chinese Must Go," 61–65, 99; Erika Lee, *At America's Gates: Chinese Immigration during the Exclusion Era, 1882–1943* (Chapel Hill: University of North Carolina Press, 2003), 175–76.
71. Lew-Williams, "The Chinese Must Go," 75; Lutz, *Makúk*, 96.
72. "The Mate Peached: Rogues Fall Out and Aid the Ends of Justice," ca 1891, RG 36 U.S. Customs Service, Puget Sound Collection, Inspectors Notices of Seizures, 1886–1897, Box 1, Series 38, Vol 1, NARA Seattle; Lew-Williams, "The Chinese Must Go," 75, 90–91; "U.S. vs T. Yamasaki," May 25, 1899, RG 21, U.S. District Courts Western District Washington Northern Division Seattle, Box 88, Folder 1497, NARA Seattle; John Melzett to A. W. Bash, October 9, 1883, RG 36, U.S. Customs Service, Puget Sound, Box 109, Letters Received From SubPorts and Inspectors, San Juan, File 4, NARA Seattle.
73. E. A. Heaman, *Tax, Order, and Good Government: A New Political History of Canada, 1867–1917* (Montreal: McGill-Queen's University Press, 2017), 98, 115, 174.
74. United States, "An Act to Execute Certain Treaty Stipulations Relating to Chinese [Chinese Restriction Act]."
75. Abraham E. Smith to David J. Hill, "No. 164," April 11, 1900, RG 59, Despatches from U.S. Consuls in Victoria, T130, Volume 13, Reel 14, NARA College Park; Lee, *At America's Gates*, 175–76.
76. James G. Swan, "United State vs. Ah Jack—United States Commissioners Court, State of Washington, County of Jefferson, City of Port Townsend," September 26, 1890, RG 21, UDC WDW, Box 8, Folder 144, U.S. vs Ah Jack, NARA Seattle.
77. Lew-Williams, "The Chinese Must Go," 371–73.
78. "U.S. vs Eng Hong," October 25, 1890, RG 21, UDC WDW, Box 8, Folder 153, NARA Seattle.
79. "U.S. vs Wong Sing et Al," September 24, 1890, RG 21, UDC WDW, Box 8, Folder 143, NARA Seattle.
80. C. H. Hanford, "No 154 Order of Deportation, US vs Wong Sing, United States District Court, District of Washington—Northern Division," c 1890, RG 21, UDC WDW, Box 8, Folder 154, U.S. vs Wong Sing, NARA Seattle.
81. "U.S. vs Wong Sing et Al."
82. C. B. Bash to A. W. Bash, August 9, 1883, RG 36, U.S. Customs Service, Puget Sound, Box 109, Letters Received From SubPorts and Inspectors, San Juan, File 4, NARA Seattle.
83. A. L. Blake to A. W. Bash, May 7, 1884, RG 36, U.S. Customs Service, Puget Sound, Box 110, Letters Recived from Subports and Inspectors, Osooyoos, Ft. Colville, Sehome, Seattle, 1882–1885, Folder 2, NARA Seattle.

84. A. L. Blake to A. W. Bash, July 1, 1884, RG 36, U.S. Customs Service, Puget Sound, Box 110, Letters Received from Subports and Inspectors, Osooyoos, Ft. Colville, Sehome, Seattle, 1882–1885, Folder 2, NARA Seattle.
85. A. L Blake to A. W. Bash, December 4, 1883, RG 36, U.S. Customs Service, Puget Sound, Box 109, Letters Received From SubPorts and Inspectors, San Juan, File 5, NARA Seattle; A. L. Blake to A. W. Bash, December 8, 1883, RG 36, U.S. Customs Service, Puget Sound, Box 109, Letters Received From SubPorts and Inspectors, San Juan, File 5, NARA Seattle; J. H. Price to A. W. Bash, November 28, 1882, RG 36, U.S. Customs Service, Puget Sound, Box 109, Letters Received From SubPorts and Inspectors, San Juan, File 5, NARA Seattle.
86. A. L. Blake to A. W. Bash, November 29, 1883, RG 36, U.S. Customs Service, Puget Sound, Box 109, Letters Received From SubPorts and Inspectors, San Juan, File 5, NARA Seattle.
87. Blake to Bash, December 4, 1883; Lew-Williams, "The Chinese Must Go," 82–83.
88. Grover Cleveland, "Message from the President of the United States, Relative to the Act to Execute Certain Treaty Stipulations with China, October 1, 1888," in *Papers Relating to the Foreign Relations of the United States*, by United States, vol. 1 (Washington, DC: Government Printing Office, 1889), 359; Lew-Williams, *The Chinese Must Go*, 1, 118, 129, 156–60, 183; Lew-Williams, "The Chinese Must Go," 125, 153.
89. Chang, *Pacific Connections*, 48–49.
90. Cleveland, "Message from the President of the United States, Relative to the Act to Execute Certain Treaty Stipulations with China, October 1, 1888," 357.
91. United States, Department of State, "Chap. 1222 An Act Making an Appropriation for the Enforcement of the Chinese Exclusion Act," in *The Statutes at Large of the United States December 1887 to March 1889 and Recent Treaties, Postal Conventions, and Executive Documents*, vol. 25 (Washington, DC: Government Printing Office, 1889), 615.
92. J. G. Carlisle, "Letter from the Secretary of the Treasury in Answer to a Resolution of the Senate of the 7th Instant, and Transmitting a Statement of the Amounts Appropriated and Expended in the Enforcement of the Chinese Exclusion Acts," September 12, 1893, 1, 53 Cong., 1 Sess., Ex. Doc 13; Lew-Williams, "The Chinese Must Go," 378.
93. Quincy A. Brooks and Secretary of Treasury, "Submitting Suggestions Relative to Chinese Restriction," May 28, 1888, RG 85, INS, Entry 134 Custom Case File 3358d Related to Chinese Immigration 1877–1891, Box 1 A1, Folder 1, NARA DC; United States, "An Act to Prohibit the Coming of Chinese Persons into the United States [Geary Act]," 52nd Congress, Sess I, CHS 60 § (1892); Lew-Williams, *The Chinese Must Go*, 205; Lee, *At America's Gates*, 153–55.
94. A. W. Bash to Charles J. Folger, September 24, 1882, 255–57, RG 36, U.S. Customs Service, Puget Sound, Box 37 Letters sent to the Secretary of the Treasury 1881–1886, Book 1, NARA Seattle; I. W. Powell to Superintendent General of Indian Affairs, November 22, 1881, 147, DIA ARO, LAC; Canada, Department of Indian Affairs, *Annual Report of the Department of Indian Affairs For the Year Ended 31st December 1881* (Ottawa: MacLean, Roger & Co., 1882), 147.
95. Michael Phillipps to Superintendent General of Indian Affairs, July 2, 1888, 110, DIA ARO, LAC.
96. Blake to Bash, July 1, 1884; Lomas to unknown [likely Superintendent General of Indian Affairs], August 16, 1882, 54; M. S. Drew to Geo. S. Boutwell, October 23, 1871, RG 36, U.S. Customs Service, Puget Sound, Box 3 Letters Received From Department of Treasury, Folder 1, NARA Seattle; J. T. Harley to M. S. Drew, October 27, 1871, RG 36, U.S. Customs Service, Puget Sound, Box 3 Letters Received From Department of Treasury, Folder 1, NARA Seattle; A. L. Blake to A. W. Bash, July 19, 1883, RG 36, U.S. Customs Service, Puget Sound, Box 109, Letters Received From SubPorts and Inspectors, San Juan, File 4, NARA Seattle; James Douglas to Archibald Barclay, "On the Affairs of Vancouver Island," October 5, 1852, 101, James Douglas Fond, A/C/20/Vi/2A, BCA.
97. A. L. Blake to A. W. Bash, May 5, 1883, RG 36, U.S. Customs Service, Puget Sound, Box 109, Letters Received From SubPorts and Inspectors, San Juan, File 3, NARA Seattle.
98. Abraham E. Smith to Herbert H. D. Peirce, September 13, 1905, RG 59, Despatches from U.S. Consuls in Victoria, T130, Volume 15, Reel 16, NARA College Park.
99. John P. McGlinn to Commissioner of Indian Affairs, "Report of Neah Bay Agency," August 19, 1892, 495, OIA ARO, UWDC; Canada, *The Revised Statutes of Canada: Proclaimed and*

Published Under the Authority of the Act 49 Vic Chap 4, Ad. 1886, vol. 1 (Ottawa: Brown Chamberlin, 1887), 683.

100. Robert B. Jimmie, Stó:lō Nation Traditional Use Study, interview by Pat John and Ernie Victor, March 13, 1997, 19 (79), TUS, JRO-I-1 (JRO-I.TRN), Jimmie Robert Transcript, Stó:lō Library and Archive; Lutz, *Makúk*, 105.
101. Jimmie, Stó:lō Nation Traditional Use Study, 36 (96).
102. Keith Carlson, "Innovation, Tradition, Colonialism, and Aboriginal Fishing Conflicts in the Lower Fraser Canyon," in *New Histories for Old: Changing Perspectives on Canada's Native Past*, ed. Ted Binnema and Susan Neylan (Vancouver: UBC Press, 2007), 159–62.
103. "White Fisherman Are Best for B.C.," *Vancouver New Advertiser*, December 17, 1911, Henry Doyle Collection, Acc. 861, box 3, Book 1908–1911, University of Washington Special Collections; Lutz, *Makúk*, 239.
104. Lutz, *Makúk*, 186; Unknown to Annie, June 30, 1891, Traill Family Fonds, Box 3, Folder 16, Glenbow Archives.
105. B.C. Packers Association, "Documents Related to Japanese Fishermen," 1916, Chung Collection, File CC-TX-101-8, University of British Columbia Rare Books and Special Collections; Boxberger, "In and out of the Labor Force," 187; Doyle, "British Columbia Fish and Fisheries," 2.
106. Wadewitz, *The Nature of Borders*, 78, 125; Daniel L. Boxberger, "Ethnicity and Labor in the Puget Sound Fishing Industry, 1880–1935," *Ethnology* 33, no. 2 (April 1, 1994): 183.
107. "Indian Rising," *News Advertiser*, August 30, 1906, Henry Doyle Collection, Acc. 861, box 2, Scrapbook 1905–1908, University of Washington Special Collections; Canada, Department of Indian Affairs, *Annual Report of the Department of Indian Affairs For the Year Ended 31st December 1881*, 150; H. Moffat to Superintendent General of Indian Affairs, October 28, 1889, 150, DIA ARO, LAC; Harry Guillod to Superintendent General of Indian Affairs, September 7, 1886, 90, DIA ARO, LAC; Wadewitz, *The Nature of Borders*, 83, 85.
108. Wadewitz, *The Nature of Borders*, 81–87; Lutz, *Makúk*, 239–42.
109. McNeff Brothers to John W. Summers, July 20, 1925, RG 85, INS, Entry 9, Box 6585, 55466/182, NARA; Great Britain. Foreign Office, *Diplomatic and Consular Reports. Annual Series. United States, San Francisco*, vol. 906, 1891, 27; D. C. Govan to Commissioner of Indian Affairs, August 28, 1896, RG 75, Annual Reports Tulalip Agency, Box 1 1863–1908, Folder 1896, NARA Seattle; Lutz, *Makúk*, 190.

Chapter 7

1. Roderick C. Macleod, "Walsh, James Morrow," in *Dictionary of Canadian Biography*, vol. 13 (University of Toronto/Université Laval, 1994).
2. The document is ambiguous as to whether Walsh was referring to the Métis, the Sioux, or First Nations in general. James Morrow Walsh, "Miscellaneous," n.d., 2, Morton Manuscripts Collection, MSS-C550-1-22-4 (Box 35) [online], University of Saskatchewan Library Special Collections.
3. Richard White, *The Republic For Which It Stands: The United States During Reconstruction and the Gilded Age, 1865–1896* (Oxford: Oxford University Press, 2017), 59.
4. White, *The Republic For Which It Stands*, 357–59.
5. United States, Treasury Department, *Annual Report of the Secretary of the Treasury on the State of the Finances, 1885 Volume I: Finance* (Washington, DC: Government Printing Office, 1885), 518, 693.
6. United States, Treasury Department, *Annual Report Treasury 1885, Vol. 1*, vi; White, *The Republic For Which It Stands*, 631.
7. United States, Treasury Department, *Annual Report Treasury 1885, Vol. 1*, 518, 693.
8. United States, Treasury Department, *Annual Report Treasury 1885, Vol. 1*, vi, 516–17. *Annual Report of the Secretary of the Treasury on the State of the Finances for the Year 1886 Volume I: Finance* (Washington, DC: Government Printing Office, 1886), xcvii–xcviii, cviii; United States, Department of the Treasury, *Annual Report Treasury 1885, Vol. 1*, vi, 517.
9. E. A. Heaman, *Tax, Order, and Good Government: A New Political History of Canada, 1867–1917* (Montreal: McGill-Queen's University Press, 2017), 24.

10. Herbert Legg, *Customs Services in Western Canada, 1867–1925: A History* (Creston, BC: Creston Review Limited, 1962), 14.
11. Dave McIntosh, *The Collectors: A History of Canadian Customs and Excise* (Toronto: NC Press, 1984), 7.
12. Heaman, *Tax, Order, and Good*, 6, 356.
13. A. C. Phillips to J. C. B. Davis, November 15, 1869, Despatches from United States Consuls in Fort Erie, Ontario, 1865–1906, T-465, Volume 1, Reel 1, March 9, 1865–December 31, 1869, NARA.
14. A. C. Phillips to J. C. B. Davis, December 31, 1870, Despatches from United States Consuls in Fort Erie, Ontario, 1865–1906, T-465, Volume 2, Reel 2, January 11, 1870—December 22, 1882, NARA; Canada, Department of Agriculture, *Census of Canada: 1870–71*, vol. 1 (Ottawa: I. B. Taylor, 1878), 98.
15. United States, Treasury Department, *Annual Report Treasury 1885, Vol. 1*, 350–51.
16. Legg, *Customs Services in Western Canada, 1867–1925*, 14–15.
17. United States, Treasury Department, *Annual Report of the Secretary of the Treasury on the State of the Finances, 1870* (Washington, DC: Government Printing Office, 1870), 257–68.
18. Peter Andreas, *Smuggler Nation: How Illicit Trade Made America* (New York: Oxford University Press, 2013), 178.
19. United States, Treasury Department, *Annual Report Treasury 1870*, 257–68.
20. United States, Treasury Department, *Annual Report of the Secretary of the Treasury on the State of the Finances, 1890* (Washington, DC: Government Printing Office, 1890), 760–76.
21. Canada, *The Civil Service List of Canada 1889* (Ottawa: Brown Chamberlin, 1890), 41–78.
22. United States, Treasury Department, *Annual Report of the Secretary of the Treasury on the State of the Finances, 1885 Volume II: Collection of Duties* (Washington, DC: Government Printing Office, 1885), 240–41.
23. P. L. Prentis to Commissioner General of Immigration, August 21, 1925, RG 85, INS, Entry 9, Box 6585, 55466/182, NARA; H. Vassal to Superintendent General of Indian Affairs, November 28, 1882, 159, DIA ARO, LAC.
24. Eithne Luibhéid, *Entry Denied: Controlling Sexuality at the Border* (Minneapolis: University of Minnesota Press, 2002), 1–2.
25. United States, *Official Register of the United States Containing a List of Officers and Employees in the Civil, Military, and Naval Service on the First of July, 1895*, vol. 1 (Washington, DC: Government Printing Office, 1895), 149–54; United States, Treasury Department, *Annual Report Treasury 1890*, 760–76; United States, Immigration Service, *Annual Report of the Superintendent of Immigration to the Secretary of the Treasury, 1892* (Washington, DC: Government Printing Office, 1892), 10.
26. White, *The Republic For Which It Stands*, 398–400.
27. United States, Immigration Service, *Annual Report of the Commissioner-General of Immigration to the Secretary of the Treasury, 1897* (Washington, DC: Government Printing Office, 1897), 12; United States, Bureau of Immigration, *Annual Report of the Commissioner-General of Immigration, 1899* (Washington, DC: Government Printing Office, 1899), 32; United States, Bureau of Immigration, *Annual Report of the Commissioner-General of Immigration, 1900* (Washington, DC: Government Printing Office, 1900), 42; White, *The Republic For Which It Stands*, 399, 522; Timothy J. Meagher, *The Columbia Guide to Irish American History* (New York: Columbia University Press, 2005), 297.
28. United States, Department of the Treasury, *Annual Report of the Commissioner-General of Immigration to the Secretary of the Treasury, 1898* (Washington, DC: Government Printing Office, 1898), 46.
29. United States, Bureau of Immigration, *Annual Report of the Commissioner-General of Immigration, 1903* (Washington, DC: Government Printing Office, 1903), 3.
30. David R. Smith, "Structuring the Permeable Border: Channeling and Regulating Cross-Border Traffic in Labor, Capital, and Goods," in *Permeable Border: The Great Lakes Basin as Transnational Region 1650–1990*, ed. John J. Bukowczyk, Nora Faires, David R. Smith, and Randy William Widdis (Pittsburgh: University of Pittsburgh Press, 2005), 130.
31. United States, Department of the Treasury, *Annual Report Immigration 1898*, 37–38; United States, Immigration Service, *Annual Report of the Commissioner-General of Immigration*

to the Secretary of the Treasury, 1896 (Washington, DC: Government Printing Office, 1896), 13–14.

32. Deirdre M. Moloney, *National Insecurities: Immigrants and U.S. Deportation Policy Since 1882* (Chapel Hill: University of North Carolina Press, 2012), 13; Katherine Unterman, *Uncle Sam's Policemen: The Pursuit of Fugitives Across Borders* (Cambridge, MA: Harvard University Press, 2015), 178.
33. United States, Bureau of Immigration and Naturalization, *Annual Report of the Commissioner-General of Immigration, 1910* (Washington, DC: Government Printing Office, 1910), 148–49.
34. Joseph Doutre, *Constitution of Canada: The British North America Act, 1867* (Montreal: John Lovell & Son, 1880), 117, 330; Patrick A. Dunae, "Promoting the Dominion: Records and the Canadian Immigration Campaign, 1872–1915," *Archivaria* 19 (1985/1984): 75.
35. Canada, *The Civil Service List of Canada 1896* (Ottawa: S. E. Dawson, 1896), 22–25; Canada, *The Civil Service List of Canada 1905* (Ottawa: S. E. Dawson, 1905), 16–19, 30; Canada, *The Civil Service List of Canada 1915* (Ottawa: J. de L. Taché, 1915), 46–53; United States, *Official Register of the United States Containing a List of Officers and Employees in the Civil, Military, and Naval Service on the First of July, 1895*, 1:149–54.
36. Canada, *The Civil Service List of Canada 1915*, 46–53.
37. Canada, *The Civil Service List of Canada 1915*, 46–53.
38. Sheila McManus, *The Line Which Separates: Race, Gender, and the Making of the Alberta-Montana Borderlands* (Lincoln: University of Nebraska Press, 2005), 108, 120; Dunae, "Promoting the Dominion," 76–77, 81; Canada, *The Civil Service List of Canada 1910* (Ottawa: C. H. Parmalee, 1910), 35–40.
39. Barbara Roberts, *Whence They Came: Deportation from Canada 1900–1935* (Ottawa: University of Ottawa Press, 1988), 195, 199–200; Unterman, *Uncle Sam's Policemen*, 178.
40. Roberts, *Whence They Came*, 72, 115–16, 122, 129.
41. Luibhéid, *Entry Denied*, 9.
42. Roberts, *Whence They Came*, 118–19.
43. Roberts, *Whence They Came*, 182.
44. Roberts, *Whence They Came*, 184.
45. Roberts, *Whence They Came*, 192.
46. Nayan Shah, *Stranger Intimacy: Contesting Race, Sexuality, and the Law in the North American West* (Berkeley: University of California Press, 2011), 208, 228–29; Luibhéid, *Entry Denied*, 11.
47. Canada, "The Laws and Regulations of Canada Respecting Immigration of Immigrants May 16, 1910," 1910, 24, RG 85, INS, Entry 9, Box 135, file 51648/1, NARA; Roberts, *Whence They Came*, 12.
48. Moloney, *National Insecurities*, 13–14.
49. Moloney, *National Insecurities*, 10.
50. United States, Immigration Service, *Annual Report of the Superintendent of Immigration to the Secretary of the Treasury, 1894* (Washington, DC: Government Printing Office, 1894), 17.
51. United States, Immigration Service, 17–18; Marian L. Smith, "The Immigration and Naturalization Service (INS) at the U.S.–Canadian Border, 1893–1993: An Overview of Issues and Topics," *Michigan Historical Review* 26, no. 2 (2000): 128–31.
52. United States, Bureau of Immigration and Naturalization, *Annual Report of the Commissioner-General of Immigration to the Secretary of Commerce and Labor, 1912* (Washington, DC: Government Printing Office, 1912), 37–38.
53. United States, Bureau of Immigration and Naturalization, *Annual Report of the Commissioner-General of Immigration to the Secretary of Commerce and Labor, 1911* (Washington, DC: Government Printing Office, 1911), 158.
54. Smith, "The Immigration and Naturalization Service," 130.
55. Rachel St. John, *Line in the Sand: A History of the Western U.S.–Mexico Border* (Princeton, NJ: Princeton University Press, 2011), 104, 106.
56. St. John, *Line in the Sand*, 109.
57. Erika Lee, *At America's Gates: Chinese Immigration during the Exclusion Era, 1882–1943* (Chapel Hill: University of North Carolina Press, 2003), 161–62, 171; Erika Lee, "Enforcing

the Borders: Chinese Exclusion along the U.S. Borders with Canada and Mexico, 1882–1924," *Journal of American History* 89, no. 1 (June 1, 2002): 59.
58. White, *The Republic For Which It Stands*, 115, 632.
59. United States, Treasury Department, *Report of the Secretary of the Treasury on the State of the Finances, 1860* (Washington, DC: Thomas H. Ford, 1860), 229.
60. United States, Treasury Department, 229.
61. "Case 30 Private Porter E. Laflan," December 4, 1905, P2239 U.S. Infantry 28th Regiment, Summary Court Records, 1906, Box 1, Folder Orders 1-2, 6-50 Jan-Feb1906, MHS.
62. "Case 30 Private Porter E. Laflan."
63. Sam Seer and Watceu, Qu'Appelle Agency #4, interview by D. G. Mandelbaum, trans. Andrew Gordon, July 10, 1934, 3–4, O CPRC, IH-DM.17, Transcript disc 135, University of Regina.
64. Digitized versions of the post/soldier records from the United States' Annual Report of the Secretary of War 1870–1896 are available at Benjamin Hoy, "Building Borders: Visual Representations of the Canada–United Border 1860–1915," 2019, www.buildingborders.com. In addition, the data has been permanently hosted by the University of Saskatchewan: https://harvest.usask.ca/handle/10388/12153 .
65. Hoy, "Building Borders."
66. Major-General George B. Davis, *A Treatise on the Military Law of the United States Together with the Practice and Procedure of Courts-Martial and Other Military Tribunals*, 3rd ed. (New York: John Wiley & Sons, 1915), 335.
67. Michel Hogue, "Disputing the Medicine Line: The Plains Crees and the Canadian–American Border, 1876–1885," *Montana: The Magazine of Western History* 52, no. 4 (Winter 2002): 8; Michel Hogue, "Crossing the Line: Race, Nationality, and the Deportation of the 'Canadian' Crees in the Canada–U.S. Borderlands 1890–1900," in *The Borderlands of the American and Canadian Wests: Essays on Regional History of the Forty-Ninth Parallel*, ed. Sterling Evans (Lincoln: University of Nebraska Press, 2006), 156, 161.
68. J. M. Walsh to J. T. MacLeod, July 25, 1879, RG 10, Indian Affairs, Black Series, Reel C-10114, Volume 3652, File 8589, pt 1, LAC; E. Dewdney to Superintendent General of Indian Affairs, December 17, 1885, 144, DIA ARO, LAC; Warren M. Elofson, *Cowboys, Gentlemen, and Cattle Thieves: Ranching on the Western Frontier* (Montreal: McGill-Queen's University Press, 2000), 102; Marian C. McKenna, "Above the Blue Line: Policing the Frontier in the Canadian and American West, 1870–1900," in *The Borderlands of the American and Canadian Wests: Essays on Regional History of the Forty-Ninth Parallel*, ed. Sterling Evans (Lincoln: University of Nebraska Press, 2006), 96–97.
69. Canada, Parliament, "Part II North-West Mounted Police Report Commissioner's Report 1880," in *Sessional Papers, 1880–1881*, vol. 3, 3rd session of the 4th Parliament (Ottawa: Maclean, Roger, & Co, 1881), 5; Canada, Parliament, *Sessional Papers, 1886*, Report of the Commissioner of the North-West Mounted Police Force 1885, Volume 6, 4th Session, 5th Parliament, No. 8, 1886, 13; Canada, Parliament, *Sessional Papers 1896*, Report of the Commissioner of the North-West Mounted Police 1895, No 15, volume 11, 6th session of the 7th Parliament (Ottawa: S. E. Dawson, 1896), 154; Canada, Parliament, *Sessional Papers, 1911*, Report of the Royal Canadian Mounted Police 1910, No 28, 1911, 204–207; Canada, Parliament, *Sessional Papers 1906–1907*, Report of the Royal Mounted Police 1906, Part II Strength and Distribution of RNWMP, Paper No 28, Vol. 11, 1907, 3–9.
70. Superintendent to J. F. Macleod, December 19, 1879, A113 Innes Collection, III. (a) 15. Mounted Police Barracks, Battleford, 1936–1942, PAS.
71. Canada, Parliament, *Sessional Papers 1896*, 78.
72. Barry M Gough, *Gunboat Frontier: British Maritime Authority and Northwest Coast Indians, 1846–90* (Vancouver: UBC Press, 1984), 12–15, 170.
73. Edwin Clark to R. B. Van Valkenburgh, "Chippewas of the Mississippi No 184," August 22, 1865, 444, OIA ARO, UWDC.
74. W. W. Miller to W. P. Dole, "Washington Superintendency No 66," September 15, 1861, 176, OIA ARO, UWDC.
75. Miller to Dole, "Washington Superintendency No 66," 176.

76. For digitized employment records (including occupations) see Hoy, "Building Borders: Visual Representations of the Canada–United Border 1860–1915." A permanent link to the database is also available http://hdl.handle.net/10388/12153.
77. For digitized employment records (including occupations) see Hoy. "Building Borders," A permanent link to the database is also available http://hdl.handle.net/10388/12153.
78. James Daschuk, *Clearing the Plains: Disease, Politics of Starvation, and the Loss of Aboriginal Life* (Regina: University of Regina Press, 2013), xxi.
79. Fred C. Morgan to Commissioner of Indian Affairs, August 21, 1913, Rocky Boy Collection, M7937, Glenbow Archives; Tyla Betke, "Cree (Nêhiyawak) Mobility, Diplomacy, and Resistance in the Canada–Us Borderlands, 1885—1917 (Forthcoming)" (MA, University of Saskatchewan, 2019).
80. A. E. Forget to Superintendent of Indian Affairs, November 20, 1897, 216, DIA ARO, LAC; Ed Stamper, Helen Windy Boy, and Ken Morsette Jr., eds., *The History of the Chippewa Cree of Rocky Boy's Indian Reservation* (Box Elder: Stone Child College, 2008), 11–12; Little Bear to Commissioner of Indian Affairs, April 24, 1914, Rocky Boy Collection, M7937, Glenbow Archives; Hogue, "Crossing the Line," 161–62.
81. Robert Goodvoice, Robert Goodvoice Interview #3, interview by Robert Goodvoice, 1977, 9, O CPRC, IH-104-5, Transcript Disc 10 (Originals held at PAS, R-A1336), University of Regina.
82. "35. Duck Lake Agency. Permits to Leave Reserve, 1889–1901, 1904–1905, 1932–1934," n.d., SE 19, Department of Indian Affairs, PAS.
83. Antoine Lonesinger, Antoine Lonesinger Interview #5, interview by Alphonse Littlepoplar, trans. Alphonse Littlepoplar, November 21, 1974, 9, O CPRC, IH-054, Transcript Disc 16, University of Regina; Goodvoice, Robert Goodvoice Interview #3, 9.
84. Cecile Many Guns and Annie Buffalo, Interview with Mrs. Cecile Many Guns (Grassy Water) and Mrs. Annie Buffalo (Bear Child), interview by Dila Provost and Albert Yellowhorn, trans. Dila Provost, 1973, O CPRC, IH-236, Transcript Disc 26, University of Regina.
85. C. T. Hauke to John T. Frater, June 19, 1911, RG 75, BIA, Leech Lake, Correspondence 1899–1921, Entry 1075, Box 6, Folder 1911, NARA Chicago.
86. W. S. Juner to U.S. Indian Agent, January 8, 1902, RG 75, BIA, Leech Lake, Correspondence 1899–1921, Entry 1075, Box 2, Folder 1902, NARA Chicago.
87. C. T. Hauke to John T. Frater, July 18, 1911, RG 75, BIA, Leech Lake, Correspondence 1899–1921, Entry 1075, Box 6, Folder 1911, NARA Chicago.
88. United States, Treasury Department, *Annual Report of the Secretary of the Treasury on the State of the Finances, 1888* (Washington, DC: Government Printing Office, 1888), xli; White, *The Republic For Which It Stands*, 357.
89. "When Whiskey Smugglers Invaded the Canadian Northwest. The Arrest and Escape of the Notorious E. Ornom," *Dillon Examiner*, November 12, 1924, 4–7, Southern Alberta Research Project, M4561, Box 1, Folder 36, Glenbow Archives.
90. Fred R. Hussey and P. Stues, October 26, 1891, 164, British Columbia Provincial Police Force, GR 0001, Outward Correspondence Reel B2568, Volume 4, August 11 1893–September 17 1894, BCA.
91. St. John, *Line in the Sand*, 62.
92. W. H. Cox, "Diary of a Mountie from 1880 to '85 [Transcribed by Innes]," 1885, 10, A113 Innes Papers, II. (b) Manuscripts, Diary of a Mountie, PAS; Bill Waiser, *A World We Have Lost: Saskatchewan Before 1905* (Markham, ON: Fifth House Limited, 2016), 596; "Two Men Desert," May 10, 1847, Isaac Cowie Fond, E 86/18, Scrap Book 1911–1912, AM.
93. Bradley Miller, *Borderline Crime: Fugitive Criminals and the Challenge of the Border, 1819–1914* (Toronto: University of Toronto Press, 2016), 46; Andrea Geiger, "Caught in the Gap: The Transit Privilege and North America's Ambiguous Borders," in *Bridging National Borders in North America*, ed. Benjamin H. Johnson and Andrew R. Graybill (Durham, NC: Duke University Press, 2010), 207; Andreas, *Smuggler Nation*, 186.
94. Levi W. Myers to Josiah Quincy, "No 262," December 27, 1893, Despatches from United States Consuls in Victoria, T130 Roll 11, Volume 11, NARA.

95. Benjamin Hoy, "Dispensing Irregular Justice: State Sponsored Abductions, Prisoner Surrenders, and Extralegal Renditions Along the Canadian–United States Border," *Law and History Review* 35, no. 2 (2017): 321–50.
96. Unterman, *Uncle Sam's Policemen*, 51; David Ricardo Williams, *Call in Pinkerton's: American Detectives at Work for Canada* (Toronto: Dundurn Press, 1998), 13, 31.
97. Unterman, *Uncle Sam's Policemen*, 55, 183.
98. Unterman, *Uncle Sam's Policemen*, 54.
99. Great Britain, *Further Correspondence Respecting the Termination of the Fishery Articles of the Treaty of Washington of the 8th May, 1871* (London: HMSO, 1888), 39–40; Williams, *Call in Pinkerton's: American Detectives at Work for Canada*, 121–22.
100. White, *The Republic For Which It Stands*, 468, 592.
101. United States, Bureau of Immigration, *Annual Report of the Commissioner General of Immigration* (Washington, DC: Government Printing Office, 1914), 306.
102. United States, Bureau of Immigration, *Annual Report of the Commissioner General of Immigration*, 21.

Chapter 8

1. United States, Treasury Department, *Annual Report of the Secretary of the Treasury on the State of the Finances, 1885 Volume I: Finance* (Washington, DC: Government Printing Office, 1885), xxxiv.
2. United States, Treasury Department, *Annual Report of the Secretary of the Treasury on the State of the Finances, 1875* (Washington, DC: Government Printing Office, 1875), xxxii.
3. United States, Treasury Department, *Annual Report of the Secretary of the Treasury on the State of the Finances, 1889* (Washington, DC: Government Printing Office, 1889), xxxvi–xxxvii.
4. Canada, Parliament, *Sessional Papers, 1889*, Report of the Commissioner of the North-West Mounted Police Force 1888, Paper No 17, Vol 13, 1889, 59, 156, 158; United States, Treasury Department, *Report of the Secretary of the Treasury on the State of the Finances, 1866* (Washington, DC: Government Printing Office, 1866), 85; Priscilla Murolo, "Wars of Civilization: The US Army Contemplates Wounded Knee, the Pullman Strike, and the Philippine Insurrection," *International Labor and Working-Class History* 80, no. 1 (2011): 78; A. L. Blake to A. W. Bash, September 8, 1884, RG 36, U.S. Customs Service, Puget Sound, Box 110, Letters Received from Subports and Inspectors, Osooyoos, Ft. Colville, Sehome, Seattle, 1882–1885, Folder 2, NARA Seattle; A. W. Bash to Charles J. Folger, July 24, 1884, RG 36, U.S. Customs Service, Puget Sound, Box 37 Letters sent to the Secretary of the Treasury 1881–1886, Book 2, NARA Seattle.
5. W. H. Cox, "Diary of a Mountie from 1880 to '85 [Transcribed by Innes]," 1885, 1–2, 8, A113 Innes Papers, II. (b) Manuscripts, Diary of a Mountie, PAS.
6. Richard White, *The Republic For Which It Stands: The United States During Reconstruction and the Gilded Age, 1865–1896* (Oxford: Oxford University Press, 2017), 116.
7. W. H. Cox, "Diary of a Mountie from 1880 to '85 [Transcribed by Innes]," 7.
8. W. H. Cox, "Diary of a Mountie from 1880 to '85 [Transcribed by Innes]," 8.
9. White, *The Republic For Which It Stands*, 116.
10. Charles E. Monteith to J. B. Moore, January 10, 1898, Despatches from United States Consuls in Chatham, Canada, 1879–1906 Collection, vol. 2 December 12, 1890—November 19, 1901, NARA.
11. United States, Treasury Department, *Annual Report of the Secretary of the Treasury on the State of the Finances, 1885 Volume II: Collection of Duties* (Washington, DC: Government Printing Office, 1885), 237; Murolo, "Wars of Civilization," 78–79; Kelly Lytle Hernández, *Migra!: A History of the U.S. Border Patrol* (Berkeley: University of California Press, 2010), 5.
12. United States, Treasury Department, *Annual Report Treasury 1885, Vol. 2*, 237.
13. United States, Bureau of Immigration and Naturalization, *Annual Report of the Commissioner-General of Immigration, 1907* (Washington, DC: Government Printing Office, 1907), 86.
14. United States, Bureau of Immigration, *Annual Report of the Commissioner-General of Immigration, 1903* (Washington, DC: Government Printing Office, 1903), 52.

15. United States, Bureau of Immigration and Naturalization, *Annual Report of the Commissioner-General of Immigration, 1908* (Washington, DC: Government Printing Office, 1908), 142.
16. United States, Bureau of Immigration and Naturalization, 142.
17. United States, Treasury Department, *Annual Report of the Secretary of the Treasury on the State of the Finances, 1874* (Washington, DC: Government Printing Office, 1874), 222.
18. W. P. Carlin to Commanding Officer Fort Seward, August 11, 1875, McLaughlin Papers, MF 970.1 M219As, Reel 31, Fort Totten, Letters Received 1870–1875, Perdue University.
19. Murolo, "Wars of Civilization: The US Army Contemplates Wounded Knee, the Pullman Strike, and the Philippine Insurrection," 79.
20. White, *The Republic For Which It Stands*, 115.
21. United States, Treasury Department, *Annual Report Treasury 1885, Vol. 2*, 142, 145, 156.
22. United States, Treasury Department, *Annual Report Treasury 1885, Vol. 2*, 168–70.
23. United States, Treasury Department, *Annual Report Treasury 1885, Vol. 2*, 165–66.
24. E. D. Dewdney to L. V. Vankoughnet, October 9, 1887, "Indians who Crossed the International Boundary were Returned to Canadian Soil by the United States Authorities," RG 10, Indian Affairs, Volume 3791, file 44, 833, LAC.
25. Peter Hourie to Indian Commissioner, October 30, 1887, "Indians who Crossed the International Boundary were Returned to Canadian Soil by the United States Authorities," RG 10, Indian Affairs, Volume 3791, file 44, 833, LAC; Lawrence Herchmen to North West Mounted Police Headquarters, October 24, 1887, "Indians who Crossed the International Boundary were Returned to Canadian Soil by the United States Authorities," RG 10, Indian Affairs, Volume 3791, file 44, 833, LAC.
26. Hourie to Indian Commissioner, October 30, 1887; Herchmen to Headquarters, October 24, 1887.
27. Herchmen to Headquarters, October 24, 1887; Hourie to Indian Commissioner, October 30, 1887; E. Dewdney to Superintendent General of Indian Affairs, December 28, 1887, "Indians who Crossed the International Boundary were Returned to Canadian Soil by the United States Authorities," RG 10, Indian Affairs, Volume 3791, file 44, 833, LAC.
28. United States, Bureau of Immigration, *Annual Report of the Commissioner General of Immigration* (Washington, DC: Government Printing Office, 1914), 296.
29. United States, Bureau of Immigration, *Annual Report Immigration 1903*, 45, 51.
30. L. F. Hewgill, "In the Days of Pioneering: Crossing the Plains in the Early 70's The Prairie Black with Buffalo," March 1, 1894, 6, MG1 B23/5, AM; Brian Hubner, "Horse Stealing and the Borderline: The NWMP and the Control of Indian Movement, 1874–1900," *Prairie Forum* 20, no. 2 (1995): 293; Martha E. Plassmann, "White Men Stole Horses from Indians," *Montana Newspaper Association*, n.d., 3–4, Southern Alberta Research Project, M4561, Box 1, Folder 65, Glenbow Archives; Alexander Morris to Secretary of State, December 21, 1876, Alexander Morris (Lieutenant-Governor's collection) MG 12 B2, Microfilm Reel M141, No 208, AM.
31. Bradley Miller, *Borderline Crime: Fugitive Criminals and the Challenge of the Border, 1819–1914* (Toronto: University of Toronto Press, 2016), 8.
32. "La Mack Goes Back: Cree Accused of Murder Left in Custody for Canada Last Night," *The Butte Inter Mountain*, January 14, 1902, 5, CAHAN, LOC.
33. Miller, *Borderline Crime*, 70; "Vengeance of the Law: Marion Brown Was Hanged at London, Ont., Wednesday," *The L'Anse Sentinel*, May 20, 1899, 1, CAHAN, LOC; "East Canadian News," *The Sandon Paystreak*, July 16, 1898, 3, BC Historical Newspapers, UBC Special Collections.
34. Miller, *Borderline Crime*, 69, 73.
35. United States, Treasury Department, *Annual Report Treasury 1875*, 672.
36. United States, Treasury Department, 673.
37. Edward Barnett, "Reminiscences of Edward Barnett," n.d., 1–10, Edward Barnett Fonds, M3876, Glenbow Archives; Fred Bagley, "Fred Bagley's Diary," 1884, June 6, 1874 to June 19th 1874, Fred Bagley fonds, M44, Glenbow Archives; Ralph A. Barnett, *A Biography of Ed Barnett Pioneer of the Canadian West* (Calgary: Alberta, 1980), 15–17; Hewgill, "In Days of Pioneering," 10.

38. G. M. Sproat to Superintendent General of Indian Affairs, "Indian Reserve Commission," July 16, 1877, RG 10, Indian Affairs, Black Series, Reel C-10114, Volume 3651, File 8540, LAC; Richard A. Preston, *The Defence of the Undefended Border: Planning for War in North America 1867–1939* (Montreal: McGill-Queen's University Press, 1977), 23–24, 102.
39. Rodolphe Boudreau, "Enclosure in No 14. A Report of the Committee of the Privy Council," July 6, 1909, 14, RG 25, F-4, Vol 1004, Hecate Strait, LAC.
40. Jno. W. Bubb to Commissioner of Indian Affairs, August 16, 1895, 313, OIA ARO, UWDC; Abraham E. Smith to Thomas W. Cridler, August 12, 1899, RG 59, Despatches from U.S. Consuls in Victoria, T130, Volume 13, Reel 14, NARA College Park; L. Edwin Dudley to David J. Hill, "Marking of Boundary Line on Puget Sound Between United States and Canada," May 10, 1900, RG 59, Despatches from U.S. Consuls in Vancouver, T114, Volume 3, Reel 3, NARA College Park.
41. Assistant Secretary to Collector of Customs, September 3, 1898, RG 36, U.S. Customs Service, Puget Sound, Letters Received from the Department of the Treasury, Box 22, Folder 2, NARA Seattle.
42. Assistant Secretary to Collector of Customs.
43. Miller, *Borderline Crime*, 27.
44. "Influence of Canneries Prevents B.C. Fishermen from Export of Sockeyes," *Vancouver Sun*, February 1913, Henry Doyle Collection, Acc. 861, box 3, Book 1912–1913, University of Washington Special Collections; Smith to Cridler, August 12, 1899.
45. Lissa K. Wadewitz, *The Nature of Borders: Salmon, Boundaries, and Bandits on the Salish Sea* (Seattle: University of Washington Press, 2012), 153.
46. Smith to Cridler, August 12, 1899.
47. Smith to Cridler.
48. "Influence of Canneries Prevents B.C. Fishermen from Export of Sockeyes"; Wadewitz, *The Nature of Borders*, 153–54; Abraham E. Smith to Thos. W. Cridler, January 21, 1899, RG 59, Despatches from U.S. Consuls in Victoria, T130, Volume 13, Reel 14, NARA College Park; Smith to Cridler, August 12, 1899.
49. Alfred Mishibinijima, Alfred (Albert) Mishibinijima Interview #2, interview by Tony Snowsill and Christine Welsh, trans. Ernest Debassigae, February 20, 1984, 4, O CPRC, IH-OM.04A, Transcript Disc 81, University of Regina.
50. Mishibinijima, Alfred (Albert) Mishibinijima Interview #2.
51. United States, Bureau of Immigration and Naturalization, *Annual Report of the Commissioner-General of Immigration, 1909* (Washington, DC: Government Printing Office, 1909), 192.
52. Chas J. Folger to A. W. Bash, August 23, 1882, 227, RG 36, U.S. Customs Service, Puget Sound, Box 37 Letters sent to the Secretary of the Treasury 1881–1886, Book 1, NARA Seattle.
53. United States, Bureau of Immigration, *Annual Report of the Commissioner-General of Immigration, 1901* (Washington, DC: Government Printing Office, 1901), 46–47; for racial passing along the Mexican border see Catherine Cocks, "The Welcoming Voice of the Southland: American Tourism across the U.S.–Mexico Border, 1880–1940," in *Bridging National Borders in North America*, ed. Benjamin H. Johnson and Andrew R. Graybill (Durham, NC: Duke University Press, 2010), 226.
54. George Swanaset, "George Swanaset: Narrative of a Personal Document," 1951, 1–2, 8, 10, 12, Melville Jacobs Collection, 1693-91-13-001 Box 112, V 206, Folder 10, University of Washington Special Collections.
55. John H. Sutherland to Honorable Commissioner of Indian Affairs, July 19, 1898, 176–77, RG 75, BIA, White Earth Agency, Letters Sent to the Comm. of Ind. Affairs 1885–1914, NAI 5239141, Entry 1248, Vol 10, NARA Chicago.
56. Robert M. Allen to Commissioner of Indian Affairs, August 1, 1895, 37, RG 75, BIA, White Earth Agency, Letters Sent to the Comm. of Ind. Affairs 1885–1914, NAI 5239141, Entry 1248, Vol 8, NARA Chicago.
57. Lydney Church, "Crime Report Re C. Marker, Frank Fester, and Ed Fester . . . Taking Possession of, Fraudulently Purchasing, and Appropriating Estray," June 22, 1908, R-986, Department of the Attorney General, General Files, I.6a, PAS; John Torpey, *The Invention of the Passport: Surveillance, Citizenship, and the State* (Cambridge: Cambridge University Press,

2000), 17; *Century Edition of The American Digest: A Complete Digest of All Reported American Cases from the Earliest Times to 1896*, vol. 2 (St. Paul: West Publishing Company, 1897), 430.
58. Torpey, *The Invention of the Passport*, 17; Craig Robertson, *The Passport in America: The History of a Document* (Oxford: Oxford University Press, 2010), 183.
59. Torpey, *The Invention of the Passport*, 5.
60. United States, Bureau of Immigration, *Annual Report of the Commissioner-General of Immigration, 1900* (Washington, DC: Government Printing Office, 1900), 4.
61. United States, Bureau of Immigration and Naturalization, *Annual Report Immigration 1909*, 135–36.
62. United States, Treasury Department, *Annual Report of the Secretary of the Treasury on the State of the Finances, 1890* (Washington, DC: Government Printing Office, 1890), 792.
63. United States, "Official Register of the United States Containing a List of the Officers and Employees in the Civil, Military, and Naval Service," Vol 1, 1895, 149–54; United States, Treasury Department, *Annual Report Treasury 1890*, 760–76.
64. United States, Bureau of Immigration, *Annual Report of the Commissioner-General of Immigration, 1902* (Washington, DC: Government Printing Office, 1903), 39–40.
65. United States, Bureau of Immigration, *Annual Report of the Commissioner-General of Immigration, 1902*, 39–41.
66. United States, Bureau of Immigration, *Annual Report of the Commissioner-General of Immigration, 1902*, 42.
67. United States, Treasury Department, *Annual Report of the Secretary of the Treasury on the State of the Finances, 1888* (Washington, DC: Government Printing Office, 1888), 854–55.
68. Sarah M. Griffith, "Border Crossings: Race, Class, and Smuggling in Pacific Coast Chinese Immigrant Society," *Western Historical Quarterly* 35, no. 4 (2004): 480, 485, 490; "For Smuggling Chinese," *The Portland Daily Press*, December 26, 1893, 1, CAHAN, LOC; *The Daily Morning Astorian*, May 29, 1895, 4.
69. United States, Treasury Department, *Annual Report of the Secretary of the Treasury on the State of the Finances, 1879* (Washington, DC: Government Printing Office, 1879), xxiii; United States, Treasury Department, *Annual Report Treasury 1875*, xxix–xxx; Miller, *Borderline Crime*, 33; "Seized at Prison Door," *Condon Globe*, August 24, 1906, 2, CAHAN, LOC; "Indicted Silk Importers," *The Savannah Morning News*, December 11, 1902, 5, CAHAN, LOC.
70. United States, Treasury Department, *Annual Report of the Secretary of the Treasury on the State of the Finances, 1886 Volume II: Collection of Duties* (Washington, DC: Government Printing Office, 1886), 8; United States, Treasury Department, *Annual Report Treasury 1888*, 853–54.
71. E. A. Heaman, *Tax, Order, and Good Government: A New Political History of Canada, 1867–1917* (Montreal: McGill-Queen's University Press, 2017), 172–73, 346; United States, Treasury Department, *Annual Report Treasury 1886, Vol. 2*, 8.
72. V. Smith to Secretary of Treasury, July 9, 1885, 49–51, RG 36, U.S. Customs Service, Duluth MN, Letters Sent, Entry 1707, Box 1, Mar 13, 1885 to Sept 1, 1887, NARA Chicago.
73. United States, Treasury Department, *Annual Report Treasury 1875*, 583; White, *The Republic For Which It Stands*, 357–58; United States, Treasury Department, *Annual Report of the Secretary of the Treasury on the State of the Finances, 1870* (Washington, DC: Government Printing Office, 1870), 260.
74. United States, Treasury Department, *Annual Report Treasury 1874*, 222.
75. United States, Treasury Department, *Annual Report Treasury 1874*, 222.
76. United States, Treasury Department, *Annual Report of the Secretary of the Treasury on the State of the Finances, 1878* (Washington, DC: Government Printing Office, 1878), 46; White, *The Republic For Which It Stands*, 357; Peter Andreas, *Smuggler Nation: How Illicit Trade Made America* (New York: Oxford University Press, 2013), 179.
77. United States, Treasury Department, *Annual Report of the Secretary of the Treasury on the State of the Finances, 1877* (Washington, DC: Government Printing Office, 1877), xxix.
78. United States, Treasury Department, *Annual Report of the Secretary of the Treasury on the State of the Finances, 1881* (Washington, DC: Government Printing Office, 1881), xxi; United States, Treasury Department, *Annual Report of the Secretary of the Treasury on the State of the Finances, 1880* (Washington, DC: Government Printing Office, 1880), xxxviii.
79. United States, Treasury Department, *Annual Report Treasury 1880*, xxxviii.

80. United States, Treasury Department, *Annual Report Treasury 1886, Vol. 2*, 590.
81. United States, Department of Treasury, *Customs Regulations of the United States Prescribed for the Instruction and Guidance of Officers of Customs* (Washington, DC: Government Printing Office, 1892), 210; Emil Olund to Secretary of the Treasury, November 29, 1895, RG 36, U.S. Customs Service, Duluth MN, Letters Sent (Series #2), Entry 1707, Box 3, Sept. 27, 1892—Jan, 25, 1896, NARA Chicago.
82. Olund to Secretary of the Treasury, November 29, 1895.
83. Emil Olund to G. H. Young, October 17, 1895, RG 36, U.S. Customs Service, Duluth MN, Letters Sent (Series #2), Entry 1707, Box 3, Sept. 27, 1892—Jan, 25, 1896, NARA Chicago.
84. Olund to Secretary of the Treasury, November 29, 1895.
85. Olund to Secretary of the Treasury.
86. C. H. Johnson to W. W. Bates, June 20, 1891, 393–97, RG 36, U.S. Customs Service, Duluth MN, Letters Sent, Entry 1707, Box 1, July 24, 1890 to Aug 8, 1891, NARA Chicago.
87. Johnson to Bates, 393–97.
88. United States, Bureau of Immigration and Naturalization, *Annual Report Immigration 1908*, 158; Erika Lee, *At America's Gates: Chinese Immigration during the Exclusion Era, 1882–1943* (Chapel Hill: University of North Carolina Press, 2003), 4–5.
89. United States, Bureau of Immigration, *Annual Report Immigration 1903*, 98; United States, Bureau of Immigration and Naturalization, *Annual Report Immigration 1907*, 109–10.
90. A. C. Philips to John Hay, January 20, 1880, Despatches from United States Consuls in Fort Erie, Ontario, 1865–1906, T-465, Volume 2, Reel 2, January 11, 1870—December 22, 1882, NARA.

Chapter 9

1. "Protected," *The Phoenix Pioneer*, March 7, 1903, BC Historical Newspapers [online], The University of British Columbia.
2. "Protected," 3.
3. L. Edwin Dudley to David J. Hill, "Amity between Americans & Canadians in This Vicinity," July 6, 1900, RG 59, Despatches from U.S. Consuls in Vancouver, T114, Volume 3, Reel 3, NARA College Park.
4. Brandon Dimmel, "'Shutting Down the Snake Ranch': Battling Booze at the BC Border, 1910–1914," in *Beyond the Border: Tensions across the Forty-Ninth Parallel in the Great Plains and Prairies*, ed. Kyle Conway and Timothy James Pasch (Montreal: McGill-Queen's University Press, 2013), 93.
5. "Business Portion of Fernie in Ashes," *The Salt Lake Herald*, April 30, 1904, 1, CAHAN, Library of Congress.
6. L. Edwin Dudley to Assistant Secretary of State, July 7, 1903, RG 59, Despatches from U.S. Consuls in Vancouver, T114, Volume 4, Reel 4, NARA College Park.
7. Dudley to Assistant Secretary of State.
8. L. Edwin Dudley to Francis B. Loomis, "Person Pulling down the Flag at Fernie," July 15, 1903, RG 59, Despatches from U.S. Consuls in Vancouver, T114, Volume 4, Reel 4, NARA College Park.
9. Dudley to Loomis.
10. Bruno Ramirez, *Crossing the 49th Parallel: Migration from Canada to the United States, 1900–1930* (Ithaca, NY: Cornell University Press, 2001), 44; Adam Shortt and Arthur G. Doughty, eds., *Canada and Its Provinces*, vol. VI (Toronto: Glasgow, Brook, & Company, 1914), 361.
11. Julie Cruikshank, *Do Glaciers Listen? Local Knowledge, Colonial Encounters, & Social Imagination* (Vancouver: UBC Press, 2005), 214.
12. Cruikshank, *Do Glaciers Listen?*, 222.
13. Cruikshank, *Do Glaciers Listen?*, 214.
14. Richard Wayne Parker, "The Alaska Boundary Question," *North American Review* 176, no. 559 (June 1903): 916; James White, "Boundary Disputes and Treaties," in *Canada and Its Provinces*, ed. Adam Shortt and A. G. Doughty, vol. IV (Toronto: Glasgow, Brook & Company, 1914), 930; C. B. Bourne and D. M. McRae, "Maritime Jurisdiction in the Dixon

Entrance: The Alaska Boundary Re-Examined," *Canadian Yearbook of International Law* 14 (1976): 175–76, 181, 185; Cruikshank, *Do Glaciers Listen?*, 223–27.

15. David Mills, *The Canadian View of the Alaskan Boundary Dispute as Stated by Hon. David Mills Minister of Justice In an Interview with the Correspondent of the Chicago Tribune on the 14th August, 1899* (Ottawa: Government Printing Bureau, 1899), 9; Richard A. Preston, *The Defence of the Undefended Border: Planning for War in North America 1867–1939* (Montreal: McGill-Queen's University Press, 1977), 150.
16. Parker, "The Alaska Boundary Question," 915.
17. Cruikshank, *Do Glaciers Listen?*, 226–27.
18. Cruikshank, *Do Glaciers Listen?*, 34, 223, 227–28, 234.
19. Cruikshank, *Do Glaciers Listen?*, 225.
20. Cruikshank, *Do Glaciers Listen?*, 31, 234.
21. O. H. Tittmann and W. F. King, "Enclosure in No 4: Fifth Joint Report of the Commissioners for the Demarcation of the Meridian of the 141st Degree of West Longitude," December 29, 1911, RG 25, F-4, Vol 1004, Correspondence Relating to Alaska Boundary 1904–1919, LAC.
22. Martin Kitchen, "The Empire, 1900–1939," in *A Companion to Early Twentieth Century Britain*, ed. Chris Wrigley (Malden, MA: Wiley-Blackwell, 2003), 193; John Herd Thompson and Stephen J. Randall, *Canada and the United States: Ambivalent Allies*, 4th ed. (Athens: University of Georgia Press, 2008), 72; Gordon T. Stewart, *The American Response to Canada Since 1776* (East Lansing: Michigan State University Press, 1992), 4.
23. Stewart, *The American Response to Canada Since 1776*, 4; Timothy C. Winegard, *For King and Kanata: Canadian Indians and the First World War* (Winnipeg: University of Manitoba Press, 2012), 42; Daniel Drache, *Borders Matter: Homeland Security and the Search for North America* (Halifax: Fernwood, 2004), 25, 34–35.
24. Stewart, *The American Response to Canada Since 1776*, 128, 191.
25. Ramirez, *Crossing the 49th Parallel*, 49–50; S. Deborah Kang, "Crossing the Line: The INS and the Federal Regulation of the Mexican Border," in *Bridging National Borders in North America*, ed. Benjamin H. Johnson and Andrew R. Graybill (Durham, NC: Duke University Press, 2010), 170; Samuel Truett and Elliott Young, "Making Transnational History: Nations, Regions, and Borderlands," in *Continental Crossroads: Remapping U.S. Mexico Borderlands History* (Durham, NC: Duke University Press, 2004), 19.
26. "Banish 'Uncle Sam's' Silver," *The Ladysmith Daily Ledger*, March 6, 1906, Open Library University of British Columbia, BC Historical Newspapers.
27. "Banish 'Uncle Sam's' Silver," 1.
28. *Miss Canada [Puck Magazine, December 26, 1888 Cover]*, 1888, Lithograph, 1888, LC-USZ62-58804, LOC, http://hdl.loc.gov/loc.pnp/cph.3b06605.
29. Louis Dalrymple, *Patient Waiters Are No Losers*, January 13, 1897, Lithograph, January 13, 1897, LC-USZC4-4133, LOC, http://hdl.loc.gov/loc.pnp/cph.3g04133.
30. Newspapers had used the imagery of a ripening fruit to visualize annexation since at least 1869. In a cartoon published in the Diogenes, for example, an MP from Shefford Quebec reaches for a forbidden fruit labelled "independence." The fruit, while tempting, threatens to lead to American control. J. W. Bengough, *A Caricature History of Canadian Politics Events From the Union of 1841 As Illustrated by Cartoons from "Grip" and Various Other Sources*, vol. 1 (Toronto: The Grip Printing and Publishing Co., 1886), 107; Drache, *Borders Matter: Homeland Security and the Search for North America*, 38.
31. Peter Sullivan, David Bernhardt, and Brian Ballantyne, "The Canada–United States Boundary: The Next Century" (International Boundary Commission, 2009), 8–9.
32. "Special Agreement for the Submission to Arbitration of Pecuniary Claims Outstanding Between the United States and Great Britain. Signed August 18, 1910; Ratifications Exchanged April 26, 1912," in *Reports of International Arbitral Awards*, vol. 6 (United Nations, 2006), 9.
33. "Great Britain and Others (Great Britain) v. United States (Canadienne Case) May 1, 1914," in *Reports of International Arbitral Awards*, vol. 6 (United Nations, 2006), 29–30.
34. "Great Britain and Others (Great Britain) v. United States (Canadienne Case) May 1, 1914," 30.
35. "Special Agreement for the Submission to Arbitration of Pecuniary Claims Outstanding Between the United States and Great Britain. Signed August 18, 1910; Ratifications

Exchanged April 26, 1912," 11, 14; "Laughlin McLean (Great Britain) v. United States Favourite Case. December 9, 1921," in *Reports of International Arbitral Awards*, vol. 6 (United Nations, 2006), 82.

36. "Special Agreement for the Submission to Arbitration of Pecuniary Claims Outstanding Between the United States and Great Britain. Signed August 18, 1910; Ratifications Exchanged April 26, 1912," 11, 14.
37. E. J. Lemaire to The Deputy of His Excellency, "P.C. 695 At The Government House at Ottawa," March 21, 1931, 1200-0354-001, COS Archives; "P.C. 185," January 31, 1923, 1200-0354-001, COS Archives.
38. Nora Soney, Mrs. Nora Soney Interview, interview by Joanne Greenwood, 1974, 1–2, O CPRC, IH-OL.05, Transcript Disc 194, University of Regina.
39. Holly M. Karibo, *Sin City North: Sex, Drugs, and Citizenship in the Detroit–Windsor Borderland* (Chapel Hill: University of North Carolina Press, 2015), 23.
40. Charles S. Kelly, interview by Margaret Robertson, September 24, 1986, 19–20, Minnesota Environmental Issues Oral History Project: Interview with Charles S. Kelly, OH 58, AV1988.99.15, MHS; Craig Robertson, *The Passport in America: The History of a Document* (New York: Oxford University Press, 2010), 13.
41. United States, Bureau of Immigration, *Annual Report of the Commissioner General of Immigration* (Washington, DC: Government Printing Office, 1914), 199–200; United States, Bureau of Immigration and Naturalization, *Annual Report of the Commissioner-General of Immigration to the Secretary of Commerce and Labor, 1912* (Washington, DC: Government Printing Office, 1912), 35; Nayan Shah, *Stranger Intimacy: Contesting Race, Sexuality, and the Law in the North American West* (Berkeley: University of California Press, 2011), 125.
42. United States, Bureau of Immigration and Naturalization, *Annual Report Immigration 1912*, 35.
43. Minister of Justice to Governor General in Council, January 9, 1908, RG 13-A-2, Vol. 149, Folder 64-83 (1908), No. 83/08, LAC; W. J. White to Frank Oliver, January 8, 1908, RG 13-A-2, Vol. 149, Folder 64-83 (1908), No. 83/08, LAC.
44. Minister of Justice to Governor General in Council, January 9, 1908; White to Oliver, January 8, 1908; Robert Bacon to Department of State, February 26, 1908, RG 13-A-2, Vol. 149, Folder 64-83 (1908), No. 83/08, LAC.
45. Minister of Justice to Governor General in Council, January 9, 1908; Bacon to Department of State, February 26, 1908; White to Oliver, January 8, 1908.
46. A. E. Dyment to F. Oliver, December 23, 1907, RG 13-A-2, Vol. 149, Folder 64-83 (1908), No. 83/08, LAC.
47. United States, Bureau of Immigration and Naturalization, *Annual Report of the Commissioner-General of Immigration, 1907* (Washington, DC: Government Printing Office, 1907), 64; Andrea Geiger, "Caught in the Gap: The Transit Privilege and North America's Ambiguous Borders," in *Bridging National Borders in North America*, ed. Benjamin H. Johnson and Andrew R. Graybill (Durham, NC: Duke University Press, 2010), 203; Barbara Roberts, *Whence They Came: Deportation from Canada 1900–1935* (Manitoba: University of Ottawa Press, 1988), 118.
48. United States, Bureau of Immigration and Naturalization, *Annual Report Immigration 1912*, 34–35; Eithne Luibhéid, *Entry Denied: Controlling Sexuality at the Border* (Minneapolis: University of Minnesota Press, 2002), 15.
49. Shah, *Stranger Intimacy*, 39–40, 76, 229–30.
50. Charles I. Bevans, ed., *Treaties and Other International Agreements of the United States of America, 1776–1949*, vol. 12 (Washington, DC: Government Printing Office, 1974), 393, 483.
51. Shah, *Stranger Intimacy*, 251.
52. Kathleen S. Sullivan, "Marriage and Federal Police Power," *Studies in American Political Development* 20, no. 1 (2006): 50–51.
53. United States, "An Act to Limit the Immigration of Aliens into the United States, and for Other Purposes [National Origins Act]," May 26, 1924, 159, 68th Congress, Session 1, Ch. 190, H.R. 7995 Public No 139; Kelly Lytle Hernández, *Migra!: A History of the U.S. Border Patrol* (Berkeley: University of California Press, 2010), 26, 28; Ramirez, *Crossing the 49th*

Parallel, 56; Deirdre M. Moloney, *National Insecurities: Immigrants and U.S. Deportation Policy Since 1882* (Chapel Hill: University of North Carolina Press, 2012), 26.

54. United States, "National Origins Act," 162; Hernández, *Migra*, 2, 89; Katherine Unterman, *Uncle Sam's Policemen: The Pursuit of Fugitives Across Borders* (Cambridge, MA: Harvard University Press, 2015), 38; Mae M. Ngai, *Impossible Subjects: Illegal Aliens and the Making of Modern America* (Princeton, NJ: Princeton University Press, 2004), 60; Ramirez, *Crossing the 49th Parallel*, 56.
55. United States Congress, "An Act to Authorize the Secretary of the Interior to Issue Certificates of Citizenship to Indians," June 2, 1924, RG 11, General Records of the United States, Enrolled Acts and Resolutions of Congress, Public Law 68-175, 43 STAT 253, NARA.
56. n.a., "Bulletin File 45 [Bulletin 20 (1922)] Indian Citizenship," c 1922, Record 266, Box 14 Montana Governor's Office: Montana Indian Reservations Historical Jurisdiction Study, folder Crow Reservation 1916–1923, C-135, MHS.
57. Canadian officials had wavered as to what relationship Native Americans would have to the armed forces. They initially restricted their service but began to accept volunteers by 1915 as military demands mounted and casualties began to pour in. Clinton Rickard, *Fighting Tuscarora: The Autobiography of Chief Clinton Rickard*, ed. Barbara Graymont (Syracuse: Syracuse University Press, 1973), 14, 53; Winegard, *For King and Kanata*, 5–9, 49.
58. United States, "National Origins Act," 162; United States Congress, "An Act to Authorize the Secretary of the Interior to Issue Certificates of Citizenship to Indians."
59. Rickard, *Fighting Tuscarora*, 65.
60. Gerald F. Reid, "Illegal Alien? The Immigration Case of Mohawk Ironworker Paul K. Diabo," *Proceedings of the American Philosophical Society* 151, no. 1 (March 2007): 65–66; A. W. Ferrin to Commissioner of Indian Affairs, "Report of Agent in New York," September 15, 1892, 344, OIA ARO, UWDC; Yuka Mizutani, "Indigenous Peoples and Borderlands," in *Immigrants in American History: Arrival, Adaptation, and Integration*, ed. Elliott Robert Barkan, vol. 4 (Santa Barbara: ABC-CLIO, 2013), 1445.
61. Laurence M. Hauptman, *Seven Generations of Iroquois Leadership: The Six Nations Since 1800* (New York: Syracuse University Press, 2008), 127.
62. Also known as Levi General. Deskaheh is a chiefly title.
63. Hauptman, *Seven Generations of Iroquois Leadership: The Six Nations Since 1800*, 124, 127, 129.
64. Deskaheh, *Chief Deskaheh Tells Why He Is over Here Again* (London: Kealeys Ltd, 1923), 3.
65. Hauptman, *Seven Generations of Iroquois Leadership: The Six Nations Since 1800*, 130, 135.
66. Hauptman, 140–42; Bruce Elliott Johansen, *Native Americans Today: A Biographical Dictionary* (Santa Barbara: ABC-CLIO, 2010), 81–82; Susan M. Hill, *The Clay We Are Made Of: Haudenosaunee Land Tenure on the Grand River* (Winnipeg: University of Manitoba Press, 2017), 214–15, 236.
67. Hauptman, *Seven Generations of Iroquois Leadership: The Six Nations Since 1800*, 141–42; Hill, *The Clay We Are Made Of: Haudenosaunee Land Tenure on the Grand River*, 230.
68. Deskaheh, "The Last Speech of Des-Ka-Heh, March 10, 1925," in *[I Am a Cayuga] The Story of Des-Ka-Heh, Iroquois Statesman and Patriot*, ed. Carl Carmer (St. Regis Mohawk Reservation: Akwesane Mohawk Counselor Organization, n.d.).
69. Deskaheh, "The Last Speech of Des-Ka-Heh."
70. Deskaheh, "The Last Speech of Des-Ka-Heh."
71. Hauptman, *Seven Generations of Iroquois Leadership: The Six Nations Since 1800*, 142; Rickard, *Fighting Tuscarora*, 64–65; Joëlle Rostkowski, "The Redman's Appeal to Justice: Deskaheh and the League of Nations," in *Indians and Europe: An Interdisciplinary Collection of Essays*, ed. Christian F. Feest (Lincoln: University of Nebraska Press, 1989), 452.
72. Clinton Rickard to W. W. Husband, August 3, 1925, RG 85, INS, Entry 9, Box 6585, 55466/182, NARA.
73. Rickard, *Fighting Tuscarora*, 72, 76–77.
74. Rickard, *Fighting Tuscarora*, 72.
75. J. Warren Brayley to John J. Davis, January 26, 1926, RG 85, INS, Entry 9, Box 6585, 55466/182, NARA; Rickard, *Fighting Tuscarora*, 72–73, 79.
76. Rickard, *Fighting Tuscarora*, 81.

77. The exact timeline of their initial arrest differs widely by source, but may have begun as early as 1924. Court proceedings against them begin in March 1926 at which point they are taken into custody. Reid, "Illegal Alien," 61–64.
78. The exact date he first came to the United States is listed as either 1902 or 1912 depending on the immigration/court records. Reid, "Illegal Alien," 62–63.
79. Reid, "Illegal Alien," 61, 64–65, 70, 73.
80. "'Red's' Uncle Sam Can't Keep Out," *The New York Literary Digest*, May 7, 1927; Rickard, *Fighting Tuscarora*, 83.
81. Reid, "Illegal Alien," 64–65; United States ex rel. Diabo v. McCandless (District Court, E.D. Pennsylvania, 18 F.2d 282; 1927 U.S. Dist. LEXIS 1053 March 18, 1927).
82. Frederick Boughton to W. W. Husband, February 14, 1927, RG 85, INS, Entry 9, Box 6585, File 55466/182, NARA.
83. Robe Carl White to R. H. Codd, April 11, 1927, RG 85, INS, Entry 9, Box 6585, 55466/182, NARA.
84. White to Codd; Harry E. Hull to Frederick Boughton, February 25, 1927, RG 85, INS, Entry 9, Box 6585, 55466/182, NARA; P. L. Prentis to Commissioner General of Immigration, August 21, 1925, RG 85, INS, Entry 9, Box 6585, 55466/182, NARA.
85. William E. Lockner to James W. Wadsworth, "Re: Indian Legislation," February 7, 1927, RG 85, INS, Entry 9, Box 6585, 55466/182, NARA.
86. Lockner to Wadsworth.
87. "Indians Not Included under Regulations of Immigration Laws," c 1927, RG 85, INS, Entry 9, Box 6585, 55466/182, NARA; Reid, "Illegal Alien," 71–73.
88. J. Henry Scattergood to Harry E. Hull, September 22, 1930, RG 85, INS, Entry 9, Box 6586, 55466/182b, NARA; Reid, "Illegal Alien," 73.
89. John L. Zurbrick to Commissioner General of Immigration, November 26, 1929, RG 85, INS, Entry 9, Box 6586, 55466/182b, NARA; John D. Johnson, "Admission into the United States of American Indians Born in Canada," n.d., RG 85, INS, Entry 9, Box 6586, 55466/182b, NARA.
90. Scattergood to Hull, September 22, 1930.
91. Scattergood to Hull.
92. Albert Nelson Marquis, *Who's Who In America: A Biographical Dictionary of Notable Living Men and Women of the United States*, vol. 15: 1928–1929 (London: Stanley Paul, 1928), 1100.
93. Harry E. Hull to J. Henry Scattergood, September 22, 1930, RG 85, INS, Entry 9, Box 6586, 55466/182b, NARA.
94. Keith Richotte Jr., *Claiming Turtle Mountain's Constitution: The History, Legacy, and Future of a Tribal Nation's Founding Documents* (Chapel Hill: University of North Carolina Press, 2017), 104; Rickard, *Fighting Tuscarora*, 112–13, 119.
95. Peter Andreas, *Smuggler Nation: How Illicit Trade Made America* (New York: Oxford University Press, 2013), 227, 229–30.
96. Karibo, *Sin City North*, 28–29.
97. Karibo, *Sin City North*, 28.
98. Andreas, *Smuggler Nation*, 245–46.
99. Andreas, *Smuggler Nation*, 231, 237, 241, 246.
100. Andreas, *Smuggler Nation*, 232.
101. Andreas, *Smuggler Nation*, 245.
102. Stephen T. Moore, "Refugees from Volstead: Cross-Boundary Tourism in the Northwest during Prohibition," in *The Borderlands of the American and Canadian Wests: Essays on Regional History of the Forty-Ninth Parallel*, ed. Sterling Evans (Lincoln: University of Nebraska Press, 2006), 253–54; Andreas, *Smuggler Nation*, 246, 248; Karibo, *Sin City North*, 33.
103. Roberts, *Whence They Came*, 38.
104. Roberts, *Whence They Came*, 8, 170–71.
105. "Family in Tears as Jobless Man to Be Deported," *Saskatoon Star Phoenix*, June 12, 1939, Box 1069-763 to 1069-777, folder 1200-0177-001, COS Archives; District Supt Immigration to Andrew Leslie, "Telegram," June 12, 1939, Box 1069-763 to 1069-777, folder 1200-0177-001, COS Archives; "Wife Bids Farewell—Pratt Taken Away from Family Deported to States," *Saskatoon Star Phoenix*, July 12, 1939, Box 1069-763 to 1069-777, folder

1200-0177-001, COS Archives; "Family in Tears as Jobless Man to Be Deported"; "Can't Find Deportee M. B. Pratt."

106. "Family in Tears as Jobless Man to Be Deported"; "Can't Find Deportee M. B. Pratt."
107. "Family in Tears as Jobless Man to Be Deported."
108. "Family in Tears as Jobless Man to Be Deported"; "At Meeting of the Appeal Board on June 26th 1939," June 26, 1939, Box 1069-763 to 1069-777, folder 1200-0177-001, COS Archives.
109. "Family in Tears as Jobless Man to Be Deported."
110. "Police Aid Sought to Find Pratt: Warrant Has Been Issued for Arrest of 32-Year-Old U.S. Citizen For Deportation," *Saskatoon Star Phoenix*, June 14, 1939, Box 1069-763 to 1069-777, folder 1200-0177-001, COS Archives; "Can't Find Deportee M. B. Pratt."
111. District Supt Immigration to Andrew Leslie, "Telegram," June 12, 1939; "Police Aid Sought to Find Pratt: Warrant Has Been Issued for Arrest of 32-Year-Old U.S. Citizen For Deportation"; "Can't Find Deportee M. B. Pratt."
112. "Wife Bids Farewell—Pratt Taken Away from Family Deported to States."
113. "Can't Find Deportee M. B. Pratt."
114. "Can't Find Deportee M. B. Pratt."
115. "Wife Bids Farewell—Pratt Taken Away from Family Deported to States."
116. Myron to [Mrs. Pratt], December 1, 1939, Box 1069-763 to 1069-777, folder 1200-0177-001, COS Archives.
117. Ramirez, *Crossing the 49th Parallel*, 45–56; Thomas A. Klug, "The Immigration and Naturalization Service (INS) and the Making of a Border-Crossing Culture on the US–Canada Border, 1891–1941," *American Review of Canadian Studies* 40, no. 3 (September 2010): 408; Ngai, *Impossible Subjects*, 17–18.

Chapter 10

1. Mildred Redmond, Mildred Redmond Interview, interview by Evelyn Sit, June 21, 1983, 1 and 13, O CPRC, IH-OT.033, Transcript Disc 115, University of Regina.
2. Redmond, Mildred Redmond Interview, 2–3.
3. Redmond, Mildred Redmond Interview, 15.
4. Gratia Alta Countryman, "Notes [Trip Diary]," 1934, June 18, 22, 23, 30 and July 3, 7, 9, 10, 1934, P315, Gratia Alta Countryman Papers, Box 6a, vol. 2, MHS.
5. Countryman, June 19, 20, and 21, 1934.
6. Countryman, June 19, 1934.
7. Countryman, July 11, 1934.
8. Countryman, July 11, 1934.
9. Countryman, July 12, 1934.
10. Countryman, July 18, 1934.
11. Holly M. Karibo, *Sin City North: Sex, Drugs, and Citizenship in the Detroit-Windsor Borderland* (Chapel Hill: University of North Carolina Press, 2015), 19.
12. Carl Lewis, Carl Lewis Interview, interview by Jamie Lee, July 5, 1982, O CPRC, IH-OT.007, Transcript Disc 104, University of Regina.
13. Brandon Dimmel, "'Shutting Down the Snake Ranch': Battling Booze at the BC Border, 1910–1914," in *Beyond the Border: Tensions across the Forty-Ninth Parallel in the Great Plains and Prairies*, ed. Kyle Conway and Timothy James Pasch (Montreal: McGill-Queen's University Press, 2013), 96.
14. Alf Weisshaar, Alf Weisshaar Interview Tape B, interview by Sandra Bingaman, June 1, 1973, GP 251 "The Americans," R-A139(B), PAS; Clara Floding, Clara Floding Interview, interview by Sandra Bingaman, June 6, 1973, GP 251 "The Americans," R-A141(A), PAS; A. Cora Houghtaling, Mrs. A. Cora Houghtaling Interview, interview by Sandra Bingaman, June 10, 1973, GP 251 "The Americans," R-A144, PAS.
15. "Tulalip Indian Agency Marriage Registers 1907–1918," n.d., 9, RG 75, Box 1, Folder 1907–1914, NARA Seattle.
16. "Tulalip Indian Agency Marriage Registers 1907–1918," n.d., 30, 39, 47, 77, RG 75, Box 1, Folder 1914–1917, NARA Seattle; "A-66 Marriage Licenses + Returns," n.d., c. 64, RG 75 General Subject "A" Files: Fy 1910, 37–74, Colville Indian Agency, box 125a, NARA Seattle; "Tulalip Marriage Registers 1907–1914," 47, 77, 88, 98.

17. “Tulalip Marriage Registers 1907–1914,” page cut off c. 64.
18. Sidonia Elizabeth Black, interview by David Vassar Taylor, Malik Simba, and W. J. Musa Foster, July 9, 1975, 1–4, MBHP, OH 43.3, MHS, http://collections.mnhs.org/cms/display.php?irn=10445825.
19. Weisshaar, Alf Weisshaar Interview Tape B.
20. Alf Weisshaar, Alf Weisshaar Interview Tape A, interview by Sandra Bingaman, June 1, 1973, GP 251 “The Americans,” R-A139(A), PAS.
21. Evelyn Ballard, “Ballard and Branches” (Prairie Graphics, 1984), 153, A579 Ballard Family, PAS.
22. Mrs. Edward Kershaw, Mrs. Edward Kershaw Interview 237b, interview by Sandra Bingaman, July 10, 1973, GP 251 “The Americans,” R-A237(B), PAS.
23. Rose Nilson, Rose Nilson Interview 147b, interview by Sandra Bingaman, n.d., GP 251 “The Americans,” R-A147(B), PAS.
24. Nilson, Rose Nilson Interview 147b.
25. Edward Henry Dienst, Edward Henry Dienst Interview 237a, interview by Sandra Bingaman, July 9, 1973, GP 251 “The Americans,” R-A237(A), PAS.
26. Mary Jourdain, interview by Tracy Dagen, trans. Janice Jordain, December 7, 1996, 3–5, 8, and 10, The Vermilion Lake People: Vermilion Lake Bois Forte Oral History Project: Interview with Mary Jourdain, OH 108, 16099, MHS.
27. Phyllis Strong Boshey, interview by Tracy Dagen, December 1, 1996, 1 and 10, The Vermilion Lake People: Vermilion Lake Bois Forte Oral History Project: Interview with Phyllis Strong Boshey, OH 108 16099, MHS; Ernestine Hill, interview by Gerald [Jerre] Pete, n.d., 1–2, The Vermilion Lake People: Vermilion Lake Bois Forte Oral History Project: Interview with Ernestine Hill, OH 108, 16099, MHS; Boshey, interview, 1.
28. Jourdain, interview, 6–8.
29. Max Ireland, Max Ireland Interview #2, interview by Alex Cywink, July 27, 1983, 3, O CPRC, IH-OT.024A, Transcript Disc 118, University of Regina.
30. Kaniswiwitay (Two Voices), Crooked Lake #1, interview by D. G. Mandelbaum, trans. Leo & Norbert, June 21, 1934, 3, O CPRC, IH-DM.01, Transcript Disc 133, University of Regina.
31. Fine Day, Fine Day Interview #7, interview by D. G. Mandelbaum, August 17, 1934, 5, O CPRC, IH-DM.46, Transcript Disc 137, University of Regina.
32. Louis mentions that “I was a kid, about sixty-five years ago” during an interview in 1967 putting his birth somewhere around the 1890s. Joe Louie, Joe Louie Interview #1, interview by Imbert Orchard, 1967, 13, O CPRC, IH-BC.53, Transcript Disc 176, University of Regina.
33. Joe Louie, Joe Louie Interview #2, interview by Imbert Orchard, 1967, 8, O CPRC, IH-BC.54, Transcript Disc 176, University of Regina.
34. Louie, Joe Louie Interview #2, 8.
35. Louie, Joe Louie Interview #2, 8.
36. Fine Day, Fine Day Interview #19, interview by D. G. Mandelbaum, trans. Solomon, September 11, 1934, 2, O CPRC, IH-DM.62, Transcript Disc 139, University of Regina; Fine Day, Fine Day Interview #31, interview by D. G. Mandelbaum, trans. George Poplar, August 5, 1935, 2, O CPRC, IH-DM.87, Transcript 144, University of Regina.
37. Cecile Many Guns and Annie Buffalo, Interview with Mrs. Cecile Many Guns (Grassy Water) and Mrs. Annie Buffalo (Bear Child), interview by Dila Provost and Albert Yellowhorn, trans. Dila Provost, 1973, 4, O CPRC, IH-236, Transcript Disc 26, University of Regina.
38. George First Rider, Tipi Flag/Medicine Pipe, interview by J. C. Hellson, trans. Dave Melting Tallow, March 26, 1969, 2, O CPRC, IH-AA.078, Transcript Disc 55, University of Regina; George First Rider, The Medicine Pipe of the Blood Indians, interview by John C. Hellson, trans. Dave Melting Tallow, April 30, 1969, 4–5, O CPRC, IH-AA.085, Transcript Disc 56, University of Regina.
39. First Rider, Tipi Flag/Medicine Pipe, 2–3; First Rider, The Medicine Pipe of the Blood Indians, 5; George First Rider, Personal History, interview by J. C. Hellson, trans. Dave Melting Tallow, June 20, 1969, 1, O CPRC, IH-AA.094, Transcript Disc 57, University of Regina.
40. First Rider, Tipi Flag/Medicine Pipe, 3.
41. George Clutesi and Annie Hayes, George Clutesi and Annie Hayes Interview #1A, interview by Imbert Orchard, n.d., 3, O CPRC, IH-BC.31A, Transcript Disc 174, University of Regina.

42. William Scow, Chief William Scow Interview #1, interview by Imbert Orchard, c 1967, 2–3, O CPRC, IH-BC.60, Transcript Disc 178, University of Regina.
43. Scow, Chief William Scow Interview #1, 4.
44. Jim Windigo, interview by Gerald [Jerre] Pete, January 15, 1997, 1, 7, The Vermilion Lake People: Vermilion Lake Bois Forte Oral History Project, OH 108 16099, MHS.
45. Windigo, interview by Gerald [Jerre] Pete, 9–10.
46. Windigo, interview by Gerald [Jerre] Pete, 2.
47. Windigo, interview by Gerald [Jerre] Pete, 3.
48. Windigo, interview by Gerald [Jerre] Pete, 2.
49. Windigo, interview by Gerald [Jerre] Pete, 1, 3, 9.
50. Windigo, interview by Gerald [Jerre] Pete, 2.
51. Letitia B. Caldwell, interview by Anthony Godfrey, November 9, 1991, i, 1, 17–18, 27, Mille Lacs Indian Trading Post Oral History Project: Interview with Letitia B. Caldwell, OH 35, AV1993.198.2, MHS.
52. Caldwell, interview by Anthony Godfrey, 18.
53. Caldwell, interview by Anthony Godfrey, 1, 3.
54. Caldwell, interview by Anthony Godfrey, i, 1, 4, 28.
55. Caldwell, interview by Anthony Godfrey, 10–11, 56–57.
56. Caldwell, interview by Anthony Godfrey, i, 1, 10–11.
57. Caldwell, interview by Anthony Godfrey, 59.
58. Caldwell, interview by Anthony Godfrey, 59.
59. Caldwell, interview by Anthony Godfrey, 59–60.

Epilogue

1. Special thank you to Tyla Betke for discovering this material "Untitled," *San Francisco Argenaut*, Jan 25, Mss. 55, Joseph M. Dixon Papers, Box 109, Scrapbook, UM Mansfield; "To Fence Boundary Line," *The Fort Benton River Press*, December 23, 1903, 5, CAHAN, LOC.
2. "Too Much Press Agent," *Helena Independent*, n.d., Mss. 55, Joseph M. Dixon Papers, Box 109, Scrapbook, UM Mansfield.
3. "Anent Boundary Fence," *Big Timber Pioneer*, January 28, 1904, Mss. 55, Joseph M. Dixon Papers, Box 109, Scrapbook, UM Mansfield.
4. "Purpose of the Boundary Fence Intent of Dixon's Resolution," n.p., Jan 25, Mss. 55, Joseph M. Dixon Papers, Box 109, Scrapbook, UM Mansfield.
5. "Purpose of the Boundary Fence Intent of Dixon's Resolution."
6. "One of Dixon's Fences!" Dec 29, Mss. 55, Joseph M. Dixon Papers, Box 109, Scrapbook, UM Mansfield.
7. "Too Much Press Agent."
8. Donald J. Trump, "SECURE THE BORDER! BUILD A WALL!," August 5, 2014, Twitter, https://twitter.com/realDonaldTrump/status/496756082489171968?ref_src=twsrc%5Etfw%7Ctwcamp%5Etweetembed%7Ctwterm%5E496756082489171968&ref_url=https%3A%2F%2Fwww.nytimes.com%2F2018%2F01%2F18%2Fus%2Fpolitics%2Ftrump-border-wall-immigration.html.
9. Linda Qiu and Ron Nixon, "Trump's Evolving Words on the Wall," January 18, 2018, https://www.nytimes.com/2018/01/18/us/politics/trump-border-wall-immigration.html.
10. Donald J. Trump, "We Don't Have a Country—If We Don't Have Borders," March 14, 2016, Twitter, https://twitter.com/realdonaldtrump/status/709362309819404289?lang=en.
11. George M. Hatch to Jos Moore Dixon, January 6, 1903, Mss. 55, Joseph M. Dixon Papers, Box 5, File 7, UM Mansfield.
12. Bonnie Berkowitz, Shelly Tan, and Kevin Uhrmacher, "Beyond the Wall: Dogs, Blimps and Other Things Used to Secure the Border," *Washington Post*, February 8, 2019, https://www.washingtonpost.com/graphics/2019/national/what-is-border-security/?noredirect=on&utm_term=.f487e1921679.; Kelly Lytle Hernández, *Migra!: A History of the U.S. Border Patrol* (Berkeley: University of California Press, 2010), 105.
13. Keren Weitzberg, *We Do Not Have Borders: Greater Somalia and the Predicaments of Belonging in Kenya* (Athens: Ohio University Press, 2017), 3.

14. Cintio, *Walls*, 59.
15. Sinae Hyun, "Building a Human Border: The Thai Border Patrol Police School Project in the Post-Cold War Era," *Sojourn: Journal of Social Issues in Southeast Asia* 29, no. 2 (2014): 334.
16. N. S. Jamwal, "Border Management: Dilemma of Guarding the India-Bangladesh Border," *Strategic Analysis* 28, no. 1 (2004): 8–9.
17. Daniel Drache, *Borders Matter: Homeland Security and the Search for North America* (Halifax: Fernwood, 2004), 22; Marcello Di Cintio, *Walls: Travels Along the Barricades* (Fredericton: Goose Lane, 2012), 76.
18. Statistics Canada, "Table 24-10-0002-01 Number of Vehicles Travelling between Canada and the United States," May 29, 2019, https://www150.statcan.gc.ca/t1/tbl1/en/tv.action?pid=2410000201; Canada, The Canadian Trade Commissioner Service, "2018 Canada–Florida Economic Impact Study" (Canadian Trade Commissioner Service, December 10, 2018), https://www.tradecommissioner.gc.ca/united-states-of-america-etats-unis-amerique/market-facts-faits-sur-le-marche/0002354.aspx?lang=eng.
19. "Cigarette Ads Reappear in Magazines Read by Canadian Teens," *CBC News*, September 12, 2013, www.cbc.ca.
20. Shane Dingman and Jeff Gray, "What's a VPN, Are They Legal and Does Netflix Care Canadians Use Them?," *Toronto Globe and Mail*, January 8, 2015, http://www.theglobeandmail.com; Alex Hern, "Why Netflix Won't Block VPN Users—It Has Too Many of Them," *The U.K. Guardian*, January 9, 2015, http://www.theguardian.com; For other ways technology has pushed border control agents to rethink their mandates see Kris Constable, "Are You Obligated to Provide Your Password at the Border?," *Huffington Post*, March 10, 2015, Canada edition, http://www.huffingtonpost.ca; Dave McIntosh, *The Collectors: A History of Canadian Customs and Excise* (Toronto: NC Press, 1984), 185.
21. The Associated Press, "Is Fetal Tissue from B.C. Used to Power Oregon Homes?," *CBC News*, April 24, 2014, www.cbc.ca; Erin Ellis, "Oregon Incinerator Stops Accepting B.C. Medical Waste Because It Contains Aborted Fetuses," *Vancouver Sun*, April 24, 2014, http://www.vancouversun.com.
22. Daniel Drache, *Borders Matter: Homeland Security and the Search for North America* (Halifax: Fernwood, 2004), 4, 23; Zalfa Feghali, "Border Studies and Indigenous Peoples: Reconsidering Our Approach," in *Beyond the Border: Tensions across the Forty-Ninth Parallel in the Great Plains and Prairies*, ed. Kyle Conway and Timothy Pasch (Montreal: McGill-Queen's University Press, 2013), 159; Shannon Gleeson, "Unauthorized Immigration to the United States," in *Immigrants in American History: Arrival, Adaptation, and Integration*, ed. Elliott Robert Barkan, vol. 4 (Santa Barbara: ABC-CLIO, 2013), 1545; James M. Hundley, "We Are Coast Salish: Politics and Society across a Settler Colonial Border in the Post–9/11 World" (PhD diss., State University of New York–Binghamton, 2017), 43–44.
23. Mexico's border with the United States did allow for economic connections to form particularly after the North American Free Trade Agreement cut away tariffs between Canada, the United States, and Mexico. Gleeson, "Unauthorized Immigration to the United States," 1540; Mary E. Burfisher, Sherman Robinson, and Karen Thierfelder, "The Impact of NAFTA on the United States," *Journal of Economic Perspectives* 15, no. 1 (2001): 125–44; Sterling Evans, *The Borderlands of the American and Canadian Wests: Essays on Regional History of Forty-Ninth Parallel* (Lincoln: University of Nebraska Press, 2006), 347.
24. As it Happens, CBC Radio, "This Canadian-Born Artist Is Building a Wall of Cheese along the U.S.–Mexico Border," *CBC*, March 27, 2019, https://www.cbc.ca/radio/asithappens/as-it-happens-wednesday-edition-1.5073703/this-canadian-born-artist-is-building-a-wall-of-cheese-along-the-u-s-mexico-border-1.5073710; "Chocolate Jesus under Wraps for Now" (CBC, April 2, 2007), https://www.cbc.ca/news/entertainment/chocolate-jesus-under-wraps-for-now-1.667553.
25. Lucinda Froman, Lucinda Froman Interview, interview by Jocelyn Keeshig, July 19, 1982, O CPRC, IH-OT.003, Transcript Disc 104, University of Regina; Robert Goodvoice, Robert Goodvoice Interview #10, interview by Helga Reydon, October 10, 1979, O CPRC, IH-114, Transcript Disc 12 (Originals held at PAS, R-5761 to R-5763), University of Regina; Casper Solomon, Casper Solomon Interview #1, interview by Jocelyn Keeshig, August 11, 1982, O

CPRC, IH-OT.011, Transcript Disc 108, University of Regina; Bruce Sam, D1, interview by Sabina Trimble, May 29, 2013, D.1 29.05.2013, Stó:lō Library and Archive.
26. Solomon Wilson, Solomon Wilson Interview #1, interview by Imbert Orchard, 1969, 6, O CPRC, IH-BC.67, Transcript Disc 180, University of Regina.
27. Solomon Wilson, Solomon Wilson Interview #2, interview by Imbert Orchard, 1969, 6, O CPRC, IH-BC.68, Transcript Disc 182, University of Regina.
28. Raymond Owen, interview by Deborah Locke, April 20, 2011, 24, DW OHP, AV2011.45.23, MHS.
29. David Pashe, interview by Deborah Locke, January 19, 2012, 4, DW OHP, AV2011.45.44, MHS.
30. Clayton Maxwell Smoke, interview by Deborah Locke, January 18, 2012, 7, DW OHP, AV2011.45.47, MHS.
31. Clifford Canku, interview by Deborah Locke, June 10, 2011, 8, DW OHP, AV2011.45.6, MHS.
32. Canku, interview by Deborah Locke, 9–10.
33. Vincent Stogan, Stó:lō Nation Traditional Use Study, interview by Val Joe and Ernie Victor, September 16, 1996, 1–2, SV-i-1, Stó:lō Library and Archive.
34. Bruce Miller, "The 'Really Real' Border and the Divided Salish Community," *BC Studies* 112 (1996): 69; Bruce Granville Miller, "Conceptual and Practical Boundaries: West Coast Indians/First Nations on the Border of Contagion in the Post–9/11 Era," in *The Borderlands of the American and Canadian Wests: Essays on Regional History of the Forty-Ninth Parallel*, ed. Sterling Evans (Lincoln: University of Nebraska Press, 2006), 59.
35. Sheryl Lightfoot, "The International Indigenous Rights Discourse and Its Demands for Multilevel Citizenship," in *Multilevel Citizenship*, ed. Willem Maas (Philadelphia: University of Pennsylvania Press, 2013), 143; Hundley, "We Are Coast Salish," 125–26.
36. Joanna Smith, "Six Nations Passport More than Travel Document, Say Users," *The Star*, July 15, 2010, http://www.thestar.com; Feghali, "Border Studies and Indigenous Peoples: Reconsidering Our Approach," 156.
37. Gale Courey Toensing, "Canadian Border Agent Confiscated Haudenosaunee Passport, Called It 'Fantasy Document,'" *Indian Country Today Media Network*, August 17, 2011, http://indiancountrytodaymedianetwork.com.
38. Kelsey Johnson, "First Nations Close Borders over Coronavirus, Using 'Isolation as a Strength,'" *The Globe and Mail*, March 19, 2020, https://www.theglobeandmail.com/canada/article-first-nations-close-borders-over-coronavirus-using-isolation-as-a/; Jill Macyshon and Nicole Bogart, "Indigenous Communities Close Their Borders in Hopes of Preventing COVID-19 Spread," *CTVNews*, March 21, 2020, https://www.ctvnews.ca/health/coronavirus/indigenous-communities-close-their-borders-in-hopes-of-preventing-covid-19-spread-1.4863166.

Appendix: Terminology Guide

1. Bruce Trigger, ed., *Handbook of North American Indians*, vol. 15 (Washington, DC: Smithsonian Institution, 1978), 743.
2. Laura Peers, *The Ojibwa of Western Canada 1780 to 1870* (Winnipeg: University of Manitoba Press, 1994), ix, xv; Chippewa Cree Tribe, "Chippewa Cree Tribe: Rocky Boy's Indian Reservation," 2019, https://www.chippewacree-nsn.gov/.
3. Trigger, *Handbook of North American Indians*, 15:769.
4. Saugeen First Nation, "About—Saugeen First Nation," 2018, https://saugeenfirstnation.ca/about/.
5. Karl S. Hele, ed., *Lines Drawn upon the Water: First Nations and the Great Lakes Borders and Borderlands* (Wilfrid Laurier University Press, 2008), xiv.
6. Jill Doerfler, Niigaanwewidam James Sinclair, and Heidi Kiiwetinepinesiik Stark, *Centering Anishinaabeg Studies: Understanding the World Through Stories* (East Lansing: Michigan State University Press, 2013), xvi; Trigger, *Handbook of North American Indians*, 15:768.
7. DeMallie and DeMallie, *Handbook of North American Indians*, 13 part 1:572–73, 592; Legal Aid Saskatchewan and Community-engaged History Collaboratorium, "The Assiniboine" (Gladue Rights Research Database, 2019), http://drc.usask.ca/projects/gladue/assin.php.
8. DeMallie and DeMallie, *Handbook of North American Indians*, 13 part 1:592.

9. James M. Hundley, "We Are Coast Salish: Politics and Society across a Settler Colonial Border in the Post–9/11 World" (PhD diss., State University of New York–Binghamton, 2017), 13–15; Duane Champagne, *The Native North American: A Reference Work on Native North Americans in the United States and Canada* (Detroit: Gale Group, 2001), 309; Wayne Suttles, ed., *Handbook of North American Indians,* vol. 7 (Washington, DC: Smithsonian Institution, 1990), 35, 454–56, 474, 487–88, 501; Kim Baird, Laura Cassidy, Andrew Bak, Andrea Jacobs, and Remo Williams, "Declaration of Tsawwassen Identity & Nationhood," April 3, 2009, http://tsawwassenfirstnation.com/wp-content/uploads/2019/07/Declaration_of_Tsawwassen_Identity_and_Nationhood.pdf; Keith Thor Carlson, *The Power of Place, the Problem of Time: Aboriginal Identity and Historical Consciousness in the Cauldron of Colonialism* (Toronto: University of Toronto Press, 2010), 13; British Columbia Assembly of First Nations, "Soowahlie," 2019, https://www.bcafn.ca/first-nations-bc/lower-mainland-southwest/soowahlie; Ts'elxwéyeqw Tribe Management, "Our Territory," Ts'elxwéyeqw Tribe Management Ltd., n.d., https://www.ttml.ca/about-us/our-land/.
10. "Little Pine First Nation," n.d., http://www.littlepine.ca/; Raymond J. DeMallie and Raymond J. DeMallie, eds., *Handbook of North American Indians,* vol. 13 part 1 (Washington, DC: Smithsonian Institution, 2001), 638.
11. June Helm, ed., *Handbook of North American Indians,* vol. 6 (Washington, DC: Smithsonian Institution, 1981), 267.
12. Neal McLeod, *Cree Narrative Memory: From Treaties to Contemporary Times* (Saskatoon: Purich Publishing Limited, 2007), 105.
13. McLeod, *Cree Narrative Memory,* 105.
14. McLeod, *Cree Narrative Memory,* 105.
15. McLeod, *Cree Narrative Memory,* 105.
16. Susan M. Hill, *The Clay We Are Made Of: Haudenosaunee Land Tenure on the Grand River* (Winnipeg: University of Manitoba Press, 2017), 33–34, 111, 289–90.
17. Adam Gaudry, Kristin Burnett, and Geoff Read, "Respecting Métis Nationhood and Self-Determination in Matters of Métis Identity," in *Aboriginal History: A Reader,* 2nd ed. (New York: Oxford University Press, 2015), 152–56; Chris Andersen, "Moya `Tipimsook ('The People Who Aren't Their Own Bosses'): Racialization and the Misrecognition of 'Metis' in Upper Great Lakes Ethnohistory," *Ethnohistory* 58, no. 1 (2011): 39–44; Gerhard J. Ens and Joe Sawchuk, *From New Peoples to New Nations: Aspects of Metis History and Identity from Eighteenth to Twenty-First Centuries* (Toronto: University of Toronto Press, 2016), 9.
18. Jennifer Seltz, "Epidemics, Indians, and Border Marking in the Nineteenth Century Pacific Northwest," in *Bridging National Borders in North America: Transnational and Comparative Histories,* ed. Benjamin H. Johnson and Andrew R. Graybill (Durham, NC: Duke University Press, 2010), 100.
19. Suttles, *Handbook of North American Indians,* 7:282; Tsimshian First Nations (TFN) Treaty Society, "Who Are We," 2015, https://www.tfntreaty.ca/about-us.html.
20. Suttles, *Handbook of North American Indians,* 7:226.
21. Suttles, *Handbook of North American Indians,* 7:258.
22. Claire Thomson, "Lakotapteole: Wood Mountain Lakota Cultural Adaptation and Maintenance Through Ranching and Rodeo, 1880–1930" (MA thesis, University of Saskatchewan, 2014), 2, https://harvest.usask.ca/handle/10388/ETD-2014-09-1809; "About Oceti Ŝakowiŋ—The Seven Council Fires," n.d., Minnesota Historical Society, https://collections.mnhs.org/sevencouncilfires/10002460; Earl Bullhead, Gladys Hawk, Corrie Ann Campbell, Stephanie Charging Eagle, Danny Seaboy, Robert Two Crow, Lydia Whirlwind Solider, et al., *Oceti Sakowin Essential Understandings & Standards,* n.d., 27–28, https://doe.sd.gov/contentstandards/documents/18-OSEUs.pdf; David G. McCrady, *Living with Strangers. The Nineteenth-Century Sioux and the Canadian–American Borderlands* (Toronto: University of Toronto Press, 2006), xv–xvi; Sharon Malinowski and Anna Sheets, eds., *The Gale Encyclopedia of Native American Tribes,* vol. 3 (Detroit: Gale, 1998), 202; Craig Howe, Lydia Whirlwind Solider, and Lanniko L. Lee, eds., *He Sapa Woihanble: Black Hills Dream* (St. Paul: Living Justice Press, 2011), 3; The application of the term "Nakoda" to the Yankton and Yanktonai has a complex and contested history. It remains here based on how these communities continue to represent themselves. Raymond J. DeMallie, Bruce

Trigger, and Smithsonian Institution, eds., *Handbook of North American Indians*, vol. 13 part 2 (Washington, DC: Smithsonian Institution, 2001), 750.

23. Sheila McManus, *The Line Which Separates: Race, Gender, and the Making of the Alberta-Montana Borderlands* (Lincoln: University of Nebraska Press, 2005), xi; Betty Bastien and Jürgen W. Kremer, *Blackfoot Ways of Knowing: The Worldview of the Siksikaitsitapi* (Calgary: University of Calgary Press, 2004), 9, 212.
24. DeMallie and DeMallie, *Handbook of North American Indians*, 13 part 1:623.
25. DeMallie, Trigger, and Smithsonian Institution, *Handbook of North American Indians*, 13 part 2:677, 693.
26. Hoxie, *Encyclopedia of North American Indians*, n.d., 1.
27. Tseshaht First Nation, "History," 2020, https://tseshaht.com/history-culture/history/; Hupacasath First Nations, "History," 2020, https://hupacasath.ca/who-we-are/history/.
28. Apache Tribe of Oklahoma, "History," 2020, https://apachetribe.org/history/; DeMallie, Trigger, and Smithsonian Institution, *Handbook of North American Indians*, 13 part 2:938–39.
29. Hoxie, *Encyclopedia of North American Indians*, 32; DeMallie, Trigger, and Smithsonian Institution, *Handbook of North American Indians*, 13 part 2:840, 859; "Official Website of the Cheyenne and Arapaho Tribes—History," 2019, https://cheyenneandarapaho-nsn.gov/project/tribal-history/.
30. Shoshone-Bannock Tribe, "Fort Hall Indian Reservation," n.d., http://www2.sbtribes.com/ ; Warren L. D'Azevedo, ed., *Handbook of North American Indians*, vol. 11 (Washington, DC: Smithsonian Institution, 1986), 305–306.
31. "Official Website of the Cheyenne and Arapaho Tribes—History"; DeMallie, Trigger, and Smithsonian Institution, *Handbook of North American Indians*, 13 part 2:881.
32. Colville Tribes, "The Confederate Tribes of the Colville Reservation," 2019, https://www.colvilletribes.com/.
33. DeMallie, Trigger, and Smithsonian Institution, *Handbook of North American Indians*, 13 part 2:902; Comanche Nation, "Comanche Nation: Lords of the Plains," 2019, https://comanchenation.com/.
34. "Crow Tribe of Indians: Official Webpage of the Crow Tribe Executive Branch," 2017, http://www.crow-nsn.gov/; DeMallie, Trigger, and Smithsonian Institution, *Handbook of North American Indians*, 13 part 2:714–15.
35. Helm, *Handbook of North American Indians*, 6:161, 168.
36. Native Village of Eyak, "The Native Village of Eyak," n.d., https://nveyak.com/about/.
37. British Columbia Assembly of First Nations, "Fort Nelson," 2019, https://www.bcafn.ca/first-nations-bc/northeast/fort-nelson.
38. Harvey Markowitz, ed., *American Indians*, vol. II (Pasadena, CA: Salem Press, 1995), 406.
39. Kiowa Tribe, "Kiowa Tribe," 2018, https://kiowatribe.org/; DeMallie, Trigger, and Smithsonian Institution, *Handbook of North American Indians*, 13 part 2:922.
40. Deward E. Walker Jr., ed., *Handbook of North American Indians*, vol. 12 (Washington, DC: Smithsonian Institution, 1998), 327, 348.
41. Walker, *Handbook of North American Indians*, 12:236.
42. Suttles, *Handbook of North American Indians*, 7:359, 376.
43. Muscogee (Creek) Nation, "Muscogee (Creek) Nation History," 2016, https://www.mcn-nsn.gov/culturehistory/; Raymond D. Fogelson, ed., *Handbook of North American Indians*, vol. 14 (Washington, DC: Smithsonian Institution, 2004).
44. Nez Perce Tribe, "Nez Perce Tribe," 2018, https://www.nezperce.org/about/.
45. Nlaka'pamux Nation Tribal Council, "About Nlaka'pamux Nation Tribal Council," n.d., https://www.nntc.ca/pages/aboutus.aspx; Walker, *Handbook of North American Indians*, 12:201.
46. Nuu-Chah-Nulth Tribal Council, "Nuu-Chah-Nulth Tribal Council," 2019, https://nuuchahnulth.org/video-player/281.
47. Pawnee Nation, "Pawnee Nation of Oklahoma," 2019, https://www.pawneenation.org/page/home/pawnee-history/pawnee-nation-flag-and-seal; Pawnee Nation, "Official Publication of the Pawnee Nation—Chatiks Si Chatiks—Men of Men," September 2019, https://www.pawneenation.org/files/chaticks-si-chaticks/2019-Sept-Chaticks-Si-Chaticks-web.pdf.
48. Trigger, *Handbook of North American Indians*, 15:135.

49. Walker, *Handbook of North American Indians,* 12:297–98, 312; Confederated Salish & Kootenai Tribes, "Cultural Preservation," 2020, http://www.csktribes.org/history-and-culture/cultural-preservation.
50. Mandan, Hidatsa and Arikara Nation, "MHA Nation History," 2018, https://www.mhanation.com/history; DeMallie and DeMallie, *Handbook of North American Indians,* 13 part 1:388.
51. Walker, *Handbook of North American Indians,* 12:202.
52. Tsuut'ina Nation, "Tsuut'ina Nation Official Website," 2017, https://tsuutinanation.com/; Harvey Markowitz, ed., *American Indians,* vol. III (Pasadena, CA: Salem Press, 1995), 695.
53. Kathryn Magee Labelle, *Dispersed but Not Destroyed: A History of the Seventeenth-Century Wendat People* (Vancouver: UBC Press, 2013), 1, 10.
54. "Six Points Master Plan," Wyandot of Anderdon Nation, n.d., https://www.wyandotofanderdon.com/wp/?page_id=385.
55. Yakama Nation, "Yakama Nation History," 2010, http://www.yakamanation-nsn.gov/history.php; Walker, *Handbook of North American Indians,* 12:327, 348.

BIBLIOGRAPHY

Oral Histories

OURSPACE CANADIAN PLAINS RESEARCH CENTRE (O CPRC), UOFR

1981 Elders' Conference with Ernest Tootoosis; Ada Ladue and Beatrice Nightraveller; Alfred (Albert) Mishibinijima; Antoine Lonesinger; Augustine Yellow Sun, Joe Poor Eagle; Carl Lewis; Carlton Agency; Casper Solomon; Chief William Scow; Coming Day; Crooked Lake; Elder's Interviews: Support From Anthropological Sources; Ernest L. Debassigae; File Hills Agency; Fine Day; Five Elders of the Sarcee Reserve; Frank Paul; George Clutesi and Annie Hayes; Harry Tremayne; Isabel Smallboy; James Mason; James Takes A Gun Strong; Jim Bottle; Joe Louie; John Yellowhorn (Hereditary Chief); Lucinda Froman; Many Guns, Cecile (Grassy Water), and Annie (Bear Child) Buffalo; Max Ireland; J. B. Sparvey and kaniswiwetag; Mildred Redmond; Moose Mountain; Mrs. Buffalo; Mrs. Nora Soney; Mrs. Widow Crane; Personal History; Qu'Appelle Agency; Robert Goodvoice; Round Lake Indian School; Saddle Lake; Sally Provost; Samuel Buffalo; Solomon Wilson; Summary of Elders' Interview: "Land and Land Surrenders"; Summary of Elders' Interviews Treaty 6; Sundance; The Medicine Pipe of the Blood Indians; Tipi Flag/ Medicine Pipe; Useless Good Runner.

MINNESOTA HISTORICAL SOCIETY

Minnesota Black History Project (MBHP): Sidonia Elizabeth Black
The Vermilion Lake People: Phyllis Strong Boshey; Ernestine Hill; Mary Jourdain; Jim Windigo
U.S.-Dakota War of 1862 Oral History Project (DW OHP): Carolynn Schommer; Clayton Maxwell Smoke; Clifford Canku; Dallas Ross; David Pashe; Dean Blue, Ed LaBelle; Elsie Noel; Evelyn Eischen; Frederick Juni; LaVonne Swenson; Marina James; Melvin Littlecrow; Michael Childs; Pamela Halverson; Raymond Owen; Walter LaBatte
Mille Lacs Indian Trading Post Oral History Project: Letitia B Caldwell
Minnesota Environmental Issues Oral History Project: Charles S. Kelly

PROVINCIAL ARCHIVES OF SASKATCHEWAN

GP 251 "The Americans": Edward Henry Dienst; Clara Floding; Mrs. A. Cora Houghtaling; Mrs. Edward Kershaw; Rose Nilson; Alf Weisshaar
Stó:lō Library and Archive: Bruce Sam; Larry Commodore; Robert B Jimmie and Vincent Stogan (Traditional Use Study)

Archival Sources

ARCHIVE MANITOBA (AM)

B 200/b 39 Fort Simpson Letter Books 1875–1878
MG 12 B1 and MG 12 B2: M135, M136, M141 Alexander Morris (Lieutenant-Governor's collection)
MG1 B23/5
MG1 D8
MG6 A3 Arthur French Papers
MG9 A50 Hamilton Papers
RG 2/42/f/5

ARCHIVE OF ONTARIO (AO)

RG 22-1863, Essex County Sheriff's Correspondence and Jail Reports

BRITISH COLUMBIA ARCHIVE (BCA)

C/AA/10.6/1 542502 "Colony of Vancouver Island," 1863
A/C/20/Vi/2A James Douglas Fond
GR 0001 British Columbia Provincial Police Force
T 0429 Attorney General Records
GR-0429, British Columbia, Attorney General
GR 426 Sergeants Report Book Victoria

CITY OF SASKATOON ARCHIVES (COS ARCHIVES)

1200-0177-001
1200-0354-001

DETROIT PUBLIC LIBRARY

Burton Historical Collection, George Ironside Papers

GLENBOW ARCHIVES

M1241 Traill Family Fonds
M3636 Walsh Fonds
M3876 Edward Barnett Fonds
M43 to M44 Fred Bagley Fonds
M4561 Southern Alberta Research Project
M6608 Joseph J. Carscadden Fonds
M7937 Rocky Boy Collection
M9460 Wood Family Fonds

GUELPH CIVIC MUSEUM ARCHIVE

Mount Forest: The Confederate

LIBRARY AND ARCHIVES CANADA (LAC)

Canadian Illustrated News 1869–1883
Department of Indian Affairs Annual Reports Online (DIA ARO) 1864–1913

MG 16-FO 5 Foreign Office
MG 24 J14 William King Collection
Northeast Boundary Papers, Papers
RG 6 Secretary of State Correspondence
RG 8 C Series Rebellion, 1837–1838
RG 10 Department of Indian Affairs
RG 13 Department of Justice
RG 13-A-2 Numbered central registry files
RG 18 Royal Canadian Mounted Police
RG 25-F-4 Department of External Affairs
Sir John A. Macdonald Papers
The Upper Canada Law Journal and Local Courts' Gazette. Vol. 8. Toronto: W. C. Chewett, 1862.

LIBRARY OF CONGRESS (LOC)

Dalrymple, Louis. Patient Waiters Are No Losers. January 13, 1897. Lithograph. LC-USZC4-4133. LOC.

Deball, Z. He Wants the Revenue—Is the Game Worth the Bait? c1919. Lithograph. Cph 3c18171. LOC.

Frank Leslie's illustrated newspaper. The Only One Barred Out [Caricature of Chinese Man Seated Outside Golden Gate of Liberty]. 1882. Wood Engraving. Illus. in AP2.L52 1882 (Case Y) [P&P]. LOC.

John S. Pughe. How John May Dodge the Exclusion Act -Illus. in: Puck, v. 57, No. 1480 (1905 July 12), Centerfold. July 12, 1905. Ppmsca 25972. LOC.

Miss Canada [Puck Magazine, December 26, 1888 Cover]. 1888. Lithograph. LC-USZ62-58804. LOC.

Opper, Frederick Burr. The Custom-House Code of Morals under Our Beautiful Tariff System. October 14, 1885. Ppmsca 28135. LOC.

The Reason of the Indian Outbreak General Miles Declares That the Indians Are Starved into Rebellion. December 20, 1890. Cph 3g04101. LOC.

The Reconstruction Policy of Congress, as Illustrated in California. 1867. Lithograph. PC/US—1867.A000, no. 24 (A size) [P&P]. LOC.

Three Siwash Indian Hop Pickers Posed with Hops, Snoqualmie, Washington. c1906. LC-USZ62-67675. LOC.

MAINE HISTORICAL SOCIETY

Coll. S-6365 Journal of the Commission to Explore the North Eastern Boundary

MINNESOTA HISTORICAL SOCIETY (MHS)

M68 U.S. Army Judge Advocate General Papers, Re Trials of Medicine Bottle and Little Six
P1548 U.S. Interior Department Indian Division, Select Files Relating to Minnesota and Northern Plains
P2239 U.S. Infantry 28th Regiment, Summary Court Records
P2309 Lewis Stowe and Family Papers, 1819–1954
P315 Gratia Alta Countryman Papers

MONTANA HISTORICAL SOCIETY ARCHIVE

Record 266 Montana Governor's Office: Montana Indian Reservations

NATIONAL ARCHIVES AND RECORDS ADMINISTRATION D.C. (NARA DC)

Despatches from United States Consuls: Fort Erie (T-465) and Chatham (T-546)
Records Relating to the Northwest Boundary, 1853–1901 (T606)

RG 11, General Records of the United States Government, 1778–2006
RG 85 Immigration and Naturalization Service

NATIONAL ARCHIVES AND RECORDS ADMINISTRATION CHICAGO (NARA CHICAGO)

RG 36 U.S. Customs Service, Duluth MN
RG 75 Bureau of Indian Affairs (BIA): White Earth Agency, Leech Lake
RG 110 Provost Marshal General's Bureau, Minnesota

NATIONAL ARCHIVES AND RECORDS ADMINISTRATION COLLEGE PARK (NARA COLLEGE PARK)

RG 59 Despatches from U.S. Consuls: Vancouver, T114; Victoria, T130
RG 59 General Records of Department of State, Extradition Papers

NATIONAL ARCHIVES AND RECORDS ADMINISTRATION SEATTLE (NARA SEATTLE)

RG 21, U.S. District Courts Western District Washington (UDC WDW)
RG 36, U.S. Customs Service, Puget Sound
RG 75 Bureau of Indian Affairs: Tulalip Agency

PERDUE UNIVERSITY

MF 970.1 M219As McLaughlin Papers

PROVINCIAL ARCHIVES OF SASKATCHEWAN (PAS)

A113 Innes Papers
A579 Ballard Family
R-304-2 Department of the Attorney General, Regina Judicial Centre: Court Records
R-986 Department of the Attorney General, General Files
SE 19 Department of Indian Affairs, Duck Lake Agency
S-E1 Department of the Interior, Dominion Land Branch

STÓ:LŌ LIBRARY AND ARCHIVE

001246 Report of Henry Custer, Assistant of Reconnaissances Made in 1859 over the Routes in the Cascade Mountains

UNIVERSITY OF BRITISH COLUMBIA RARE BOOKS AND SPECIAL COLLECTIONS

Chung Collection

UNIVERSITY OF CALGARY LIBRARY

Despatches from U.S. Consuls in Hamilton, T470

UNIVERSITY OF MONTANA MANSFIELD

Mss. 55, Joseph M. Dixon Papers

UNIVERSITY OF SASKATCHEWAN LIBRARY SPECIAL COLLECTIONS

MSS-C550-1-22-4 Morton Manuscript Collection

UNIVERSITY OF WASHINGTON SPECIAL COLLECTIONS

Edmond S. Meany Papers
Hecht Collection
Henry Doyle Collection
Tulalip Reservation Washington, Annual Reports

UNIVERSITY OF WATERLOO

CA1 IA H5P37 Papers Relating to the Sioux

UNIVERSITY OF WISCONSIN DIGITAL COLLECTION (UWDC)

Office of Indian Affairs Annual Reports Online (OIA ARO) 1826–1895

Newspapers/Social Media

Many of the historic newspapers are available online through repositories such as the Library of Congress and British Columbia Historical Newspapers.

Active History
Alexandria Gazette
Alpena Weekly Argus
BBC
Butte Weekly Miner
CBC News
CTV News
Condon Globe
Daily Press
Global News
Globe and Mail
Huffington Post
Indian Country Today Media Network
Mineral Independent
National Post
National Public Radio
National Republican
News Advertiser
NY Times
Perthshire Advertiser
Press and Daily Dakotaian
Saskatoon Star Phoenix
Seattle Daily Intelligencer
SFGate
The Benton Weekly Record
The Butte Inter Mountain
The Cleveland Weekly Herald
The Daily Morning Astorian
The Fairfield Herald

The Fort Benton River Press
The L'Anse Sentinel
The Ladysmith Daily Ledger
The Maysville Evening Bulletin
The New York Literary Digest
The Northern Pacific Farmer
The Phoenix Pioneer
The Portland Daily Press
The Salt Lake Herald
The Sandon Paystreak
The Savannah Morning News
The Star
The Toronto Globe
The U.K. Guardian
The Vancouver Independent
The Washington Post
Toronto Globe and Mail
Twitter
Utica Morning Herald
Vancouver Sun
Vermont Phoenix
Washington National Republican
Winnipeg Free Press
Winnipeg Liberal
Woodstock Spirit of the Age

Government Publications

"Great Britain and Others (Great Britain) v. United States (Canadienne Case) May 1, 1914." In Reports of International Arbitral Awards, 6:29–32. United Nations, 2006.

"Laughlin McLean (Great Britain) v. United States Favourite Case. December 9, 1921." In Reports of International Arbitral Awards, 6:82–85. United Nations, 2006.

"Special Agreement for the Submission to Arbitration of Pecuniary Claims Outstanding Between the United States and Great Britain. Signed August 18, 1910; Ratifications Exchanged April 26, 1912." In Reports of International Arbitral Awards, 6:9–15. United Nations, 2006.

Canada. "An Act to Amend and Consolidate the Laws Respecting Indians Assented to 12th April, 1876." In Acts of the Parliament of the United Kingdom of Great Britain and Ireland. Ottawa: Brown Chamberlin, 1876.

Canada. "An Act to Amend and Continue the Act 32 and 33 Victoria, Chapter 3; and to Establish and Provide for the Government of the Province of Manitoba—Assented 12th May, 1870 [Manitoba Act]." In Statutes of Canada Vol 2. Ottawa: Brown Chamberlin, 1870.

Canada. Canadian Census 1901 and 1911

Canada. Report of the Commissioners Appointed to Consider the Defences of Canada, 1862. London: G. E. Eyre and W. Spottiswoode, 1862.

Canada. Sessional Papers 1889–1896.

Canada. The Civil Service List of Canada 1889.

Canada. Debates of the Senate of the Dominion of Canada. Vol. 2. Third Session—Fifth Parliament. Ottawa: A. S. Woodburn, 1885.

Canada. The Canadian Trade Commissioner Service. "2018 Canada–Florida Economic Impact Study." Canadian Trade Commissioner Service, December 10, 2018. https://www.tradecommissioner.gc.ca/united-states-of-america-etats-unis-amerique/market-facts-faits-sur-le-marche/0002354.aspx?lang=eng.

Carlisle, J. G. "Letter from the Secretary of the Treasury in Answer to a Resolution of the Senate of the 7th Instant, and Transmitting a Statement of the Amounts Appropriated and Expended in the Enforcement of the Chinese Exclusion Acts," September 12, 1893. 53 Cong., 1 Sess., Ex. Doc 13.

Cleveland, Grover. "Message from the President of the United States, Relative to the Act to Execute Certain Treaty Stipulations with China, October 1, 1888." In Papers Relating to the Foreign Relations of the United States, by United States, Vol. 1. Washington, DC: Government Printing Office, 1889.

Davis, J. C. Bancroft. Treaties and Conventions Concluded Between the United States of America and Other Powers Since July 4, 1776. Washington, DC: Government Printing Office, 1873.

Earl of Durham. "Report on the Affairs of British North America," 1839.

Featherstonhaugh, Capt. Narrative of the Operations of the British North American Boundary Commission, 1872–1876. Woolwich England: A. W. and J. P. Jackson, 1876.

Great Britain, and United States. "A Treaty of Peace and Amity between His Britannic Majesty and the United States of America [Treaty of Ghent]." R. G. Clarke, December 24, 1814.

Great Britain. British and Foreign State Papers 1883–1884. London: William Ridgway, 1891.

Great Britain. "British North America (Arms, &c.): Return Showing the Number of Arms, &c., Sent to British North America, from December 1861, and Ordered in Consequence of the Affair of the 'Trent.'" HMSO, 1863.

Great Britain. "Copy of a Despatch from Lieutenant-Governor Sir George Arthur to Lord Glenelg, 28 September 1838." In British North America: Copies or Extracts of Correspondence Relative to the Affairs of British North America. London: HMSO, 1839.

Great Britain. "Enclosure 1, in No. 87 Declaration by Robert Nelson." In British North America: Copies or Extracts of Correspondence Relative to the Affairs of British North America. London: HMSO, 1839.

Great Britain. "Inclosure 4 No. 72 Province of British Columbia—Report of a Committee of the Honourable the Executive Council, Approved by His Honour the Lieutenant-Governor on the 9th September, 1887 by JNO Robson." In Further Correspondence Respecting the Termination of the Fishery Articles of the Treaty of Washington of the 8th May, 1871: October to December 1887. London: HMSO, 1888.

Great Britain. "No. 2 Upper Canada Gazette Extraordinary By Authority—Toronto, Friday, November 16, 1838." In British North America: Copies or Extracts of Correspondence Relative to the Affairs of British North America. London: HMSO, 1839.

Great Britain. Correspondence Respecting the Operations of the Commission for Running and Tracing the Boundary Line Between Her Majesty's Possessions in North America and the United States Under the VIth Article of the Treaty Signed at Washington, August 9, 1842. London: T. R. Harrison, 1845.

Great Britain. First Statement on the Part of Great Britain, According to the Provisions of the Convention Concluded Between Great Britain and the United States, on the 29th September 1827 in Regulating the Reference to Arbitration of the Disputed Points of Boundary Under the Fifth Article of the Treaty of Ghent. J. Harrison and Son, 1829.

Great Britain. Diplomatic and Consular Reports. Annual Series. United States, San Francisco. Vol. 906, 1891.

Johnson, Andrew. "Detailed Statement of Disbursements on Account of Northwest Boundary Survey, From February 14, 1857 to December 31, 1868." In Message from the President of the United States Concerning the Northwest Boundary Commission, 40th Congress, 3d Session, Ex. Doc. No. 86., 1869.

Johnston, Andrew. "Message from the President of the United States Concerning the Northwest Boundary Commission, February 13, 1869," 1869. 40th Congress, 3d Session, Ex. Doc. No. 86.

Michigan, William Blair Lord, and David Wolfe Brown. The Debates and Proceedings of the Constitutional Convention of the State of Michigan: Convened at the City of Lansing, Wednesday, May 15th, 1867. Vol. II. John A. Kerr & Co., 1867.

Michigan. "Constitution of Michigan 1835," 1835. Legislature of Michigan. http://www.legislature.mi.gov/documents/historical/miconstitution1835.htm.

Michigan. The Revised Constitution of the State of Michigan. Lansing: R. W. Ingals, 1850.

Mills, David. *The Canadian View of the Alaskan Boundary Dispute as Stated by Hon. David Mills Minister of Justice In an Interview with the Correspondent of the Chicago Tribune on the 14th August, 1899*. Ottawa: Government Printing Bureau, 1899.

Narrative of the Survey by the British Commission of the Boundary Between the British Possessions in North America and the United States of America under the Treaty of Washington of 9th August, 1842. S.l.: s.n., 1846.

Reports of Cases Determined in the Practice Court and Chambers. Toronto: Roswell & Hutchison, 1872.

Schoolcraft, Henry R. "Report of H. R. Schoolcraft, Agent at Mackinac, and Acting Superintendent[,] Michigan." In Message from the President of the United States to the Two Houses of Congress at the Commencement of the Second Session of the Twenty-Sixth Congress. Washington, DC: Blair and Rives Printer, 1840.

Statistics Canada. "Table 24-10-0002-01 Number of Vehicles Travelling between Canada and the United States," May 29, 2019. https://www150.statcan.gc.ca/t1/tbl1/en/tv.action?pid=2410000201.

Sullivan, Peter, David Bernhardt, and Brian Ballantyne. "The Canada–United States Boundary: The Next Century." International Boundary Commission, 2009.

The Canada Year Book 1911. Second Series. Ottawa: C. H. Parmelee, 1912.

The Statutes of the Province of Upper Canada 1792–1831: Together with Such British Statutes, Ordinances of Quebec, and Proclamations, as Relate to the Said Province. Kingston: Francis M. Hill, 1831.

Timothy D. McNeff. Letter to Hon. Wm. B. West, November 1865. Message of the President of the United States, 40th Congress, 2nd Session, House of Representatives, Ex. Doc 157, Part 2, Trial and Conviction of American Citizens in Great Britain.

Twining, William Johnson, and Archibald Campbell. Reports upon the Survey of the Boundary between the Territory of the United States and the Possessions of Great Britain from the Lake of the Woods to the Summit of the Rocky Mountains. Washington, DC: Government Printing Office, 1878.

United Nations. United Nations Declaration on the Rights of Indigenous Peoples. United Nations, 2008. http://www.un.org/esa/socdev/unpfii/documents/DRIPS_en.pdf.

United States Congress. Congressional Record, V. 153, Pt. 1, January 4, 2007 to January 17, 2007. Washington, DC: Government Printing Office, 2007.

United States ex rel. Diabo v. McCandless (District Court, E.D. Pennsylvania, 18 F.2d 282; 1927 U.S. Dist. LEXIS 1053 March 18, 1927).

United States, and Great Britain. "Treaty of Amity, Commerce, and Navigation, between His Britannic Majesty, and the United States of America [Jay Treaty]," November 19, 1794.

United States, and Great Britain. "Convention between the United States of America and Great Britain. Concluded September 29, 1827. Ratified April 2, 1828. Proclaimed May 15, 1828." In Treaties and Conventions Concluded Between the United States of America and Other Powers Since July 4, 1776, edited by John Chandler Bancroft Davis. Washington, DC: Government Printing Office, 1871.

United States, and Great Britain. "Convention Respecting Fisheries, Boundary, and Restoration of Slaves, Signed October 20 1818." In Treaties and Conventions Concluded Between the United States of America and Other Powers Since July 4, 1776. Washington, DC: Government Printing Office, 1873.

United States, and Great Britain. "Definitive Treaty of Peace and Friendship between His Britannic Majesty and the United States of America [Treaty of Paris]," September 3, 1783.

United States, and Great Britain. "Extradition Convention Between the United States of America and Her Britannic Majesty, Supplementary to the Tenth Article of the Treaty, Concluded Between the Same High Contracting Parties on the Ninth Day of August, 1842. Convention

Signed at Washington July 12, 1889, Ratifications Exchanged March 11, 1890, Entered into Force April 4, 1890." In Treaties and Other International Agreements of the United States of America, 1776–1949, Vol. 12. Department of State Publication 8761. Washington, DC: Government Printing Office, 1974.

United States. "An Act Respecting Alien Enemies," July 6, 1798. The Avalon Project. Yale University Law School.

United States. "CIA and Nazi Warcrim. and Col. Chap. 1–10, Draft Working Paper_0003," n.d. Special Collection, Nazi War Crimes Disclosure Act, FOIA/ESDN (Crest) 519697e8993294098d50c2a3. CIA Freedom of Information Act Electronic Reading Room. https://www.cia.gov/library/readingroom/document/519697e8993294098d50c2a3.

United States. Annual Report of the Commissioner-General of Immigration 1895–1914

United States. Annual Report of the Secretary of the Treasury 1860–1890

United States. "An Act to Execute Certain Treaty Stipulations Relating to Chinese [Chinese Restriction Act]," May 6, 1882. U. S. Statutes at Large, Vol. XXII, p. 58 ff. 22 Stat. 58.

United States. "An Act to Limit the Immigration of Aliens into the United States, and for Other Purposes [National Origins Act]," May 26, 1924. 68th Congress, Session 1, Ch. 190, H.R. 7995 Public No 139.

United States. "An Act to Prohibit American Vessels from Proceeding to or Trading with the Enemies of the United States, and for Other Purposes," July 6, 1812. The Avalon Project. Yale University Law School.

United States. "An Act to Provide for the Allotment of Lands in Severalty to Indians on the Various Reservations, and to Extend the Protection of the Laws of the United States and the Territories over the Indians, and for Other Purposes [Dawes Act]." 49th Cong., 2nd sess., 1887.

United States. "Chap 141—An Act Supplementary to the Acts in Relation to Immigration [Page Act], 18 Stat L., 477, March 3, 1875." In Supplement to the Revised Statutes of the United States 1874–1891, edited by William A Richardson, 2nd ed. Vol. 1. Washington, DC: Government Printing Office, 1891.

United States. "Chap. 1222 An Act Making an Appropriation for the Enforcement of the Chinese Exclusion Act." In The Statutes at Large of the United States December 1887 to March 1889 and Recent Treaties, Postal Conventions, and Executive Documents, Vol. 25. Washington, DC: Government Printing Office, 1889.

United States. "Fugitive Slave Act 1850," September 18, 1850. The Avalon Project. Yale University Law School.

United States. "Naturalization; Signed in London May 13, 1870, Came into Force August 10, 1870." In Treaties and Other International Agreements of the United States of America 1776–1949, edited by Charles I. Bevans, Vol. 12. Washington, DC: Department of State, 1968.

United States. An Act to prohibit the coming of Chinese persons into the United States [Geary Act], 52nd Congress, Sess I, CHS 60 § (1892).

United States. Annual Report of the Commissioner General of Immigration. Washington, DC: Government Printing Office, 1914.

United States. Annual Report of the Superintendent of Immigration to the Secretary of the Treasury 1893–1894

United States. Compendium of the Eleventh Census: 1890. Part 1—Population. Washington, DC: Government Printing Office, 1892.

United States. Compendium of the Tenth Census of the United States. Vol. 1. Washington, DC: Government Printing Office, 1883.

United States. Customs Regulations of the United States Prescribed for the Instruction and Guidance of Officers of Customs. Washington, DC: Government Printing Office, 1892.

United States. Office of Indian Affairs. Annual Report of the Commissioner of Indian Affairs, 1860–1880.

United States. Official Register of the United States, Containing a List of Officers and Employees in the Civil, Military, and Naval Service. 1899–1895

United States. Register of the Department of State. Washington, DC: Government Printing Office, 1925.

United States. Report of the Secretary of War Being Part of the Message and Documents Communicated to the Two Houses of Congress at the Beginning of the First Session of the Forty-Third Congress. Vol. 1. Washington, DC: Government Printing Office, 1873.

United States. Statement on the Part of the United States, of the Case Referred in Pursuance of the Convention of 29th September, 1827 between the Said States and Great Britain to His Majesty, the King of the Netherlands for His Decision Thereon. Washington, DC: Office of the United States Telegraph, 1829.

United States. Testimony Taken by the Joint Selection Committee to Inquire into the Conditions of Affairs in the Late Insurrectionary States—South Carolina. Vol. III. Washington, DC: Government Printing Office, 1872.

United States. Thirteenth Census of the United States 1910: Bulletin Population: United States—Color or Race, Nativity, Parentage, and Sex. Washington, DC: Government Printing Office, 1913.

United States. President. Executive Orders Relating to Indian Reservations : From May 14, 1855 to July 1, 1912. Washington, DC: Government Printing Office, 1912.

West, Wm. B. Letter to Patrick S. Walsh, November 22, 1865. Message of the President of the United States, 40th Congress, 2nd Session, House of Representatives, Ex. Doc 157, Part 2, Trial and Conviction of American Citizens in Great Britain, 1868.

Tribal Websites

"About Oceti Ŝakowiŋ—The Seven Council Fires," n.d. Minnesota Historical Society. https://collections.mnhs.org/sevencouncilfires/10002460.

"Official Website of the Cheyenne and Arapaho Tribes—History," 2019. https://cheyenneandarapaho-nsn.gov/project/tribal-history/.

Apache Tribe of Oklahoma. "History," 2020. https://apachetribe.org/history/.

Baird, Kim, Laura Cassidy, Andrew Bak, Andrea Jacobs, and Remo Williams. "Declaration of Tsawwassen Identity & Nationhood," April 3, 2009. http://tsawwassenfirstnation.com/wp-content/uploads/2019/07/Declaration_of_Tsawwassen_Identity_and_Nationhood.pdf.

British Columbia Assembly of First Nations. "Fort Nelson," 2019. https://www.bcafn.ca/first-nations-bc/northeast/fort-nelson.

British Columbia Assembly of First Nations. "Soowahlie," 2019. https://www.bcafn.ca/first-nations-bc/lower-mainland-southwest/soowahlie.

Chippewa Cree Tribe. "Chippewa Cree Tribe: Rocky Boy's Indian Reservation," 2019. https://www.chippewacree-nsn.gov/.

Colville Tribes. "The Confederate Tribes of the Colville Reservation," 2019. https://www.colvilletribes.com/.

Comanche Nation. "Comanche Nation: Lords of the Plains," 2019. https://comanchenation.com/.

Confederated Salish & Kootenai Tribes. "Cultural Preservation," 2020. http://www.csktribes.org/history-and-culture/cultural-preservation.

Crow Tribe. "Crow Tribe of Indians: Official Webpage of the Crow Tribe Executive Branch," 2017. http://www.crow-nsn.gov/.

Earl Bullhead, Gladys Hawk, Corrie Ann Campbell, Stephanie Charging Eagle, Danny Seaboy, Robert Two Crow, Lydia Whirlwind Solider, et al. *Oceti Sakowin Essential Understandings & Standards*, n.d. https://doe.sd.gov/contentstandards/documents/18-OSEUs.pdf.

Hupacasath First Nations. "History," 2020. https://hupacasath.ca/who-we-are/history/.

Little Pine First Nation. "Little Pine First Nation," n.d. http://www.littlepine.ca/.

Kiowa Tribe. "Kiowa Tribe," 2018. https://kiowatribe.org/.

Mandan, Hidatsa, and Arikara Nation. "MHA Nation History," 2018. https://www.mhanation.com/history.

Muscogee (Creek) Nation. "Muscogee (Creek) Nation History," 2016. https://www.mcn-nsn.gov/culturehistory/.
Native Village of Eyak. "The Native Village of Eyak," n.d. https://nveyak.com/about/.
Nez Perce Tribe. "Nez Perce Tribe," 2018. https://www.nezperce.org/about/.
Nlaka'pamux Nation Tribal Council. "About Nlaka'pamux Nation Tribal Council," n.d. https://www.nntc.ca/pages/aboutus.aspx.
Nuu-Chah-Nulth Tribal Council. "Nuu-Chah-Nulth Tribal Council," 2019. https://nuuchahnulth.org/video-player/281.
Pawnee Nation. "Official Publication of the Pawnee Nation—Chatiks Si Chatiks—Men of Men," September 2019. https://www.pawneenation.org/files/chaticks-si-chaticks/2019-Sept-Chaticks-Si-Chaticks-web.pdf.
Pawnee Nation. "Pawnee Nation of Oklahoma," 2019. https://www.pawneenation.org/page/home/pawnee-history/pawnee-nation-flag-and-seal.
Saugeen First Nation. "About—Saugeen First Nation," 2018. https://saugeenfirstnation.ca/about/.
Shoshone-Bannock Tribe. "Fort Hall Indian Reservation," n.d. http://www2.sbtribes.com/.
Ts'elxwéyeqw Tribe Management. "Our Territory." Ts'elxwéyeqw Tribe Management Ltd., n.d. https://www.ttml.ca/about-us/our-land/.
Tseshaht First Nation. "History," 2020. https://tseshaht.com/history-culture/history/.
Tsimshian First Nations (TFN) Treaty Society. "Who Are We," 2015. https://www.tfntreaty.ca/about-us.html.
Tsuut'ina Nation. "Tsuut'ina Nation Official Website," 2017. https://tsuutinanation.com/.
Wyandot of Anderdon Nation. "Six Points Master Plan," n.d. https://www.wyandotofanderdon.com/wp/?page_id=385.
Yakama Nation. "Yakama Nation History," 2010. http://www.yakamanation-nsn.gov/history.php.

GIS Territorial Boundary Datasets

Manson, Steven, Jonathan Schroeder, David Van Riper, and Tracy Kugler. *IPUMS National Historical Geographic Information System: Version 15.0 [Dataset]*. Minneapolis, MN: IPUMS, 2020. http://doi.org/10.18128/D050.V15.0.
Nicholson, Norman L., Charles F. J. Whebell, Robert Galois, and Michael Stavely. *Territorial Evolution, 1670-2001: Version 1 [Dataset]*, 2020.

MA/PhD Dissertations

Betke, Tyla. "Cree (Nêhiyawak) Mobility, Diplomacy, and Resistance in the Canada–Us Borderlands, 1885—1917." MA thesis, University of Saskatchewan, 2019.
Francis, James M. "Business, Enterprise, and National Policy: The Role of T. C. Power & Brother and I. G. Baker & Company in the Political and Economic Development of the Southwest Canadian Prairies and Northern Montana, 1870–1893." MA thesis, University of British Columbia, 1978. Glenbow Archives (M4498).
Hundley, James M. "We Are Coast Salish: Politics and Society across a Settler Colonial Border in the Post—9/11 World." PhD diss., State University of New York–Binghamton, 2017.
Lew-Williams, Elizabeth Rose. "The Chinese Must Go: Immigration, Deportation and Violence in the 19th-Century Pacific Northwest." PhD diss., Stanford University, 2011.
Rensink, Brenden. "Native But Foreign: Indigenous Transnational Refugees and Immigrants in the U.S.–Canadian and U.S.–Mexican Borderlands 1880–Present." PhD diss., University of Nebraska, 2010.
Sossoyan, Mathieu. "The Kahnawake Iroquois and the Lower-Canadian Rebellions, 1837–1838." MA thesis, McGill University, 1999.
Thomson, Claire. "Lakotapteole: Wood Mountain Lakota Cultural Adaptation and Maintenance Through Ranching and Rodeo, 1880–1930." MA thesis, University of Saskatchewan, 2014.

Published Material

A. N. Marquis Company. *Who's Who In America with World Notables: Biographical Dictionary of Notable Living Men and Women*. Vol. 35 (1968–1969). Chicago: A. N. Marquis Company, 1968.

Abbott, Frederick H. *The Administration of Indian Affairs in Canada*. Washington, DC: Board of Indian Commissioners, 1915.

Adelman, Jeremy, and Stephen Aron. "From Borderlands to Borders: Empires, Nation-States, and the Peoples in between in North American History." *American Historical Review* 104, no. 3 (June 1, 1999): 814–41.

Andersen, Chris. "From Nation to Population: The Racialisation of 'Métis' in the Canadian Census." *Nations and Nationalism* 14, no. 2 (2008): 347–68.

Andersen, Chris. "Moya `Tipimsook ('The People Who Aren't Their Own Bosses'): Racialization and the Misrecognition of 'Metis' in Upper Great Lakes Ethnohistory." *Ethnohistory* 58, no. 1 (2011): 37–63.

Andreas, Peter. *Smuggler Nation: How Illicit Trade Made America*. New York: Oxford University Press, 2013.

Androff, David K., and Kyoko Y. Tavassoli. "Deaths in the Desert: The Human Rights Crisis on the U.S.–Mexico Border." *Social Work* 57, no. 2 (2012).

Anzaldúa, Gloria E. *Borderlands: La Frontiera the New Mestiza*. 2nd ed. San Francisco: Aunt Lute Books, 1999.

Assu, Harry. Assu of Cape Mudge: *Recollections of a Coastal Indian Chief*. Vancouver: UBC Press, 1989.

Barkan, Elliott Robert. *Immigrants in American History: Arrival, Adaptation, and Integration*. Vol. 4. Santa Barbara: ABC-CLIO, 2013.

Barman, Jean. *The West Beyond the West: A History of British Columbia*. Toronto: University of Toronto Press, 1991.

Barnett, Ralph A. *A Biography of Ed Barnett Pioneer of the Canadian West*. Calgary: Alberta, 1980.

Barron, F. Laurie. "The Indian Pass System in the Canadian West 1882–1885." *Prairie Forum* 13, no. 1 (1988): 25–42.

Barsh, Russel Lawrence. "Puget Sound Indian Demography, 1900–1920: Migration and Economic Integration." *Ethnohistory* 43, no. 1 (winter 1996): 65–97.

Basson, Lauren L. "Savage Half-Breed, French Canadian or White US Citizen? Louis Riel and US Perceptions of Nation and Civilisation." *National Identities* 7, no. 4 (December 2005): 369–88.

Bastien, Betty, and Jürgen W. Kremer. *Blackfoot Ways of Knowing: The Worldview of the Siksikaitsitapi*. Calgary: University of Calgary Press, 2004.

Bengough, J. W. *A Caricature History of Canadian Politics Events From the Union of 1841 As Illustrated by Cartoons from "Grip" and Various Other Sources*. Vol. 1. Toronto: The Grip Printing and Publishing Co., 1886.

Bengough, J. W. *A Caricature History of Canadian Politics Events from the Union of 1841 As Illustrated by Cartoons from "Grip" and Various Other Sources. Vol. 2*. Toronto: The Grip Printing and Publishing Co., 1886.

Benjamin, L. N., ed. *The St. Albans Raid; or, Investigation into the Charges against Lieut. Bennett H. Young and Command, for Their Acts at St. Albans, Vt., on the 19th October, 1864*. Montreal: John Lovell, 1865.

Berkman, Paul Arthur. *Baseline of Russian Arctic Laws*. New York: Springer, 2019.

Bessler, John D. *Legacy of Violence: Lynch Mobs and Executions in Minnesota*. Minneapolis: University of Minnesota Press, 2003.

Bevans, Charles I., ed. *Treaties and Other International Agreements of the United States of America, 1776–1949*. Vol. 12. Washington, DC: Government Printing Office, 1974.

Bingham, Tom. "The Alabama Claims Arbitration." *International and Comparative Law Quarterly* 54, no. 1 (2005): 1–25.

Binnema, Ted, and Susan Neylan. In *New Histories for Old: Changing Perspectives on Canada's Native Past*. Vancouver: UBC Press, 2007.

Boulton, Charles Arkoll. *Reminiscences of the North-West Rebellions: With a Record of the Raising of Her Majesty's 100th Regiment in Canada, and a Chapter on Canadian Social & Political Life*. Toronto: The Grip Printing and Publishing Co., 1886.

Bourne, C. B., and D. M. McRae. "Maritime Jurisdiction in the Dixon Entrance: The Alaska Boundary Re-Examined." *Canadian Yearbook of International Law* 14 (1976): 175–223.

Bowman, John S. *Chronology of War*. New York: Infobase Publishing, 2003.

Boxberger, Daniel L. "Ethnicity and Labor in the Puget Sound Fishing Industry, 1880–1935." *Ethnology* 33, no. 2 (April 1, 1994): 179–91.

Boxberger, Daniel L. "In and Out of the Labor Force: The Lummi Indians and the Development of the Commercial Salmon Fishery of North Puget Sound, 1880–1900." *Ethnohistory* 35, no. 2 (April 1, 1988): 161–90.

Boyko, John. *Blood and Daring: How Canada Fought the American Civil War and Forged a Nation*. Toronto: Knopf, 2013.

Brebner, John Bartlet. *North Atlantic Triangle: The Interplay of Canada, the United States and Great Britain*. 5th ed. New York: Columbia University Press, 1958.

Brown-Kubisch, Linda. *The Queen's Bush Settlement: Black Pioneers 1839–1865*. Toronto: Natural Heritage, 2004.

Brundage, David. *Irish Nationalists in America: The Politics of Exile, 1798–1998*. New York: Oxford University Press, 2016.

Bruyneel, Kevin. "Exiled, Executed, Exalted: Louis Riel, Homo Sacer and the Production of Canadian Sovereignty." *Canadian Journal of Political Science* 43, no. 3 (2010).

Bukowczyk, John J., Nora Faires, David R. Smith, and Randy William Widdis. *Permeable Border: The Great Lakes Basin as Transnational Region 1650–1990*. Pittsburgh: University of Pittsburgh Press, 2005.

Bumsted, J. M. "Louis Riel and the United States." *American Review of Canadian Studies* 29, no. 1 (1999): 17–41.

Burfisher, Mary E., Sherman Robinson, and Karen Thierfelder. "The Impact of NAFTA on the United States." *Journal of Economic Perspectives* 15, no. 1 (2001): 125–44.

Burroughs, Peter. "Tackling Army Desertion in British North America." *Canadian Historical Review* 61, no. 1 (1980): 28–68.

Cadava, Geraldo. *Standing on Common Ground: The Making of the Sunbelt Borderland*. Cambridge, MA: Harvard University Press, 2013.

Cahill, Cathleen D. *Federal Fathers & Mothers: A Social History of the United States Indian Service, 1869–1933*. Chapel Hill: University of North Carolina Press, 2011.

Campbell, Robert A. "Making Sober Citizens: The Legacy of Indigenous Alcohol Regulation in Canada, 1777–1985." *Journal of Canadian Studies* 42, no. 1 (2008): 105–26.

Carlson, Keith Thor, Albert (Sonny) McHalsie, and Jan Perrier. *A Stó:Lo-Coast Salish Historical Atlas*. Vancouver: Douglas & McIntyre, 2001.

Carlson, Keith Thor. *The Power of Place, the Problem of Time: Aboriginal Identity and Historical Consciousness in the Cauldron of Colonialism*. Toronto: University of Toronto Press, 2010.

Carlson, Keith, ed. *You Are Asked to Witness: The Stó:Lō in Canada's Pacific Coast History*. Chilliwack B.C.: Stó:lō Heritage Trust, 1997.

Carmer, Carl. *[I Am a Cayuga] The Story of Des-Ka-Heh, Iroquois Statesman and Patriot*. St. Regis Mohawk Reservation: Akwesane Mohawk Counselor Organization, n.d.

Carroll, Francis M. *A Good and Wise Measure: The Search for the Canadian–American Boundary, 1783–1842*. Toronto: University of Toronto Press, 2001.

Carter, Sarah, and Patricia McCormack, eds. *Recollecting: Lives of Aboriginal Women of the Canadian Northwest and Borderlands*. Edmonton: Athabasca University Press, 2011.

Carter, Sarah. *Lost Harvests: Prairie Indian Reserve Farmers and Government Policy*. Montreal: McGill-Queen's University Press, 1990.

Carter, Sarah. *The Importance of Being Monogamous: Marriage and Nation Building in Western Canada in 1915*. Alberta: University of Alberta Press, 2014.

Century Edition of The American Digest: A Complete Digest of All Reported American Cases from the Earliest Times to 1896. Vol. 2. St. Paul: West Publishing Company, 1897.

Chabot, Richard, Yves Roby, and Jacques Monet. "Nelson, Robert." In *Dictionary of Canadian Biography*, Vol. 10, 1972.

Champagne, Duane. *The Native North American: A Reference Work on Native North Americans in the United States and Canada*. Detroit: Gale Group, 2001.

Chang, Kornel S. *Pacific Connections*. Berkeley: University of California Press, 2012.

Chomsky, Carol. "The United States-Dakota War Trials: A Study of Military Injustice." *Stanford Law Review* 43, no. 1 (November 1990): 13–98.

Cintio, Marcello Di. *Walls: Travels Along the Barricades*. Fredericton: Goose Lane, 2012.

Clark, Richard. *Point Roberts, U.S.A. The History of a Canadian Enclave*. Bellingham, WA: Textype, 1980.

Collins Jr., Charles D. *Atlas of the Sioux Wars*. Fort Leavenworth: Combat Studies Institute Press, 2006.

Conway, Kyle, and Timothy Pasch, eds. *Beyond the Border: Tensions Across the Forty-Ninth Parallel in the Great Plains and Prairies*. Montreal: McGill-Queen's University Press, 2013.

Cott, Nancy F. *Public Vows: A History of Marriage and the Nation*. Cambridge, MA: Harvard University Press, 2000.

Cruikshank, Julie. *Do Glaciers Listen? Local Knowledge, Colonial Encounters, & Social Imagination*. Vancouver: UBC Press, 2005.

Cunfer, Geoff, and Bill Waiser, eds. *Bison and People on the North American Great Plains*. College Station: Texas A&M Press, 2016.

Daschuk, James. *Clearing the Plains: Disease, Politics of Starvation, and the Loss of Aboriginal Life*. Regina: University of Regina Press, 2013.

Davis, Major-General George B. *A Treatise on the Military Law of the United States Together with the Practice and Procedure of Courts-Martial and Other Military Tribunals*. 3rd ed. New York: John Wiley & Sons, 1915.

DeLay, Brian. *War of a Thousand Deserts: Indian Raids and the U.S.–Mexican War*. New Haven, CT: Yale University Press, 2008.

Deskaheh. *Chief Deskaheh Tells Why He Is over Here Again*. London: Kealeys Ltd, 1923.

Doerfler, Jill, Niigaanwewidam James Sinclair, and Heidi Kiiwetinepinesiik Stark. *Centering Anishinaabeg Studies : Understanding the World Through Stories*. East Lansing: Michigan State University Press, 2013.

Donald, Leland. *Aboriginal Slavery on the Northwest Coast of North America*. Berkeley: University of California Press, 1997.

Douaud, Patrick C. *The Western Métis: Profile of a People*, Regina: Canadian Plains Research Center, 2007.

Doutre, Joseph. *Constitution of Canada: The British North America Act, 1867*. Montreal: John Lovell & Son, 1880.

Drache, Daniel. *Borders Matter: Homeland Security and the Search for North America*. Halifax: Fernwood, 2004.

Dusenberry, Verne. "The Rocky Boy Indians." *Montana: The Magazine of Western History* 4, no. 1 (Winter 1954): 1–15.

Elias, Peter Douglas. *The Dakota of the Canadian Northwest: Lessons for Survival*. Regina: Canadian Plains Research Center, 2002.

Elofson, W. M. Cowboys, *Gentlemen, and Cattle Thieves: Ranching on the Western Frontier*. Montreal: McGill-Queen's University Press, 2000.

Ens, Gerhard J. *Homeland to Hinterland: The Changing World of the Red River Metis in the Nineteenth Century*. Toronto: University of Toronto Press, 1996.

Ens, Gerhard J., and Joe Sawchuk. *From New Peoples to New Nations: Aspects of Metis History and Identity from Eighteenth to Twenty-First Centuries*. Toronto: University of Toronto Press, 2016.

Errington, Elizabeth Jane. *The Lion, the Eagle, and Upper Canada: A Developing Colonial Ideology*. Montreal: McGill-Queen's University Press, 1994.

Evans, Sterling, ed. *The Borderlands of the American and Canadian Wests: Essays on Regional History of the Forty-Ninth Parallel*. Lincoln: University of Nebraska Press, 2006.

Feest, Christian F. *Indians and Europe: An Interdisciplinary Collection of Essays*. Lincoln: University of Nebraska Press, 1989.

Ferguson, Julie H. *James Douglas: Father of British Columbia*. Toronto: Dundurn Press, 2009.

Fisher, Robin. "Indian Warfare and Two Frontiers: A Comparison of British Columbia and Washington Territory during the Early Years of Settlement." *Pacific Historical Review* 50, no. 1 (February 1, 1981): 31–51.

Flanagan, Thomas, and Claude Rocan, eds. *The Collected Writings of Louis Riel*. Vol. 5. Alberta: University of Alberta Press, 1985.

Flanagan, Thomas. "Louis Riel and the Dispersion of American Métis." *Minnesota History* 49, no. 5 (1985): 179–90.

Flanagan, Thomas. *Riel and the Rebellion: 1885 Reconsidered*. Toronto: University of Toronto Press, 2000.

Ford, Clellan S. *Smoke from Their Fires: The Life of a Kwakiutl Chief*. 2nd ed. Hamden: Archon Books, 1968.

Foster, Hamar, and Grove Alan. "'Trespassers on the Soil': United States v. Tom and A New Perspective on the Short History of Treaty Making in Nineteenth-Century British Columbia." *BC Studies* 138/139 (2003): 51–84.

Foucault, Michel. *Discipline & Punish: The Birth of the Prison*, trans. Alan Sheridan, 2nd ed. (New York: Vintage Books, 1995

Friday, Chris. *Organizing Asian American Labor: The Pacific Coast Canned-Salmon Industry, 1870–1942*. Philadelphia: Temple University Press, 1994.

Gaffen, Fred. *Cross-Border Warriors: Canadians in American Forces, Americans in Canadian Forces From the Civil War to the Gulf*. Toronto: Dundurn Press, 1995.

Galbraith, John S. "The Early History of the Puget's Sound Agricultural Company, 1838–43." *Oregon Historical Quarterly* 55, no. 3 (1954): 234–59.

Garrison, Tim Alan. *The Legal Ideology of Removal: The Southern Judiciary and the Sovereignty of Native American Nations*. Athens: University of Georgia Press, 2002.

Gaudry, Adam, Kristin Burnett, and Geoff Read. "Respecting Métis Nationhood and Self-Determination in Matters of Métis Identity." In *Aboriginal History: A Reader*, 2nd ed., 152–63. New York: Oxford University Press, 2015.

Gills, Bradley J. "Navigating the Landscape of Assimilation: The Anishnabeg, the Lumber Industry, and the Failure of Federal Indian Policy in Michigan." *Michigan Historical Review* 34, no. 2 (2008): 57–74.

Gluek, Alvin C. "The Sioux Uprising: A Problem in International Relations." *Minnesota History* 34, no. 8 (Winter 1955): 317–24.

Gorsline, Jeremiah, ed. *Shadows of Our Ancestors: Readings in the History of Klallam-White Relations*. Port Townsend, WA: Empty Bowl, 1992.

Gough, Barry M. *Gunboat Frontier: British Maritime Authority and Northwest Coast Indians, 1846–90*. Vancouver: UBC Press, 1984.

Grant, Ulysses S. *The Papers of Ulysses S. Grant*. Edited by John Y. Simon. Vol. 28 November 1, 1876–September 30, 1878. Carbondale: Southern Illinois University Press, 2005.

Graybill, Andrew R. *Policing the Great Plains: Rangers, Mounties, and the North American Frontier 1875–1910*. Lincoln: University of Nebraska Press, 2007.

Green, Joyce. "Canaries in the Mines of Citizenship: Indian Women in Canada." *Canadian Journal of Political Science* 34, no. 4 (2001): 715–38.

Greenwald, Emily. *Reconfiguring the Reservation: The Nez Perces, Jicarilla Apaches, and the Dawes Act*. Albuquerque: University of New Mexico Press, 2002.

Greer, Allan. "1837–38 Rebellion Reconsidered." *Canadian Historical Review* 76, no. 1 (1995): 1–18.

Griffith, Sarah M. "Border Crossings: Race, Class, and Smuggling in Pacific Coast Chinese Immigrant Society." *Western Historical Quarterly* 35, no. 4 (2004): 473–92.

Haag, Larry, and Lawrence Barkwell. *The Boundary Commission's Metis Scouts The 49th Rangers.* Winnipeg: Louis Riel Institute, 2009.

Hämäläinen, Pekka, and Samuel Truett. "On Borderlands." *Journal of American History* 98, no. 2 (2011): 338–61.

Hämäläinen, Pekka. *The Comanche Empire.* New Haven, CT: Yale University Press, 2008.

Hansen, Marcus Lee. *The Mingling of Canadian and American People.* New Haven, CT: Yale University Press, 1940.

Hargrave, Joseph James. *Red River.* Montreal: John Lovell, 1871.

Harmon, Alexandra. *Indians in the Making: Ethnic Relations and Indian Identities Around Puget Sound.* Berkeley: University of California Press, 1998.

Harmon, Alexandra. "Lines in Sand: Shifting Boundaries between Indians and Non-Indians in the Puget Sound Region." *Western Historical Quarterly* 26, no. 4 (Winter 1995): 429–53.

Harris, Cole. *Making Native Space: Colonialism, Resistance, and Reserves in British Columbia.* Vancouver: UBC Press, 2002.

Harris, Cole. *The Resettlement of British Columbia: Essays on Colonialism and Geographical Change.* Vancouver: UBC Press, 1997.

Hauptman, Laurence M. *Seven Generations of Iroquois Leadership: The Six Nations Since 1800.* Syracuse: Syracuse University Press, 2008.

Hauptman, Laurence M. *The Iroquois in the Civil War: From Battlefield to Reservation.* Syracuse: Syracuse University Press, 1993.

Heaman, E. A. *Tax, Order, and Good Government: A New Political History of Canada, 1867–1917.* Montreal: McGill-Queen's University Press, 2017.

Hele, Karl S., ed. *Lines Drawn Upon the Water: First Nations and the Great Lakes Borders and Borderlands.* Waterloo: Wilfrid Laurier University Press, 2008.

Hepburn, Sharon A. Roger. "Following the North Star: Canada as a Haven for Nineteenth-Century American Blacks." *Michigan Historical Review* 25, no. 2 (Fall 1999): 91–126.

Hepburn, Sharon A. Roger. *Crossing the Border: A Free Black Community in Canada.* Urbana: University of Illinois Press, 2007.

Hernández, Kelly Lytle. *Migra!: A History of the U.S. Border Patrol.* Berkeley: University of California Press, 2010.

Hill, Susan M. *The Clay We Are Made Of: Haudenosaunee Land Tenure on the Grand River.* Winnipeg: University of Manitoba Press, 2017.

Hirota, Hidetaka. *Expelling the Poor: Atlantic Seaboard States and the Nineteenth-Century Origins of American Immigration Policy.* New York: Oxford University Press, 2017.

Hogue, Michel. "Disputing the Medicine Line: The Plains Crees and the Canadian–American Border, 1876–1885." *Montana: The Magazine of Western History* 52, no. 4 (Winter 2002): 2–17.

Hogue, Michel. *Metis and the Medicine Line: Creating a Border and Dividing a People.* Regina: University of Regina Press, 2015.

Howard, James Henri. *The Canadian Sioux.* Lincoln: University of Nebraska Press, 1984.

Howe, Craig, Lydia Whirlwind Solider, and Lanniko L. Lee, eds. *He Sapa Woihanble: Black Hills Dream.* St. Paul: Living Justice Press, 2011.

Howell, Alfred. *Naturalization and Nationality in Canada: Expatriation and Repatriation of British Subjects: Aliens, Their Disabilities and Their Privileges in Canada.* Toronto: Carswell & co, 1884.

Hoxie, Frederick E. *Encyclopedia of North American Indians.* Boston: Houghton Mifflin Company, 1996.

Hoy, Benjamin. "A Border without Guards: First Nations and the Enforcement of National Space." *Journal of the Canadian Historical Association* 25, no. 2 (2014): 89–115.

Hoy, Benjamin. "Dispensing Irregular Justice: State Sponsored Abductions, Prisoner Surrenders, and Extralegal Renditions Along the Canadian–United States Border." *Law and History Review* 35, no. 2 (2017): 321–50.

Hoy, Benjamin. "Uncertain Counts: The Struggle to Enumerate First Nations in Canada and the United States 1870–1911." *Ethnohistory* 62, no. 4 (2015): 729–50.

Hubbard, Bill. *American Boundaries: The Nation, the States, the Rectangular Survey.* Chicago: University of Chicago Press, 2008.

Hubner, Brian. "Horse Stealing and the Borderline: The NWMP and the Control of Indian Movement, 1874–1900." *Prairie Forum* 20, no. 2 (1995): 281–300.

Hyun, Sinae. "Building a Human Border: The Thai Border Patrol Police School Project in the Post-Cold War Era." *Sojourn: Journal of Social Issues in Southeast Asia* 29, no. 2 (2014): 332–63.

Jacobs, Lesley A. *Mapping the Legal Consciousness of First Nations Voters: Understanding Voting Rights Mobilization.* Ottawa: Elections Canada, 2009.

Jamwal, N. S. "Border Management: Dilemma of Guarding the India-Bangladesh Border." *Strategic Analysis* 28, no. 1 (2004): 5–36.

Jefferson, Thomas. *The Jeffersonian Cyclopedia: A Comprehensive Collection of the Views of Thomas Jefferson.* Edited by John P. Foley. New York: Funk & Wagnalls Company, 1900.

Johansen, Bruce Elliott. *Native Americans Today: A Biographical Dictionary.* Santa Barbara: Greenwood Press, 2010.

Johnson, Benjamin H., and Andrew R. Graybill, eds. *Bridging National Borders in North America: Transnational and Comparative Histories.* Durham, NC: Duke University Press, 2010.

Johnston, William, William G. P. Rawling, Richard H. Gimblett, and John MacFarlane. *The Seabound Coast: The Official History of the Royal Canadian Navy, 1867–1939.* Vol. 1. Toronto: Dundurn Press, 2010.

Josephy, Alvin M. *Nez Perce Country.* Lincoln: University of Nebraska Press, 2007.

Kantrowitz, Stephen. *More than Freedom: Fighting for Black Citizenship in a White Republic, 1829–1889.* New York: Penguin, 2012.

Karibo, Holly M. *Sin City North: Sex, Drugs, and Citizenship in the Detroit-Windsor Borderland.* Chapel Hill: University of North Carolina Press, 2015.

Kennedy, Dorothy. "Quantifying 'Two Sides of a Coin': A Statistical Examination of the Central Coast Salish Social Network." *BC Studies*, no. 153 (2007): 3–34.

Keyssar, Alexander. *The Right to Vote: The Contested History of Democracy in the United States.* New York: Basic Books, 2009.

Kirby, Rollin. *Highlights: A Cartoon History of the Nineteen Twenties.* New York: William Farquhar Payson, 1931.

Klug, Thomas A. "The Immigration and Naturalization Service (INS) and the Making of a Border-Crossing Culture on the US–Canada Border, 1891–1941." *American Review of Canadian Studies* 40, no. 3 (September 2010): 395–415.

Labelle, Kathryn Magee. *Dispersed but Not Destroyed: A History of the Seventeenth-Century Wendat People.* Vancouver: UBC Press, 2013.

LaDow, Beth. *The Medicine Line: Life and Death on a North American Borderland.* New York: Routledge, 2001.

Landon, Fred. "The Kidnapping of Dr. Rufus Bratton." *Journal of Negro History* 10, no. 3 (1925): 330–33.

Laviolette, Gontran. *The Sioux Indians in Canada.* Regina: Saskatchewan Historical Society, 1944.

Laxer, James. *The Border: Canada, the U.S. and Dispatches from the 49th Parallel.* Toronto: Doubleday Canada, 2003.

Lee, Erika. *At America's Gates: Chinese Immigration during the Exclusion Era, 1882–1943.* Chapel Hill: University of North Carolina Press, 2003.

Legal Aid Saskatchewan, and Community-engaged History Collaboratorium. *Gladue Rights Research Database*, 2019. http://drc.usask.ca/projects/gladue/

Legg, Herbert. *Customs Services in Western Canada, 1867–1925: A History.* Creston: Creston Review Limited, 1963.

Lew-Williams, Beth. *The Chinese Must Go: Violence, Exclusion, and the Making of the Alien in America.* Cambridge, MA: Harvard University Press, 2018.

Little, John Irvine. *Loyalties in Conflict: A Canadian Borderland in War and Rebellion 1812–1840.* Toronto: University of Toronto Press, 2008.

Luibhéid, Eithne. *Entry Denied: Controlling Sexuality at the Border.* Minneapolis: University of Minnesota Press, 2002.

Lutz, John Sutton. *Makúk: A New History of Aboriginal-White Relations.* Vancouver: UBC Press, 2008.

Maas, Willem. *Multilevel Citizenship.* Philadelphia: University of Pennsylvania Press, 2013.

Macdougall, Brenda. *One of the Family: Metis Culture in Nineteenth-Century Northwestern Saskatchewan.* Vancouver: UBC Press, 2010.

Macleod, Roderick C. "Walsh, James Morrow." In *Dictionary of Canadian Biography,* Vol. 13. Toronto: University of Toronto/Université Laval, 1994.

Major, Frederick Wm. *Manitoulin: The Isle of the Ottawas Being a Handbook of Historical and Other Information and Other Information on the Grand Manitoulin Island.* Gore Bay: The Recorder Press, 1934.

Malinowski, Sharon, and Anna Sheets, eds. *The Gale Encyclopedia of Native American Tribes.* Vol. 3. Detroit: Gale, 1998.

Margolies, Daniel S. *Spaces of Law in American Foreign Relations: Extradition and Extraterritoriality in the Borderlands and Beyond, 1877–1898.* Athens: University of Georgia Press, 2011.

Markowitz, Harvey, ed. *American Indians.* Vol. II and III. Pasadena, CA: Salem Press, 1995.

Marquis, Albert Nelson. *Who's Who In America: A Biographical Dictionary of Notable Living Men and Women of the United States.* Vol. 15: 1928–1929. London: Stanley Paul, 1928.

Martel, Gilles, ed. *The Collected Writings of Louis Riel.* Vol. II. Alberta: University of Alberta Press, 1985.

Martinez, J. Michael. *Carpetbaggers, Calvary, and the Ku Klux Klan.* Lanham, MD: Rowman & Littlefield, 2007.

Mathieu, Sarah-Jane. *North of the Color Line: Migration and Black Resistance in Canada, 1870–1955.* Chapel Hill: University of North Carolina Press, 2010.

Mawani, Renisa. "Cross-Racial Encounters and Juridical Truths: (Dis)Aggregating Race in British Columbia's Contact Zone." *BC Studies,* 2007 2008, 141–71.

May, Samuel. *The Fugitive Slave Law and Its Victims.* Vol. 15. Anti-Slavery Tracts. New York: American Anti-Slavery Society, 1861.

Mayers, Adam. *Dixie and the Dominion: Canada, the Confederacy, and the War for the Union.* Toronto: Dundurn Group, 2003.

McArthur, Alexander. *The Causes of the Rising in the Red River Settlement 1869–1870.* Winnipeg: Manitoba Free Press, 1882.

McClurken, James M. "Ottawa Adaptive Strategies to Indian Removal." *Michigan Historical Review* 12, no. 1 (1986): 29–55.

McCoy, Robert Ross. *Chief Joseph, Yellow Wolf, and the Creation of Nez Perce History in the Pacific Northwest.* New York: Routledge, 2004.

McLeod, Neal. *Cree Narrative Memory: From Treaties to Contemporary Times.* Saskatoon: Purich Publishing Limited, 2007.

McCrady, David G. *Living with Strangers: The Nineteenth-Century Sioux and the Canadian–American Borderlands.* Lincoln: University of Nebraska Press, 2006.

McDermott, John D. "Were They Really Rogues? Desertion in the Nineteenth-Century U.S. Army." *Nebraska History* 78 (1997): 165–74.

McInnis, Edgar W. *The Unguarded Frontier: A History of American–Canadian Relations.* Garden City, NY: Doubleday, 1942.

McManus, Sheila. *The Line Which Separates: Race, Gender, and the Making of the Alberta-Montana Borderlands.* Lincoln: University of Nebraska Press, 2005.

Meagher, Timothy J. *The Columbia Guide to Irish American History.* New York: Columbia University Press, 2005.

Meeker, Ezra. *Pioneer Reminiscences of Puget Sound: The Tragedy of Leschi.* Seattle: Lowman & Hanford Stationary and Printing Co., 1905.

McIntosh, Dave. *The Collectors: A History of Canadian Customs and Excise*. Toronto: NC Press, 1984.
McLeod, Neal. *Cree Narrative Memory: From Treaties to Contemporary Times*. Saskatoon: Purich Publishing Limited, 2007.
McManus, Sheila. *The Line Which Separates: Race, Gender, and the Making of the Alberta-Montana Borderlands*. Lincoln: University of Nebraska Press, 2005.
Meter, Jan R. Van. "Fifty-Four Forty or Fight!" In *Tippecanoe and Tyler Too*. Chicago: University of Chicago Press, 2008.
Meyer, Edith Patterson. *The Friendly Frontier: The Story of the Canadian–American Border*. Toronto: Little, Brown, 1962.
Miller, Bradley. *Borderline Crime: Fugitive Criminals and the Challenge of the Border, 1819–1914*. Toronto: University of Toronto Press, 2016.
Miller, Bruce. "An Ethnographic View of Legal Entanglements on the Salish Sea Borderlands." *UBC Law Review* 47, no. 3 (2014): 991–1023.
Miller, Bruce. "The 'Really Real' Border and the Divided Salish Community." *BC Studies* 112 (1996): 63–79.
Miller, Bruce Granville, ed. *Be of Good Mind : Essays on the Coast Salish*. Vancouver: UBC Press, 2007.
Moloney, Deirdre M. *National Insecurities: Immigrants and U.S. Deportation Policy Since 1882*. Chapel Hill: University of North Carolina Press, 2012.
Moore, John Bassett. *A Treatise on Extradition and Interstate Rendition*. Vol. 1. Boston: Boston Book Company, 1891.
Morse, Alexander Porter. *A Treatise on Citizenship, by Birth and by Naturalization: With Reference to the Law of Nations, Roman Civil Law, Law of the United States of America, and the Law of France*. Boston: Little Brown, 1881.
Morton, Desmond. "Cavalry or Police: Keeping the Peace on Two Adjacent Frontiers, 1870–1900." *Journal of Canadian Studies* 12, no. 2 (1977): 27–37.
Mumford, Jeremy Ravi. "Why Was Louis Riel, a United States Citizen, Hanged as a Canadian Traitor in 1885?" *Canadian Historical Review* 88, no. 2 (2007): 237–62.
Murolo, Priscilla. "Wars of Civilization: The US Army Contemplates Wounded Knee, the Pullman Strike, and the Philippine Insurrection." *International Labor and Working-Class History* 80, no. 1 (2011): 77–102.
Nadasdy, Paul. *Hunters and Bureaucrats: Power, Knowledge and Aboriginal-State Relations in the Southwest Yukon*. Vancouver: UBC Press, 2003.
Nadelmann, Ethan A. *Cops Across Borders: The Internationalization of U.S. Criminal Law Enforcement*. University Park: Penn State University Press, 1997.
Neering, Rosemary. *The Pig War: The Last Canada–US Border Conflict*. Toronto: Heritage House Publishing, 2011.
Neihardt, John Gneisenau. *The Sixth Grandfather: Black Elk's Teachings Given to John G. Neihardt*. Edited by Raymond J. DeMaille and Hilda Neihardt Petri. Lincoln: University of Nebraska Press, 1985.
Nevitt, Richard Barrington. *Frontier Life in the Mounted Police: The Diary Letters of Richard Barrington Nevitt, NWMP Surgeon, 1874–78*. Calgary: Alberta Records Publication Board, Historical Society of Alberta, 2010.
Newman, David. "On Borders and Power: A Theoretical Framework." *Journal of Borderlands Studies* 18, no. 1 (2003): 13–25.
Ngai, Mae M. *Impossible Subjects: Illegal Aliens and the Making of Modern America*. Princeton, NJ: Princeton University Press, 2004.
Ormsby, Margaret A. "Douglas, Sir James." In *Dictionary of Canadian Biography*, Vol. 10. Toronto: University of Toronto Press/Université Laval, 1972.
Parker, Richard Wayne. "The Alaska Boundary Question." *North American Review* 176, no. 559 (June 1903): 913–26.
Parsons, John. *West on the 49th Parallel: Red River to the Rockies, 1872–1876*. New York: William Morrow and Company, 1963.

Patrick A. Dunae. "Promoting the Dominion: Records and the Canadian Immigration Campaign, 1872–1915." *Archivaria* 19 (1985–1984): 73–93.

Pearen, Shelley J. *Exploring Manitoulin*. 3rd ed. Toronto: University of Toronto Press, 1993.

Peers, Laura. *The Ojibwa of Western Canada 1780 to 1870*. Winnipeg: University of Manitoba Press, 1994.

Peterson, Hans. "Imasees and His Band: Canadian Refugees after the North-West Rebellion." *Western Canadian Journal of Anthropology* 8, no. 1 (1978): 21–37.

Preston, Richard A. *The Defence of the Undefended Border: Planning for War in North America 1867–1939*. Montreal: McGill-Queen's University Press, 1977.

Pyle, Christopher H. *Extradition, Politics, and Human Rights*. Philadelphia: Temple University Press, 2001.

Raibmon, Paige. "The Practice of Everyday Colonialism: Indigenous Women at Work in the Hop Fields and Tourist Industry of Puget Sound." *Labour* 3, no. 3 (2006): 23–56.

Ramirez, Bruno. *Crossing the 49th Parallel: Migration from Canada to the United States, 1900–1930*. Ithaca, NY: Cornell University Press, 2001.

Ray, Arthur. *I Have Lived Here Since the World Began: An Illustrated History of Canada's Native People*. 3rd ed. Montreal: McGill-Queen's University Press, 2011.

Rees, Tony. *Arc of the Medicine Line: Mapping the World's Longest Undefended Border Across the Western Plains*. Lincoln: University of Nebraska Press, 2007.

Reid, Gerald F. "Illegal Alien? The Immigration Case of Mohawk Ironworker Paul K. Diabo." *Proceedings of the American Philosophical Society* 151, no. 1 (March 2007): 61–78.

Reid, Richard M. *African Canadians in Union Blue: Volunteering for the Cause in the Civil War*. Vancouver: UBC Press, 2014.

Richotte Jr., Keith. *Claiming Turtle Mountain's Constitution: The History, Legacy, and Future of a Tribal Nation's Founding Documents*. Chapel Hill: University of North Carolina Press, 2017.

Rickard, Clinton. *Fighting Tuscarora: The Autobiography of Chief Clinton Rickard*. Edited by Barbara Graymont. Syracuse: Syracuse University Press, 1973.

Roberts, Barbara. *Whence They Came: Deportation from Canada 1900–1935*. Manitoba: University of Ottawa Press, 1988.

Robertson, Craig. *The Passport in America: The History of a Document*. New York: Oxford University Press, 2010.

Salyer, Lucy. *Laws Harsh as Tigers: Chinese Immigration and the Shaping of Modern Immigration Law*. Chapel Hill: University of North Carolina Press, 1995.

Samito, Christian G. *Becoming American Under Fire: Irish Americans, African Americans, and the Politics of Citizenship During the Civil War Era*. Ithaca, NY: Cornell University Press, 2009.

Senior, Hereward. *The Last Invasion of Canada : The Fenian Raids, 1866–1870*. Toronto: Oxford; Dundurn Press in collaboration with the Canadian War Museum Canadian Museum of Civilization, 1991.

Shah, Nayan. *Stranger Intimacy: Contesting Race, Sexuality, and the Law in the North American West*. Berkeley: University of California Press, 2011.

Shepard, R. Bruce. "Diplomatic Racism: Canadian Government and Black Migration from Oklahoma, 1905–1912." *Great Plains Quarterly* 1, no. 1 (Winter 1983): 5–16.

Shortt, Adam, and A. G. Doughty, eds. *Canada and Its Provinces*. Vol. IV and VI. Toronto: Glasgow, Brook & Company, 1914.

Smearman, Claire A. "Second Wives' Club: Mapping the Impact of Polygamy in U.S. Immigration Law." *Berkeley Journal of International Law* 27, no. 2 (2009): 382–447.

Smith, Marian L. "The Immigration and Naturalization Service (INS) at the U.S.–Canadian Border, 1893–1993: An Overview of Issues and Topics." *Michigan Historical Review* 26, no. 2 (2000): 127–47.

Smith, Michael Thomas. "The Most Desperate Scoundrels Unhung: Bounty Jumpers and Recruitment Fraud in the Civil War North." *American Nineteenth Century History* 6, no. 2 (2005): 149–72.

Sohi, Seema. "Race, Surveillance, and Indian Anticolonialism in the Transnational Western U.S.–Canadian Borderlands." *Journal of American History* 98, no. 2 (September 2011): 420–36.
St. John, Rachel. *Line in the Sand: A History of the Western U.S.–Mexico Border*. Princeton, NJ: Princeton University Press, 2011.
Stamper, Ed, Helen Windy, and Ken Morsette Jr., eds. The *History of the Chippewa Cree of Rocky Boy's Indian Reservation*. Montana: Stone Child College, 2008.
Stead, Robert J. C. "Canada's Immigration Policy." *Annals of the American Academy of Political and Social Science* 107 (1923): 56–62.
Stephen, Scott. "Manitoba History: James McKay (1828–1879): Métis Trader, Guide, Interpreter and MLA." *Manitoba Historical Society* 58 (2008).
Stewart, Gordon T. *The American Response to Canada Since 1776*. East Lansing: Michigan State University Press, 1992.
Strong, Josiah. *Our Country Its Possible Future and Its Present Crisis*. New York: The Baker & Taylor Co., 1885.
Sturtevant, William C., series ed.. *Handbook of North American Indians*. Vol. 5–15. Washington, DC: Smithsonian Institution, 1986–2001.
Sullivan, Kathleen S. "Marriage and Federal Police Power." *Studies in American Political Development* 20, no. 1 (2006): 45–56.
Swan, Ruth, and Edward A. Jerome. "Unequal Justice: The Metis in O'Donoghue's Raid of 1871." *Manitoba History* 39 (Spring 2000): 24–38.
Taylor, Alan. *The Civil War of 1812: American Citizens, British Subjects, Irish Rebels, & Indian Allies*. New York: Knopf, 2010.
The Fenian Raid at Fort Erie, June the First and Second, 1866: With a Map of the Niagara Peninsula, Shewing the Route of the Troops, and a Plan of the Lime Ridge Battle Ground. Toronto: W. C. Chewett & co, 1866.
Thelen, David. "The Nation and Beyond: Transnational Perspectives on United States History." *Journal of American History* 86, no. 3 (December 1, 1999): 965–75.
Thompson, John Herd, and Stephen J. Randall. *Canada and the United States: Ambivalent Allies*. 4th ed. Athens: University of Georgia Press, 2008.
Thrush, Coll. *Native Seattle: Histories from the Crossing-Over Place*. Seattle: University of Washington Press, 2007.
Tollefson, Kenneth D. "The Political Survival of Landless Puget Sound Indians." *American Indian Quarterly* 16, no. 2 (April 1, 1992): 213–35.
Torpey, John. *The Invention of the Passport: Surveillance, Citizenship, and the State*. Cambridge: Cambridge University Press, 2000.
Trimble, Sabina. "Storying Swí:Lhcha: Place Making and Power at a Stó:Lō Landmark." *BC Studies* 190 (2016): 39–66.
Truett, Samuel, and Elliott Young. *Continental Crossroads: Remapping U.S. Mexico Borderlands History Nations, Regions, and Borderlands*. Durham, NC: Duke University Press, 2004.
Tyler, Kenneth J. "KIWISĀNCE." In *Dictionary of Canadian Biography*, Vol. 11. Toronto: University of Toronto Press/Université Laval, 2003.
Unterman, Katherine. *Uncle Sam's Policemen: The Pursuit of Fugitives Across Borders*. Cambridge, MA: Harvard University Press, 2015.
Urvashi, Butalia. *The Other Side of Silence: Voices from the Partition of India*. Durham, NC: Duke University Press, 2000.
Uttley, Jim. "The Cypress Hills Massacre: A Tragedy Hidden Too Long." *Indian Life* 31, no. 3 (December 2010): 2.
Wadewitz, Lissa K. *The Nature of Borders: Salmon, Boundaries, and Bandits on the Salish Sea*. Seattle: University of Washington Press, 2012.
Waiser, Bill. *A World We Have Lost: Saskatchewan Before 1905*. Markham, ON: Fifth House Limited, 2016.
Walker, Barrington. *The History of Immigration and Racism in Canada*. Toronto: Canadian Scholars' Press, 2008.

Walker, Francis A. "The Indian Question." *North American Review* 66, no. 239 (1873): 329–88.

Warrick, W. Sheridan. "The American Indian Policy in the Upper Old Northwest Following the War of 1812." *Ethnohistory* 3, no. 2 (1956): 109–25.

Wayne, Michael. "The Black Population of Canada West on the Eve of the American Civil War: A Reassessment Based on the Manuscript Census of 1861." *Social History* 28, no. 56 (1995): 465–85.

Weitzberg, Keren. *We Do Not Have Borders: Greater Somalia and the Predicaments of Belonging in Kenya*. Athens: Ohio University Press, 2017.

West, Elliott. *The Last Indian War: The Nez Perce Story*. New York: Oxford University Press, 2009.

West, Jerry Lee. *The Reconstruction Ku Klux Klan in York County, South Carolina, 1865–1877*. Jefferson, NC: McFarland and Company Inc, 2002.

White, Richard. *Railroaded: The Transcontinentals and the Making of Modern America*. New York: Norton, 2011.

White, Richard. *The Middle Ground: Indians, Empires, and Republics in the Great Lakes Region, 1650–1815*. Cambridge: Cambridge University Press, 1991.

White, Richard. The *Republic For Which It Stands: The United States During Reconstruction and the Gilded Age, 1865–1896*. New York: Oxford University Press, 2017.

Wigmore, Gregory. "Before the Railroad: From Slavery to Freedom in the Canadian–American Borderland." *Journal of American History* 98, no. 2 (2011): 437–54.

Williams, David Ricardo. *Call in Pinkerton's: American Detectives at Work for Canada*. Toronto: Dundurn Press, 1998.

Williams, Lou Falkner. *The Great South Carolina Ku Klux Klan Trials 1871–1872*. Athens: University of Georgia Press, 1996.

Winegard, Timothy C. *For King and Kanata: Canadian Indians and the First World War*. Winnipeg: University of Manitoba Press, 2012.

Winks, Robin W. *The Civil War Years: Canada and the United States*. 4th ed. Montreal: McGill-Queen's University Press, 1998.

Wise, Stephen R. *Lifeline of the Confederacy: Blockade Running During the Civil War*. Columbia: University of South Carolina Press, 1988.

Wolfe, Patrick. "Race and Citizenship." *OAH Magazine of History* 18, no. 5 (2004): 66–71.

Wrigley, Chris. *A Companion to Early Twentieth Century Britain*. Massachusetts: Wiley-Blackwell, 2003.

INDEX

For the benefit of digital users, indexed terms that span two pages (e.g., 52–53) may, on occasion, appear on only one of those pages.

Tables, figures, and boxes are indicated by an italic *t*, *f*, and *b* following the page number

CPSIA information can be obtained
at www.ICGtesting.com
Printed in the USA
BVHW031501190622
639809BV00001B/1

9 780197 528693